MW01007881

"Few people in the world have a richer knowledge of C. S. Lewis's works or a more energetic intellectual curiosity than Jerry Root. Both qualities inform this unique exploration of evil through genres ranging from literary criticism to theological fantasy. What were Lewis's ideas on audience and how did he propose to connect with his readers? How did his rhetorical approach square with his theological understanding and life experience of pain and evil? Dr. Root will take you on an extended exploration of these questions and more."

—Wayne Martindale, author of *Beyond the Shadowlands: C. S. Lewis on Heaven and Hell*

# C. S. Lewis and a Problem of Evil

# Princeton Theological Monograph Series

K. C. Hanson, Charles M. Collier, and
D. Christopher Spinks, Series Editors

*Recent volumes in the series*

Linda Hogan and Dylan Lehrke, editors
*Religion and the Politics of Peace and Conflict*

Lisa E. Dahill
*Reading from the Underside of Selfhood: Bonhoeffer and Spiritual Formation*

Gale Heide
*System and Story: Narrative Critique and Construction in Theology*

Jeanne M. Hoeft
*Agency, Culture, and Human Personhood: Pastoral Thelogy and
Intimate Partner Violence*

Christian T. Collins Winn
*"Jesus Is Victor!": The Significance of the Blumhardts for the
Theology of Karl Barth*

Philip Ruge-Jones
*Cross in Tensions: Luther's Theology of the Cross as Theolgico-social Critique*

Michael S. Hogue
*The Tangled Bank: Toward an Ecotheological Ethics of Responsible
Participation*

Charles Bellinger
*The Trinitarian Self: The Key to the Puzzle of Violence*

Steven B. Sherman
*Revitalizing Theological Epistemology: Holistic Evangelical Approaches
to the Knowledge of God*

# C. S. Lewis and a Problem of Evil

*An Investigation of a Pervasive Theme*

JERRY ROOT

PICKWICK *Publications* · Eugene, Oregon

C. S. LEWIS AND A PROBLEM OF EVIL
An Investigation of a Pervasive Theme

Princeton Theological Monograph Series 96

Pickwick Publications
A Division of Wipf and Stock Publishers
199 W. 8th Ave., Suite 3
Eugene, OR 97401

www.wipfandstock.com

ISBN 13: 978-1-55635-720-6

*Cataloging-in-Publication data:*

Root, Jerry, 1959–

C. S. Lewis and a problem of evil : an investigation of a pervasive theme / Jerry Root.

xxii + 284 p. ; 23 cm. —Includes bibliographical references and index.

Princeton Theological Monograph Series 96

ISBN 13: 978-1-55635-720-6

1. Lewis, C. S. (Clive Staples), 1898–1963—Philosophy. 2. Metaphysics in literature. 3. Good and evil. I. Title. II. Series.

BX4827. L44   R66 2009

Manufactured in the U.S.A.

*For my sister, Kathy Hamlin,*
*who brought me to the door of the*
*Wardrobe and said "Look!"*

# Contents

*Acknowledgements*    *ix*

*Preface*    *xi*

1  Objectivity and Evil    1

2  The Problem of Pain    46

3  Lewis's Literary Criticism and a Problem of Evil    95

4  The Rhetorical Aim of Lewis's Fiction in Light of a Problem of Evil    149

5  Literary Analysis    187

6  Conclusions    239

*Permissions*    249

*Bibliography*    253

*Index*    273

# Acknowledgements

THE INVESTMENT OF TIME AND ENERGY NECESSARY TO COMPLETE THIS book has revealed to me the limitations of my personal resources. While this project demanded many sacrifices of varying proportions, I have been humbled by the sacrifices others around me have made on my behalf while I was engaged in writing. I would like to thank my wife Claudia and my children, Jeremy, Alicia, Grady and Jeffrey, for the weeks, months, and years of their lives I missed. Of all who gave of themselves for me to complete my work, they gave the most. I would like to thank my sister Kathy for first telling me about C. S. Lewis and in effect setting a trajectory for my life. Thanks also go to my parents Chester and Jessie Root and my wife's parents Dr. Raymond and Mabel Biel for their continued encouragement and support.

I want to thank Professors Basil Mitchell, Lyle Dorsett, Jeffry Davis, Steven Beebe, and Chris Mitchell. I have been fortunate to have academic friends knowledgeable in their fields who knew the right balance between criticism and encouragement. Their insights were always timely and helpful. They were models of scholarship connecting intellect and heart, mediated through patience and goodness. I would also like to thank Drs. Bernard Farr and Andrew Walker for their feedback concerning revisions of this manuscript.

My gratitude also extends to the community at the Oxford Centre for Missions Studies. I would like to thank Canon Dr. Vinay Samuel, Canon Dr. Christopher Sugden, Dr. Carl Armerding and his wife Betsy, Dr. Ben Knighton, and Hillary Guest.

I would like to thank others in the Oxford community: Steve and Michele Connor, Stephen and Alice Lawhead, and their sons Ross and Drake. I am grateful to the David Young family and the supportive congregation at St. Aldate's. Thanks as well goes to the Oxford C. S. Lewis society for their kindness in allowing me to read several of these chapters at their society meetings and for their thoughtful responses to my work. I'm especially grateful to Walter Hooper, Michael Ward, Peter

Cousin, and Andrew and Erika Cuneo. Professor Stephen Mann and his wife Cindy were also encouraging.

In Wheaton, Illinois, I would like to thank Drs. Steve and Ruth Gieser for their support and encouragement. I am also grateful to Wheaton College for a generous grant from the Aldeen Fund. I'm grateful to Wendy Alderfer, Becs Richart, and Holly Sutton for their technical support. I am grateful to faculty members at Wheaton College who gave me feedback on the various chapters I presented at faculty forums: David Cook, Wayne Martindale, Tom Martin, Bruce Benson, Alan Jacobs, Bud Williams, Ward Kriegbaum, and Mark Noll. Thanks also goes to Marj Mead, Heidi Truty, Shawn Mrakovic, and the staff of the Marion E. Wade Center at Wheaton College, Wheaton, Illinois.

I am also grateful to dear friends in Santa Barbara, California: Tim and Marcia Tremblay, Vic and Barbara Batastini, Dan and Julie Michealsen, Gerda Inger, and Joan Frederickson for their friendship and support. I'm grateful to Steve and Reed Jolley for their pastoral encouragement. I must thank Cassandra Sternthall for her counsel and wisdom. For additional encouragement, I am also grateful to Jeff Frazer, Karen Erkel, Debby and Robby Edwards, Michael Anthony, Greg Pritchard, James Stamoolis, Jeff Nelson, Greg Campbell, and the Mead Men: Lon Allison, Chris Mitchell, Rick Richardson, and Brian Medaglia.

# Preface

## Introduction

IN HIS LIFETIME, C. S. LEWIS MASTERED MULTIPLE MODES OF COM-
munication. A sound and clear academic writer, able to engage in dialectic and debate on a high level, he gained the respect of those in his
field of medieval literature. An admired popularizer of Christianity, he
fashioned works in Christian apologetics that are still appreciated and
widely read today. A skilled imaginative writer, he crafted a wide range
of fiction and poetry, which demonstrates his enduring creative vision.
A brilliant teacher, lecturer, and preacher, Lewis often channeled his
skills via the medium of radio broadcast with great success. And as an
active and proficient public debater, Lewis was rightly called Oxford's
"bonny fighter," by his friend Austin Farrer, because of the rhetorical
skill he demonstrated at the weekly meetings of the Oxford Socratic
Club.[1] In each of these realms of communication, Lewis was not merely
experienced; he proved himself to be greatly skilled in each mode of
expression and, as a result, enjoyed remarkable success.

There are many reasons for Lewis's success as a communicator and
for his appeal to a wide audience, not the least of which is his facility
with language. Indeed, the thing that generates Lewis's holding power
is his rhetoric—the ability to use words well and with pervasive force.
Lewis always appears to be rhetorical, whether explicitly or implicitly
so. Professor James Como, Lewis scholar and rhetorician, emphatically
asserts that Lewis writes with explicitly rhetorical aims, calling him a
"rhetorical genius." Como notes, "Most at home with a rhetoric of demonstration, Lewis was obliged to elicit belief from particular people, at
particular times, under particular circumstances. He epitomized the
rhetor as defined by that old Roman teacher Quintilian, in his Institutes

---

1. Farrer, "The Christian Apologist," 25.

of Oratory: 'The good man speaking well.'"[2] Indeed, because Lewis had a rhetorical interest in his readers, he was particularly aware of his audience. He desired to persuade them to see the world in fresh ways, using multiple modes of communication. Consequently, he often succeeded at engaging his readers and moving them toward noble action.

Certainly, there were early formative experiences that shaped Lewis as a rhetorician. He was raised in an environment where a rhetorical approach to life was as native to him as the Irish air he breathed. At home, Lewis could not help but be affected by watching his father, who was the Sessional Solicitor of the Belfast City Council, as well as an effective political speaker for the Conservative Party.[3] In school, the young Lewis was classically trained, receiving an education informed by the medieval trivium, with its attention to rhetoric. Furthermore, at the university he worked as a literary historian, aware as any man of the power that rhetoric had over the conventions of writing and speaking.

Although Como observes that Lewis was a natural rhetorician, he is surprised that the books written by rhetoricians in Lewis's library are lacking the marginalia so characteristic of other books that most clearly influenced Lewis. This mystery may be easily solved, however. First, not all of the books from Lewis's library were sent to the Wade Center in Wheaton, Illinois, the library collection Como reviewed. In light of this, missing marginalia may not be significant. Second, the works of the rhetoricians may not be the only means by which Lewis could have learned the canons of rhetoric. Lewis himself writes of the Middle Ages, "Everything we should now call criticism belonged either to Grammar or to Rhetoric."[4] Clearly, Lewis knew the conventions of criticism from that epoch, and his books from this period are full of marginalia. His familiarity with the influence of rhetoric upon medieval works gave him the authority to say that the precepts of rhetoric were "addressed quite as much to poets as to advocates."[5] Almost as if he is defending

---

2. Como, *Branches to Heaven*, 16.

3. Ibid., 24.

4. C. S. Lewis, *Discarded Image*, 190.

5. Ibid. As Lewis continues the discussion here, he indicates that the poets learned rhetoric from one another. He sites as an example that "Virgil is for Dante the poet who taught him his *bello stilo.*" He notes that Petrarch had a similar influence on Chaucer, for "Petrarch in the *Clerk's Prologue* is for Chaucer the man who illuminated all Italy with his 'rethoryke swete.'" Lewis also observes the passing on of the tradition through

himself as a rhetorician, he further notes that one could not help but learn rhetorical theory by reading Dante, Chaucer, Lydgate, and others.[6] Lewis writes that "In rhetoric, more than anything else, the continuity of the old European tradition was embodied."[7] Furthermore, he says that "Nearly all our older poetry was written and read by men to whom the distinction between poetry and rhetoric, in its modern form, would have been meaningless."[8] Rhetorical study, then, was afforded to Lewis from a variety of sources.

Given Lewis's rhetorical training, in the broadest sense, and considering the way in which his written work operates with rhetorical purposes, it is only natural that the type of literary critical methodology I will use for this study is rhetorical. British literary scholar Terry Eagleton convincingly makes the case for a return to rhetoric as a form of "discursive theory," claiming that it is the oldest form of literary criticism. He writes, "Rhetoric, which was the received form of critical analysis all the way from ancient society to the eighteenth century, examined the way discourses are constructed in order to achieve certain effects."[9] Even so, Lewis argues in *An Experiment in Criticism*, books must be judged by the way they are read (that is by the way readers are affected by them). Likewise, a rhetorical approach to literature considers how an audience (even a reading audience) might be affected.

Why might rhetorical methodology be useful in analyzing the writing of Lewis? Most important, it must be understood that historically, rhetoric is "the art of persuasion." (Heretofore, most references to "rhetoric" in this study will signify "persuasion toward a view of reality.") As Eagelton accurately observes, "Rhetoric wanted to find out the most effective ways of pleading, persuading and debating, and rhetoricians studied such devices in other people's language in order to use

---

the poets, for Lydgate learned his rhetoric from Chaucer. As Lewis notes, "Chaucer in the *Book of Thebes* is for Lydgate the 'flour' of poets in Britain by his 'excellence in rethorike and in eloquence." The rhetorical influence is clear and, in some ways, absolute, for Lewis observes that "All Chaucer's medieval successors speak of him in this way." The rhetoric of the middle ages was literary and it had a clear influence on Lewis.

6. Ibid.

7. C. S. Lewis, *English Literature in the Sixteenth Century*, 61.

8. Ibid.

9. Eagleton, *Literary Theory*, 179.

them more productively in their own."[10] Lewis was well aware of the limitations of exposition, and likewise he saw the natural constraints of each genre of literature. Therefore, when he wrote, he sought to write using the written form most capable of bearing the weight of his purpose. His full and fertile mind had much to express, and he employed many forms of writing to do it—from lectures to literary criticism, from preaching to poetry. This enabled him not only to write about many things, but to provide his readers with a wide variety of vantage points so they might see more clearly what it was that Lewis saw. A voracious reader himself, Lewis wrote well, in part, because he read often. As rhetorician Doug Brent observes, "Reading and writing are intimately connected."[11] Much of Lewis's writing is focused on his own reading. Similarly, his writing is centered in his Christian faith; in other words, his writing is theological. Theologian David Cunningham rightly notes that "Whenever people attempt to communicate through language, they will find themselves disagreeing with one another; and, when their language concerns God, they may find themselves disagreeing quite frequently." Since this is the case, one should expect that "the enterprise of theology necessarily involves the construction and dissection of arguments and argumentative strategies."[12] This is a further reason why rhetorical criticism is the best methodology for the study of Lewis: he has a theological mind constructed from both deep personal reflection as well as discursive argument. The distinguished University of Chicago Professor, Wayne Booth, a former President of the Modern Language Association, convincingly argues that fiction is itself a means of rhetoric.[13] As a master of fiction, Lewis created his imaginative worlds to convince his readers not only of their plausibility, but also of the gravity of the issues at stake between his characters. "For Lewis every critical posture is always an implicit ontology, teleology, and an eschatology," argues Lewis scholar Bruce Edwards. This being so, "the critic is always defining the relationship of mankind not only to texts, but also to ultimate matters: the ground of being, the locus of meaning, and the possibility of transcendence. For Lewis, the Christian, this means

10. Ibid., 180.

11. Brent, *Reading As Rhetorical Invention*, xi.

12. Cunningham, *Faithful Persuasion*, xiii.

13. Booth, *Rhetoric of Fiction*.

that literary inquiry is always in some sense apologetics, though rarely explicitly so."[14] Without question, if Lewis's literary work is apologetical, then it is also rhetorical in nature.

## The Rhetorical Tradition

Lewis's rhetorical approach places him in an old and venerated tradition. Its longevity is attributed to the fact that human beings are communal and seek to communicate persuasively with one another. Rhetoric is about persuasion. Undoubtedly, every time Lewis put his pen to paper, he was interested in persuading readers to see a particular point of view. He was not seeking to manipulate his readers, for the key tool in the rhetorician's toolbox is dialectic. Dialectic functions as the art of debate and supplies rhetoric with its power to persuade. Lewis was a brilliant debater, and he was not afraid of opposition; rather, he encouraged it. Dialectic and the deepening of understanding require debate among able-minded disputants. Lewis was a part of this tradition. He embraced the canons of classical rhetoric as his own. Schooled in the art of invention, he knew how to craft strong argument, looking not only for the main flow of a river of thought but paying attention, as well, to the detailed tributaries and rivulets which supported it. He was a master of arrangement, capable of crafting his written word in such a way that he expressed himself with clarity, making even complex ideas easy to follow. Whatever criticisms one might find with Lewis's work, "lack of clarity" is never a concern. He crafted his imaginative prose with precision and style. His early practice of reading poetry and his lifetime love of poetry composition enabled him to develop a rhythm to his writing that makes it a delight to read out loud and easy to read in silence. Not only did he write for the ear, but he wrote visually, too. Metaphor and analogy serve to create word pictures that are not mere decoration; they are part of Lewis's rhetorical craft. Their use, in his hands, brings imaginative sight.

Lewis also understood the rhetorician's three classical modes of appeal, as developed in the Aristotelian tradition: pathos, logos, and ethos. Lewis sought to move his audiences by means of pathos, rooted in his own passions, sorrows, disappointments, joys, and expectations. There are some who believe that Lewis was not in touch with such emo-

---

14. B. Edwards, *A Rhetoric of Reading*, 110.

tions, but a close read of Lewis leads one to experience a heightened sense of emotion. Lewis, the letter writer, who answered all of his mail out of tender respect for those who happened to write him, is never far from any of his other publications, as well. Lewis's mind, prepared for debate not only by his training in logic but also in his wide knowledge of languages—Greek, Latin, Anglo-Saxon, French, German, Italian and a limited use of old Icelandic—knew the power of the word. He used logos to develop his content. One never gets the idea that he is fumbling for something to say. His mind was fertile, manifesting fruit whenever he put his pen to paper. Perhaps the mode most strongly evident in him is ethos. He is honest, and he displays in his work that authenticity of character that is full of genuine humility and childlike wonder. His ethos is exhibited when he wrestles with thorny passages in the Psalms that others tend to avoid because of their difficulty. It is seen as he announces to his readers that there is much about prayer he does not understand, or when he confesses that academic study should end in some degree of doubt. His ethos is equally evident by the confidence with which he presses a point that he has developed discursively, championing it with bulldog tenacity. Clearly, Lewis was in touch with the rhetorician's skill; he benefited by its tradition, and others benefited by his rhetoric, as well.

## Lewis's Rhetorical Aim

Considering C. S. Lewis as a rhetorician, what primary concern occupies his persuasive endeavors most often? Actually, there is one theme that is seldom addressed by scholars: Lewis's concern about subjectivism. He believed that if subjectivism were left unchecked, it would tend toward evil. While he writes about the problem of evil often enough, and about that aspect of it he defines as subjectivism, it is interesting to note that virtually all of the evil characters in his fiction attempt to justify their actions by means of subjectivist rhetoric. On the other hand, those protagonists caught in the balances between evil and good begin to emerge from temptations to evil when they reconcile themselves to the objective world about them and surrender to its demands. Evil characters seek to conform the world to their wishes; good characters grow out of the conformity of thought and will to habits of harmonious concord with the world in which they find themselves. Lewis's rhetorical concern about that aspect of the problem of evil he calls subjectivism is a theme which is pervasive in his writing and which is the focus of this investigation.

Subjectivism, as I define it for the purposes of this study, must be distinguished from the word subjective. The subjective refers to the subject's attempt to respond to objects with thoughts, feelings and motives appropriate to those objects. The objects are points of reference by which thoughts, feelings and motives may be assessed and judged. Subjectivism, on the other hand, is a point of view isolated from, and unresponsive to, objective reality. In its worst examples, subjectivism may even refer to those attempts to shape reality in order to make it fit preconceived notions about it; or, subjectivism may seek to shape reality in order to maintain evil motives. Lewis's concern about subjectivism and its connection with evil is stated explicitly in "The Poison of Subjectivism:"

> One cause of misery and vice is always present with us in the greed and pride of men, but at certain periods of history this is greatly increased by the temporary prevalence of some false philosophy. Correct thinking will not make good men out of bad ones; but a purely theoretical error may remove the ordinary checks to evil and deprive good intentions of their natural support. An error of this sort is abroad at present. . . . I am referring to Subjectivism.[15]

Lewis was an objectivist and argued that others should be, as well. His rhetoric against subjectivism is demonstrated in both discursive and imaginative writing.

## Methodology

Throughout this analysis, I will utilize the rhetorical ideas of Richard M. Weaver in order to make critical judgments about Lewis's writing and his own rhetorical endeavors. I have chosen to employ Weaver's theoretical perspective for several reasons. First, he was a contemporary of Lewis; they died the same year—1963. There is no indication that Lewis ever read anything by Weaver, but Weaver was familiar with Lewis. On rare occasions he quotes him, and on one occasion he wrote

---

15. C. S. Lewis, "The Poison of Subjectivism," in *Christian Reflections*, 72.

a favorable book review of Lewis's *Studies in Words*.[16] Although Weaver was from America and Lewis from Ireland, they were both affected by similar global issues and concerns. They were also both academics in rigorous academic environments, Lewis at Oxford and later Cambridge, Weaver at the University of Chicago. Both authors published in several literary genres and wrote across several disciplines. As Weaver scholar Ted J. Smith III notes, Weaver was one of the last century's leading rhetorical theorists, and he was a traditionalist.[17] He was a critic of his own culture, as, in his way, Lewis was also. Like Lewis, Weaver appears to have made an enduring contribution to letters, though not in as wide-ranging a manner as Lewis. Furthermore, scholar Robert Preston writes that Weaver was influenced by "the Western tradition, that of the high Middle Ages from the 10th to the 14th centuries." This interest in the medieval period also links Weaver to Lewis, and like Lewis, he was opposed to Nominalism to the degree that it denied the objective reality of universal principles. In other words, Weaver was also concerned about the dangers of subjectivism and promoted objective values, as a result.[18]

## A Summary of Richard Weaver's Salient Thought

Robert Preston writes that "Weaver's vision is based on two premises: the world is intelligible and the human person is free."[19] Weaver, like Lewis, accepts the idea that there is an objective world that exists independent of anyone's thoughts about it. He believes that the universe has design and therefore possesses this quality of intelligibility. Preston further observes of Weaver, "In appealing to the intelligibility of the universe, Weaver is siding with the philosophical realists against the nominalists."[20] His realist convictions put him in a position contrary to subjectivism and relativism. Weaver also believes that this world is moral. If man is a free and communicating being, and if the world is complex, then it is necessary for man to enter into a dialectical development in order to enrich his understanding of the world in which he lives. This process is a rhetorical one.

16. Weaver, "A Moral In a Word," from *In Defense of Tradition*, 448–49.

17. Ted Smith, introduction in Weaver, *In Defense of Tradition*, xix–xlviii.

18. Preston, "'Ideas Have Consequences' Fifty Years Later," 47 and 51.

19. Ibid., 47.

20. Ibid., 47–48.

Weaver believes in three levels of knowledge. First, there are facts, or ideas. Second, there are beliefs; these include interpretations of those facts which one holds with a degree of conviction. Third, there is the Metaphysical Dream; this is a kind of world view that informs the interpretations of facts; including antecedent assumptions about the world as those assumptions are embraced by a culture. According to Weaver, the "Metaphysical Dream" unifies a culture: the "dream" is communicated and refined through language. Dialectic is the means employed by the rhetorician in the hopes of persuading the culture to understand the "dream" more thoroughly and to discard those things that are unhealthy for the culture. It is possible for a false "dream" to emerge, which is not maintained by reasonable dialectic and debate over the meaning of facts. It is maintained by the use of what Weaver calls Ultimate Terms. There are, likewise, "god terms." These are words that have an attributed sacredness to them, and to depart from them is to risk being shunned by the culture. Similarly, there are "devil terms." These are the reverse of the "god terms;" they are little more than dismissive ad hominems, allowing a detractor to condemn without reason, to persuade without dialectic.

In Weaver's schema, a proper dialectic is maintained by various forms of argument, each with an ethical gradation of effectiveness. The most ethical form of argument is the argument from "Genus and Definition." Such an argument seeks to understand the essence and nature of a thing, as well as the purpose to which that thing serves. This dialectic approach has respect for the object as a thing in itself. It is ethical because, though the full truth of a thing may never be known, its approximations are based on the thing itself. The second most ethical type of argument is the argument from "Similitude." This argument seeks to understand the thing itself by use of comparison and analogy. When done well, it may establish an understanding that approximates the argument from definition; this is due to its comparisons to real things. The third type of argument—and the least ethical—is the argument from "Cause and Effect," or the argument from "Circumstance." For Weaver, this is the least ethical, for it appeals to something that has not yet occurred. Consequently, that something may be little more than the subjectivist's imagined concern. The rhetorician using this type of argument may use rhetoric manipulatively to secure responses in order to fulfill his own desires. Finally, there is a fourth type of argument to which Weaver refers; it is an appeal to "Authority and Testimony."

This type of argument depends on the traditions and dialectic of others; it appeals to history and tradition for authority and support. These concepts are at the core of Weaver's rhetorical theory, and will serve to orient the methodological analysis that will follow.

## Development of the Argument

Lewis was an objectivist and wrote at least one essay, "The Poison of Subjectivism," and one book, *The Abolition of Man*, to declare rhetorically that he was committed to this principle. These works, however, do not reflect the totality of Lewis's objectivist stance, as it appears also in many other bits and pieces of his writing. I have sought, for the purposes of this study, to pull together a systematic exposition of the more salient ideas of Lewis. If the tendency to slip into subjectivism and its potential for evil is a genuine risk, one might suppose that its allure is subtle. Was Lewis himself conscious of this? Does he seek to make accommodation for these risks by developing checks and balances helpful for himself, as well as his readers? I argue that Lewis was conscious of subjectivism's subtlety and that he uses his rhetoric to make the danger more evident.

Lewis was interested in the larger problem of evil, as is attested by his publications *The Problem of Pain* and *A Grief Observed*. Lewis rejected the faith of his childhood for its failure to console him after his mother died, when he was merely nine years old. He also had a deformity of his thumbs that made him awkward and the brunt of abuses in school. As he looked at his difficulties and the deficiencies of Christianity to provide satisfactory answers to his questions, he turned to atheism. Clearly, he was in a position to project onto the world an understanding driven by his own subjectivist assessments. However, it is important to note that he was an objectivist before his conversion to Christianity. His attempt to understand reality drove him from his childhood faith, and it also brought him back to faith as an adult convert. He was willing to modify his intellectual position. Although his conversion to Christianity has been discussed at great length, scholars have not pointed out that Lewis's own modifications of thought were due to his objectivist commitments. As he writes about the problem of evil, he is constantly asking his readers to consider more deeply what is involved in understanding the problem properly, and in doing this he offers fresh and helpful insights. These insights are not without flaws, and they are far from being last words on the subject, but they do reveal that Lewis's thinking about such things was "under construction," so to speak, as he sought to conform his thinking, as best he might, to the objective world. With the death of his wife, Joy Davidman, Lewis was forced to reconsider these matters more deeply, seeking for satisfactory answers—not only for the mind, but also for the heart. In looking at these matters, I argue that Lewis is cognizant of the problems of subjectivism, and his wrestling with these things is an example of one committed to the benefits of an objective pursuit of truth.

Lewis's professional career as an Oxford don and Cambridge Professor of Medieval and Renaissance Literature demanded that he attend to literary historical and critical matters related to this period. If subjectivism concerned Lewis, as I argue it did, then it is reasonable to suspect that he sees the need to address rhetorically the dangers of subjectivism in his literary critical work as well. I will examine how Lewis addresses subjectivist habits as he sees them practiced by literary critics and what he does in an effort to address them rhetorically. His literary critical work stands as a warning to the academy regarding the dangers of subjectivism.

Some have suggested that Lewis's interest in writing fiction was a retreat from his failed attempts as a Christian apologist. Certainly few, if any, would argue that Lewis was never an influential apologist. Many, on the other hand, would argue that Lewis could write popular works for the masses who lacked the technical skill to see through the weaknesses of his reasoning, but he lacked the background to keep up with the debates of the academy in areas of philosophy and theology. Due to his deficiencies, there are some, such as Lewis biographers George Sayer and A. N. Wilson, as well as Inkling and Tolkien biographer Humphrey Carpenter, who are convinced that fiction enabled him to press his ideas in a less threatened medium. I argue that Lewis continued producing works of apologetics throughout his life, and his interest in writing fiction resulted because that form of literature worked best for what it was he sought to convey rhetorically. One of the things he concerns himself with in his fiction is how subjectivism, unchecked, supports evil. It is one thing to state this as a proposition, but there is something of richer interest in portraying a supposal, in fiction, about how such a slide might occur. Lewis is not fleeing from the arena of debate as he does this; rather, he adds more texture to his body of work, and, in essence, he fleshes the significance of his ideas out as he does this.

Upon discovering the level of Lewis's concern about subjectivism, I will give attention to Lewis's fiction. Lewis has rhetorical interests in making it clear to his readers that evil is likely to grow from unchecked subjectivism. While he does not say this explicitly, it is implied in the argument of his work. Using Weaver's ideas about objective value, I will analyze several texts gathered from Lewis's fiction. The breadth of Lewis's fiction provides more data than can possibly be analyzed in this study; therefore I will take examples from four different decades, from the 1920s through to the 1950s. When these examples resemble similar instances in other texts, I will make note of the similarities as a means of highlighting other works with similar motifs. Lewis is concerned about a problem of evil, particularly subjectivism, and this idea is supported by the fact that he addresses its significance rhetorically in his fiction.

# 1

## Objectivity and Evil

### Introduction

IN THIS CHAPTER I EXAMINE C. S. LEWIS'S OBJECTIVIST COMMITMENTS. Lewis stated his objectivist position in the essay *The Poison of Subjectivism* and in the book *The Abolition of Man*, but additional evidence for his position is scattered throughout his work. It is necessary, for the argument of this study, to understand the significance of Lewis's objectivist position because of its unifying effect on his writing. Furthermore, it opens the door immediately to the principal topic of this investigation that Lewis believed subjectivism, left unchecked, leads to evil. Therefore, what follows is a systematic exposition of Lewis's thinking, based upon his published texts. Rhetoric scholar Richard M. Weaver's work on the ethics of rhetoric will provide a methodological approach to investigate and evaluate Lewis's objectivist stance. According to Weaver, by its very nature "language is sermonic," and rhetoric seeks to persuade; therefore, the rhetorician has ends in mind that he believes to be ethical. Weaver's insights are relevant to Lewis's writing. In his writing, Lewis has persuasive ends in mind, for he is conscious of his readers. Objectivity is the means by which he maintains an ethical rhetorical position, honest with the facts as he understands them, and with his readers. If, as I assert, Lewis believed subjectivism could lead to evil, it will be necessary to answer this question: What prevents the objectivist from undergoing such a slide himself? Mere objectivist sentiments are no guarantee that one can negotiate through the risks of self-deception, denial, or failure to recognize the human tendency for personal predilection to influence judgment. Does Lewis provide checks and balances in the configuration of his own objectivist stance, which, when in place, help to minimize these risks? I assert that he does. This is important for my overall argument, for eventually these checks will also be seen to be present in the good characters in his fiction, and absent in those characters that have succumbed to subjectivism and evil.

## Scholarly Views Concerning the One and the Many

Is there a common thread that unites all of Lewis's writing? To answer this question, a consideration of scholarly views is in order. In her doctoral dissertation, Jody R. Woerner notes this about Lewis's fiction: "There does seem to be an unmistakable quality that pervades all his fictional works as if he had left behind the scent of some familiar breeze—bright, bracing, and borne from a distant clime."[1] Similarly, author and Lewis critic David Downing observes that "One always senses in Lewis's books 'the one in the many.'"[2] While there is a wide variety of suggestions as to what accounts for this "one in many," most would agree with Downing when he writes that there is a "fascinating interconnectedness in all the books . . . reading any one of them casts light on all the others." This observation is commonly made. For example, J. A. W. Bennett, Lewis's student at Oxford, and later the man who would take up his Chair at Cambridge after Lewis retired, acknowledged this interconnectedness of his writing and called attention to it in his inaugural address at Cambridge. Speaking of Lewis, he noted, "The whole man was in all his judgments and activities. . . . His works are all of a piece: a book in one genre will correct, illumine or amplify what is latent in another."[3] Familiarity with Lewis continues to reveal this characteristic of his work. Concepts defined in his non-fiction are illustrated in his imaginative works. A self-effacing comment in one of his literary critical works may merit an entire chapter in one of his religious books. A thought in bud, found in a letter, is manifest in full bloom in an essay. An idea presented by means of an essay becomes the subject of a book. Interconnections reverberate throughout Lewis's work. Such internal amplification suggests that, in many ways, the best interpreter of his work is Lewis. Downing sees that this is so and, for example, asserts that the best approach for interpreting Lewis's science fiction is

1. Woerner, *Quest for Joy*, 1.
2. Downing, *Planets in Peril*, 8.
3. J. Bennett, "Humane Medievalist," 74.

to look to his autobiography. He posits that one will discover there that "Lewis shaped his early life experiences into a coherent narrative." The observation is true. What is it that informed 'the one in the many' and gave to Lewis's writing a single voice, and how did that voice shape the ethics of his rhetoric—his persuasive view of reality?

The quest for the unifying element in Lewis's work has led to many suggestions. Downing believes it is found in the fact that Lewis was a deeply imaginative man; he posits that Lewis's own writing supports this claim. He quotes from one of Lewis's published letters: "The list of my books which I send . . . will I fear strike you as a very mixed bag . . . (but) there is a guiding thread. The imaginative man in me is older, more continuously operative, and in that sense more basic than either the religious writer or the critic."[4] Lewis's words, here, are certainly significant, and I will develop their importance in a later chapter on Lewis's use of fiction. Nevertheless, Downing's judgment about the unifying element requires greater consideration.

Others, such as Donald Glover in *C. S. Lewis: The Art of Enchantment*, Michael H. Macdonald and Andrew A. Tadie in *C. S. Lewis: The Riddle of Joy*, and Corbin Scott Carnell in *Bright Shadow of Reality: C. S. Lewis and the Feeling Intellect*, claim that what unifies Lewis's work is his interest in the longing he describes as joy. According to Lewis, this longing is deeply rooted in all humans and is satisfied only when it is tethered to its proper object, that is, to God. Margaret Hannay also sees the importance of this longing in Lewis, and uses it as a means to judge his literary success. She sees *Perlandra* succeeding where *That Hideous Strength* fails, for the former develops this longing and the latter does not. However, such a judgment speaks against joy as the source of unity in Lewis, for by Hannay's own critique, it is inadequate to account for a book such as *That Hideous Strength*.[5] If a cause sufficient enough to explain this 'one in many' phenomenon exists at all, it will have to be found elsewhere.

Scott Oury also wonders what the source of this perceived unity in Lewis might be. He dismisses the idea that it should be located in his conversion to Christianity, for "Certainly he did not suddenly, or subsequently, become all he was from that point on. Nor can the liter-

4. Downing, *Planets in Peril*, 11.
5. Hannay, *C. S. Lewis*, 99.

ary man be understood entirely from the perspective of his beliefs."[6] It is at this point that Oury explains, and I believe rightly so, that the common thread linking all of Lewis's writing is an attempt to pay close attention to what Oury calls "the object itself." The object itself would include anything to which Lewis gave his attention, be it material object, literary text, idea, philosophy or doctrine. The object was always something outside of Lewis which he sought to understand as best as he might. Oury adds, "C. S. Lewis's conversion, first to theism and then to Christianity, was due in good part to his attention to 'the object itself.' The result was to confirm this habit of attention and establish it as a basis for his subsequent life and work."[7] One of the most central facts about Lewis, a fact necessary to understand his work, is that he was an objectivist. Lewis's rhetorical objectivism may be understood via Richard Weaver, who rightly maintains that rhetoric is sermonic. In other words, all rhetoric seeks to persuade an audience to accept a particular point of view. Consequently, Lewis uses his writing to persuade his readers towards his "sermonically" objectivist position. Oury argues that "This emphasis on 'otherness,' objectivity, attention to 'the object itself,' appears throughout Lewis's theological, apologetical, and critical works."[8] While this seems to be so, it may also be argued that attention to "the other," in this regard, also appears in his fiction. I am arguing that this is particularly evident in the way his evil characters are unwilling to surrender to the objects of their respective worlds; that is to say, they are plagued by their own subjectivism.

## Objections to the Argument Considered

Not all Lewis scholars would agree with Oury. Robert Houston Smith concedes that Lewis was an objectivist, but he means something very different by the idea than anything Oury has in mind. Smith asserts that Lewis was a Platonist, and he argues that having read Charles Williams's *The Place of the Lion*, Lewis "came to a richer awareness of the potential relevance of Platonism for his Christian world view."[9] Smith even goes so far as to assert, "Platonism, as the mature Lewis perceived it,

6. Oury, "The Thing Itself," 2.

7. Ibid., 2.

8. Ibid., 6.

9. R. Smith, *Patches of Godlight*, 4.

was a philosophical embodiment of the same absolute truth that was to be found in Christianity."[10] Certainly, Lewis is at times sympathetic to Plato, but he sees the areas that distinguish Christianity from Platonism, and he rejects Plato soundly at such places.[11] Though Smith sees Lewis's objectivist position grounded in Platonism, an argument which I believe is too simple and incorrect, he does concede that it is Lewis's belief in objective value that provides a clue for understanding 'the one in the many.' Smith confidently asserts that "Running through much of Lewis's writing is the belief that the greatest danger to human beings is that of losing sight of objective value, of degenerating into self-centered creatures wallowing in subjectivism, making gods of the appetites and irrational preferences."[12] This self-centeredness turns man into a mere consumer; what exists has value only as far as it serves his utilitarian interests, and beyond these he senses no moral responsibility within the objective world. Furthermore, Smith notes, "A great many times in his writing Lewis used the words *object* and *objective* when elucidating the philosophical dimensions of his thought, and always favorably."[13]

Another objection comes from Peter Schakel. He also concedes that Lewis was an objectivist, but he appears to believe that Lewis's brand of objectivism sought to suppress his own subjectivity. This will be discussed in greater depth in the chapter on Lewis's literary criticism, in the context of Lewis's controversy with E. M. W. Tillyard and "the personal heresy." Here, it is necessary, however, to visit the topic briefly as it relates to Lewis's objectivism in order to gain further clarity about his objectivist position. Lewis's life-long friend, Owen Barfield, wrote about a change he observed in Lewis between 1930 to 1940, "which roughly coincided with his conversion to theism and then to Christianity, but which did not appear . . . naturally connected with it."[14] Barfield says of this change "that at a certain stage in his life [Lewis] deliberately ceased

---

10. Ibid., 5.

11. C. S. Lewis, *Letters*. There is one such example dated 17 January 1940; Lewis, writing to a former student, marks the difference between Christianity and Platonism where the Platonists are closer to the Gnostics and the Docetics than they are to Christianity. Lewis then comments, "But I fear Plato thought the concrete flesh and grass bad, and have no doubt he was wrong" (175).

12. R. Smith, *Patches of Godlight*, 13–14.

13. Ibid., 12.

14. Barfield, Introduction to *Light on C. S. Lewis*, edited by Jocelyn Gibb, ix.

to take any interest in himself."[15] Schakel fixes on this comment in order to suggest that Lewis chose to suppress his subjectivity. According to Schakel, objectivity for Lewis was a means of denying his feeling side, which did not evidence signs of reawakening until Lewis met his wife, Joy Davidman, and until he wrote *Till We have Faces*.[16] Schakel says that "the place [Lewis] allows to the imagination is limited at this point by his conception of the 'objective.'"[17] Later, Schakel adds that Lewis had a "tendency to concretize the 'objective' and to isolate it from the subjective element."[18] While this argument is interesting, Schakel seems to have overlooked some important data.

The publication of *The Allegory of Love* occurs during the period of Lewis's life in which Barfield says he noted this change in Lewis. Whatever Barfield may have meant by his comment, *The Allegory of Love* would seem to count against Schakel's interpretation of Barfield's statement. In his book, Lewis traces the development of the allegory during the late medieval period. He credits Chretien de Troyes as the creator of allegory, noting that he "can hardly turn to the inner world without, at the same time, turning to allegory." Then Lewis explains, "Allegory, besides being many other things, is the subjectivism of an objective age."[19] These comments about allegory as the means to express the interior life are repeated often enough. The Middle Ages looked forward, anticipating a form by which it might express the interior life, and this expectancy was nurtured by Augustine's *Confessions* and its "turning inward." Lewis writes that this "turning inward," or personalistic style in the *Confessions*, "is the very moment of a transition more important, I would suggest, than any that is commonly recorded in our works of 'history.'"[20] Augustine "wanders hither and thither in his own mind as he speaks the very language of a traveller."[21] Here, Lewis writes as if he values this subjective element, alive, at full play, a chance to look over one's life, an object needing interpretation. Following these early

15. Ibid., xvi.
16. Schakel, *Reason and Imagination*, 160–62.
17. Ibid., 108.
18. Ibid., 115.
19. C. S. Lewis, *Allegory of Love*, 30.
20. Ibid., 65.
21. Ibid.

developments in Augustine and de Troyes, Lewis adds, "Hence the development of allegory, to supply the subjective element in literature, to paint the inner world, followed inevitably."[22] With clear appreciation for this development, Lewis writes words that are hardly those of one who is seeking to suppress subjectivity in pursuit of objectivity. Contrary to Schakel's assessment, Lewis, at the very time in question, sees subjectivity in a positive light. Subjectivity is not eclipsed by objectivity. Objects properly perceived invite a subjective response which is necessary if they are to be understood. *Subjectivism*, in contradistinction to subjectivity, does not take its lead from objects. It seeks to force reality to fit preconceived notions.

I have been arguing that the unity in Lewis, observed by so many, can be accounted for by the fact that he was an objectivist. His commitment to objectivity, however, was not to be seen as synonymous with the suppression of any subjective or emotional capacities within him.

## A Systematic Examination of Lewis's Views about Objectivity

Lewis's views about objectivity can be compiled from many of his books, so significant is this theme in his work. A grasp of his general thinking about this topic is necessary to understand his commitment to objectivity. Additionally, this understanding is also significant for situating his views about subjectivism and its potential for evil.

### *Truth Is Objective*

Richard Weaver rejects the position of the Nominalists. He believes that "universals have a real existence."[23] The issue between the Nominalists and realists like Weaver "is whether there is a source of truth higher than, and independent of, man: and the answer to the question is decisive for one's view of the nature and destiny of humankind."[24] Like Weaver, Lewis assumes that the universe is intelligible. Consequently, Lewis writes, "The first qualification for judging any piece of workmanship from a corkscrew to a cathedral is to know what it is—what it was

22. Ibid.
23. Weaver, *Ideas*, 3.
24. Ibid.

intended to do and how it is meant to be used."[25] From this statement at least four things can be observed about Lewis as a rhetorician—a man making a pervasive claim about reality.

First, Lewis believed in the objectivity of truth—thought must conform to its object.[26] This does not overlook issues of perspective. For example, four people seated at a square table, in a home for a meal, will each have a slightly different perspective of that meal. One sees beyond the table a painting on the wall; another sees through a window into the garden; a third sees through a doorway into the kitchen; and the fourth sees the buffet and on it the dishes of food still to be served. All the views, though different in perspective, have at their centre the table on which is served their meal. And beyond the table, each sees items peculiar to a house; more specifically, to that very house where they are in fact eating. In hearing a report of the meal from three of the four, including details of the foods and features of the home, no one would take as factual a report from the fourth that claimed the meal was actually eaten as a picnic in the park. For the fourth participant to insist that he be given liberty for his point of view on the basis of perspective is to demand too much. What he says does not conform to the object of the meal in any way consistent with the report given by the others. This illustration demonstrates what Lewis understood: belief in objective truth does not discount perspective; neither should perspective be construed as mere relativism.

Second, Lewis believed it is important to discover what an object is intended to do. The word *definition* essentially means, "Of the finite." As Weaver explains, "One way to interpret a subject is to define its nature—to describe the fixed features of its being."[27] Things are defined by their limitations; in that way, they can be distinguished from other things. For a thing to be defined, it must be small enough to wrap words around it. Lewis also observes that a characteristic distinguishing one object from some other object is function. It is one thing to recognize the truth of an object by virtue of its limitations, and another thing to

---

25. C. S. Lewis, *Preface to Paradise Lost*, 1.

26. C. S. Lewis, *Abolition of Man*, 29. Lewis develops the idea of "the doctrine of objective value, the belief that certain attitudes are really true, and others really false, to the kind of thing the universe is and the kind of things we are." For brevity's sake, he calls this the *Tao*.

27. Weaver, "Language is Sermonic," 1354.

understand the truth of that object in relation to its function, the purpose or ends to which it serves. This is true of material objects, objects of thought, and even the words used to describe them.

Third, Lewis believed that an understanding of the truth of an object is more fully grasped when one possesses the skill to use the object for its intended purposes. The person who possesses the skill of horsemanship will have an understanding of horses different than the person who can merely distinguish a horse from other animals. The horseman will know the proper care and treatment of the horse. He will be able to develop the animal's trust. He will know how to saddle and ride it, how to change leads, and so on. His knowledge of the horse will be experiential and more fully developed.

Fourth, to say what a thing is does not imply that one has spoken the last word about that object. I doubt whether anyone is capable of speaking a last word about anything. If I look at a pen and say, "That is a pen," I have not uttered a last word about the object as a pen. Certainly more could be discovered about it. Is it a fountain pen, or a ballpoint, or a felt tipped pen? What color is it? What color does it write? Who made it, and from what was it made? What is its molecular structure? How much ink does it hold? And so it goes, on and on. The fact that I do not have a last word about the pen does not mean that I cannot have a sure word about it. If I do not possess all the details about the pen, my lack of full knowledge does not invalidate my statement, "That is a pen."

From these observations about Lewis, more can be concluded. First, in the pursuit of truth, subjectivism is undesirable; this occurs when the subject no longer surrenders to the object, choosing, rather, to believe arbitrarily whatever he will about the object, without sense of obligation that his thoughts ought to conform to the object as it is. Second, a misunderstanding of the function, purpose or ends for which a thing exists can radically minimize what truth is known about it, making less substantive any judgments that might be made concerning it. Finally, lack of firsthand familiarity with the object may prove to be an obstacle standing in the way of understanding practical truth about it. The person skilled in the use of a particular object is in a position of advantage when seeking to understand the truth about that object. This does not guarantee he will always do well. He may have become lazy since acquiring his skill, and therefore not always careful in its application. He may have endangered his clarity of thought about the object and compromised its integrity by using it in a way contrary to the purposes for which it was designed. Still, the fact that he is skilled in the use of that object means that he has concentrated on that object in the acquisition of his skill in a way that another, lacking that skill, has not.

It is possible that the subject, as a perceiver of an object, can himself get in the way of perceiving a thing properly; that is to say, in a way that is inconsistent with the being of the object itself. Such hindrances can be those of limitation, due to lack of knowledge of facts related to the object. They may also be due to conflicts of interests, moral compromises that can cloud perception. Hindrances may be the result of psychological maladjustment; they can also be the result of cultural presuppositions or prejudices. To know the truth about an object, one must recognize that he can, and sometimes does, misunderstand what it is and how it is to be used. Therefore, it is important to minimize those things that would distract one from getting at the object itself, and maximize those conditions that would allow the conformity of thought to the object, in order to know more of the truth about it. Weaver underscores this importance when he acknowledges that "With the denial of objective truth there is no escape from the relativism of 'man the measure of all things.'"[28] Such a subjectivist position is exactly what Lewis the rhetorician encourages his readers to avoid.

## Truth Is Narrow

Lewis writes, "We should never ask of anything 'Is it real?,' for everything is real. The proper question is 'A real *what*?' e.g. a real snake or real *delirium tremens*?"[29] Getting at the object for what it really is, as best he might, is essential to Lewis's objective approach to truth, the basis of his rhetoric. Without the conformity of thought to object, truth cannot be known nor error corrected. He writes, "Truth is always *about* something, but reality is that *about which* truth is."[30] He develops this objective view of truth in *The Abolition of Man*, stating, "It is the sole source of all value judgements. If it is rejected, all value is rejected. If any value is retained, it is retained."[31] Lewis held this position, at this

28. Weaver, *Ideas*, 4.

29. C. S. Lewis, *Letters to Malcolm*, 107

30. C. S. Lewis, *God in the Dock*, 66.

31. C. S. Lewis, *Abolition of Man*, 56.

point, as a non-negotiable. He believed tenaciously that truth is objective. This view should not be dismissed as unduly narrow for at least two reasons.

If truth is found in the conformity of thought to object, then it stands to reason that truth will be narrow. That which can be truly thought will be limited to the object itself and how it may be understood in relation to other objects. Though it may be possible to gain a fuller understanding of the object, any thought not conforming to the object *per se* will not be true of it.

Also, though Lewis may be intentionally narrow in matters concerning the nature of truth, he recognizes that it is consistent with the nature of opinion to allow for differences.[32] Objectivist philosopher Mortimer Adler identifies three useful characteristics of opinions which are relevant here. First, they are based on probability rather than certainty. There must be good reasons for one's opinion, or it is simply prejudice. A distinction also ought to be made between what is believed because good reasons support it, and what is believed as certainty. Second, opinions are subject to doubt. And third, reasonable people can differ on matters of opinion.[33] Lewis was on the whole careful to mark the difference between truth and opinion, as is evident throughout his published work. While knowledge may be extended through the use of opinions and probabilities, Lewis's dogma is reserved for, and appropriate to, matters of truth and certainty as best he understood them; his openness and broadmindedness was directed towards matters of opinion, probabilities, and possibilities.

32. Ibid., 60. He writes, "An open mind, in questions that are not ultimate, is useful. But an open mind about ultimate foundations either of Theoretical or Practical Reason is idiocy. If a man's mind is open on these let his mouth at least be shut." Elsewhere, Lewis writes to those who would engage in Christian Apologetics, warning them that they must be careful to defend the Faith and not mere opinions about it. "Each of us has his individual emphasis: each holds, in addition to the Faith, many opinions which seem to him to be consistent with it and true and important. And so perhaps they are. But as apologists, it is not our business to defend *them*. We are defending Christianity; not 'my religion.' When we mention our personal opinions, we must always make quite clear the difference between them and the Faith itself" (C. S. Lewis, *God in the Dock*, 90).

33. Adler, *Great Ideas*, 6.

## Lewis's Explanation for the Existence of Objective Reality

The fact that objects exist, as well as knowers and things to be known, suggests another issue important to Lewis's thought. What does the existence of objects and of knowers suggest about what can be known concerning the world? In *Miracles*, he writes, "If anything exists, something must be eternal; if any reason exists, some reason must be self existent, non-contingent."[34] In a world of contingencies, Lewis agrees with Thomas Aquinas in observing, "It is clear that there never was a time when nothing existed; otherwise nothing would exist now."[35] What can account for the existence of things as they are? Here the connection between knowing and metaphysics must be acknowledged.

Though there may be many answers to the ontological question, it appears to Lewis that they fall into three general categories. The first category includes all attempts to explain the existence of things through a process that begins with self-creation. Things just happen on their own with no outside assistance. Of course this view is nonsense. Canvasses do not paint themselves, gardens do not organize themselves, babies do not give birth to themselves, and universes do not make themselves. Nothing is self-created. In his mature writing, Lewis never takes this view seriously. Lewis's attention is given to categories two and three.

The second category would include those explanations that suggest matter is eternal and therefore can be shown to account for the existence of things as we know them. Someone may object to this materialist position, arguing that it cannot account for things immaterial, such as thought or love. In light of this challenge, the materialist explains his position by reducing all such experiences to mere chemical phenomena. For instance, the man looks at a woman. Her image is projected on the retina of his eye. Through a series of electrical synapses the message travels along the optic nerve until it stimulates the brain. The response that follows is the secretion of particular hormones that direct the man to say he is in love. The materialist says it is not love at all, merely chemistry. It can all be explained away as a function of matter. Yet, Lewis objects to this, for if it is so, the materialist has explained away explanation

34. C. S. Lewis, *Miracles*, 27–28.

35. Ibid., 107. As generally regards the Medieval man, Lewis notes, "It was fundamental to his thought that no infinite series can be actual. We cannot therefore go on explaining one movement by another *ad infinitum*." See C. S. Lewis, *Discarded Image*, 62.

itself. The materialist observes the lovers. Their image is projected onto the retina of his eye. Through a series of synapses, the message is carried along his optic nerve to his brain. A chemical response to the incoming stimulus results in his explaining that it is not love that exists between the man and the woman, only chemistry. If the lovers cannot call their experience "love," then neither can the materialist call what he speaks an "explanation." If all phenomena can be reduced to mere chemistry, then it would appear that knowledge is impossible, because knowledge must be more than mere chemical function. Mere chemical functions cannot be said to know themselves anymore than fluctuations in the weather can be said to know themselves. Consequently, Lewis cannot accept the materialist's presuppositions. He believes that "Reason is something more than cerebral bio-chemistry."[36]

The third category of possible explanations for the existence of objective reality is, for Lewis, the view that something supernatural and immaterial caused the universe to be. He explains,

> The naturalist believes that a great process, or 'becoming,' exists 'on its own' in space and time, and that nothing else exists— what we call particular things and events being only the parts into which we analyze the great process or the shapes which that process takes at given moments and given points in space. This single, total reality he calls nature. The supernaturalist believes that one Thing exists on its own and has produced the framework of space and time and the procession of systematically connected events which fill them. This framework, and this filling, he calls nature. It may, or may not, be the only Reality which the one Primary Thing has produced.[37]

There are two major pieces of data here: first, that material objects exist in a world of flux, change, and contingencies; second, that immaterial things also exist—such as thought, love, justice—and cannot be adequately accounted for by any materialist presuppositions. Lewis

---

36. C. S. Lewis, *Miracles*, 50. Elsewhere, Lewis writes, "If I swallow the scientific cosmology as a whole, then not only can I not fit in Christianity, but I cannot even fit in science. If minds are wholly dependent on brains, and brains on bio-chemistry, and bio-chemistry (in the long run) on meaningless flux of atoms, I cannot understand how the thought of those minds should have any more significance than the sound of wind in the trees" (C. S. Lewis, *Screwtape Proposes a Toast*, 58).

37. Ibid., 19–20.

accepts the third category as valid, since it best accounts for the data.[38] He observes of the supernaturalist position, "No philosophical theory which I have yet come across is a radical improvement on the words of *Genesis*, that, 'In the beginning God made Heaven and Earth.'"[39]

## Lewis's View That Objective Reality Is Moral

The supernatural view presupposes that there is a moral intelligence responsible for the material universe.[40] Lewis writes, "If there is 'something behind' [the material world], then either it will have to remain altogether unknown to us or else make itself known in some different way."[41] Our knowledge concerning any kind of objective morality in the universe is limited. But Lewis points out that a kind of first-hand knowledge of objective morality is available to us as creatures: "In this case we have, so to speak, inside information; we are in the know. And because of that, we know that men find themselves under a moral law, which they did not make and cannot quite forget even when they try, and which they know they ought to obey."[42] Knowledge of the moral law and knowledge that we break it is consistent with the idea of objective value. The obvious danger of a subjectivist whose vision of the world is self-referential is that he is likely to be blind to any standard whereby he might evaluate his behavior. Ignorance of how evil affects him will prove to be a liability in his attempt to make sense of the problem of evil, and the subjectivist may even blame others for things they did not do. Lewis presses this point persistently throughout his published work. One of his rhetorical aims is to drive into the conscious minds of his readers that each one has moral failure which must be dealt with, and it is Lewis's belief in the moral nature of the objective universe that makes it possible for him to make such claims.

---

38. Lewis also suggests another category that I have not included here. It is found in *Mere Christianity*. Book I, Chapter 4. It is the category he calls "Emergent evolution." I did not include it here because Lewis sees it as a hybrid between the materialist position and the religious or supernatural position. When pressed, those who hold the view, Lewis experienced, moved into one of the original camps from which it was derived. He felt it was a mere convenience more than a substantive position.

39. C. S. Lewis, *Miracles*, 42.

40. C. S. Lewis, *Mere Christianity*, 17–18

41. Ibid., 18.

42. Ibid., 19.

Beside moral failure, Lewis considers emotional issues that must be accounted for when working through matters related to the problem of evil. Who could believe otherwise after reading his anguish in *A Grief Observed*, or reading his explanations of the imprecatory Psalms in *Reflections on the Psalms*? Emotional anguish should find its voice, rather than be suppressed. If resolution is to be found, perhaps it is best when this voice, with its complaints, is directed toward God.[43] If reasoned arguments lead one to believe that God does not exist, the emotional problems associated with pain and suffering do not cease. Atheists and agnostics still complain to God of such things, and religious believers may still trust Him. Certainly more is at play here than meets the eye. Further, one may even be less likely to make sense of the problem without some kind of belief in God.[44]

For Lewis, truth is objective. It is found in the conformity of thought to object. Thoughts and objects exist, and this fact points to intelligence behind the universe. One of the ways that this intelligence can be known is through the personal experience of sensing that one "ought" to do certain things which one tends not to do. Lewis sees in this experience an awareness of a Moral Law. He speculates that the intelligence behind the universe has placed this awareness within human conscience. Notwithstanding all this, subjectivism may blind one to these moral obligations.

## Obstacles to Seeing Objectively

If humans have some kind of insider's information that confirms a supernatural cause and moral order in the universe, and if it is as obvious as Lewis suggests, why does not everyone readily accept it? Lewis gives many possible explanations.

43. This is the kind of thing Lewis does in *A Grief Observed*, and the kind of thing Queen Orual does in *Till We Have Faces*.

44. In his autobiography, Lewis observes that this was, in part, his own predicament having rejected the existence of God over the problem of evil. He writes, "I was at this time living, like so many Atheists or Antitheists, in a whirl of contradictions. I maintained that God did not exist. I was also very angry with God for not existing. I was equally angry with Him for creating a world" (C. S. Lewis, *Surprised By Joy*, 115).

## Ignorance

Lewis believes that one reason an individual might be unresponsive to his moral obligation in the universe might be due to ignorance.[45] Perhaps the data with which a person is working is presently insufficient. However, if this is so, it would appear to be an exception to Lewis's concept of the Moral Law acting upon human conscience generally, and he would therefore appear to be inconsistent in his reasoning. Ignorance of this sort might make violations of the Moral Law excusable. If this is the case, it would certainly be difficult to charge offenders with intentional violations, for again the ignorance may be due to data that is deficient. Or it may be that an individual is not developmentally able to discern the "voice" of the Moral Law upon the conscience, or has not yet identified whatever might be the transcendent source of that voice. In these instances, it might be possible that the voice of conscience may be speaking, but that ignorance as to its source may be a legitimate excuse for not attending to it. However, on closer inspection it appears that there is no real ignorance of the Moral Law. We may make excuses for the actions we do that are hurtful to others. But as soon as we experience similar ill treatment from others that hurt us, our complaints betray our claim to ignorance. In cases like these, ignorance is no longer an acceptable excuse. This double standard leaves us condemned, as Lewis well understood, for we have acknowledged that we do not like to receive what we have been willing to give.

## Inattention

Lewis suggests that inattention may be a second possible reason for missing the voice of conscience.[46] Perhaps moral sensitivity must be cultivated and developed. It may be that serious attention has never been paid to the conscience when it has spoken and its impressions are, therefore, misunderstood or neglected. These things could be the consequence of laziness or disinterest, perhaps motivated by the fear that, should a transcendent source be behind the prompting of conscience, it may likely mean a change in one's behavior. Lewis writes personally of his own days as an Agnostic, citing that he doubted his position was one of genuine honesty. "Amiable Agnostics will talk cheerfully about

45. C. S. Lewis, *Christian Reflections*, 67.
46. Ibid., 68.

'man's search for God.' To me, as I then was, they might as well have talked about the mouse's search for the cat."[47] Inattention may be a habit of purposeful neglect, and to that degree it is dishonest.

## INEFFICIENCIES IN THE SYSTEM OF SYMBOLS

A third type of misunderstanding of one's obligation to the moral order of the universe, according to Lewis, may be due to "inefficiencies in the system of symbols (linguistic or otherwise) which we are using."[48] Lewis divides this problem into further subcategories. The first subcategory of *inefficient symbols* is that of equivocation, and results from a misunderstanding caused by failures of definition. With both errors of reason and moral error, the process necessary to make corrections requires a return to the very place where the error was originally made.[49] Failure to define an important term may lead to equivocation and skew one's thinking about a matter. So too, lack of clear moral definition in those places where morality can be known leads to moral ambiguity. Failure to correct inconsistencies of reason or morality, the kind of failure supported by subjectivity, may turn misunderstanding into serious error. This may still be the fruit of intellectual misunderstanding more than moral failure *per se*. Moral failure would be evidenced by acknowledging the need to correct an error and then refusing to do so. Weaver explains that people travelling down a path of decadence "develop an insensibility which increases with their degradation."[50] Moral lapse, it appears, tends towards increasing self-justification, and this will find easy support in subjectivism.

47. C. S. Lewis, *Surprised By Joy*, 227.

48. C. S. Lewis, *Christian Reflections*. 68.

49. Lewis observes, "We all want progress. But progress means getting nearer to the place where you want to be. And if you have taken a wrong turning, then to go forward does not get you any nearer. If you are on the wrong road, progress means doing an about-turn and walking back to the right road; and in that case the man who turns back soonest is the most progressive man. We have all seen this when doing arithmetic. When I have started a sum the wrong way, the sooner I admit this and go back and start over again, the faster I shall get on. There is nothing progressive about being pig-headed and refusing to admit a mistake. And I think if you look at the present state of the world, it is pretty plain that humanity has been making some big mistake. We are on the wrong road. And if that is so, we must go back. Going back is the quickest way on" (*Mere Christianity*, 22).

50. Weaver, *Ideas*, 10.

The second subcategory found under *inefficient symbols* describes misunderstanding made from the kinds of language we use and what our intentions are with that language. In his essay, *The Language of Religion*,[51] Lewis exhibits his rhetorical insight regarding the function of three kinds of language, each identified by its particular use. The first is ordinary language as it is used every day. The second is scientific language; it improves upon ordinary language by being precise in quantification.[52] The third is poetic language, which is directed toward conveying quality, and as Lewis observes, "...contains a great many more adjectives."[53] In comparing scientific language with poetic, Lewis writes the following:

> I think Poetic language does convey information, but it suffers from two disabilities in comparison with Scientific. (I) It is verifiable or falsifiable only to a limited degree and with a certain fringe of vagueness. Not all men, only men of some discrimination, would agree, on seeing Burn's mistress that the image of 'a red, red rose' was good, or (as might be) bad. In that sense, Scientific statements are, as people say now, far more easily 'cashed.' But the poet might of course reply that it always will be easier to cash a cheque for 30 shillings than one for 1,000 pounds, that the scientific statements are cheques, in one sense, for very small amounts, giving us, out of the teeming complexity of every concrete reality only 'the common measurable features.' (2) Such information as Poetic language has to give can be received only if you are ready to meet it half-way. It is no good holding a dialectical pistol to the poet's head and demanding how the deuce a river could have hair, or thought be green, or a woman a red rose.[54]

Lewis classifies theological language as something like scientific language because it is used "for purposes of instruction, clarification, controversy and the like."[55] He then describes a further category, the language of religion: "The language in which we express our religious beliefs and other religious experiences, is not a special language, but

51. C. S. Lewis, *Christian Reflections*, 129–41.
52. Ibid., 130.
53. Ibid., 131.
54. Ibid., 135.
55. Ibid., 135.

something that ranges between the Ordinary and the Poetical."[56] Lewis observes that "there is a special region of experiences which can be communicated *without* Poetic language, namely, its 'common measurable features,' but most experience cannot." Lewis argues, "To be incommunicable by Scientific language is, so far as I can judge, the normal state of experience."[57] He notes further, "The very essence of our life as conscious beings, all day and every day, consists of something which cannot be communicated except by hints, similes, metaphors, and the use of those emotions (themselves not very important) which are pointers to it."[58] Lewis reveals a rhetorical mastery and facility with each of these types of language. His precision of the "scientific" is evident in his apologetics and his literary criticism. His skill at ordinary language and the use of the vernacular contributes to his success as a popular writer. And his imaginative use of the "poetic" enables him to put "flesh" on religious themes.

If a Supernatural Being stands behind the world as Creator, and if he is active in its natural order, how can this be talked about? Although God is a being whose very nature transcends description, this does not mean that such a Being cannot be described at all, but only that certain concessions must be made which account for the complexities peculiar to the object itself and to the limited capacities of human communication. As was mentioned previously, definition means *of the finite*, and objects are defined by their limitation and function. Given this, how does the language of definition, even the language of theology, let alone science, function to describe God? If God is Infinite Being, then he is something that defies the categories of this type of description. How can the infinite be defined? How do we describe that which is not natural but supernatural? How do we talk about that which is not typical but archetypal? Lewis suggests, and I concur, that God *can* be talked about; however, to do it properly one has to have respect for the object itself and the kind of language appropriate to it. To challenge whether or not God exists or His character is good, because his activities are not describable by the kinds of language that have by their very nature a scope too narrow for the task, begs the question. Still, assertions about God

56. Ibid.
57. Ibid., 138.
58. Ibid., 140.

that use the language of Religion can be judged to be valid or invalid. The canons of rhetoric that govern any reasonable discourse will still apply. It does mean, however, that we will become less proficient in our ability to say anything meaningful about God, His work in the world, or His character without respect for the differences in kinds and uses of language. In other words, to speak of God requires a particular kind of rhetoric—a language that conveys a distinct view of reality.

Lewis concedes at the end of *The Language of Religion* that his thoughts are tentative and he has his doubts.[59] But he acknowledges that if anyone wants to discover truths concerning religious sayings, "You will not get it on any other terms."[60] Consequently, in relation to the problem of evil, three things are apparent. First, the nature of language, as Lewis understands it, does not permit final judgments. Whatever is known can be plumbed deeper. It is more likely that the subjectivist, not the objectivist, will be misled to think he understands a matter entirely. Lewis writes, "To say that Reason is objective is to say that all our false reasonings could in principle be corrected by more Reason."[61] Furthermore, though judgments can be made, they will be tentative and therefore must necessarily be open to modification. Even a sure word can be refined further. Finally, we should recognize that Lewis thinks about the problem of evil with openness to modification of his thinking to account for new developments within his thought process. His views about the problem of evil develop with respect to time and experience, and they are expressed in a variety of ways that are conditioned by rhetorical need as well as the literary genre in which he is working. One thing must be said at this point which is critical to the development of my argument: Changes that do occur in Lewis, as reflected in his writing, occur because of his belief that truth is objective. Each modification in his thinking about evil and suffering represents Lewis's attempt to get at reality, to the degree that it can be known. He does not always do it well, and that is why modifications are necessary. But the fact that modifications can be made at all is consistent with his belief that truth is objective. This will be developed further in chapter two.

59. Ibid., 141.
60. Ibid.
61. Ibid., 68.

"The Language of Religion," as Lewis develops the concept, makes understanding about God's work in the universe something that can be approximated. It may not be perfect sight. But "seeing through a glass darkly" is better than not seeing at all.

Lewis develops a third subcategory of *insufficient symbols* in his *Preface* to D. E. Harding's *The Hierarchy of Heaven and Earth*.[62] He explains his concerns about the use of language by those who were engaged in "linguistic analysis," seeking by it to discredit the study of Metaphysics and matters related to Metaphysics. Lewis calls his readers, or at least the readers of Harding's book, to re-think their response to that critique. His *Preface* echoes many themes that can be found in his apologetics, his fiction, and his essays. Even more, Lewis, in this long but important excerpt, writes with a keen linguistic awareness of how the rhetoric of the subject supplants the rhetoric of the object:

> The process whereby man has come to know the universe is from one point of view extremely complicated; from another it is alarmingly simple. We can observe a single one-way progression. At the outset the universe appears packed with will, intelligence, life and positive qualities; every tree is a nymph and every planet a god. Man himself is akin to the gods. The advance of knowledge gradually empties this rich genial universe: first of its gods; then of its colours, smells, sounds and tastes, finally of solidity itself as solidity was originally imagined. As these items are taken from the world, they are transferred to the subjective side of the account; classified as sensations, thoughts images or emotions. The Subject becomes gorged, inflated at the expense of the Object. But the matter does not rest there. The same method which has emptied the world now proceeds to empty ourselves. The masters of the method soon announce that we were just as mistaken (and mistaken in much the same way) when we attributed 'souls,' or 'selves' or 'minds' to human organisms, as when we attributed Dryads to the trees. We, who have personified all other things, turn out to be ourselves mere personifications. Man is indeed akin to the gods: that is, he is no less phantasmal than they. And just as we have been broken of our bad habit of personifying trees, so we must now be broken of our bad habit of personifying men: a reform already effected in the political field. There never was a Subjective account into which we could transfer the items which the Object had lost.

---

62. Harding, *Hierarchy of Heaven and Earth*.

For we are given to understand that our mistake was a linguistic one. All our previous theologies, metaphysics, and psychologies were a by-product of our bad grammar. Max Muller's formula (Mythology is a disease of language) thus returns with a wider scope than he ever dreamed of. We were not talking these things, we were only talking confusedly. All the questions which humanity has hitherto asked with deepest concern for the answer turn out to be unanswerable; not because the answers are hidden from us like 'goddes privitee,' but because they are nonsense questions like 'How far is it from London Bridge to Christmas day.'

This sort of error is of course very common in debate or even in our solitary thought. We start with a view which contains a good deal of truth, though in a confused or exaggerated form. Objections are then suggested and we withdraw it. But hours later we discover that we have emptied the baby out with the bath and that the original view must have contained certain truths for lack of which we are now entangled in absurdities. So here. In emptying out the dryads and the gods (which, admittedly, 'would not do' just as they stood) we appear to have thrown out the whole universe, ourselves included. We must go back and begin again: this time with better chance of success, for of course we can now use all particular truths and all improvements of method which our argument may have thrown up as by-products in its otherwise ruinous course.[63]

As this passage reveals, Lewis is very aware of the *inefficiency of symbols* and how this phenomenon limits the way things can be communicated.

### The Secret Influence of Our Unconscious Wishes or Fears

The fourth reason why one may be distracted from the voice of conscience, Lewis says, may be due to "the secret influence of our unconscious wishes or fears,"[64] which may result from an individual's psychological state. If things are not well within the mind, it may lead to the loss of objective focus, thus preventing one from seeing something as it really is. The literary critic whose book or review tells nothing of

63. Ibid., 9–10, 12. This is what Lewis has developed in greater breadth in *Abolition of Man*, *That Hideous Strength*, *The Great Divorce*, and his essay in *Christian Reflections*, "The Poison of Subjectivism."

64. C. S. Lewis, *Christian Reflections*, 68.

the work under scrutiny, but everything about the author's particular likes and dislikes (even hatreds), may signal that something within him is awry. The critic has called his reader's attention away from the literature and riveted it on himself.[65] Lewis explains this phenomenon by noting that "the strength of our dislike is itself a probable symptom that all is not well within; that some raw place in our psychology has been touched, or else that some personal or partisan motive is secretly at work." He warns, "If we were simply exercising judgement we should be calmer; less anxious to speak. And if we do speak, we shall almost certainly make fools of ourselves."[66] When one is in such a state, if the voice of conscience is speaking, there is a high degree of probability it will be disregarded. The wish to avoid pain may also distract one from the voice of conscience, for if its voice is obeyed, it might lead to discomfort. While the rewards for temperance may be manifest over time, the benefits of intemperance are more immediately proximate, and therefore they truncate the development of character. Another reason one may allow his unconscious fears to drown out the voice of conscience centers on the nature of human fallenness. We have a propensity toward what Lewis calls "penal blindness."[67] The Moral Law makes its demands, but if one does not attend to them, he may pretend that he did not see what was expected by those very demands. He may even make excuses for what he knows is wrong behavior. At first it is a matter of choice; in time it is something that cannot be stopped. Eventually, it is etched into one's character. Lewis says, "Continued disobedience to conscience makes conscience blind."[68] In places where 'penal blindness' has set in, it becomes difficult to scrutinize one's own moral judgments. These compromises make it all but impossible to judge confidently what others may be doing, let alone make moral judgments about what God is doing in the world. Attempts to make sense of evil and suffering may be at risk because of one's own moral condition. As Lewis notes, "All that is made seems planless to the darkened mind, because there are more plans than it looked for."[69]

65. C. S. Lewis, *Studies in Words*, 330.
66. Ibid., 331.
67. C. S. Lewis, *Surprised By Joy*, 76–77.
68. C. S. Lewis, *A Preface to Paradise Lost*, 11.
69. C. S. Lewis, *Perelandra*, 218.

## Objectivity and the Problem of Evil

Lewis believes that if truth is objective, then denial of the claims of God on one's life leads to the rejection of the central fact of the universe. He writes, "God is basic Fact or Actuality, the source of all other facthood."[70] To deny Him is to respond to the objective world with selective interest. One will probably keep to the rules of the road when seeing a police car in the rear view mirror—a reminder that those rules are likely to be enforced. But one might make other kinds of compromises—moral compromises—if he thinks he can get away with them: for example, an unreported sum on a tax form, or a personal long distance call on company time and at company expense. The act is excused by saying, "Nobody will mind," or, "I've given them lots of extra hours, they owe it to me," or "I'm not the only one who does it; it's as if the company expects it of its employees." The compromises work themselves into the fabric of one's life. Eventually, these can easily become habit, seldom needing rationalization, because they have become so common to one's routine. At this point the state of "penal blindness" has nearly been reached. But the blindness is only in relation to one's own acts. Let someone try to take advantage of the individual described above, and clarity of sight comes rushing in as soon as that misdeed becomes known. There are no shades of grey now. Very pronounced moral distinctions are employed for use on the behavior of others, especially if one has been the victim of those misdeeds. In such a situation, the one judging is twice condemned: first, because he soft-peddles and excuses his own compromises. Lewis recognizes this pattern in his own life and confesses, "I do not succeed in keeping the Law of nature very well, and the moment anyone tells me I'm not keeping it, there starts up in my mind a string of excuses as long as your arm."[71] Second, in judging the failures of others, one acknowledges that morally speaking he is not utterly blind, and therefore he can claim no exemptions or excuses. Lewis writes, "How difficult it is to avoid having a special standard for oneself."[72] To the degree this is done, one becomes isolated in his subjectivism, picking and choosing the morality that suits him best in any given the situation.

70. C. S. Lewis, *Miracles*, 93.
71. C. S. Lewis, *Mere Christianity*, 6.
72. C. S. Lewis, *American Lady*, 58.

Lewis believes that the whole process of moral decline either begins or is sustained by the denial of God as the central fact of the universe. And this denial may be active and intentional, or passive and indifferent. If he is right, then one's ability to be objective is affected by moral compromises. Hence, for Lewis, issues related to one's thinking about any aspect of the problem of evil cannot be separated from his thinking about moral objectivity. If one's thought processes are skewed by these kinds of moral limitations, how can he be confident in his thinking about any issue where he might be tempted to support his moral compromises by increasing subjectivism? Although it may be possible to think about the problem of evil and suffering with various degrees of approximate success, if one's thinking is affected by one's own compromises, then these compromises make discussions about evil more difficult. Therefore, I argue that subjectivism itself, in the way that Lewis is concerned about it, becomes an aspect of the problem of evil.

In this regard, Lewis's work on the problem of evil establishes a standard that may inform the attempts and endeavors of others. He does not neglect to discuss the moral weaknesses of man, a quality often missing in other work on the subject. Whatever his weaknesses of argument may be, the fact that he seeks to account for the presence of human moral failure, not merely as an interesting idea but as a daily struggle, remains a refreshingly honest feature in Lewis's writing. One cannot help but wonder if his Christian faith provided him the security to look at the issue of evil from this angle. Because Lewis believed in the forgiveness of sins, he writes honestly about his own. Divine forgiveness is not an excuse for compromised behavior, but it may liberate one from the practice of hiding moral failure behind any kind of pretence. A non-Christian attempt to understand evil may be more at risk of failure to account for 'penal blindness.' Certainly a non-Christian recognizes hypocrisy in the world and may even acknowledge its presence in his own life, but what would he suggest by way of honestly dealing with the problem? And if he sees the problem of pain as reason enough to doubt the existence of God, thereby questioning any soteriological benefit in the Incarnation, what helpful suggestions can he offer for dealing with this matter? Of course this is not merely a problem for the non-Christian approach to the problem of evil. Moral compromises are commonplace enough among Christians as well as non-Christians. Since this is so, it is important to investigate whether or not Lewis accounts for these compromises by developing a system of checks and balances for this kind of behavior. I argue that he does, but first it will be necessary to evaluate his arguments for objectivity as they are laid out in the *Abolition of Man*. For this exercise, Weaver will provide the theoretical means to make critical judgments.

## Richard M. Weaver: The Ethics of Rhetoric

Richard Weaver provides a methodological means for interpreting Lewis's ideas about objectivity. Weaver, a University of Chicago professor of rhetoric, was a contemporary of Lewis. Although there is no evidence that Lewis ever read anything by Weaver, an extant review reveals that Weaver wrote about Lewis's *Studies in Words*.[73] What is undeniable, however, is that they share an interest in objective thought. In *The Ethics of Rhetoric*, Weaver identifies three 'different orders of knowledge.' First, there are "facts about existing physical entities." Second come "statements about these facts; these are the propositions or theories of science." And third come "statements about these statements." Quoting philosopher Mortimer Adler, Weaver asserts that "The propositions which these last statements express form a partial universe of discourse which is the body of philosophical opinion."[74] In *Ideas Have Consequences*, Weaver writes that "Every man participating in a culture has three levels of conscious reflection: his specific ideas about things, his general beliefs or convictions, and his metaphysical dream of the world."[75] The metaphysical dream "is an intuitive feeling about the immanent nature of reality, and this is the sanction to which both ideas and beliefs are ultimately referred for verification."[76] According to Weaver, ideas look outward, beyond mere subjectivist impressions, for their confirmations.

Facts are to be understood through dialectic in Weaver's schema of things. Dialectic is "a method of investigation whose object is the establishment of truth about doubtful propositions," writes Weaver.[77] "Facts

---

73. Weaver, *Defense of Tradition*, 448–49. This has been mentioned (page 23 above) and Weaver does refer to Lewis in one other place in this book, 416.

74. Weaver, *Ethics*, 30–31.

75. Weaver, *Ideas*, 18.

76. Ibid.

77. Weaver, *Ethics*, 15.

are never dialectically determined—although they may be elaborated in a dialectical system."[78] Dialectic secures possibility:[79] "What rhetoric thereafter accomplishes is to take any dialectically secured position . . . and show its relationship to the world of prudential conduct."[80] The rhetorician, seeing the implications of dialectic, speaks to persuade. It is because of this that Weaver says "language is sermonic." Scholars Bernard K. Duffy and Martin Jacobi observe that Weaver believes this "sermonic" characteristic of language which is inherently persuasive, is to be regarded as its defining characteristic. Therefore, one ought to appeal to objective value and do so as persuasively as one is able.[81]

There are at least four forms of argument by which the rhetor seeks to persuade. For Weaver, the highest form of persuasion is that of definition, or genus. Objects provide topics for dialectic. The arguer seeks to define an object by means of its limits; he attempts to name the object and speak of its essential quality. An argument from genus "Begins with the nature of the thing and then makes the application."[82] It argues from "the nature of the thing,"[83] and "involves a philosophy of being."[84] The second form of argument is that from similitude. "Those who argue from similitude invoke essential (though not exhaustive) correspondences."[85] They use "similitude to establish a probability." It is "thinkers of the analogical sort [who] use this argument chiefly."[86] The reason why Weaver places this form of argument second to that of definition rests on his belief that "behind every analogy lurks the possibility of a general term."[87] In other words, while the genus or class of a thing may elude me, I can come closer to discovering the definition of that thing by means of an analogy or metaphor. Its nature becomes clearer by use of comparisons and contrasts. The third form of argument is that which appeals to circumstance. "This argument merely reads the

78. Ibid., 27.

79. Ibid.

80. Ibid., 27–28.

81. Duffy and Jacobi, *Politics of Tradition*, 171.

82. Ibid., 56.

83. Ibid., 86.

84. Ibid., 87.

85. Ibid., 57.

86. Ibid.

87. Weaver, *Language is Sermonic*, 1355–56.

circumstances—the 'facts standing around'—and accepts them as coercive, or allows them to dictate the decision."[88] According to Weaver, this form of argument has two subcategories, that of consequence and that of circumstance. An "argument from consequence attempts a forecast of results," while an "argument from circumstance attempts only an estimate of current conditions or pressures."[89] This third form of argument is, by Weaver's estimation, the weakest form because "it is grounded in the nature of a situation rather than in the nature of things."[90] This is also the least philosophical of all sources of argument, "since theoretically it stops at the level of fact;"[91] furthermore, supposed consequences are not even facts, and therefore no reality supports the claims of this kind of rhetoric. This form of argument can tend to be utilitarian in its designs, and as Weaver says, coercive. There is also a fourth form of argument built on an appeal to authority. "If we are not in a position to see or examine, but can procure the deposition of some one who is, the deposition may become the substance of our argument."[92] Weaver's four forms of argument are the methodological standard by which I will evaluate Lewis's ideas about objectivity as he presents them in *The Abolition of Man*.

## A Critical Evaluation of the Arguments in *The Abolition of Man*

I have been examining Lewis's objectivist commitments as they are presented in one form or another throughout his published work. The purpose of this investigation has been to verify that Lewis is frequently reminding his readers, either explicitly or implicitly, that he holds to the objectivist position. It is in *The Abolition of Man*, however, that Lewis sets forth his most boldly sustained argument for objectivism. What follows is an evaluation of the strength of Lewis's presentation and an assessment of his effectiveness, based upon Weaver's four forms of argument.

---

88. Weaver. *Ethics*, 57.
89. Ibid.
90. Ibid., 83.
91. Ibid., 7.
92. Weaver, *Language is Sermonic*, 1354.

*The Abolition of Man*, published in 1947, contains three chapters, each corresponding to one of the three Riddell Memorial Lectures delivered by Lewis at Durham University in February 1943. The book also includes an appendix full of passages from ancient religious and philosophical texts that, on one level, also contributes to Lewis's rhetorical aims.

*Men Without Chests* is the title of the first chapter. In it, Lewis says he became concerned while reading an English grammar textbook for education in the upper forms of school. Lewis calls this textbook *The Green Book*, and gives the names Giaus and Titius to its authors. In fact, the book was *The Control of Language*, written by Alec King and Martin Ketley. Lewis believes the book does much to inculcate subjectivist assumptions into the minds of its readers. The chapter begins by recounting an incident when the poet Coleridge paused with some tourists to look at a waterfall. Coleridge endorsed the first tourist's remark that the waterfall was sublime, and was displeased by the other tourist's comment that the waterfall was merely pretty. Gaius and Titius inform their readers that Coleridge had no right to register such judgments, as the remarks had nothing to do with the waterfall, but only with the tourists' feelings about the waterfall. Lewis says that what the student learns from such instruction are two things: "firstly, that all sentences containing a predicate of value are statements about the emotional state of the speaker, and secondly, that all such statements are unimportant."[93] Here Lewis sees subjectivist philosophy manifest by the authors of *The Green Book* without thought of the contradictions of their own position; if Coleridge had no right to judge between the comments made by the two tourists, then certainly Gaius and Titius have no right to judge Coleridge.

In pointing out the inconsistencies of judgments made without regard for the objective world, Lewis sets forth an appeal to objectivism. He uses the term "Tao" as a kind of shorthand for his position, and defines it as "the doctrine of objective value, the belief that certain attitudes are really true, and others really false, to the kind of thing the universe is and the kind of things we are."[94] Lewis supports this definition not only by pointing out the inconsistencies in *The Green Book*, but

93. C. S. Lewis, *Abolition of Man*, 15.
94. Ibid., 29.

also by appealing to traditions which support the doctrine of objective value, as diverse as Hindu, Chinese, Jewish, Platonic, Aristotelian, Stoic, Oriental, Christian and so forth. The key point to notice is that Lewis is seeking to argue from the standpoint of definition, as Weaver would describe it. He wants to find validation for the objectivist position, so he borrows from a wide range of supports and then establishes his definition of the *Tao*. From here he argues the need to maintain objectivist commitments in the educational enterprise. If we deny objectivity, we leave no basis for judgments at all. It is as if we have surgically removed an organ and still expected its function. How can a teacher have any kind of expectations at all if there is no standard to appeal to? Outcomes in such an environment are nonsensical. The plumb line by which to judge a proper response is removed, and all that is left is mere subjectivist predilection and the lust for power to implement one's point of view over conflicting points of view.

Of the three chapters of the book, chapter 1's argument, by Weaver's standard, is the strongest. It is most convincing due to Lewis's ability to build his argument upon the definition of the *Tao*. Lewis reasons his way towards this definition discursively. He sets out facts and seeks to interpret them in a manner that validates his conclusions and supports his definition. Because Lewis appeals to that which is definitive, his argument has ethical credence, or as Weaver asserts concerning this type of rhetor, "he is making the highest order of appeal when basing his case on definition or the nature of the thing."[95] Furthermore, Weaver argues, "if it is possible to determine unchanging essences or qualities and to speak in terms of these, one is appealing to what is most real in so doing."[96] Clearly, Lewis argues in this way from a position that transcends the circumstance of time and place, and because of this, the value of his claims maintain their relevancy many decades after their publication.

Lewis opens chapter 2 by questioning the end to which Giaus and Titius create such a book. The fact that they write it indicates that they have some rhetorical ends based upon values they believe are valid. Here Lewis compares three possible rivals for the *Tao*, looking at them as possible bases of value which Giaus and Titius might embrace as sub-

---

95. Weaver, *Sermonic*, 1355.
96. Ibid.

stitutes. He explores the capability of utilitarian philosophies as possibly supplying a sound foundation for judgments. He recognizes, however, that because these build on what may be best for the greatest number, they have little to empower them to judge what the best might be. How is it possible to determine that good for some will be found in what is not good for others? Such a judgment demands a standard outside of mere utility. Another suggestion is that perhaps instinct could provide what the authors of *The Green Book* truly need to make their case. Again, Lewis sees that this will do no better than utility, for instincts often speak with competing voices and the knowledge to chose one over the other in such cases cannot be supplied by instinct itself. There must be an appeal to something that transcends instinct. Lastly, Lewis considers economic value as a third possible innovation in values. Here, too, the relativity of such a standard breaks down, for mere accumulation cannot provide a standard as to how much is enough or how what is acquired should be used. But each of these innovations does supply Lewis with an opportunity to test the validity of the doctrine of objective value against other subjectivist philosophies. The comparisons allow for something like Weaver's argument from similitude. Weaver says that one may use similitude—or dissimilitude as the case may be—to establish probability.[97] By examining competing philosophies in order to identify their dissimilarities with the *Tao*, Lewis is able to hone his definition of the *Tao* and to clarify the rhetorical strength of his appeal to objective value.

In the third chapter of *The Abolition of Man*, Lewis asserts that education in the spirit of *The Green Book* will produce people whose subjectivist values will render them incapable of appealing to an objective standard; consequently, it will be necessary for some to ascend to positions of power over others in order to make sure that their will and their point of view prevails. Having forsaken the *Tao*, these men will be driven by instinct; in the end, the rejection of objective value will not entail man's power over nature but nature's power over man. Lewis writes, "When all that says 'it is good' has been debunked, what says 'I want' remains."[98] The chapter paints a very grave account of what a future society is likely to look like if subjectivism becomes the prevailing

97. Weaver, *Ethics*, 57.
98. Ibid., 77–78.

basis for making judgments. What Lewis describes would make for good science fiction, and in fact it plays into the themes developed in Lewis's *That Hideous Strength*. Unfortunately, his argument is situated in consequence, and it appeals to the future; no objective reality exists to support the claim. The appeal is to speculation, not to certainty. Furthermore, as Weaver reminds us, this kind of speculation is the least convincing, because it is not rooted in anything as stable as definitions based on the nature of things. The futuristic speculation cannot be validated, nor the argument verified. Consequently, though the chapter is interesting, it may be judged to be the weakest in the book. Here, Weaver provides an insightful way to judge critically, and soundly, the weaknesses of Lewis's argument in this chapter. Nevertheless, the weakness is less distracting when seen in the context of Lewis's total endeavor.

It may be valuable to note here that Lewis's *Appendix* also carries with it some degree of rhetorical substance. Lewis cites references to a variety of literary sources from many cultures and over a wide range of time. These references give significant support to the idea that belief in the *Tao* has been foundational to cultures throughout history. Here, also, Lewis makes his case by employing what Weaver would call *the argument appealing to authority*. Chapter one, with its appeal to definition, is the strongest, based on Weaver's standards. Chapter two, for its appeal to similitude, comparisons, and contrasts, ranks second in Weaverian persuasiveness. The argument in chapter 3, rooted as it is in consequence, is the feeblest of the book. However, the appendix provides a source of support that has significant merit for its appeal to authority. Despite his testimony to the importance of affirming the doctrine of objective value, such affirmations are no guarantee that one has the capacity to live consistently with objectivist commitments. Humans are weak and prone to moral error, as well as errors of reason. Does Lewis account for such things?

## Checks and Balances

The finite and fallen condition evident in human experience will require some kind of device to minimize the hazards of thought and maximize attempts at better and better approximations in objectivity. Some kind of system of checks and balances on one's thinking is necessary to get somewhere near success in the endeavor. Lewis certainly recognizes this, and his belief that truth is objective encourages him in the effort to find checks on his own thought processes. There are at least three forms of checks and balances to be found in Lewis: 1) those of Authority, Reason and Experience; 2) those of Humility, Faith and Obedience; and 3) those of Community.

## Authority, Reason, and Experience

Lewis writes, "Authority, reason, experience; on these three, mixed in varying proportion all our knowledge depends."[99] At this point he is drawing on the checks and balances of these three, working together, to confirm a matter. He sees this triad in use throughout history and employs it himself with confidence, encouraging his readers to do the same.

### AUTHORITY

Regarding Authority, Lewis writes, "Believing things on authority only means believing them because you have been told them by someone you think trustworthy."[100] He believes that ninety-nine percent of the facts with which our reason works come to us by means of some kind

99. C. S. Lewis, *Christian Reflections*, 41. The use of authority, reason and experience to confirm a matter occurs, not infrequently, in Lewis's work. His essay, *Weight of Glory*, is developed throughout on a practical application of authority, reason and experience. Lewis writes that affirmations in literary criticism come from history, i.e., authority; scholarship, i.e., reason; and experience. They are aids to "Enable the reader to enter more fully into the author's intentions" (C. S. Lewis, *Selected Literary Essays*, 307). He writes, "In the Middle Ages, there are three kinds of proof: from Reason, from Authority, and from Experience. We establish a geometrical truth by reason; an historical truth, by authority, by *auctours*. We learn by experience that oysters do or do not agree with us" (C. S. Lewis, *Discarded Image*, 189). In the portion of *Discarded Image* on "The Seven Liberal Arts," specifically the section on *Dialectic*, Lewis clarifies that *Dialectic* in the Medieval sense of the word has nothing to do with "The modern Marxist sense . . . Hegelian in origin" (189). Lewis clarifies that the *Dialectic* he speaks of "*Is* concerned with proving," and sets forth three kinds of proof: reason, authority and experience. Certainly one of the most well known applications of this triad by Lewis grows out of his development of the *aut Deus aut malus homo* argument for the Deity of Christ. C. S. Lewis, *God in the Dock*, 101. In *Mere Christianity*, Lewis supports the argument with authority, reason and experience. First, Jesus claimed to be God (authority); second, his life and teaching appeared to confirm it (experience); third, it appears that he couldn't be mad or evil (reason). (C. S. Lewis, *Mere Christianity*, 42).

100. C. S. Lewis, *Mere Christianity*, 49.

of authority,[101] and that "few of us have followed the reasoning on which even ten percent of the truths we believe are based."[102] Therefore, Lewis recognizes, "A man who jibbed at authority in other things as some people do in religion would have to be content to know nothing all his life."[103] Furthermore, if creatures are ever to know their creator, the initiative[104] can never rest on the side of the creature. The creator will have to reveal Himself (or creaturely knowledge of Him will be impossible), and these revelations will have authoritative value. Lewis believes that God reveals Himself several ways: generally in Nature and in the Laws of Nature;[105] in human conscience and the Moral Law;[106] and also in other human beings.[107] God reveals Himself specifically in several ways also: the Word of God Incarnate; in the Word of God written; and, in some ways, through individual inspiration.[108]

Even though Lewis believes that God has revealed Himself in many ways, he also believes it is possible for the revelation of God to be abused. Anyone can attach the words "Thus saith the Lord" to his own opinions, invoking divine authority to sustain his own views and

---

101. "Of every hundred facts upon which to reason, ninety-nine depend on authority" (Lewis, *The Weight of Glory*, 54). He also writes, "Ninety-nine percent of the things you believe are believed on authority. I believe there is such a place as New York. I have not seen it myself. I could not prove it by abstract reasoning that there must be such a place. I believe it because reliable people have told me so. The ordinary man believes in the Solar System, atoms, evolution, and the circulation of the blood on authority—because the scientists say so. Every historical statement in the world is believed on authority. None of us has seen the Norman Conquest or the defeat of the Spanish Armada. None of us could prove them by pure logic as you prove a thing in mathematics. We believe them simply because people who did see them have left writings that tell us about them: in fact, on authority" (C. S. Lewis, *Mere Christianity*, 49).

102. C. S. Lewis, *The Weight of Glory*, 55.

103. C. S. Lewis, *Mere Christianity*, 49–50.

104. C. S. Lewis, *Surprised By Joy*, 227.

105. C. S. Lewis, *Christian Reflections*, 78–81.

106. C. S. Lewis, *Mere Christianity*, 4–5, 19–25.

107. C. S. Lewis, *The Weight of Glory*, 40. Lewis writes, "Next to the Blessed Sacrament itself, your neighbour is the holiest object presented to your senses. If he is your Christian Neighbour, he is holy in almost the same way, for in him also Christ *vere latitat*—the glorifier and the glorified, Glory Himself, is truly hidden."

108. Of Bunyan's particular genius Lewis observes, "'*It* came.' I doubt if we shall ever know more of the process called 'inspiration' than those two monosyllables tell us" (Lewis, *Selected Literary Essays*, 147).

produce a kind of tyranny.[109] This cannot be held as an objection against authority *per se*, but only to the misuse of authority. The nature of the abuse is the subjectivist use of Divine authority to buttress the opinions of manipulators and power mongers. Thus, though authority is of vital importance in knowing, to be of value it must be checked by reason and experience.

## REASON

Lewis recognizes that "all possible knowledge . . . depends on the validity of reasoning."[110] He thinks that there is a rationality existing in the universe from which all human rationality is derived; it is objective and not a consequence of reading into the universe what is not there intrinsically.[111] For Lewis, Reason involves three aspects: 1) the reception of facts; 2) the perception of self-evident truths and axioms; and 3) "the art or skill of arranging the facts so as to yield a series of such intuitions which linked together produce a proof of the truth or falsehood of the proposition we are considering."[112] This last aim is a rhetorical one, for it employs invention and arranges the argument for persuasive ends. Furthermore, Lewis believes, for instance, that "primary moral principles on which all others depend are rationally perceived."[113] "We 'just see' that there is no reason why my neighbour's happiness should be

109. Lewis writes, "On those who add 'Thus saith the Lord' to their merely human utterances descends the doom of conscience that seems clearer the more it is loaded with sin. All this comes from pretending that God has spoken when He has not." Meditations on the Third Commandment (*God in the Dock*, 198). Lewis also recognizes, "Even for adults, it is 'sweet, sweet, sweet poison' to feel able to imply 'Thus saith the Lord' at the end of every expression of our pet aversions" (*Christian Reflections*, 31). He adds, "The danger of mistaking our merely natural, though perhaps legitimate enthusiasms for holy zeal, is always great" (*God in the Dock*, 198). It is a kind of borderline blasphemy. I say borderline because when this is done, I hardly believe that it is done as an act of intentional blasphemy. Nonetheless, it is done all too often, and has its own kind of negative consequence in both the doer and the one done by.

110. Lewis, *Miracles*, 19. Lewis also writes, "We may state it as a rule that *no thought is valid if it can be fully explained as the result of irrational causes*" (*Miracles*, 20–21).

111. "Unless all that we take to be knowledge is an illusion, we must hold that in thinking we are not reading rationality into an irrational universe, but responding to a rationality with which the universe has always been saturated" (C. S. Lewis, *Christian Reflections*, 65).

112. Ibid., 54.

113. C. S. Lewis, *Miracles*, 35.

sacrificed to my own, as we 'just see' that things which are equal to the same thing are equal to one another." Lewis adds, "If we cannot prove either axiom, that is not because they are irrational but because they are self-evident and all proofs depend on them. Their intrinsic reasonableness shines by its own light."[114] This leads him to conclude, "It is because all morality is based on such self-evident principles that we say to a man, when we would recall him to right conduct, 'be reasonable.'"[115] He believes that wrong conduct has something in it that is unreasonable. Therefore, it is a precursor to subjectivism.

Lest he be misunderstood, it must also be noted that, for Lewis, moral failure is not synonymous with utter moral blindness or rational lapse, as he explains: As regards the Fall, I submit that the general tenor of scripture does not encourage us to believe that our knowledge of the Law has been depraved in the same degree as our power to fulfil it. . . . our perceptions of right . . . may, no doubt, be impaired; but there is a difference between imperfect sight and blindness. A theology which goes about to represent our practical reason as radically unsound is headed for disaster.[116]

If we are utterly blind, morally, we can never be judged for our moral lapses. The blind man must be treated with sympathy when he stumbles, not with contempt. He cannot help himself. However, if one can judge the moral failures he observes in others, he is not in the same condition as the blind man. Our own failures are without excuse, especially when we find ourselves doing the very thing we have condemned in others. Of course, it may be that our judgments against others are not as refined as we first suppose. If we can be blind to our own lapses and misunderstand how morally short-sighted we are, then it is possible that we might misjudge the actions and intentions of others as well. We might condemn a relatively innocent behavior simply because we misunderstand it or find ourselves inconvenienced by it. If this can be the case, then we will have to admit the possibility that cosmic activity can also be misunderstood and misjudged.

114. Ibid.
115. Ibid.
116. C. S. Lewis, *Christian Reflections*, 79.

Lewis observes, "Unless we allow ultimate reality to be moral we cannot morally condemn it."[117] He understands that "our very condemnation of reality carries in its heart an unconscious act of allegiance to that same reality as the source of our moral standards."[118] Consequently, "The pell-mell of phenomena, as we first observe them, seems to be full of anomalies and irregularities; but being assured that reality is logical we go on framing and trying out hypotheses to show the apparent irregularities are not really irregular at all."[119] Lewis writes, "The process whereby, having admitted that reality in the last resort must be moral, we attempt to explain evil, is the history of theology."[120] Reason, despite its deficiencies in its work with available and ever expanding data, allows for approximate answers to the problem of evil, and should constantly be used for better and better approximations. Reason, as helpful as it is, cannot give a final word on the matter because of the limitations under which it operates. There are too many variables. Good attempts at dealing with the issue of evil may be judged by their scope and the degree to which they account for the complexities involved. It is enough for some critics to see evidence in the problem of evil and suffering to conclude that God (at least the Christian God) cannot exist. One wonders if the complexities of knowledge, generally, and the issues relating to the limits of reason, justify such a definitive position on the matter. Furthermore, one wonders if the numbers of problems created by denying the existence of God, as well as the problems that occur in attempts to try and explain the phenomena of evil and suffering without a belief in God, can be surmounted. It would appear that the most substantial work done on this matter (with the most reasonable approaches) has been done by those who take the existence of God as valid, and the many problems of evil as matters which must be tackled. Lewis is among those who believe this: reason is necessary for working through issues essential to this problem, but reason cannot properly function in isolation from authority and experience.

117. Ibid., 70.
118. Ibid.
119. Ibid., 70–71.
120. Ibid., 71.

### Experience

Lewis believes that experience, despite all of its benefits, should not be trusted on its own. It needs the checks of authority and reason. Hume argues, "The *ultimate* standard by which we determine *all* disputes . . . is *always* derived from experience and observation [italics mine]."[121] Lewis takes issue with this kind of thought. He writes, "We never start from a *tabula rasa*: if we did, we should end, ethically speaking, with a *tabula rasa*."[122] The *tabula rasa*, like a movie screen, cannot retain any of the images projected on it unless it has some power to retain those images. It can never make sense of the images retained unless it has some capacity to sort, classify, compare, and contrast those images. The power to retain and to sort must be a power that precedes the experience itself. Thus, to make any sense of experience *a posteriori*, there must exist something *a priori*. As William James observes, "Without selective interest, experience is an utter chaos."[123] Experience must operate with the checks and balances of reason and authority, or it seems destined to fall into various forms of subjectivism or skepticism.

Lewis writes, "The senses are not infallible."[124] While he sees the risks of emphasizing experience over reason and authority, he also recognizes the value of experience as part of a whole epistemological operation. In his autobiography, Lewis notes the valuable part that experience played in his own pilgrimage. "What I like about experience is that it is such an honest thing." Then he adds, "You may take any number of wrong turnings; but keep your eyes open and you will not be allowed to go very far before warning signs appear. You may have deceived yourself, but experience is not trying to deceive you. The uni-

121. Hume, *An Inquiry Concerning Human Understanding*, section 10, "Of Miracles," part 1.

122. C. S. Lewis, *Christian Reflections*, 53.

123. James, *Principles of Psychology*, 490. Mark Twain writes, "We should be careful to get out of an experience only the wisdom that is in it—and stop there; lest we be like the cat that sits down on a hot stove-lid. She will never sit on a hot stove-lid again—and that is well; but also she will never sit down on a cold one anymore." *Pudd'nhead Wilson's New Calendar*. Lewis writes, "consciousness is, from the outset, selective, and ceases when selection ceases . . . not to attend to one part of our experience at the expense of the rest, is to be asleep" (C. S. Lewis, *Preface to Paradise Lost*, 136).

124. C. S. Lewis, *God in the Dock*, 25. He says further, "Experience by itself proves nothing" (ibid., 25–26). And, "Experience proves this, or that, according to the preconceptions we bring to it" (ibid., 26).

verse rings true wherever you fairly test it."[125] The fair test, for Lewis, includes the checks and balances of authority, reason, and experience. In his attempts to resolve the problems of objectivity, Lewis, whether successful or not, sought to respect this balance.

## Humility, Faith, and Obedience

Besides authority, reason, and experience, Lewis identified the importance of humility, faith, and obedience as necessary checks and balances for sound thinking. These may also help to prevent a slip into subjectivism.

### HUMILITY

Lewis believed that most truths come with prescriptions and ethical implications. The significance of the prescription varies with the significance of the truth. To violate the prescription by living contrary to it is precarious, for it brings with it a loss of objectivity regarding the truth that supports the prescription. This may lead to a blinding subjectivity, a diminishing concern for the correspondence between a thought and its object. The emphasis shifts from the balance of the object-subject relation to an imbalance on the side of the subject. And this kind of subjectivity may lead to an increasing inability to correct one's thinking at the point of moral compromise. Lewis notes in *The Abolition of Man* that corrupted men cannot usefully study ethics. Because they are corrupted, the whole science of ethics is invisible to them.[126] He footnotes the reference to the text in the *Ethics*, where Aristotle observes that "Vice is unconscious of itself."[127] Lewis sees that this is not only a problem for individuals, but could affect entire cultures. He believes that history can sustain his judgment at this point. Writing in *The Discarded Image*, he describes what he calls the "Great process of Internalisation:"

> Always, century by century, item after item is transferred from the object's side of the account to the subject's, And now, in some extreme forms of Behaviourism, the subject himself is discounted as merely subjective; we only think that we think.

125. C. S. Lewis, *Surprised By Joy*, 177.

126. C. S. Lewis, *Abolition of Man*, 26.

127. Aristotle *Nicomachean Ethics* 1095b, cited in C. S. Lewis, *Abolition of Man*, 26. See also Aristotle *Nichomachean Ethics* 6.3 1139b.

Having eaten up everything else, he eats himself up too. And where we 'go from that' is a dark question.[128]

For Lewis, this process of internalization characterizes his idea of pride. He calls Pride "The Great Sin."[129] It is an inordinate estimation of self. He explains, "The characteristic of lost souls is 'their rejection of everything that is simply not themselves.'" The antidote to pride, as Lewis affirms, is humility, and he claims that "If anyone would like to acquire humility . . . The first step is to realize that one is proud."[130] A characteristic of a person with humility will be that he will not be thinking of himself as a humble person. This is principally because he will be thinking less about himself and more about other people and other things around him. Such was the case with Lewis's medieval man, whose "humility," he writes, "was rewarded with the pleasures of admiration."[131] He advises, "To love and admire anything outside yourself is to take one step away from utter spiritual ruin."[132] Such humility is less and less accessible to the subjectivist.

Lewis may, or may not, be right about pride being "The Great Sin." Certainly Christians have believed something along those lines throughout history. It seems, however, that the matter is so much more complicated than this. Perhaps pride comes at the end of a line, following much that precedes it. If pride is preceded by pretence, then perhaps pretence seeks to cover up more deeply seated fears and insecurities. Concern for what may actually be right could be compromised, leading one to ignore some pieces of data significant for a larger understanding. One might imagine circumstances in which pride grows out of the need to be right. Psychological issues may be at stake. Certainly these things can also be in operation while one is engaged in any intellectual pursuit, including attempts to resolve the problem of evil. Pride may affect one's ability to be objective, and humility may be an antidote to pride. Nevertheless, how would it be possible to break free from this kind of pride in the first place? Even more, how is it possible to prevail in the battle against pride in one's life? Here Lewis sees faith as an important virtue.

128. C. S. Lewis, *Discarded Image*, 215, 42.
129. C. S. Lewis, *Mere Christianity*, 101.
130. Ibid., 101.
131. C. S. Lewis, *Discarded Image*, 185.
132. C. S. Lewis, *Mere Christianity*, 100.

## FAITH

Faith is crucial as a significant check and balance in Lewis's approach to objectivity. He writes:

> When we exhort people to Faith as a virtue, to the settled intention of continuing to believe certain things, we are not exhorting them to fight against reason. The intention of continuing to believe is required because, though Reason is divine, human reasoners are not. When once passion takes part in the game, the human reason, unassisted by Grace, has about as much chance of retaining its hold on truths already gained as a snowflake has of retaining its consistency in the mouth of a blast furnace. The sort of arguments against Christianity which our reason can be persuaded to accept at the moment of yielding to temptation are often preposterous. Reason may win truths; without faith she will retain them just so long as Satan pleases. There is nothing we cannot be made to believe or disbelieve. If we wish to be rational, not now and then, but constantly, we must pray for the gift of Faith for the power to go on believing not in the teeth of reason but in the teeth of lust and terror and jealousy and boredom and indifference that which reason, authority, or experience, or all three, have once delivered to us for truth.[133]

In Lewis's scheme of things, faith is not antithetical to reason. It is antithetical to sin, and especially pride. This does not mean that people of faith will automatically become particularly clever. It does mean that as long as believers walk according to this kind of faith, they will be working to remove one significant barrier to sound reason.

## OBEDIENCE

In addition to humility and faith, Lewis makes room in his approach to knowledge for another of his checks and balances—obedience. His anthology of George MacDonald includes the observation that "Obedience is the opener of eyes."[134] When he writes that "Virtue—even attempted virtue—brings light; indulgence brings fog,"[135] he is in agreement with MacDonald. A person may not be anything near virtuous, but he will seldom be so clear about his deficiencies as when he is try-

---

133. C. S. Lewis, *Christian Reflections*, 43.

134. Macdonald, *Anthology*, 42.

135. C. S. Lewis. *Mere Christianity*, 81.

ing hard and still failing. There is a kind of light that can come in the midst of such a struggle. It is the awareness that one needs help beyond himself. Attempts at virtue, both those attempts that approximate success and those that underscore deficiencies, are helpful. It is clear in his writing that when Lewis addresses obedience, he is referring to obedience to God. Let it suffice here to point out that Lewis believes there is an advantage to be gained through obedience to God, as nearly as one might practice it. Obedience works as a kind of splint on both the reason and the character.[136] Authority, reason, and experience; humility, faith, and obedience: all are, in Lewis's thinking, helpful checks and balances toward sound thinking. But there is at least one more.

## Community

Lewis regards community as another necessary aid for thinking objectively. To listen to people who differ, to weigh the things they say and believe against my own thoughts and attitudes, works as a kind of corrective; and in this way, the community works as a means of growth towards maturity. As a rhetorician of the written word, Lewis also sees that community is an essential environment necessary for dialectic and the shaping of ideas, as well as shaping character. For Lewis, the community is essentially a good thing. Even so, he sees it can become perverted. The perversion is manifest, in part, when the means which the community exists to serve becomes autonomous and separated from its ends. Weaver asserts that "the substitution of means for ends is the essence of fanaticism;"[137] and Lewis believes that this is always dangerous.[138] He makes this matter clear in two different essays. In one essay, *The Inner Ring*,[139] he describes *the inner ring* as an exclusive group that exists for itself and for its own self-interest. Of course, there are times when it is necessary for circles to form in order to accomplish some task

136. Lewis writes, "A *perfect* man w[oul]d never act from a sense of duty; he'd always *want* the right thing more than the wrong one. Duty is only a substitute for love (of God and of other people), like a crutch, which is a substitute for a leg. Most of us need the crutch at times; but of course it's idiotic to use the crutch when our own legs (our own loves, tastes, habits etc.) can do the journey on their own" (*Letters to Children*, 72).

137. Weaver, *Ideas*, 60.

138. Lewis writes, "When the means are autonomous, they are deadly" (*Reflections on the Psalms*, 58). See also C. S. Lewis, *Arthurian Torso*, 133.

139. C. S. Lewis, *Weight of Glory*, 107–18.

or because some common interest has bound the members together. It is when the group has lost sight of the task or initial interest that trouble starts. The band becomes a clique. In at least three places it runs the risk of going very much awry. First, when the desire to become a part of the ring takes the form of an all-consuming desire, at which point other, higher ends may be sacrificed. Any amount of moral compromise may be made to get inside. Second, "Of all passions the passion for the Inner Ring is most skilful in making a man who is not yet a very bad man do very bad things."[140] Third, Lewis reminds his readers that the "Inner Ring exists for exclusion."[141] Lewis warns,

> The quest of the Inner Ring will break your hearts unless your hearts break it. But if you break it, a surprising result will follow. If in your working hours you make the work your end, you will presently find yourself all unawares inside the only circle in your profession that really matters. You will become one of the sound craftsmen, and the other craftsmen will know it.[142]

The Inner Ring is portrayed in all of its evil proportion in Lewis's novel *That Hideous Strength*.[143] It is the N. I. C. E., a nefarious community, which Lewis contrasts with another group gathered around his hero, Elwin Ransom at St. Anne's. The gathering at St. Anne's is emblematic of all that is good about community. The members share a common end, they are inclusive, and they contribute towards the growth and maturation of one another.

In the second essay, "'Membership,'"[144] he highlights the value of healthy community, which he sees exhibited at its best moments in the Church. The Church ought to be a place where we come with our rough edges and, in the context of a loving community, have those rough edges smoothed out. This is done not only through the patience, love, and mercy of others toward all of our idiosyncrasies, but also as we learn patience, love, and mercy toward others with all of their idiosyncrasies. It is not the patience of mere endurance, but the patience that loves, nurtures, and aids in the mutual growth of each member. This kind of

---

140. Ibid., 116.
141. Ibid., 117.
142. Ibid., 116.
143. C. S. Lewis, *That Hideous Strength*.
144. C. S. Lewis, *The Weight of Glory*, 119–31.

community is healthy not because it is perfect, but because it is aware of its weaknesses, and dedicated to the growth and development of its members. This kind of community, when fostering open-ended dialogue among its members, provides the kind of forum where objectivity and intellectual growth can happen. In relation to the problem of pain and suffering, with all of its emotional dynamics, such a forum is vital. In fact, as Lewis wrote *The Problem of Pain*, he read it in installments to the Inklings, a weekly gathering most of whom were Oxford academics and also Christians.[145] As he developed his thinking about the problem of evil and suffering rhetorically for his *Inkling* audience, he sought both criticisms and encouragement from this group. Acknowledging his debt, Lewis dedicated the book to the *Inklings*.

## Conclusion

Lewis is right to be concerned about the degree to which finite man can grasp the purposes and intentions of the Infinite. At best, we make approximations in understanding questions related to the problem of evil. The actions of God have been questioned throughout history; even the Scriptures themselves record them.[146] Interesting answers and responses to those challenges have come in the past and more will certainly come in the future. With each round of debate and discussion, some very helpful insight has developed; still, the last word has not been spoken. Each generation seems to be faced with new twists and turns concerning this issue, nuancing the complexities. This all seems consistent with Lewis's thought on the matter. He writes in *A Grief Observed* that he wants God, not merely his idea of God.[147] There is honesty here. Lewis recognizes, with a certain degree of humility, his own limitations when it comes to discussing this subject, and expresses an openness to keep at it until he arrives at better and better approximations. He is convinced that the facts, as he understands them, give him enough encouragement to press on. He believes, for good reason, that there is a God, and that He is good, although that goodness is not entirely understood. Knowledge of God has characteristics about it which are similar to

145. Sayer, *Jack*, 162. Sayer misattributes the dedication to Robert Havard and J. R. R. Tolkien, when in fact Lewis dedicated it to the Inklings.

146. See, for example, Job, Jonah, Habakkuk, and many of the Psalms.

147. C. S. Lewis, *Grief Observed*, 56.

knowledge of a good friend, for more can always be known. Any given circumstances that might arise, calling into question the character of that friend, must be considered in light of the full experience of that relationship. Certainly ambiguities and misunderstandings will come in any good friendship, but satisfactory reasons and deeper commitments lead to the willingness to seek resolutions to the difficulties that might arise. Through these circumstances, many new discoveries are made. Lewis's attempt to understand God, although substantially magnified, is not unlike this. His approach proves to be honest and encouraging.

Lewis is also helpful in his recognition that humans are themselves complex, not only as rational beings, varied in personality, temperament, and aptitude, but also as fallen beings. His willingness to account for the possibilities to go wrong morally and intellectually, not only because we are finite, but also because we are flawed, brings a helpful dimension to his discussion of theodicy. Here again, Lewis does not give a last word on the matter, but he does give a helpful one; it is helpful because it is aware of the complexities to an extent greater than those who might neglect human fallenness and fail to make allowances for it. Lewis's attempt at checks and balances, in an effort to better approximate objectivity, is a step in a healthy direction, for it acknowledges the limitations any individual will bring to the discussion and seeks to address these in a way that makes it possible to proceed with humility. I think the most significant thing for this study is not so much the extent of Lewis's contribution to objectivity and the problem of evil, but the fact that in his writing he is concerned with this issue. It is a guard against subjectivism, not only for others but for himself.

It is necessary now to investigate Lewis's ideas about the problem of evil as he developed them throughout the course of his life. This provides a way to see how his objectivist commitments caused his thinking to change, allowing him to avoid the pitfall of subjectivism.

# 2

## The Problem of Pain

### Introduction

IN THE PREVIOUS CHAPTER I SET FORTH LEWIS'S OBJECTIVIST COMMIT-
ments and explained that he believed that evil is likely to occur through
subjectivism. In this chapter I argue that C. S. Lewis's ideas concerning the topic of evil and suffering are developing; therefore, significant
personal experiences in his life, and his response to them, furnish an
example of how he adjusts his thoughts to the objective reality of evil.
In so doing, Lewis embodies his objectivist views, avoiding that kind
of subjectivism that would otherwise lead him to squeeze his experience into the mould created by prior perceptions of the world. In fact,
readers of Lewis see in him a willingness to adjust his preconceptions
to fit a growing and dynamic view of the world. We would be in error
to suggest that he does this perfectly, but the fact that he does it at all
testifies to his desire to respond to things as they are, and not merely as
he would have them be. Consequently, his rhetoric about evil becomes
more convincing when viewed as dialectic developed in life's crucible.
Richard Weaver truly observes, "Whenever the rhetorician actualizes an
event . . . , he is making it mean something to the emotional part of us,
but that part is involved whenever we are deliberating about goodness
and badness."[1] So too, as Lewis embodies his objectivist commitments,
particularly in relation to evil and suffering, his rhetoric displays an
ethos which is compelling, not so much in its philosophical exactness
but in its ability to speak authentically about life, with both its discoveries and its ambiguities.

---

1. Weaver, "Language is Sermonic," 1358.

Lewis was a rhetorician who shaped his writing to persuade his readers to action. Weaver writes that "Rhetoric has a relationship to the world which logic does not have and which forces the rhetorician to keep his eye upon reality as well as on the character and situation of his audience."[2] In other words, the rhetorician, while looking at objective reality, seeks to describe the world as he sees it to his audience, and to persuade them to adjust their thoughts and actions accordingly. In this way, rhetoric is situated; the exigencies of personal circumstance inform the rhetor, making it possible for him or her to connect a message to an audience. Rhetorician Gerard A. Hauser defines rhetorical situations as "Situations that present problems that can be resolved meaningfully through the uses of speech and writing. Problems that require changes of belief or attitude or require cooperation are typically ones in which skill in the management of language can make a difference."[3] Hauser explains that "every rhetorical situation is composed of three elements: an *exigence*, an *audience*, and *constraints*."[4] Hauser defines an exigence as "an imperfection marked by urgency," and adds that "any undesirable element in a situation can satisfy the demands of this definition."[5] Furthermore, he explains that an audience is not merely composed of hearers, or readers as the case may be, but rather is made up of "individuals who are *capable of being influenced*. Such individuals have an interest in an exigence and its resolution."[6] As for constraints, Hauser notes that "each speaker has the formidable task of discovering the constraints that will aid in influencing audiences to embark on the desired course of action to remedy the exigence."[7] In this light, Lewis's writing is rhetorically situated. When he wrote about the problem of evil, autobiographically or apologetically, he had intentions for his audience. He was not interested merely in developing plausible solutions to the problem; he hoped to persuade his audience to respond to the claims of Christianity in spite of the difficulties presented by the existence of evil and suffering. These problems represent significant constraints, but the

2. Weaver, "Language is Sermonic," 1353.

3. Hauser, *Introduction*, 35.

4. Ibid.

5. Ibid., 36.

6. Ibid., 37.

7. Ibid., 38.

circumstances of Lewis's own conversion convinced him that they were not insurmountable.

Richard Weaver provides a means for better understanding Lewis's rhetorical aims; he writes that "Rhetoric comprehensively considered is an art of emphasis."[8] Whenever Lewis put his pen to paper, he was selecting out of a complex body of information those bits and pieces he believed would most honestly make his case. Lewis's argument took shape or form by drawing on available resources and configuring them according to his intentions. As Weaver observes, cultures tend to develop forms for interpreting the world in which those cultures exist. These forms represent a developing understanding, and therefore Weaver notes that "culture . . . has to be credited with a form that can be distorted."[9] Weaver recognizes the dangers of subjectivism, as these forms are shaped, and he comments that "a culture opens itself up to condemnation when it begins to attribute an immanence to the forms and institutions it has created. The source of evil we are endeavoring to isolate thus lies in a false immanentization."[10] In describing the failures of eighteenth-century European culture, Weaver observes that "it had come to believe in the immanence of its own elegant forms and was raising them to the rank of an idol."[11] This idolatry exists not only where a cultural understanding has become too rigid to explain the world the way it is; it can exist in an individual's assessment of his world, as well. Weaver believes the usefulness of forms is located in maintaining this truth: "that the vitality of a form lies in its ability to go on forming."[12] Whenever an understanding ceases to develop in response to objective reality, subjectivism is likely to occur. Thus, maladjustments resulting in idolatry ought to be corrected. "Clearly, if the question can be resolved by the intellect," writes Weaver, "it will have to be undertaken at the level of ontology, where the order of reality is envisaged."[13] And on this point, Weaver's concerns correspond to those of Lewis; for Lewis is trying to understand the significance of the existence of evil in the

8. Weaver, "Language is Sermonic," 1357.

9. Weaver, Visions of Order, 75.

10. Ibid., 78.

11. Ibid., 81.

12. Ibid., 86.

13. Ibid., 89.

universe, and his understanding ripens as he looks at objective reality. The process of Lewis's development along these lines is essential to my argument that Lewis is the embodiment of his own objectivist views.

## Lewis's Pre-Conversion Experiences with Evil and Suffering

As Lewis recounts his past, he reveals to his readers his own struggle with evil and suffering. This personal narration establishes an emotional connection with his audience and increases his persuasiveness. Rhetoric, according to Weaver, appeals to more than the rational part of a man, for "its object is the whole man."[14] Consequently, its arguments are presented to the rational man, but rhetoric also addresses the "pathetic being."[15] As Weaver writes, "Rhetoric is addressed to man in his humanity," and "a speech intended to persuade achieves little unless it takes into account how men are reacting subjectively to their hopes and fears and special circumstances."[16] Wherever Lewis recalls difficult experiences from his youth, he establishes that he is emotionally in touch with the issue of evil. As a young boy, his reaction to such difficult circumstances led to the rejection of his faith, for he recognized that his early understanding of Christianity was incapable of giving him an accurate account of the world as he was experiencing it. As a mature adult, he recounts these events in his autobiography to persuade his readers of his familiarity with the pathos surrounding evil. For the purposes of this study, some significant struggles from Lewis's life will be examined in relationship to his developing sense of the world as it is.

### *Rejecting the Faith of His Youth*

In his autobiography, Lewis explains how his interpretation of childhood experiences led to the loss of his early faith. There was the death of his mother and his subsequent estrangement from his father when Lewis was nine years old. He also struggled with a growing pessimism resulting from a deformity of his thumbs and the difficulties he faced in school because of physical awkwardness. Each of these emotional expe-

---

14. Weaver, "Language is Sermonic," 1352.
15. Ibid.
16. Ibid.

riences contributed to the shaping of his thoughts about evil and God, and he had difficulty believing in a God who would allow such things.

## The Loss of His Mother

Lewis's autobiography recounts a night in which Lewis was sick in bed, wanting his mother to comfort him; she was unable to come because she was sick in her own bed with cancer. She died on August 23, 1908.[17] The death was not quick, and consequently the agony C. S. Lewis experienced was great. He writes of the time, "We lost her gradually as she was gradually withdrawn from our life into the hands of nurses and delirium and morphia, and as our whole existence changed into something alien and menacing, as the house became full of strange smells and midnight noises and sinister whispered conversations."[18] Praying earnestly with childlike faith, he hoped she would be healed, and he petitioned with the full expectation that his needs would be answered.[19] Even after his mother died, he prayed more fervently that a miracle would occur and that she would be raised from the dead. His expectations were met with disappointment when she did not.[20] Simply put, Lewis's childhood understanding of reality led him to reject the faith that could not explain his experience. For him, the most difficult thing was his loss of 'all settled happiness, all that was tranquil and reliable."[21] He may have known times of fun and pleasure and happiness, but, as he remarks, there was "no more of the old security. It was sea and islands now; the great continent had sunk like Atlantis."[22]

## Estranged from His Father

Unfortunately, at the time Lewis lost his mother, it appears that he also experienced what he felt to be emotional abandonment from his father. He observes that her death "Divided us [Lewis and his brother] from our father as well as our mother."[23] In his own grief, Albert Lewis was

17. Green and Hooper, *Biography*, 25.
18. C. S. Lewis, *Surprised By Joy*, 19.
19. Ibid., 20.
20. Ibid., 20.
21. Ibid.
22. Ibid., 21.
23. C. S. Lewis, *Surprised By Joy*, 19.

not able to offer the kind of comfort the younger Lewis and his brother needed at the time. He tended to be short tempered and irritable; his father's unpredictable nature compounded Lewis's own suffering.[24] Eventually, the boys were both sent off to boarding school. One might expect that their returns home on vacations from school would be met with great joy, that there would be consolation in being together as a family, fractured though it was; but such was not the case. The times he shared with his brother at home were dear to him, but time spent in his father's presence was awkward and difficult. Without question, Lewis considered times with his father more like a trip to an asylum than a return home. Lewis sadly remarks, "All the happy hours of the holidays occurred during our father's absence."[25] According to Major Warren Lewis, his brother was faithful and dutiful in his correspondence to his father, "But visits to Little Lea [their boyhood home in Ireland] had always a sad penitential character."[26] The Major validates his brother's impression of their father, writing that the holidays spent at home, even after the boys were adults, were such that they eagerly anticipated the conclusion of their visits: "we were always glad to get away."[27] Years after his father died, Lewis's feelings toward him softened.[28] Even so, the impressions made during his childhood contributed to his sense that he was alone in a hostile world.

## Physical Deformity

As a result of his hardships as a young boy, Lewis became a pessimist. Though the death of his mother and his father's lack of understanding compounded this outlook on the world, he observes that "The seeds of pessimism were sown before my mother's death. Ridiculous as it may sound, I believe that the clumsiness of my hands was at the root of the matter."[29] He and his brother both shared a functional genetic deformity of the endmost joint of their thumbs. His awkwardness made him very unhappy and cynical. He admits his pessimism was not as simple as

24. Ibid., 39.
25. Ibid., 41.
26. W. H. Lewis, *Letters*, 21.
27. Ibid., 21.
28. C. S. Lewis, *Surprised By Joy*, 160.
29. Ibid., 64.

that of a child who says, "I can't cut a straight line with a pair of scissors, therefore the universe is evil."[30] Nevertheless, this negativity created in him "a settled expectation that everything would do what you did not want it to do."[31] He had not by this time read Lucretius, but writes, "I felt the force of his argument (and it is surely the strongest of all) for atheism—*Had God designed the world, it would not be/ A world so frail and faulty as we see.*"[32] At this point in his childhood, Lewis set about projecting onto the universe what he expected to find there. He explains the phenomenon of his own emerging subjectivism, "It is perhaps just these early experiences which are so fugitive and, to an adult, so grotesque, that give the mind its earliest bias, its habitual sense of what is or is not plausible."[33] It becomes clear from these experiences that Lewis embodied a lived dialectic, his struggles informing his vision of the world.

## Difficulties at School

Lewis's early schooling was a disaster, a cause of much torment and grief. Nevertheless, it also placed him in an environment where he grew through difficulties. His first bad experience (as has been mentioned) came on the heels of his mother's death, when his father sent him off to a boarding school. Warren Lewis, recounting the decision of his father, explains, "With his uncanny flair for making the wrong decision, my father had given us helpless children into the hands of a madman."[34]

The Lewis brothers, still grieving over their mother's death, found themselves in a small boarding school with a declining enrolment. The decline was due to a High Court action brought against the school by a man whose son had been brutally beaten by the headmaster. The suit was eventually settled out of court, but rumors about the school and its headmaster's maniacal tendencies were confirmed.[35] The horrible conditions, the irrational behavior of the headmaster, and the beatings are all recorded in Lewis's autobiography, where he dubs the

30. Ibid.
31. Ibid.
32. Ibid., 65.
33. Ibid.
34. W. H. Lewis, ed., *Letters*, 3–4.
35. Ibid., 3.

school "Belsen" after the Nazi concentration camp.[36] The boys wrote repeatedly to their father, asking him to remove them from the school. The father, "reading between the lines" and believing he understood what was really behind the pleas, never responded to their requests. It was not until the school was shut down nearly two years later that the Lewis brothers were relieved of their dire circumstances. And shortly after this, the headmaster was restrained, declared legally insane, and institutionalized.[37]

In retrospect, Lewis recalls that even this suffering served a purpose. Time gave him perspective on his experience, adjusting his first impressions, for good could result even from bad. "Life at a vile boarding school is in this way a good preparation for the Christian life," explains Lewis, "that it teaches one to live by hope."[38] His times at school were measured by their distance to the next term break and the respite that came with it. Later, in possession of a firm belief in the Christian God, Lewis acknowledges the significance of future hope in a life to come; it had for him a context by which it could be interpreted and its significance understood. Reflecting back on boarding school, Lewis writes,

> I think that the life of faith is easier to me because of these memories. To think, in sunny and confident times, that I shall die and rot, or to think that one day all this universe shall slip away and become memory (as Oldie [the headmaster at Belsen] slipped away into memory three times a year, and with him the canes, the cold beds)—this is easier to us if we have seen just that sort of thing happen before. We had learned not to take present things at their face value.[39]

The difficulties at this point in Lewis's life could be properly understood only with the aid of a long view. The rough boyhood experiences, as he recalls them years later, contributed to his developing thoughts about the problem of evil and subjectivism.

Another thing must be mentioned here. Although Lewis considered home to be much better than school, he still felt it could be improved. This longing for something better contributed to that pang

---

36. C. S. Lewis, *Surprised By Joy*, 22–41, 25.

37. W. H. Lewis, *Letters*, 3.

38. C. S. Lewis, *Surprised By Joy*, 36.

39. Ibid., 37.

which he later labeled as joy. Although distant and estranged from that which he desired most, Lewis became hungry for joy because of disappointments, sorrows, griefs, and dissatisfactions with the world. He wanted things to be better. Despite the fact that dissatisfaction turned him away from God when he was young, the adult Lewis found the same dissatisfaction drawing him to God. Here again, the passing of time positively affected his thinking about the evil he had endured: objective reality made its demands.

Lewis's experiences in the English public school system, though a great improvement over his previous "concentration camp" days, were still far from desirable. He did not like his years in the public school, and describes those aspects that he detested most in his autobiography. However, Major Lewis writes in his *Memoir* that his brother overstated the circumstances of his school environment. His own impression was that it was not nearly as bad a place as the junior Lewis had suggested.[40] The two boys, different in age and personality, in fact did have different experiences in the public school. C. S. Lewis recognized that his brother's perspective was different than his own.[41] However much Lewis might have been mistaken about school, perceptions, as Lewis would agree, are often treated as reality and affect the choices one makes in responding to perceived conditions. Although one may respond to situations according to one's perceptions, it is important that one comes to see things as they *really* are.

In public school, Lewis found some teachers that he thought were tolerable, and in at least one case excellent. It was, however, the social environment that Lewis found so deplorable. The hierarchical system of "fagging" allowed senior boys to take advantage of younger boys to produce a world of anxiety, compromise, and fear. Lewis describes a setting where people would claw, lie, and cheat to move into the approved social group or climb to the top of the desired hierarchy. For the young Lewis, it was oppressive nonsense. His circumstances served to create a discontent with the world as he was experiencing it. He was becoming a man against the world, and his negativity was the bad fruit of his difficult circumstances, contributing to his growing pessimism.

40. W. H. Lewis, ed., *Letters*, 5.

41. Lewis, *Surprised By Joy*, 126–27.

In the world of school, as Lewis perceived it, he was discovering that it was "every man for himself." He did not, of course, at this time see the consequences of such an outlook. Protecting himself in the world in which he was becoming more and more insecure also led him to be more self-centered. This retreat back into himself was equally an exercise in contempt towards the world. His subjectivism resulted in a contempt for authority, and manifested itself in his concern to preserve what he calls his "monstrous individualism, my lawlessness."[42] He did not want any interference in his life, and thus Christianity was especially odious to him at this time, for

> Christianity placed at the centre what then seemed to me a transcendental Interferer. If its picture were true then no sort of 'treaty with reality' could ever be possible. There was no region even in the innermost depth of one's soul (nay, there least of all) which one could surround with a barbed wire fence and guard with a notice No Admittance. And that was what I wanted; some area, however small, of which I could say to other beings, 'This is my business and mine only.'[43]

Withdrawing into a dungeon of self-centeredness, he became shackled. Something needed to be done, for as Lewis later observes, "The characteristic of lost souls is 'a rejection of everything that is not simply themselves.'"[44] He did not know the love of others, let alone the love of God. He sounded the horn of retreat, going deeper into himself. How well he came to understand this is evidenced by what he writes later in his life:

> Love anything, and your heart will certainly be wrung and possibly be broken. If you want to make sure of keeping it intact you must give your heart to no one, not even to an animal. Wrap carefully around with hobbies and little luxuries; avoid all entanglements; lock it up safe in the casket or coffin of your selfishness. But in that casket—safe, dark, motionless, airless—it will change. It will not be broken; it will become unbreakable, impenetrable, irredeemable. The alternative to tragedy, or at least to the risk of tragedy, is damnation. The only place outside

42. Ibid., 172.
43. Ibid.
44. C. S. Lewis, *Pain*, 98.

> heaven where you can be perfectly safe from all the dangers and
> perturbations of love is Hell.[45]

Rescue would come, but the way out of self was not easy, and Lewis
discovered pain was part of the process. Knowledge of this fact later
influenced his rhetoric.

Lewis's childhood understanding of Christianity proved insufficient to account for the complexities surrounding the pain he suffered.
Reflecting back, he writes of the atheism which eventually emerged
from these events: "I was at this time living, like so many Atheists or
Antitheists, in a whirl of contradictions." He explains, "I maintained
that God did not exist. I was also very angry with God for not existing. I was equally angry with Him for creating a world."[46] He did not,
at that time, scrutinize the unreasonableness of his thinking. He was
convinced that the world was the way he *configured* it to be. Clearly,
subjectivism was a strong force in interpreting his limited life experience. His thinking would change, however, as he wrestled with more of
life's complexities.

## World War I

The next set of painful circumstances which Lewis faced came with
World War I, when he fought as a soldier in the heart of the Battle of
the Somme.[47] This experience marked Lewis's life and contributed to
his developing objectivism and the rhetoric which emerged from it,
particularly as he thought about evil and suffering. Although his letters from the period make no mention of the problem of evil, Lewis's
experiences in the war greatly informed his developing vision of the
objective world. Here, again, he was placed in an environment that
communicated to him some of the worst of life's experiences. He recalls
a few of the horrors in a letter to Dom Bede Griffiths, a former pupil:

> My memories of the last war haunted my dreams for years.
> Military service, to be plain, includes the threat of every *tempo-*
> *ral* evil; pain and death which is what we fear from sickness; iso-
> lation from those we love which is what we fear from exile: toil

45. C. S. Lewis, *Four Loves*, 138–39

46. Lewis, *Surprised By Joy*. 115.

47. For a detailed account of Lewis's World War I experiences the reader may want
to consult Gilchrist, *Morning After.*

under arbitrary masters, injustice, humiliation, which is what
we fear from slavery: hunger, thirst, and exposure which is what
we fear from poverty.[48]

But, in spite of all of war's horrors, Lewis writes, "I am surprised that I
did not dislike the army more."[49] In an environment where the expectation for enjoyment was kept to a minimum, there were still joys to be
found. Lewis recounts these in the chapter of his autobiography called
"Guns and Good Company."[50] During the war, he learned that, although
the earth can promise no lasting security, it can provide many pleasures
if one does not expect too much from it. Insight grew as he reflected on
his war experience:

> If you think of this world as a place intended simply for our
> happiness, you find it quite intolerable: think of it as a place
> of training and correction and it's not so bad. Imagine a set of
> people all living in the same building. Half of them think it is
> a hotel, the other half think it is a prison. Those who think it
> is a hotel might regard it as quite intolerable, and those who
> thought it was a prison might decide it was really surprisingly
> comfortable. So that what seems the ugly doctrine is one that
> comforts and strengthens you in the end. The people who try
> to hold an optimistic view of the world will become pessimists:
> people who have a pretty stern view of it become optimistic.[51]

Certainly, hardship had its lessons to teach, and Lewis found that reflection could produce fruit. He realized that events that occur in time cannot be fully understood in the moment of their occurrence; the passage
of time can produce fresh perspective and bring to light significance
not grasped in the moment of difficulty. Lewis's wrestling, his desire to
reorder and reinterpret his perceptions over time according to objective
reality, even reality he did not initially understand fully, demonstrated
his commitment to objectivism.

In his days of service during World War I, Lewis encountered
what he perceived at the time as goodness. The passing of time did not
dim this perspective. As Lewis recounts it, not long after he arrived at
the front, he came down with what was called "trench fever." While he

48. W. H. Lewis, ed. *Letters*, 166.
49. C. S. Lewis, *Surprised By Joy*, 188.
50. Ibid., 182–86.
51. C. S. Lewis, *God in the Dock*, 52.

was hospitalized for treatment, he first discovered the writings of G. K. Chesterton. Chesterton, a Christian apologist, was not the kind of author one would expect to appeal to Lewis, the atheist. Yet, in a hospital bed in France, surrounded by the various stresses of the war, he began to read one of the authors who would most profoundly influence his own return to faith. Lewis believed it was an act of providence.[52] He liked the humor and goodness he discovered in Chesterton. Recalling this later, he writes, "A young man who wished to remain a sound atheist cannot be too careful in his reading. There are traps everywhere—'Bibles laid open, millions of surprises,' as Herbert says, 'fine nets and stratagems.' God is, if I may say it, very unscrupulous."[53] Clearly, his looking back over these war years, Lewis seems to indicate a warming up to Christian authors, if not to Christianity itself.

Lewis was also amazed at the number of people he met who embodied genuine good will. He did not discount the fact that one would encounter nasty people in the military. "But," he writes, "memory fills these months with pleasant, transitory, contacts. Every few days one seemed to meet a scholar, an original, a poet, a cheery buffoon, a raconteur or at least a man of good will."[54] These encounters enabled him to come "to know and pity and reverence the ordinary man."[55] His own heart was growing in charity in the difficult context of war. The reality of "the thing itself" was transforming his perspective.

Some years later, at the outbreak of World War II, Lewis was asked to deliver two different messages at Oxford to students who were on the threshold of despair. He spoke to them with rhetorical sensitivity— pathos—for they were beginning to wonder if civilization was on the verge of collapse and utter destruction. What was the use of continuing the futile pursuit of education in light of such circumstances? Lewis's experiences in World War I contributed to his empathetic capacity as he addressed his audiences. The first address he gave was at Magdalen College, titled "De Futilitate."[56] He began by probing what it means to

52. C. S. Lewis, *Surprised By Joy*, 190.

53. Ibid., 191.

54. Ibid., 189.

55. Ibid., 196.

56. C. S. Lewis, *Christian Reflections*, 58.

judge a thing as futile.[57] "An accusation always implies a standard."[58] To suggest that all is futile or performed in vain is to imply an expectation that things ought to be different. The judgment itself would not be possible unless things were, in fact, different than how we perceive them to be. Lewis suggests, "Unless we allow our ultimate reality to be moral, we cannot morally condemn it."[59] Lewis believed that there is always more to account for than what is first perceived in any given moment. Because there is a reasonable, theological answer to the issues of seeming futility, Lewis suggests that God has purposes, the fullness of which is not always understood while one is in the midst of its unfolding plans. Lewis delivers his address with the ethos of one who witnessed war first-hand and discovered his perceptions of reality could be modified, over time.

Under similar circumstances, Lewis preached a sermon at the University Church of St. Mary the Virgin, entitled "On Learning in Wartime." In this message, Lewis reminded his hearers that war does not increase death, given that death is total in every generation. It is imminent and can happen to anyone at any time. During the sermon, Lewis posits,

> War creates no absolutely new situation: it simply aggravates the permanent human situation so that we can no longer ignore it. Human life has always been lived on the edge of a precipice. Human culture has always had to exist under the shadow of something infinitely more important than itself. If men had postponed the search for knowledge and beauty until they were secure, the search would never have begun. We are mistaken when we compare war with normal life. Life has never been normal.[60]

For Lewis, the desire for security must find its satisfaction in something other than the world's situation as it presents itself at any given moment. One's character begins to shrivel up and shrink so as to correspond to the finite and temporal things to which it has become attached. His audience may complain of death and the pains that surround it, or they may cry to God that His world is unfair, but as Lewis reminds them, God never

---

57. Ibid., 60.

58. Ibid., 65–66.

59. Ibid., 70.

60. C. S. Lewis, *Weight of Glory*, 44.

intended for them to be satisfied in this world. Lewis's rhetoric is full of the ethos of his own life's experience; consequently, he could assert that through pain, sorrow, suffering, and even death itself, God allows us to experience the "severe mercies" that remove from us the very things that keep us from Him. Lewis's understanding grew as he adjusted his own thinking to objective values, and this adjusted thought provided the basis for the counsel he was able to give to the Oxford students.

On September 28, 1931, Lewis became a Christian.[61] Nearly thirty-three years old, he had been a fellow of Magdalen College, Oxford for five years. He was on the threshold of a distinguished academic career, in the course of which he would become an important contributor to the spread of Christianity through his lay preaching, his popular Christian books, and his B. B. C. broadcast talks. The emotional impact of evil and suffering misguided him in his younger years. Still, his objectivist commitments led him to eventual transformation. In the years following his conversion, the emotional struggles of his past enhanced his rhetorical ability, enabling him to connect with his readers, who also surely struggled.

## Lewis's *The Problem of Pain*

In "Language is Sermonic," "The rhetorician," writes Weaver, "is concerned with definite questions."[62] One question that occupied much of Lewis's thought throughout his life was the question of evil; and Lewis, always the rhetorician, seeks to explain to others the workings of evil and pain in the world. While he was sensitive to the emotional stresses related to his own youth, it is clear he also wanted to present his content in a more universal way, in hopes of reducing confusion in the minds of his audience. Weaver notes that "the very task of the rhetorician is to determine what feature of a question is most exigent and to use the power of language to make it appear so."[63] In fact, Lewis engages his readers by using language to find the most exigent features relative to the problem of evil; then he directs them to look, in a fresh way, at the objective realities surrounding the problem.

61. Green and Hooper, *Biography*, 116.

62. Weaver, *Sermonic*, 1357.

63. Ibid., 1358.

In *The Problem of Pain*, Lewis produced his first book in Christian apologetics. What was his purpose for doing so? English Professor and Lewis scholar Clyde S. Kilby writes, "Lewis is fully aware that in this book he does not solve all the problems entailed in pain and evil."[64] If Kilby is correct, and I think he is, then Lewis must have believed that his was a work in progress, not a last word on the subject, but the best word he could offer at the time. Therefore, his rhetorical claims are not inflated or overbearing. Concerning his entire output of apologetic books, Lewis scholar Richard B. Cunningham observes, "As an apologist, Lewis does not do certain things in his writings. He creates no comprehensive, all-embracing apologetic system, and yet he deals with a surprising number of apologetic problems."[65] Cunningham continues, "Nor does he thoroughly, systematically, and exhaustively deal with objections to the Christian faith. Instead he generally isolates and deals only with the main problems of a given question."[66] As a Christian, Lewis changed his views since his conversion: he came to believe that not only can God and evil both exist in the world, but belief in God is the primary way someone can make the most sense of the very phenomenon of evil. Nevertheless, in *The Problem of Pain* Lewis is not expecting to fully resolve the matter. He sets out to present an explanation that is "good enough," a work in progress.

Other scholars also recognize that Lewis's work in *The Problem of Pain* was neither complete nor meant to present itself as so. The Catholic critic John Randolph Willis perceptively notes, "Lewis shows that the universe is small indeed compared with Ultimate Reality; so how much smaller earth is when compared to the universe, and man when compared to the earth." He develops this further, remarking, "Lewis always reminds us that when we speak of the attributes of God, we speak in a supereminent fashion. What God is in actuality is simply beyond all human imagination. God is his mercy and much more; God is his justice and much more."[67] John Peters, another Lewis scholar, rightly observes, "Lewis recognizes too that there is no easy solution to the problem of pain, and that no intellectual solution or formula can do away with the

---

64. Kilby, *Christian World*, 70.

65. Cunningham, *Defender of the Faith*, 20.

66. Ibid.

67. Willis, *Pleasures Forevermore*, 20

need for patience, fortitude and courage."[68] We see, then, that Lewis does not oversimplify either the problem or the solution. Perhaps purposefully seeking to avoid a comprehensive and systematic theological or philosophical approach to the problem, Lewis introduces the image of a dance into the narrative of *The Problem of Pain* at several places. It is a good image, for it speaks of a process more than a completed act; furthermore, a dance has form with room for variety, structure as well as play. Lewis critic Joe Christopher believes that this image ties the book together. It is a significant observation and underscores the incompleteness of the book, emphasizing that it was never intended to be, for Lewis, a last word or a simple formula.[69] One only needs to recall Lewis's own comment about William Morris to make the point more clear. For here, too, Lewis uses an image of a dance to speak of something that has meaning but is both in process and incomplete in its presentation. He writes, "In Morris there are no conclusions . . . balance is attained and immediately lost; everything is beginning over again: it is a dance, not a diagram. It can no more be seized in an epigram, summed up and docketed, than experience itself."[70]

Lewis biographer A. N. Wilson observes of *The Problem of Pain* that it displays, from its opening paragraphs, a "style of rhetoric which seems more reminiscent of the Belfast police courts." He calls Lewis a "rhetorical trickster who is not thinking at all."[71] Wilson seems to be arguing that Lewis is trying to bludgeon a confession from his readers to agree with his solution to the problem. However, the criticism is too strong, discounting the skill and subtlety of Lewis's linguistic aims. Nevertheless, what can be said is that much of Lewis's apologetic work grew out of his own autobiographical struggles; thus, his work in this area represents a work in progress. But here caution must be taken, for as Lewis scholar James Como writes, and I think accurately, Lewis is not always exactly right in telling his own story: "The consideration of C. S. Lewis's self is a very great challenge. He at once hid it absolutely, distorted it, and invented parts of it to parade forth; he repressed, explored, and denied it; he indulged and overcame it; certainly he would

68. Peters, *Achievement*, 62.

69. Christopher, *C. S. Lewis*, 67–68.

70. C. S. Lewis, *Selected Literary Essays*, 229.

71. Wilson, *Biography*, 162–63.

transform, and then transcend it; almost always he used it."[72] Yet Como also points out that Lewis turns to his own life to find the *topoi* for his arguments. Where but to life—that is, to thought, reading, and experience—would he turn when looking for subject matter, suitable as the raw material for his argument?[73]

Christian apologist John Sims also sees Lewis's answer to the problem of evil (especially his treatment of Natural Evil in *The Problem of Pain*) as incomplete. This is a further indication that Lewis's ideas were still in formation. His ideas developed in the process of his life experience. Sims observes, "The only answer that Lewis could offer to this perpetual and perplexing question was that nature does not always act benevolently or even-handedly because matter has a fixed nature and obeys constant laws." Sims adds, "Christianity does not offer an easy solution or a quick fix for the pain and suffering that is experienced through nature."[74] Sims points out that "Lewis warned that it is not our experiences, our subjectivity, and our ideas that are all-important. If this were true, some of them would break us. There must be some objective truth that we can trust that transcends our experience."[75] Consequently, it is necessary to engage in a kind of public debate or dialectic if a culture hopes to make better and better approximations towards an understanding of the complex problem of evil. Still, speculation about this issue at any given moment, however helpful it might be, is insufficient. A lifetime of contemplative work, work that Lewis was himself doing, will likely produce better results, having time to accommodate itself to more and more nuances surrounding the issues.

Lewis, aware of the exigency surrounding the problem of pain, sought to address this topic out of what he felt was a common concern. He was well aware of the constraints he would have to consider for his text to be taken seriously. His own life's experience embodied these difficulties, and the fact that the issue of evil had driven him from his childhood faith was proximate in his thinking. *The Problem of Pain* reveals significant development in his thinking as he sought to resolve the conflicts that had plagued him. There are weaknesses in the book, as

72. Como, *Branches to Heaven*, 54.

73. Ibid., 140. This is what the ancients recognized as the First Canon of Rhetoric: Invention.

74 Sims, *Missionaries to the Skeptics*, 60.

75. Ibid., 64.

will be seen below. Nevertheless, Lewis's attempts to address the problem of pain reveal significant modifications in his thinking relative to
avoidance of subjectivism and adjusting his thinking to objective reality.
The fact that Lewis addresses these things to his audience shows that he
has a rhetorical interest in helping them to make similar adjustments.
It is not necessary for us to think that Lewis felt he had worked out his
conclusions to some kind of finality. Weaver wisely reminds us that "We
accept the fact frankly that most issues, including some of vital relation
to our welfare, are still in the realm of deliberative forensics."[76] Since
Lewis's attempts at addressing the problem of pain is a work in progress,
drawing on the embodiment of his own personal struggles, it is necessary to look further at the successes and failures of his argument.

It is evident to many that Lewis's ideas in *The Problem of Pain* do
not represent an attempt at a comprehensive explanation of the problem of evil. The fact is that Lewis's ideas on this matter were subject to
change. He had been unable to account for significant data by means of
his pre-Christian understanding. When he became a Christian, it was
natural that he should turn his thoughts again to the matter of evil and
address the topic rhetorically, to look afresh at the problem in light of
the objective facts. Therefore, he did not reject the Christian faith that
informed the core of his new thinking about the matter. His was an
understanding in process, as it should be.

## Features of Lewis's Argument in The Problem of Pain

Weaver asserts that a "society cannot exist without a social bond, nor a
social bond without a rhetorical impulse. There are some things which
the community needs to believe, and these beliefs come to us couched in
rhetorical terms, which tell us what attitudes to take."[77] In *The Problem
of Pain*, Lewis's rhetorical aim is to have his readers take a fresh look at
the issue of evil in a world made by God. Given that Lewis's thinking
about the matter had changed, his intention was to persuade others to
do the same. As he engages his audience in this way, he is accepting his
obligations to the community in which he lives. His rhetorical efforts
are necessary, even if they are not perfect.

76. Weaver, *Defense of Tradition*, 291.
77. Weaver, *Defense of Tradition*, 346.

The problem of evil can be stated in the following question: If God is good and all-powerful, why does He allow evil to exist in the universe? It would appear on the surface of things that if evil exists in the world, we must conclude that God is either not good or not all-powerful. Lewis stirs his readers to ask, "Is there more here than meets the eye at first glance?" He invites his audience to look more carefully at the problem, to guard against subjectivism by delving into the facts. It is important to see how Lewis uses discursive argument to establish his rhetorical claims.

## DIVINE OMNIPOTENCE

In the chapter *Divine Omnipotence*, Lewis begins with a quotation from Thomas Aquinas: "Nothing which implies contradiction falls under the omnipotence of God."[78] Throughout the rest of the chapter Lewis develops his argument around this remark. His aim is to make his readers rethink what one means when he says that God is all-powerful. It certainly does not mean that God can do anything. Given his nature, He cannot do anything self-contradictory.[79] If He is just, He cannot be unfair; if He is love, He cannot be less than charitable; if He is holy, He cannot be impious; if He is righteous, He cannot do wrong; if He is immutable, He cannot be capricious. According to Lewis, omnipotence means that God has the power to do all that is intrinsically possible.[80] He observes, "It is no more possible for God than for the weakest of His creatures to carry out both of two mutually exclusive alternatives; not because His power meets an obstacle, but because nonsense remains nonsense even when we talk it about God."[81] Later he adds, "Heaven will solve our problems, but not, I think, by showing us subtle reconciliations between all our apparently contradictory notions. The notions will all be knocked from under our feet. We shall see there never was any problem."[82] Lewis is too confident in his understanding of his readers to assert that they might think that there was never any problem at

---

78. C. S. Lewis, *Pain*, 21.

79. Ibid., 22.

80. Ibid.

81. Ibid., 23.

82. Ibid., 56.

all. He has the right idea when he challenges his readers to re-examine what it is they mean when they speak of God's Omnipotence.

From here Lewis develops his argument further by speculating that God could not create "free souls without giving them some kind of independence."[83] What would such a thing involve? The nature of this freedom must make actual relationship between creature and Creator possible. This relationship is necessary because "something analogous to society exists within the Divine Being from all eternity—that God is love, not merely in the sense of being the platonic form of love, but because within Him, the concrete reciprocities of love exist before all worlds and are thence derived to the creatures."[84] Relational attributes in a non-contingent being presuppose that relationship is necessary in that being. If relationship is necessary in God, then creatures made to bear His image must also exhibit the capacity to live in society with God and with others. The ability to choose, and the relative independence of will to make choices, makes it possible for man to love, but it also makes evil possible. In pointing this out, Lewis is clarifying for his audience that evil is the fruit of the ill-use of free-will. But, as will be shown later, he neglects to explain the origin of other kinds of evil which cannot be accounted for simply by the existence of free-will.

Lewis goes on to argue that God not only created man with a will, but also set him in a context or matrix in which those wills could operate and develop. He created an objective reality, independent of the creature's mind.[85] One finds, then, that in this matrix it is possible to make adjustments in one's thinking which are appropriate to the world in which he lives.[86] Clearly, Lewis is appealing to his audience to reconsider the matter of evil in light of a more consistent and objective approach. He is arguing that should one not make adjustments of thought and life, that is, if one turns away from reality towards subjectivism, it is a kind of rebellion which is bound to produce painful consequences. And Lewis explains, "If matter has a fixed nature and obeys constant laws, not all states of matter will be equally agreeable to the wishes of a given soul, nor all equally beneficial for that particular aggregate of

83. Ibid., 23.
84. Ibid., 23–24.
85. Ibid., 25.
86. Ibid., 26.

matter which he calls his body."[87] If God creates a world that is not ca-pricious and allows its inhabitants free will, this will provide a matrix for wonderful possibilities, but also open the door to incredible risks. Such a world is not incompatible with God's omnipotence, but should God intervene to correct the abuse of free will at each instance, this would lead to a contradiction. Lewis continues:

> But such a world would be one in which wrong actions were impossible, and in which, therefore, freedom of the will would be void; nay, if the principle were carried out to its logical con-clusion, evil thoughts would be impossible, for the cerebral matter which we use for thinking would refuse its task when we attempted to frame them. All matter in the neighbourhood of a wicked man would be liable to undergo unpredictable al-terations. That God can and does, on occasions, modify the be-haviour of matter and produce what we call miracles, is part of Christian faith; but the very conception of a common, and therefore stable, world, demands that these occasions be ex-tremely rare.[88]

Lewis makes two final points about the Divine Omnipotence. First, he argues, "Perhaps this is not the 'best of all possible' universes, but the only possible one."[89] He appears to be saying that the problem of evil, properly understood, is not so much that God's omnipotence seems incompatible with the existence of evil. The proper mode of thinking is, rather, because God is good and all-powerful, willing to create creatures with the capacity for relationships, He has willed for conditions to exist where evil is a possibility. In His wisdom, He chose these conditions under which the universe operates, and He anticipated evil would arise under these conditions. God is not responsible for evil, as if He acted in an evil manner Himself, though He can be seen to be responsible for it in that He created the conditions from which it would arise. According to Lewis, He did this in His wisdom, fully knowing that He would accomplish a greater good through it. Undoubtedly, Lewis is appeal-ing to his audience to reconsider the matter of evil in light of a more consistent and objective approach. Even so, there is a need for further explanation. Would it have been possible for God to create a world that

---

87. Ibid., 25–26.
88. Ibid., 27.
89. Ibid., 28.

minimized the risks, perhaps even eliminating them altogether? Lewis offers a response:

> Possible worlds can mean only 'worlds that God could have made but didn't.' The idea of that which God 'could have' done involves a too anthropomorphic conception of God's freedom. Whatever human freedom means, Divine freedom cannot mean indeterminacy between alternatives and choice of one of them. Perfect goodness can never debate about the end to be attained, and perfect wisdom cannot debate about the means most suited to achieve it. The freedom of God consists in the fact that no cause other than Himself produced His acts and no external obstacle impedes Him—that His own goodness is the root from which they all grow, and His own omnipotence the air in which they all flower.[90]

The eternal scope of God's purposes and plans may not be perceived by the very limited and temporal understanding of His creatures. But the inability of the creature to understand those purposes does not imply a deficiency in the power of God to accomplish them. To be sure, Lewis is using his rhetorical skill to make his readers consider the complexities surrounding the problem of evil more accurately and with greater clarity than they might have considered before.

In addition to questioning the possibility of other universes, Lewis asks, perceptively, If pain were to be part of this world, wouldn't we have been better off if we had never been created? He answers:

> I am aware of no human scales in which such a portentous question can be weighed. Some comparison between one state of being and another can be made, but the attempt to compare being and not being ends in mere words. "It would be better for me not to exist"—in what sense "for me"? How should I, if I did not exist, profit by not existing?[91]

In order to make his case rhetorically, He reasons in a way that seeks to account not only for the facts themselves, but the discursive arrangement of those facts.

90. Ibid., 28.
91. Ibid., 29.

## DIVINE GOODNESS

As Richard Weaver observes, "We have no sooner uttered words than we have given impulse to other people to look at the world, or some small part of it in our way."[92] Weaver is right in making this observation, and it has particular application to Lewis. It does no good to dismiss Lewis's argument, in *The Problem of Pain*, simply because he has rhetorical ends in mind, engaged as he is in apologetic efforts and evangelistic aims. He may, or may not, be wrong, but he must not be dismissed because he is seeking to persuade his readers. It is the responsibility of the critic—who also uses rhetoric for persuasive purposes—not to dismiss Lewis because he sounds 'preachy' but rather to point out the flaws in his dialectic that invalidate his rhetoric. If this is not done, one might assume that the critic does not understand Lewis well enough to engage him. The dismissive attitude is certainly easier than engagement, but it is also less ethical. And Lewis, believing in the goodness of God, whose nature is manifest in the objective world, seeks to be ethical in his own claims. Lewis's aim is such that he wants to convince his readers to look at facts surrounding the problem of evil in a way whereby they must re-think their idea of Divine Goodness. If God exists, it can be expected that His goodness would differ from mere human goodness.[93] He suspects that God's goodness would contrast with man's as the drawing of an architect's circle, made with a compass, would contrast with the circle drawn by the freehand of a child.[94] Lewis says that the reason some may find any measure of pain incompatible with Divine Goodness is that they confuse goodness with that mere kindness which seeks to make everyone comfortable at all times.[95] God, in His love and goodness, on the other hand, desires that His creatures actually become good, that they may be objects in which He is well pleased.

### Four Analogies of Divine Goodness

Believing that Divine Goodness may allow for suffering, Lewis looks rhetorically at four analogies taken from the Bible where the objects of love must experience some kind of correction and discomfort in order

92. Weaver, *Sermonic*, 1360
93. C. S. Lewis, *Pain*, 30.
94. Ibid., 31.
95. Ibid., 32.

that they might become more pleasing to the one who loves them. This is clearly an argument from similitude, and through these analogies he seeks to explain how God's love for His creatures may be compatible with suffering and pain. First, there is the love of the artist for his art. God's relationship to man may be compared to the potter's relationship with the clay (Jeremiah 18), or the architect's relationship to a building (1 Peter 2:5). The potter at the wheel, whenever he may perceive a flaw in his work, will mash it back down into a lump again in order that he may remake it. So, too, the architect designing his building may make any number of erasures on the blueprint as he seeks to portray on paper the ideas he has in his mind. If lumps of clay and blueprints had intelligence, emotion, and will, they might sound out a complaint in the midst of these procedures, not understanding the grander designs of their creator.[96] Significantly, Lewis does not mention that the analogy breaks down at an important point. While human potters and architects may make mistakes and therefore have to undo them, one would expect that no problems of this sort would be true of God.

His second analogy is "The love of a man for a beast."[97] If God is referred to as a shepherd, He is to His creatures as the animal husbandman is to his flock. Lewis develops the analogy by considering the relationship that exists between a man and his dog. He writes:

> In its state of nature it has a smell, and habits, which frustrate man's love: he washes it, house-trains it, teaches it not to steal, and is so enabled to love it completely. To the puppy, the whole proceeding would seem, if it were a theologian, to cast grave doubts on the "goodness" of man: but the full-grown and full-trained dog, larger, healthier, and longer-lived than the wild dog, and admitted, as it were by Grace, to a whole world of affections, loyalties, interests, and comforts entirely beyond its animal destiny, would have no such doubts.[98]

The third analogy is found in a father's love for his son. If a father never disciplined his child, one might wonder if he truly loved the child. Certainly, this life has risks and dangers beyond the child's comprehension. The father who loves his child disciplines him in hopes that the child will be protected from those dangers. It is not because he wishes

96. Ibid., 34.
97. Ibid., 35.
98. Ibid., 35.

his child to suffer, but rather because he wills the minor suffering that may come with discipline until the child acquires a level of maturity. In a letter, Lewis expresses the idea like this:

> I believe that all pain is contrary to God's will, absolutely but not relatively. When I am taking a thorn out of my own finger (or a child's finger) the pain is 'absolutely' contrary to my will; i.e. if I could have chosen a situation without pain I would have done so. But I do will what caused the pain, relative to the given situation; i.e. granted the thorn I prefer the pain rather than leaving the thorn where it is. A mother spanking a child would be in the same position; she would rather cause it this pain than let it go on pulling the cat's tail, but she would like it better if no situation which demands a smack had arisen.[99]

Lewis's fourth and final analogy is the love of a man for a woman. He cautions that the analogy is full of danger if it is not properly understood. For no one would admire a husband who intentionally causes his wife to suffer. On the other hand, Lewis explains,

> Does any woman regard it as a sign of love in a man that he neither knows nor cares how she is looking? Love may, indeed, love the beloved when her beauty is lost: but not because it is lost. Love may forgive all infirmities and love still in spite of them: but Love cannot cease to will their removal. Love is more sensitive than hatred itself to every blemish in the beloved; his 'feeling is more soft and sensible than are the tender horns of cockled snails.' Of all powers he forgives most, but he condones least: he is pleased with little, but demands all.[100]

Here again, the tenderest of loves is found to be compatible with pain.[101] Lewis believed it was necessary to challenge his readers rhetorically, to rethink what Divine Goodness must truly mean. While any one of these analogies will break down at points, together they form a compelling composite picture. The analogies strengthen Lewis's argument by use of similitude, demonstrating ways in which love is seen to be compatible with suffering. In this way, he appeals to the readers' experience in the real world where they have encountered examples revealing the

99. W. H. Lewis, *Letters*, 237, 238.
100. Lewis, *Pain*, 37.
101. Ibid.

relationship that can exist between goodness and suffering. Thus, Lewis has his readers consider objective reality in a fresh way.

## Further Clarifications of Lewis's Argument

Lewis argues that being self-existent, God has no need external to Himself. Therefore, Lewis observes, "If He who in Himself can lack nothing chooses to need us, it is because we need to be needed."[102] Could this be self-serving on God's part? Here Lewis believes that God's loves and interests must not be confused as self-serving in any way that resembles human selfishness. If there appears to be something in Him analogous to a passion or a "want, it is there by His own will and for our sakes."[103] Furthermore, His love cannot be considered selfish because He made creatures for Himself, so His desire for them is appropriate to His nature and ours. "When we want to be something other than the thing God wants us to be, we must be wanting what, in fact, will not make us happy."[104] Lewis argues that God has created humans with a deep-seeded need for Him. If they seek to fulfill themselves with anything less than God, they set themselves up for disappointments. His goodness might appear to His creatures as questionable if He should remove from them the things that keep them from Him. If the desire for Him has been tethered to other objects that cannot ultimately satisfy, God may appear as a rival to what they think they want. Lewis believes that nothing else can ultimately fulfill the creature but God. There are no other options; it is central to Lewis's argument that great disappointments come when the things one puts in God's place do not satisfy. Again, Lewis seeks to clarify his argument by appealing to the reader's objective experience of expectation and disappointment.

In Lewis's system, pain is one of God's "severe mercies"[105] to bring creatures to Himself. If this is so, then Lewis fails either to suggest or to answer a very important question: If creatures are lacking in their understanding of the Divine intention, then how can they be blamed for turning from God in that very hour that He brings pain into their lives in order to turn them to Him? An animal which is suffering from

102. Ibid., 41.
103. Ibid., 42.
104. Ibid.
105. Vanauken, *Severe Mercy*, 209.

the pain inflicted by a veterinarian may understandably bite the vet's hand. It is not surprising that the animal may likely turn to something other than the vet for comfort.

As Lewis concludes his chapter on Divine Goodness, his focus moves away from anything that might resemble the philosophical or apologetic. He seems to transition from objections to belief, in light of the problem of evil and suffering, towards the rhetoric of an evangelist, calling his audience to repentance and faith. He writes that it is the very goodness of God that seeks to transform humankind, and that transformation may mean pain if God must remove those things, keeping them from Him.

> God wills our good, and our good is to love Him (with that responsive love proper to His creatures) and to love Him we must know Him: and if we know Him, we shall in fact fall on our faces. If we do not, that only shows that what we are trying to love is not yet God—though it may be the nearest approximation to God that our thought and fantasy can attain.[106]

With this Lewis closes his chapter on the Divine Goodness.

For the purposes of my argument—that Lewis was himself the embodiment of his rhetoric concerning the problem of pain (and therefore it was a rhetoric in process)—I will conclude by considering the chapter on "Animal Pain." Though the other chapters have various strengths and weaknesses, I want to focus on this chapter because it reveals most strikingly where Lewis fails in making his point.

## Animal Pain

In what is by far the weakest chapter in the book, Lewis considers the matter of animal pain. It poses a difficulty for him, particularly in the way he has developed his argument thus far. It also reveals a specific case where his argument lacks sophistication. If animals have no wills, they cannot be responsible for rebellion and sin. Anything relative to free-will cannot apply to them. And if they are incapable of virtue and pain, suffering will not improve their character. Therefore the explanations he has developed for human pain and suffering cannot be applied to animals. Yet before he begins to attempt an explanation, he reminds his readers that it is a mistake to let the entire issue of pain and suffering

106. C. S. Lewis, *Pain*, 42–43.

rest on the problem of the animals. He concedes that it is an important issue, but stresses that it is not a matter upon which we can have clarity, since "It is outside of the range of our knowledge."[107]

I believe that Lewis's difficulty in this chapter is due to the narrow focus of his rhetorical approach to the problem of evil. Animals do not fit neatly into Lewis's argument, which posits that God uses suffering for remedial purposes to make virtuous wills that have rebelled. At least he is honest enough to consider a matter that runs against the grain of the approach he has taken so far. However, rather than concede the point or use this issue to develop his argument along different lines, he tries to work the animals into his scheme of free-will and soul-making apologetics. Unfortunately, he makes such a mess of it that readers who may take his earlier chapters seriously will be dissatisfied at this point.

Lewis says that three questions must be answered. First is the question of fact: What do animals suffer? Second, the question of origin: How did disease and pain enter into the animal world? And third, there is the question of justice: How can animal suffering be reconciled with the justice of God?[108] Lewis's argument will begin to fail as it develops along these lines, for he will have to force it onto a path that leads his readers to wonder if he has slipped into subjectivism.

Seeking to answer the first question, Lewis's asks his readers to distinguish between sentience and consciousness.[109] The feeling of sensations does not imply consciousness. To have sensation (a) followed by sensation (b) followed by sensation (c), and so on, is not to experience these things; it is merely to sense them. The experience of these sensations would demand that we are able to look at them sequentially. In order to do this, there must be something in us outside the sequence of the sensations themselves, which can perceive when each sensation begins and ends. Lewis believes that "this something is . . . Consciousness or Soul and the process I have just described is one of the proofs that the soul, though experiencing time, is not itself completely 'timeful.'"[110] If an animal has no soul, then its experience of these sensations will be without a sense of succession. Lewis writes:

107. Ibid., 103.
108. Ibid., 104.
109. Ibid., 105.
110. Ibid.

The correct description would be 'Pain is taking place in this animal'; not, as we commonly say, 'this animal feels pain,' for the words 'this' and 'feels' really smuggle in the assumption that it is a 'self' or 'soul' or 'consciousness' standing above the sensations and organizing them into an 'experience' as we do.[111]

What he has written here neglects the fact that animals seem to remember suffering pain and take care to avoid it.

When he turns his attention to answering the question, "How did disease and pain enter the animal world?" and tries to work it into the scheme of his free-will apologetic, he makes a muddle of it. He notes that if animals are not willful creatures, then the problem of explaining the origin of any evil effect in animals is a difficulty. At this point he suggests that Satan's fall, with its consequence of affecting the created order, has resulted in animal suffering. He explains that "this hypothesis is not introduced as a 'general explanation of evil': it only gives a wider application of the principle that evil comes from the abuse of free will. If there is such a power, as I myself believe, it may well have corrupted the animal creation before man appeared."[112] Lewis adds that the existence of this problem in the animal world became a burden for man at the moment of his making, as he was created with a "redemptive function to perform."[113] He was to rule over the world, subduing it and bringing order out of any chaos that might exist in it. Lewis writes, "It may have been one of man's functions to restore peace to the animal world, and if he had not joined the enemy he might have succeeded in doing so to an extent now hardly imaginable."[114] Sadly, it is not a well-developed argument. While Lewis's overall thesis in *The Problem of Pain* has value within the narrow focus he has carved for himself, the issue of animal suffering is clearly outside the scope of his argument. He drifts towards subjectivism in order to fit animal pain into his system. I do think, however, there is a way Lewis might have brought the animal issue into his argument without having to reconcile it with free-will and still maintain his objectivist commitments.

111. Ibid., 106.
112. Ibid., 107.
113. Ibid., 108.
114. Ibid., 108.

In his chapter on *Divine Omnipotence*, Lewis mentions that we experience some pain simply because we come in conflict with "a relatively independent and 'inexorable' Nature."[115] Those conflicts do not necessarily signify acts of rebellion against Nature. Certainly we can suffer because we make misjudgments concerning the world around us. We can just as easily drink from a stream where we think the water is good, only to find through the tasting that it is bitter and unhealthy. The relative pain of a bitter taste acts for us as a kind of warning device to move on and avoid grave consequences. Without even bringing up the issue of free-will, we may argue that animals may have been given the capacity of pain for reasons similar to these. If it finds that the thicket has thorns that tear at its fur, the animal experiencing pain goes around another way. Pains, in this way, may prescribe limits which, if heeded, can add to whatever quality of life might be available to animals. Lewis might have developed his argument along these lines and still brought it into the realm of his particular focus.

As to the question of justice, he recognizes that though animal pain may not be "God's handiwork,"[116] even so, "if God has not caused it, he has permitted it, and once again, what shall be done for these innocents?"[117] Here he directs his attention to "animal immorality," and engages in the most highly speculative portion of the chapter. It is his belief that an animal may gain something like self-consciousness in response and submission to its master. Just as man is redeemed in Christ, so too, the animal can be redeemed in man.[118] A reader familiar with Lewis's work can only assume that here he is not at his best. He does not deny that he writes full of doubts, and acknowledges that all the while, "When we are speaking of creatures so removed from us as wild beasts, and prehistoric beasts, we hardly know what we are talking about."[119] Though he usually writes with clarity, this chapter is full of obscurity. He would have been wiser to have refined his thoughts, in this section of the book, before publication, or left it out completely since it distracts from the strong portions of the book and diminishes Lewis's rhetoric.

---

115. Ibid., 23.
116. Ibid., 109.
117. Ibid., 109.
118. Ibid., 111–13.
119. Ibid., 113.

Since he did not, he must face further problems. Lewis's failure to deal adequately with the problem of animal pain, and the fact that his argument, if properly adjusted, can be strengthened, reveals once again that his argument is a work in progress and not a last word. Even a relatively sound rhetorician such as Lewis does not always argue infallibly. There is always room for further discursive thought.

## Criticisms of Lewis's Argument

While there is much to commend in *The Problem of Pain*, its biggest failure may be understood along rhetorical lines. Lewis's argument breaks down logically, and deficiencies occur when he fails at the level of his own objectivist commitments. In the section on animal pain, Lewis does not speak accurately about animals' suffering. As has been mentioned, it is at this place that Lewis is himself tempted by subjectivism, for he projects onto the world what he wants it to be rather than amend his speculation about it to accommodate to objective reality. Furthermore, while Lewis benefits from the rich background of his reading, both philosophically and theologically, he fails to maintain consistency with the objective traditions from which he has drawn. Austin Farrer writes that there are at least two obvious ways to approach the problem of evil, one philosophical and the other theological.[120] Farrer posits that Lewis's chapter on *Divine Omnipotence* is directed towards the philosophical, and the chapter on *Divine Goodness* is directed towards the theological.[121] As the book progresses, Farrer observes the philosophical interests of the book falling into the background. It could equally be said that the theological approach of the book also fades into the background, for Lewis abandons strictly theological concerns in the development of his argument.

Lewis's failure to fit animals into his theodicy in a reasoned way does not mean that a successful Christian defense for the problem of animal pain is impossible. Farrer addresses the issue much more convincingly, and his contribution is helpful in seeing how Lewis might have modified his own argument. Farrer's argument runs something like this: While some suffering among men is certainly justifiable due

120. Gibb, *Light on C. S. Lewis*, 35.
121. Ibid., 36.

to guilt, animal suffering could have no such justification.[122] Human suffering can produce growth in character such as "heroic endurance," "moral wisdom," and sacrifice for the sake of others; animals cannot benefit in this way, and therefore animal suffering cannot be justified in this way.[123] Furthermore, animal irrationality aggravates the problem, for "the power of reason can render physical sufferings endurable."[124] Understanding the dentist's motives makes it possible to endure his drill. Animals, lacking reason, do not possess this advantage. Farrer also notes that because animals cannot communicate their pains, they are likely to suffer longer before their needs are tended to.[125]

Farrer observes that there is a common element running through each of the items mentioned above; it is that animal pain is "sheer pain," and as such, it appears to be "an unmitigated evil, incapable of justification."[126] Here, he asks the question: Would animals be better off if they had no pains at all?[127] It would seem that they would not be better off if they had no capacity to feel pain, for animal pain is necessary to animal consciousness, and without it they would have no chance for survival. He argues that "the working of animal pain has the rough effect of defending the species and promoting evolutionary development."[128] And Farrer believes the whole process has been creatively guided.[129] God cares for each individual creature by his providence and compassion. It appears that the Christian argument can be developed much further, and certainly Farrer is more satisfying than Lewis. In fact, Lewis's unsuccessful treatment of animal pain stems from his failure to develop a satisfactory resolution for the problem of natural evil and weakens the effectiveness of his rhetoric.

---

122. Farrer, *Love Almighty*, 84.

123. Ibid., 85.

124. Ibid.

125. Ibid., 86.

126. Ibid.

127. Ibid.

128. Ibid., 97.

129. Ibid., 95.

## Lewis's Underdeveloped Concept of Natural Evil

The *logos* of Lewis's argument concerning animal pain fails because Lewis neglects to address the more foundational issue of natural evil. Consequently, his argument reveals a weakness related directly to his infidelity to objective value. Since he sees pain primarily as a corrective aimed at the flawed components of the creature brought on by the Fall, his argument takes on a remedial quality. His argument, therefore, does not seem to bother much with physical or natural evil, and when it does, Lewis's attempts to address it are unsatisfactory. When natural evils are discussed at all, they are seen as the product of a malevolent supernatural being. Lewis writes of the "Satanic corruption of the beasts," evidenced by "the fact that animals, or some animals, live by destroying each other."[130] Later, he adds that "it is possible to believe that animal pain is not God's handiwork but begun by Satan's malice and perpetuated by man's desertion of his post."[131] Lewis does not believe that Christian revelation shows "any signs of being intended as a *system de la nature* answering all questions."[132] Since he believes the Scriptures lack a system of nature, he does not see that it is incumbent upon him to supply one. He acts as an apologist charged with the task to defend what he believes is present in Scripture. He seems to be inconsistent, picking and choosing when and where he will develop an idea in an imaginative way in order to provide probable solutions to particular problems. As to the problem of natural evil, he avoids doing any imaginative speculation as to what might be helpful in resolving certain difficulties beyond the data supplied by the texts of Scripture. It could be argued that Lewis misreads the Scriptures. Certainly enough data can be found there to begin the work of natural theology, and with it develop probable resolutions to the questions of natural evil, which others have, in fact, done.[133] It is also odd that Lewis, who is quite successful in the use of his imagination, would neglect the opportunity here, at such a critical juncture in *The Problem of Pain*, to venture an attempt at some kind of explanation. On the other hand, it may be that

130. C. S. Lewis, *Pain*, 108.

131. Ibid., 109.

132. Ibid.

133. Polkinghorne, *Science and Theology*, 93–95; Ward, *God, Faith & the New Millenium*, 91–108; Farrer, *Love Almighty*, 77–105.

Lewis thought no explanation was necessary, because all the problems of natural evil may be accounted for by the existence of devils. It can be said with confidence that Lewis's primary concern in *The Problem of Pain* is to explain how his readers can be improved by the suffering they experience, thus justifying apologetically how evil can exist in a world made by a good and all-powerful God.

On a related note, Cambridge scientist and theologian John Polkinghorne has suggested that theology could address the issue of natural evil (what he also calls physical evil) along the lines of what he calls a "free process defence." God has created the universe unfinished and has permitted the created order to develop over time:

> A world allowed to make itself through the evolutionary explo-
> ration of its potentiality is a better world than one produced
> ready-made by fiat. In such an evolving world there must be
> malfunctions and blind alleys. The same biochemical processes
> that enable some cells to mutate and produce new forms of life
> will allow other cells to mutate and become malignant.[134]

While God sustains history in a single timeless act—there is, therefore, only a general providence—"God is in the overall necessity, but the de-tailed happenstance of actual historical process is just how it all chances to work out."[135] Polkinghorne believes, perhaps too strongly, that "the integrity of modern science would be breached in an arbitrary way by any other suggestion."[136] Polkinghorne's judgment may be premature. Other suggestions might become necessary by virtue of the fact that science is often developing new probabilities to account for new discov-eries. Nevertheless, as a Christian, Polkinghorne seeks to absolve the Divine will for actual evil and suffering in creation, thus relieving Him from responsibility for it. The question still remains: Why did God not take a more active role in the developing creation? To this, Polkinghorne simply replies, "The stronger one's account of Divine action, the more pressing becomes the problem of theodicy."[137] While Polkinghorne does not develop the argument as fully as one might hope, he moves in a direction that Lewis might have taken, but does not.

134. Polkinghorne, *Science and Theology*, 94.
135. Ibid., 85.
136. Ibid.
137. Ibid., 86.

A similar view is held by Oxford theologian Keith Ward, who develops it further:

> It seems probable, for example, that a universe that is truly emergent is one is one in which some measure of conflict and suffering will necessarily exist. Old forms have to die away, to make room for new. And it may be partly through competition and conflict that new forms come into existence. In this way, the distinctive values that only an emergent, evolutionary universe can realise—values of courage, tenacity, creative adventure, as well as values of compassion, co-operation and self-sacrifice—will not be able to exist without the existence of some sort of suffering that God does not directly intend.
>
> We might say that God intends the values, the goods, that only such a process can realise. Therefore God does generate the whole process intentionally. Yet God does not intend the suffering and conflict that the process entails, or at least makes unpreventable by God.[138]

Thus, God may have permitted nature to take its own course of development, just as He permitted man to go his own way. If development can be observed in nature even through a process of suffering, perhaps an apologetic can be informed, in part, by natural revelation, as well as through special revelation. In this way, even the Fall of man could be seen as developmentally necessary. Lewis's argument could benefit from discoveries related to natural development. So too scientists can benefit from theology when it suggests that providence provides an explanation for the good observed by the positive development of species through a process that includes suffering and survival in nature. These insights suggest ways that an apologetic might be developed with respect to natural evil. Lewis is not unaware of these things; by the time he writes *Miracles*, his thinking has progressed along lines such as these. He believes that nature was not created perfectly. He does not believe it to be created evil, thus involving himself in all the difficulties of ascribing evil in creation to the work of a good God. Instead, he believes that God created the universe imperfectly, in the sense that it was immature and undergoing a process towards some kind of maturity. Creation, like man, was made innocent, and like man reveals that it experiences corruption. How does it come "to be in this condition," asks Lewis?

138. Ward, *God, Faith and the New Millennium*, 93.

> By which question we may mean either how she comes to be
> imperfect—to leave 'room for improvement' as the school mas-
> ters say in their reports—or else, how she comes to be positively
> depraved. If we ask the question in the first sense, the Christian
> answer (I think) is that God, from the first, created her such as
> to reach her perfection by a process in time. He made an Earth
> at first 'without form and void' and brought it by degrees to its
> perfection. . . . In that sense a certain degree of 'evolutionism'
> or 'developmentalism' is inherent in Christianity. Her positive
> depravity calls for a very different explanation. According to the
> Christians this is all due to sin: the sin both of men and of pow-
> erful, non-human beings, supernatural but created.[139]

One wonders where Lewis might go with this idea if he would tease it
out further. However, he keeps coming back to the belief that all the
difficulties of natural evil have for their cause fallen beings, either men
or devils, and it appears that this position hinders him from making a
fuller development of his contribution to the problem of evil. His failure
occurs because he does not accommodate himself, as well as he might,
to objective reality; and to the degree that he fails in this regard, he also
fails rhetorically.

## Remedial Pain and the Humanitarian Theory of Punishment

Lewis is the embodiment of his rhetoric concerning objectivism, but
as human beings are limited by virtue of their finitude and their lack
of full development, these criticisms reveal that Lewis's embodiment is
imperfect. Further criticisms of Lewis's argument, as he develops it in
*The Problem of Pain*, come to light when considered alongside his essay
*The Humanitarian Theory of Punishment*.[140] While he believes God was
involved in the use of pain for remedial purposes, he strongly objects to
such tactics being used to treat criminals. He writes, "The Humanitarian
theory removes from punishment the concept of Desert. But the concept of Desert is the only connecting link between punishment and
justice. It is only as deserved or undeserved that a sentence can be just

---

139. C. S. Lewis, *Miracles*, 146.
140. C. S. Lewis, *God in the Dock*, 287–300.

or unjust."[141] What he says may be true, but it also shows how strongly he believes that this kind of suffering must have just cause. If God is just and his creatures suffer in a world that He has made, then the assumption is that they must deserve it. While Lewis objects strongly to any other kind of suffering for criminals, it may also be that he doubts that a just God could allow innocents in His universe to suffer undeservedly. This could show a proclivity on his part to disregard anything other than moral evil in his theodicy. It may be that he feels an obligation to defend a God of his own making, rather than the God who might allow for kinds of suffering other than soul-making. His defense lays blame for evil at the feet of humanity and devils easily enough, but he seems hesitant to consider that God might have purposes outside of the understanding he embraces at the time he published *The Problem of Pain*.

On the surface, it appears as if that which he decries in *The Humanitarian Theory of Punishment* is found acceptable in *The Problem of Pain*. In his defense, it could be argued that he might shudder at the thought of this kind of power in the hands of men while being less suspicious of the kinds of judgments made by an omniscient God. But in this Lewis would be begging the question. The whole difficulty with the problem of evil in the first place is that it grows out of some kind of doubt concerning God's love or power. Is it satisfactory simply to say that God knows what He is doing, and therefore we should trust Him? While this could in fact be true, it does not bring us any closer to solving the intellectual problem of evil. Furthermore, Lewis warns, "I think it is essential to oppose the Humanitarian theory of punishment *wherever* we encounter it."[142]

I think it would be fair to imagine that Lewis is, as a practicing Christian, impressed and awed by what he knows of the love and grace of God. His desire to steer clear of anything that might challenge the belief he holds at this time in his life is understandable. How can we make sense of this tendency in light of Lewis's honest desire to be objective? He writes in his autobiography that he came into the faith "kicking, struggling, resentful, and darting his eyes in every direction for a chance of escape."[143] While it is possible to admire Lewis's willingness to

---

141. Ibid., 288.

142. Ibid., 293 (italics mine).

143. C. S. Lewis, *Surprised By Joy*, 229.

be objective, it does not mean that he arrives at particular conclusions without a struggle. I think that in time, Lewis saw the weaknesses in his approach. The objectivist who operates consistent with his principles is likely to make many changes in his thinking as he discovers more and more data. The changes in Lewis mark the fact that he embodies his own objectivist views, and it is an appeal to objective reality that provides a basis for correction of his errors.

The Problem of Pain succeeds where Lewis is faithful to his objectivist's commitments and fails when he tries to force his argument. His failure arises when he drifts towards subjectivism. Nevertheless, the book clearly reflects his thinking about an issue that mattered to him and to others very deeply. Weaver recognizes that "Anyone who uses words which he hopes will move men in a direction which he has chosen must wade boldly into rhetoric and morality."[144] Lewis was simply trying to work his way through the problem of evil, and not for the last time. His thinking about the subject was developing, and popular apologetics was one way for him to express himself rhetorically. He is bold in what he asserts, but if he is to be moral, he must acknowledge that no present understanding of a subject as complex as evil is a final word on the matter. In what remains of this chapter, I will look at some of the ways his thinking was further modified through own his personal grief as he develops it in A Grief Observed.

## The Mature Lewis

Since Lewis was the embodiment of his objectivist commitments, it is to be expected that as he matured in his faith, his ideas concerning evil also developed. Charles Williams, Lewis's close friend, comments that The Problem of Pain resembles the theology of Job's friends. For his struggles, his impatience, and contempt Job is forgiven. But, Williams tells Lewis, "The weight of the divine displeasure had been reserved for the 'comforters,' the self-appointed advocates on God's side, the people who tried to show that all was well. . . . the sort of people who wrote books on the problem of pain."[145] Since Lewis himself passes along this anecdote, it would appear that he sees something in Williams's remark which reveals the incompleteness of Lewis's ideas about evil. The friends

144. Weaver, Defense of Tradition, 348.
145. C. S. Lewis, ed., Essays Presented to Williams, xiii.

of Job had a theology that was too simple to explain the complexities surrounding pain and suffering. Job, on the other hand, was forced, by the circumstances of his suffering, to speak about the world from a position more aware of its complexities and mysteries. As Weaver observes, "Rhetoric always comes to us in well-fleshed words, and that is because it must deal with the world, the thickness, stubbornness, and power of it."[146] Similarly, Lewis's rhetoric about evil takes on added dimension as time passes. By the time Lewis writes *Reflections on the Psalms*, he is becoming ever more careful and sensitive to the "thickness" and complexity surrounding the issue of evil. "Of all bad men religious bad men are the worst," he writes,[147] for his

> soul is filled with some great Cause, to which he will subordinate his appetites, his fortune, and even his safety. But it is out of [this] man that something really fiendish can be made; an Inquisitor, a Member of the Committee of Public Safety. It is great men, potential saints, not little men, who become merciless fanatics. Those who are readiest to die for a cause may easily become those readiest to kill for it.[148]

The reported comment made by Williams, in addition to Lewis's observation in *Reflections on the Psalms*, reveals some development in his thinking about the problem of moral evil. How is he willing to reflect more deeply on it, and do these reflections add to his *ethos* whenever he speaks rhetorically about the matter of evil?

## Friendship with Charles Williams

To understand how Lewis's thinking about the problem of evil develops, it is important to consider the influence of Charles Williams. This is necessary not only to see how Lewis's thought is clarified, but also to make sense of several passages in *A Grief Observed*, for Lewis's understanding of objective reality is informed by Williams's ideas about reality. It is worth noting here that Lewis says explicitly that Williams in fact *has* influenced him. In a letter, he notes, "Charles Williams certainly influenced me and I perhaps influenced him."[149]

146. Weaver, *Language is Sermonic*, 1353.

147. C. S. Lewis, *Reflections on the Psalms*, 32.

148. Ibid., 28.

149. W. H. Lewis, ed., *Letters*, 287.

Though Lewis had corresponded with Williams as early as 1936,[150] the friendship did not take off until World War II began. Oxford University Press moved its London offices to Oxford at this time. Williams, who was working for the Press, also made the move. When he arrived in Oxford, he was invited to join "The Inklings," an informal literary group that met for weekly meetings at "The Eagle and Child" public house.[151] It was in this context of regular meetings and extended conversations, in which they commented on and critiqued one another's work, that the friendship grew and was nourished.

Williams's first letter to Lewis reveals a common interest in a romantic approach to theology, shared by both.[152] Lewis sums up Williams's doctrine of romantic love in *The Arthurian Torso*. This doctrine is developed from Williams's interpretation of Dante's first meeting with Beatrice, as told in the *Vita Nuova* and *The Divine Comedy*. Dante, a boy of nine, sees a young girl of Florence named Beatrice. In that moment, something of great significance awakens in him. Beatrice comes to symbolize the object of his heart's desire; she represents beauty, desire, love, and longing. Although she provokes the desire; however, the object of the desire is for something, or in this case someone, beyond Beatrice herself. This "Beatrician experience" eventually leads Dante to the Beatific vision of God. Several passages from Lewis's explanation of this event, as they are filtered through Williams, are worthy of reproduction here. Lewis writes, "The intense significance which she appears to have is not an illusion; in her (at that moment) Paradise is actually revealed, and in the lover nature is renovated. The greater danger is lest he should mistake the vision, which is really a starting point, for a goal; lest he should mistake the vision of Paradise for arrival there."[153] Lewis continues:

> The Beatrician experience does not usually last; nor did the Wordsworthian. Dante's Beatrice died—but even had she lived the story would have been much the same. The glory is temporary; in that sense Beatrice nearly always dies. But a transitory vision is not necessarily a vision of the transitory. That it passes does not necessarily prove it a hallucination. It has in fact been

150. Green and Hooper, *Biography*, 133–35.

151. Ibid., 155.

152. Ibid., 135.

153. C. S. Lewis, *Arthurian Torso*, 116–17.

a glimpse of what is eternally real. The phenomenal Beatrice—
Beatrice as she is in this fallen world—has for an instant been
identical with the real Beatrice. . . .[154]

Lewis is describing in this passage the significance of Williams's doctrine of romantic love, capturing the influence of Dante on Williams,
and applying it particularly to the interpretation of Williams's Arthurian
poetry. Beatrice has value in herself as one created, but she also has
value in that God is revealed in her and through her. She is a bearer of
His glory, but she must not be confused for the glory itself.

Another facet of Williams's theology, described by Lewis, concerns
the Christian concepts of transcendence and immanence. Williams's
maxim is "This also is Thou, neither is this Thou."[155] It is possible to
say of everything encountered in a world made and sustained by God,
"This also is thou." If He creates and sustains each thing in the universe,
then in its particular way it reveals something of Him, something of
His character and nature. All of life furnishes opportunities to behold
something of the glory of God.[156] But to distinguish himself from the
Pantheist, the Christian must also say, "Neither is this Thou." To say,
"Neither is this thou" acknowledges God's transcendence.

Out of this understanding of God's transcendence and immanence,
two great ways of Christian devotion were developed. First is the way
of negation or rejection of images; second the way of affirmation of images. The way of negation is the ascetic way. It is the way of "Neither is
this Thou." It is the way that closes its eyes in prayer lest anything from
the visible world distracts from focusing on God alone. The way of affirmation is the aesthetic way. It is the way of "This also is Thou." It is the
way of praying with eyes wide open, allowing all of Creation to sound
the call to worship; it is the way of the Beatrician experience, the way
described by Lewis in *Letters to Malcolm*, when he asks, "What must be
the quality of that Being whose far-off and momentary coruscations are
like this! One's mind runs back up the sunbeam to the sun."[157] This is the

154. Ibid., 117.

155. Williams, *Descent*, 8. See also Williams, *Figure of Beatrice*, 37.

156. This is reminiscent of Julian of Norwich in the *Revelations of Divine Love*.
Julian is asked to look at a hazelnut and discover from it three truths: "God made it,
God loves it, God keeps it." For a richer development of this theme, see also C. S. Lewis,
*Letters to Malcolm*, chapter 17.

157. C. S. Lewis, *Letters to Malcolm*, 118.

sacramental way. Lewis is developing a more complex and therefore less definitive grasp of the nature of God. This understanding is consistent with his objectivist commitments allowing him to embody a rhetoric which is more convincing for its power to speak truly of the universe.

Both the ascetic and the aesthetic ways provide a kind of richness in their devotion, but both ways come with their own liabilities. The risk of the way of negation is that it can produce in its follower a kind of austerity that leads to pride. He can become condescending towards those who are less capable of his level of self-discipline. The way of affirmation has as its liability the risk of making the objects encountered in Creation the very objects of worship and devotion. It can lead to idolatry. Each way must balance the other. How should this be done? Williams's doctrine of exchange brings a resolution into view. When the follower of the way of negation begins to drift towards isolation because of his asceticism, he must open his eyes and discover of the world around him, "This also is Thou." And when the follower of the way of affirmation begins to drift towards idolatry, he must either close his eyes from the distraction or break the idol and say, "Neither is this Thou."

That Lewis highly valued his association with Williams is suggested by several things. He dedicated his work on Milton's *Paradise Lost* to Williams. Furthermore, as World War II came to a close and the Oxford University Press prepared to return to their offices in London, Lewis edited a collection of essays in honor of Williams.[158] Unfortunately, Williams died before the work was completed. Lewis wrote a poem in his honor after his death.[159] He prepared a series of lectures on Williams's poetry, which he delivered at Oxford during the Michaelmas term of 1945 and which were later published.[160] But the thing most significant to this study as it relates to Lewis's developing theodicy are the letters Lewis wrote after Williams's death. In one, written to Owen Barfield, Lewis mentions his reaction to Williams's passing:

> It has been a very *odd* experience. This, the first really severe loss I have suffered, has . . . given corroboration to my belief in immortality such as I never dreamed of—it is almost tangible

---

158. C. S. Lewis, *Essays Presented to Williams.*

159. C. S. Lewis, *Poems*, 119.

160. C. S. Lewis. *Arthurian Torso*, 1.

now. . . . To put it in a nutshell: what the idea of death has done to him is nothing to what he has done to the idea of death.[161]

Lewis felt that when the idea of Williams and the idea of death met, he was oddly comforted and encouraged. In a sense, Lewis was able to say in that moment, "This also is Thou," for God could be met there.

Lewis's darkest moments, however, were still ahead. He would have to face the death of his wife Joy Davidman. It was one thing to write about pain when it was an issue of intellectual interest. His book may have been helpful to others struggling to understand how to reconcile the power and love of God with the existence of evil in the universe, but how would his faith hold up when the crisis came? Some, as we will see later, believe that his personal crisis made a chaos of his apologetics and reduced his Christianity to mere fideism. I think it will be possible to make the most sense of Lewis's personal crisis only if we consider it in light of William's influence on Lewis's views about objective reality. Furthermore, Lewis's experiences added to his ethos as a rhetorician.

## The Death of Joy Davidman Lewis

Though Lewis had corresponded with Joy Davidman, they did not meet until September of 1952.[162] Joy was 37 and Lewis nearly 54. The unusual nature of their friendship, marriage at the Oxford Registry Office,[163] and marriage in a religious ceremony as Joy lay dying on a hospital bed[164] has all been chronicled in many places, even in a major motion picture.[165] Joy recovered from her illness and Lewis and his wife shared a little over three years of married life together. She died on July 13th, 1960.[166] This was perhaps the greatest crisis of Lewis's life, bringing him to a difficult time of testing in his faith. It was also a time when he had to wrestle more deeply still with the problem of evil. He chronicles much about his grief in *A Grief Observed*. Sims writes about the book, and I believe rightly, that though Lewis doubted during this time, "He did not succumb to doubt. His trust in God's objective reality pulled

161. W. H. Lewis, ed., *Letters*, 206.

162. Green and Hooper, *Biography*, 257.

163. Ibid., 268. The date was 23 April 1956.

164. Ibid. The date was 21 March 1957.

165. *Shadowlands*, directed by Richard Attenbourough.

166. Green and Hooper, *Biography*, 276.

him through this most difficult time in his life. His enduring conviction was that it is Christ, the object of our faith, that is ultimately important—not our subjectivity, our emotions, or our arguments."[167] Sims continues, "He had learned through experience what he already knew in his head: that the Christian cannot live out of his experiences or his circumstances. The only sure foundation is the objective reality of God and His promises."[168]

## A Grief Observed

In reading *A Grief Observed*, one discovers that Lewis did go through a time of significant and, for him, horrifying doubt. He was not on the verge of ceasing to believe in God, but rather, as he writes, he began "to believe such dreadful things about Him. The conclusion I dread is not 'So there's no God after all,' but 'So this is what God is really like. Deceive yourself no longer.'"[169] It appears on the surface that Lewis did have a case against the goodness of God. However, as noted earlier, grief is an emotional process, and Lewis had recognized that emotional challenges to faith were likely to come in the course of one's life:

> Now Faith, in the sense in which I am here using the word, is the art of holding on to things your reason has once accepted, in spite of your changing moods. For moods will change, whatever view your reason takes. I know by experience. Now that I am a Christian I do have moods in which the whole thing looks very improbable: but when I was an atheist I had moods in which Christianity looked terribly probable.[170]

Were Lewis's cries, which were critical of God, motivated by rational objection or emotional reaction? It is a question that needs to be asked. When he experienced grief before, it did not lead him to write transparent expressions of troubled feelings and doubts. However, the nature of this grief, the loss of his wife, touched him more deeply than anything he had yet experienced. Even so, his emotional reaction and the press of his emotions on his reason could not in themselves invalidate the reasonableness of his faith. The question is, How would he resolve

167. Sims, *Missionaries to the Skeptics*, 65.

168. Ibid., 66.

169. C. S. Lewis, *Grief Observed*, 8.

170. C. S. Lewis, *Mere Christianity*, 111.

the tensions in such a way that he might reconcile his experience as a Christian with his experience as a grieving husband? It is here that the theological influence of Charles Williams comes into play.

It is evident, after several readings of *A Grief Observed*, that Williams's ideas are not far from Lewis as he writes. Throughout the book, Lewis invokes the concept of images, complaining that no photograph of his wife captures for him what she was really like.[171] He is losing even his mental image of her. He uses images to explain her to his reader, describing her like a sword[172] or even a garden.[173] But these images are not Joy anymore than images we might have of God can actually be what God truly is in Himself. The maxim, "This also is Thou; neither is this Thou," as it is used of God in Williams's theology, has applications for Lewis in regard to Joy, as well. Any image that reminds him of Joy produces in him a kind of "This also is thou," response. But since no image captures fully what she was like, Lewis has to remember, "Neither is this Thou." The image must be abandoned as inadequate to the objective reality itself.

As Lewis comes to the end of the book, he acknowledges this parade of images, which come and go, as true of our understanding of anything or anyone, especially of our understanding of God. All thoughts must go through processes of re-imaging. If God exists both in the world and transcends it, then somehow this process finds meaning ultimately in Him. Thus, speaking of these images of his wife, Lewis writes that he must look "up from the garden to the Gardener, from the sword to the Smith. To the life-giving Life and the beauty that makes beautiful."[174] These ideas are not entirely new for Lewis, but they are freshly developed in this new circumstance. Years earlier he observes, "The acceptance of loss therefore combines in itself the two 'Ways,' the Romantic and the Ascetic, the Affirmation and the Rejection of images. We affirm the image at the very moment of affirming its opposite."[175] In the loss of the image, it is reclaimed as an image, thus rescuing it from slowly becoming either an idol or a god. It is affirmed by restraining it

171. C. S. Lewis, *A Grief Observed*, 15, 18, 52, 55.

172. Ibid., 37, 53.

173. Ibid., 53

174. Ibid., 53.

175. C. S. Lewis, *Arthurian Torso*, 181.

from becoming more than it is. This clarification in *A Grief Observed* is both an affirmation of Joy and a refocusing of his desire for God. Far from falsifying, it is a revivification and clarification of his faith. Lewis also writes, "since every earthly good is only an image, therefore the breaking of that image 'doesn't matter.' It is only an image."[176] He is not saying that the death of his wife does not matter. Certainly it matters; the loss is severe and the pain excruciating. Nor is he saying that Joy as a person does not matter. When Lewis says, "it doesn't matter," he means that his image of Joy does not have a value worth preserving permanently. It is not an accurate image. No image can ever fully represent the thing it symbolizes. That is not to say that it does not matter at all. It merely affirms that his image of her does not matter ultimately; what matters is Joy herself. Even more, Joy, like Dante's Beatrice, points to a reality beyond Joy herself. She exhibits something of the image of God, and Lewis comes to see from a new perspective that only the reality of God matters ultimately. Lewis's relationship with Joy is certainly an earthly good, but also an image of something more. Though he has lost her, and she is not present for him in this life any longer, he believes that she lives on in the Communion of Saints. There he might know her more accurately. Again, these ideas are not new for Lewis, but never has he felt them so deeply or seen their application in just this way.

Lewis does not stop with his wife when it comes to images. He writes of his faith in a similar manner: "The case is too plain. If my house has collapsed at one blow, that is because it was a house of cards."[177] This image of his faith as a "house of cards" appears often in *A Grief Observed*.[178] It is not that his faith has been insincere, but only that the understanding on which his faith is built has been incomplete and in the process of being remade. The house of cards must come down so that a better, though far from permanent, house might be put in its place. In time, it too will also have to come down. The blow to his faith, evidenced by his wife's death, becomes an experience through which his faith will grow less ambiguous. So it is that Weaver can write, "The good man, the man with proved allegiance to correct sentiment, has been the natural trustee of authority; the man of knowledge has been necessary for such duties as

176. Ibid.
177. C. S. Lewis, *A Grief Observed*, 32.
178. Ibid., 32, 33, 34, 45, 57.

require system and foresight."[179] The emotions of his experience, rightly processed, allow Lewis to further embody his objectivist commitments and lend greater ethos to his rhetoric about suffering and pain. Lewis has come to the place where crisis, far from destroying his faith, leads to what Mitchell has called, "maintaining a living tradition."[180] As a rhetorician, Lewis realizes there is an ethos which emerges all the more profoundly and persuasively, not because he has everything perfectly formulated when he speaks (or writes), but because his modes of expression and the images he uses are supple enough to capture objective reality as it is. The permanence is not in the images, but in the reality behind them.

Likewise, these images are necessary when speaking about God in the context of evil. For how but by the use of images is anyone to understand what God is like? And what set of images will do permanently? Once again, because he embodies his objectivist position during the time of his deepest grief, Lewis uses several images, some of them shocking. Lewis compares God to a veterinarian,[181] or, worse still, a vivisector[182] or Cosmic Sadist.[183] But even here his thinking must change and develop. The process is aided by his willingness to adjust each new image, saying, "Neither is this Thou." His understanding is stretched as he undergoes suffering. He writes,

> Images of the Holy easily become holy images—sacrosanct. My idea of God is not a divine idea. It has to be shattered time after time. He shatters it Himself. He is the great iconoclast. Could we not almost say that this shattering is one of the marks of His presence? The Incarnation is the supreme example; it leaves all previous ideas of the messiah in ruins. And most are 'offended' by the iconoclasm; and blessed are those who are not.[184]

Lewis comes to believe that this iconoclastic work of God may be a part of what some call the problem of evil. His conception of God is never quite big enough to accommodate itself to the work or the purpose of

179. Weaver, *Ideas*, 36.
180. Mitchell, *Faith and Criticism*, 167.
181. C. S. Lewis, *A Grief Observed*, 32.
182. Ibid., 26, 34, 35.
183. Ibid., 35.
184. Ibid., 55–56.

God, but he recognizes through the grieving process that what he wants is God, not his idea or image of God.[185]

## Conclusion

The exigencies surrounding the problem of pain, and highlighted by Lewis's childhood experiences, informed the pathos of his rhetoric. Weaver notes that "sentiments pass from a welter of feeling to an illumined concept of what one ought to feel."[186] Lewis's rhetoric is more confident for learning that objects could merit sentimental responses that are just and congruous. And these responses, both rational as well as emotional, are not permanent, for "reality is iconoclastic." Lewis's ethos as a rhetorician is fuller for having discovered this. Forsaking subjectivism in his own struggle to understand human suffering, he is able to have the good of his audience, and not just himself, in mind as he addresses them about the problem of evil. The word he speaks correlates with reality as it is, not as the rhetor merely wants it to be.

185. Ibid., 56.

186. Weaver, *Ideas Have Consequences*, 22.

# 3

# Lewis's Literary Criticism
# and a Problem of Evil

## Introduction

IN THE PREVIOUS CHAPTER, I ARGUED THAT THROUGH THE DIFFICULTIES
of his life Lewis came to embody his objectivist commitments. In this
chapter, I will look at C. S. Lewis's literary criticism, for in it one can
find expressions of his concern regarding that aspect of the problem of
evil he calls subjectivism. While it might appear to some that Lewis's
entire literary critical enterprise is an attempt to understand and interpret texts—and certainly this is part of his critical interest—it is more
accurate to say that he is rhetorically active in refuting the various forms
of subjectivism he observes in the academy. He seeks to engage and
convince his readers of his point of view; therefore, his literary critical work is rhetorical in nature. He draws his readers into a dialectical
development of his point of view always referencing the text as a guide
to his interpretive judgments. I will also argue that Lewis saw literary
studies moving away from the analysis of texts to discussions of many
things other than the texts themselves. This practice of subjectivist criticism was something Lewis sought to correct. Furthermore he saw literary critical practice in its larger cultural context.

Lewis would have agreed with Richard Weaver, who asserts, "The
truth is that if culture is to assume form and to bring the satisfactions
for which cultures are created, it is not culturally feasible for everyone
to do everything 'anyway he wants to.'"[1] Because of Lewis's objectivist commitments and his concerns about the dangers of subjectivism,

1. Weaver, *Visions of Order*, 11.

Lewis held similar views to those of Weaver. I will look at Lewis's judgments about the benefits of culture generally and then look at the ways
he sought to address subjectivism in literary critical practice specifically. Lewis was aware that though a full and complete understanding
and interpretation of any text is not likely, nevertheless, approximations
are possible. Any approximate interpretation of a text, however, must be
attempted with respect for the objective text itself. In this way, an object
is available to which an appeal might be made whenever disputes about
a text occur. Misguided interpretations can be corrected and incomplete interpretations can be developed further. Without this possibility
of a corrective, thinking about texts becomes little more that the whim
of the interpreter. While this may be unfortunate for literary criticism,
such practices generally applied to life could, as has been mentioned,
lead to the natural removal of useful checks on evil. Lewis marshals the
weight of his best discursive thought to challenge subjectivism before
his audience in the academy. At risk were the minds of students, who
would themselves shape the academy for future generations, and thus
prove influential in shaping the culture.

## Objectivism in Lewis's Literary Criticism

Many have recognized the objectivist commitments which appear in
Lewis's literary critical work. Jerry L. Daniel, editor of *CSL: The Bulletin
of the New York C. S. Lewis Society*, the oldest scholarly journal dedicated to Lewis scholarship, writes that Lewis "perceived most modern
critics to be busily engaged in *avoiding* the essence of the works they
criticized."[2] Additionally, Lewis scholar Bruce Edwards writes that one
of the effects of radical literacy is that "the idea of objectivity is out of
fashion." He notes, "A growing orthodoxy views traditional literacy . . .
not as liberating, self-actualizing acquisition, but as an instrument of
oppression, a tool of a technoelite primed to enslave impressionable
citizens to "advanced capitalism.""[3] When this happens, according to
Edwards, "readership collapses into authorship; and the text, long the
most stable and reliable component in the study of literature, relin-
quishes its ability to *mean* or *be*."[4] Daniel sees in Lewis the insistence

2. Daniel, "Taste of the Pineapple," 16.
3. B. Edwards. *A Rhetoric of Reading*, 20.
4. B. Edwards, *Taste of the Pineapple*, 29.

that "one must receive the work as it is." The critic cannot even begin to "discuss literature until he has seen and received it as it was intended."[5] In this kind of reception of the text, Edwards observes that Lewis "struggled to balance issues of textual objectivity and readerly subjectivity, to marry reason and imagination in the reading act."[6] To "examine Lewis's approach to the written text," Edwards states that "one may extrapolate a 'Rhetoric of reading,' i.e., a sound, comprehensive strategy for confronting texts."[7] When subjectivism gives way to the objective value of the text, true subjectivity is restored; it is in proper relation to the text. It is, as Edwards says "rehabilitated," able "to understand [its] own personhood, to become something other."[8] Edwards reads Lewis correctly, but with his reading of Lewis comes a level of urgency which can be seen in Lewis's critical enterprise. What is at stake is not only the person's capacity to understand himself but also the culture's hope for any kind of collective identity.

Richard Weaver observes that "Culture in its formal definition is one of the fulfillments of the psychic need of man. The human being is a focal point of consciousness who looks with wondering eyes upon a universe into which he is born a kind of stranger."[9] Man adjusts himself to his surroundings as an outsider; when he does this in a collective fashion, the result is the creation of culture. This cultural adjustment to objective reality develops when it is "accompanied by degrees of restlessness and pain, and it is absolutely necessary, as we must infer from the historical record, that he do something to humanize his vision and to cognize in special ways his relation to these surroundings."[10] One can certainly infer from Weaver's remarks that these degrees of adjustment can be more or less accurate, and that a culture may be judged to be good when it makes these adjustments along lines consistent with objective reality. The complexity of reality means that no society is likely to arrive at a perfect culture, and thus culture is always in a state of development. Furthermore, Weaver observes that cultures are not

5. Ibid., 21.

6. B. Edwards, *A Rhetoric of Reading*, 2.

7. Ibid., 11.

8. B. Edwards, *Taste of the Pineapple*, 35.

9. Weaver, *Defense of Tradition*, 405.

10. Ibid.

only a corporate attempt to adjust themselves to objective reality with its demands of objective value, but they seek to do this while maintaining a degree of unity. He notes, "Culture by its very nature tends to be centripetal, or to aspire toward some unity in its representational modes."[11] Unity in this regard is not to be confused with uniformity. Uniformity devalues rhetoric and the discursive thought out of which it grows. On the other hand, unity encourages persuasion. The culture acts as audience and listens to the rhetor's voice to discern if what is spoken is convincing, thereby benefiting by his word. I argue, therefore, that Lewis's literary criticism comes with a strong address to the academy, warning them of the evils of subjectivism and its ability to harm both individuals and culture.

It must be noted that the objectivists commitments evidenced in Lewis's literary criticism contributed to his clarity as a critic. Chad Walsh, scholar and friend of Lewis, may have overstated his claim when he asserts regarding Lewis that "no writer of our time has been more blessed with the gift of clarity."[12] Nevertheless, Lewis's clarity as a writer and critic has been affirmed by many including those who would disagree with his points of view. Walsh adds that "his literary criticism—a field in which turgid and tortured prose abounds—was crisp, to the point, never ambiguous."[13] Yet Walsh sees that this clarity may at times work against Lewis: "His literary judgments are sometimes too rational, too clear-cut. He can hack his way through acres of critical nonsense, but in the process he tramps down certain interesting and important little growths of insight."[14] Even so, professor Clyde Kilby, Lewis scholar and founding curator of the Wade Center, writes in the context of Lewis's critical endeavors, "If values are objective and one man may be right and another wrong, then there will be an obligation to try to discover the right value and champion it. And there can be no *ought* where there is no objective value."[15] This is precisely Lewis's concern when he calls the academy to renounce its subjectivism and return to the objectivity of texts. Lewis critic and scholar Michael Aeschliman

11. Ibid., 406.

12. Hillegas, *Shadows of Imagination*, 1.

13. Ibid., 3.

14. Ibid., 11.

15. Kilby, *Christian World*, 101–2.

correctly warns that "Assertions of personal preference disguised as Assertions Of value . . . weaken the conception of value itself."[16] These personal preferences, when cloaked in subjectivism, lead to the weakening of objective value that precedes the rise of evil. Lewis is right to be concerned about this problem, for as Weaver observes, "With the denial of objective truth, there is no escape from the relativism of 'man the measure of all things.'"[17]

Lewis's objectivist commitments, coupled with his ability to speak clearly about literary texts, whether flawed at points, as Walsh suggests, or not, contributed to his excellence as a teacher. Aeschliman writes, "A Lewis lecture was a feast, Kingsley Aims has written; 'if ever a man instructed by delighting it was he'; he was 'a masterly teacher and critic whose knowledge and feeling were in usual accord.'"[18] Daniel says that Lewis was "a soul almost intoxicated with the 'pure organic pleasure' of things as they are."[19] Daniel sees this as a cultivated habit. Citing *Surprised by Joy* for support, he quotes Lewis stressing, "We should attempt a total surrender to whatever atmosphere was offering itself at the moment." This was written about A. K. Hamilton Jenkin, a man Lewis admired and sought to emulate for his "serious, yet gleeful, determination to rub one's nose in the very quiddity of each thing, to rejoice in its being (so magnificently) what it was."[20] Then Daniel adds, "This matter is important to anyone who is concerned to analyze Lewis's approach to literature."[21] Lewis was eager to encounter objects as they are, wherever he met them. To speak of these things clearly, especially when speaking of literary texts, increased his rhetorical powers to persuade. His words, having a reference point which he made clear, allowed his audiences to see and affirm his claims in their own minds. This approach to objectivity made him a good teacher and an appealing writer. His former student, Harry Blamires, commenting on Lewis's literary critical approach, writes, "The impulse to go out of the self, to enter into other men's beliefs, and to be admitted to experience other than our own is

16. Aeschliman, *Restitution of Man*, 67.

17. Weaver, *Ideas Have Consequences*, 4.

18. Aeschliman, *Restitution of Man*, 66.

19. B. Edwards, *Taste of the Pineapple*, 9.

20. Ibid., 9, quoting C. S. Lewis, *Surprised by Joy*, 199.

21. Ibid., 10.

what is satisfied by good literature."[22] As Lewis addresses the problems of subjectivism in literary criticism, he recognizes the need to see them within the larger context of culture.

## Christianity and Culture

Since literary critical work can be affected by broader cultural concerns, and since Lewis wrote on Christianity and culture,[23] it is necessary to consider Lewis's general observations about this subject before moving to more specific literary issues. Lewis begins his essay, "Christianity and Culture," by asking, "What then is the value of culture?"[24] Weaver's insight here, may help to point in the direction I believe Lewis is leading. Weaver sees great value in culture, for it is a storehouse for the "metaphysical dream" which preserves a community by maintaining its corporate and imaginative understanding of itself. This understanding must be an imaginative one for it lacks capacities for absolute knowledge. The dream must develop or the imaginative grasp calcifies into idolatries and eventually the culture ossifies. The dream advances as the culture attends to the rhetoric of its members appealing imaginatively to the "dream"—this appeal has emotional power for it is an appeal to all that the culture holds dear. Weaver asserts that "without some comparable feeling a commonwealth does not exist, for people will act in a common cause only while they are conscious of an identity of sentiment."[25] Furthermore, sentiment may be valid, or invalid, only if there is some standard by which to judge it so. A culture may maintain its values, its shared "metaphysical dream," but it is objective value that gives credence to the "dream." The literature of a proper culture gives fresh visions of reality by clear reference to those things a culture values and respects, thus appealing to the emotion and making it possible for the culture to be moved in a way to adapt its corporate sense of itself to the objective world. If a culture is cut off from its literature, it loses one of its most important guides. As Lewis moves along these lines in his discussion of culture and literature, he is deeply concerned that literature not be diluted by subjectivist critical theories. Returning to the

22. Blamires, *Literary Criticism*. 351.

23. C. S. Lewis, *Christian Reflections*, 12–36.

24. Ibid., 14.

25. Weaver, *Defense of Tradition*, 346.

question, "What is the value of culture?" Lewis refines the discussion; here he seeks to discover whether or not culture has an intrinsic value for Christians. Is it redemptive? Can it be an aid to spiritual maturity? Is a society morally improved by its culture?

Lewis considers the ideas of Dr. I. A. Richards, an atheist literary critic who held that "good poetical taste" could provide "the means of attaining psychological adjustments which improved a man's power of effective and satisfactory living all around."[26] For Richards, "This theory of value was a purely psychological one." And Lewis adds, "This amounted to giving poetry a kind of soteriological function; it held the keys of the only heaven that Dr. Richards believed in."[27] While culture, in this way, addresses that part of the problem of evil related to human deficiency, Lewis, nevertheless, rejects Richards's position for two reasons. First, as a Christian, he rejects the inherent materialism of Richards's atheistic approach to psychology. Second, he is suspicious of anything that smacks of elitism, as if "superior taste" could become a synonym for "superior character."[28] This could open the door to pride and the evil that is likely to follow in its wake; and Lewis stands against this.

Lewis then turns his attention to the New Testament to see if he might find answers to his inquiry from the Bible. After this investigation, he concludes that the Scriptures, "if not hostile, [were] yet unmistakably cold to culture. I think we can still believe culture to be innocent after we have read the New Testament; I cannot see that we are encouraged to think it important."[29] Here, Lewis overlooks the significance of the creation by God of a particular people, the Jews through whom he would give his word and his Son to the world. If this is so, then culture may have significances that Lewis fails to identify. He also neglects the significance of culture and the Incarnation: God comes in flesh at a particular place and time to work out purposes that must be understood and translated into other places and times. Nevertheless, in Lewis's estimation, whether right or wrong, the Scriptures do not lend their authority for the resolution of this issue. He would have to look elsewhere to discover the value of culture.

26. C. S. Lewis, *Christian Reflections*, 12.
27. Ibid., 12.
28. Ibid., 13.
29. Ibid., 15.

Next, Lewis turns to authors and periods of literature with which he is familiar. Here he did not find Christian experience necessarily enhanced by the literature *per se*, though he did believe that "the sub-Christian or anti-Christian values implicit in most literature did actually infect many readers."[30] At this point, Lewis finds Newman helpful. Newman's lectures on *The Idea of a University* sternly resisted the temptation to confuse culture with things spiritual. Even so, he exhibited an appreciation of "the beauty of culture for its own sake."[31] The value of culture, according to Newman and highlighted by Lewis, is observable in four ways. First, culture is of interest for this world. Neither Newman nor Lewis was Gnostic. As Christians, they saw value in a world created by God. Civilizations, being part of the created order, could be appreciated as things in themselves, as part of a world which God had made. Lewis notes, "The cultivation of the intellect, according to [Newman], is 'for this world.'"[32] In other words, the development of the intellectual life has cultural value, even though temporary. Second, culture cannot make Christians, but it can develop gentlemen. If such cultivation looks like virtue, this, according to Lewis, is an observation made at a distance. Newman "will not for an instant allow 'that it makes men better.'"[33] Refinement must not be confused with virtue. Third, spiritual guides may encourage participation in cultural activities. This is not because these activities make a participant more pleasing to God, but rather because they may provide "innocent distraction at those moments of spiritual relaxation which would otherwise lead to sin."[34] Fourth, Lewis observes through Newman that theology as an intellectual activity, encouraged by culture, may provide gains in "meritoriousness," but could also lead to losses in "liberality."[35] He sees in Newman a concession to a kind of goodness that is not necessarily moral but has a developmental value. The clever man is preferred to the dull one and any man to the chimpanzee.[36]

---

30. Ibid., 16.
31. Ibid., 18.
32. Ibid.
33. Ibid.
34. Ibid.
35. Ibid., 19.
36. Ibid.

Though Lewis appreciates Newman's distinctions, he cannot see how accepting Newman's understanding could motivate anyone to spend time investing in the temporal pursuits offered by culture when eternal matters ought to demand a greater concentration of our time and energies. "Christianity and Culture" first appeared in *Theology* in March of 1940.[37] In the autumn of 1939, just before he published the article, Lewis preached a University Sermon at the Church of St. Mary the Virgin. Hitler had invaded Poland, and Europe was at war. Lewis had been asked to address the issue of the apparent futility of pursuing a university education when Western civilization and culture appeared to be on the threshold of collapse. In the sermon titled "Learning in War Time," he reminded his listeners that war does not increase death: death is total in every generation.[38] War, danger, disease, famine and accidents are reminders of the age-old situation that human life and human culture have always been fragile. It is no use waiting till all was secure before engaging in the pursuits of culture; such times never come.[39] "Life has never been normal."[40] He reminded his hearers that cultural pursuits in the midst of cataclysmic conditions are not a mere fiddling while Rome burns. "To a Christian, the true tragedy of Nero must be not that he fiddled while the city was on fire but that he fiddled on the brink of hell."[41] It is not "a compromise between the claims of God and the claims of culture, or politics, or anything else. God's claim is infinite and inexorable."[42] Even so, Christianity sets forth the dignity of human endeavor and activity. "Learning and the arts flourish" in most times and places where the Church has gained a foothold. He suggests that the reason for this may be found in the text, "whether ye eat or drink or whatsoever ye do, do all to the glory of God."[43]

Clearly Lewis considers cultural participation important, but it is not yet clear why. He continues to look for reasons why with life and death in the balance, Christians should concern themselves with mat-

37. Ibid., xii. Also, see Lewis, "Christianity and Culture," 166–79.

38. C. S. Lewis, *Weight of Glory*, 53.

39. Ibid., 45.

40. Ibid., 44.

41. Ibid., 43.

42. Ibid., 47.

43. Ibid., 47–48. See 1 Cor 10:31.

ters of culture. Lewis's rhetorical appeals at this point are attempts to ground themselves in objective value. The first reason why Christians should concern themselves with culture, he confesses, is not too exciting, but is nonetheless validated in Scripture: It is the task of earning a living. Since Christians are instructed to do their work (1 Thessalonians 4:11; Ephesians 4:28), they are expected to participate in the life of the culture as active in its workaday world.[44] Second, Lewis acknowledges that though cultural activity could be harmless, it can also be harmful. Since this is the case, Christians who recognize an abuse must also see that "the task of resisting that abuse might be not only lawful but obligatory."[45] Proper judgment and moral discernment are necessary, for, "if you don't read good books you will read bad ones. If you don't go on thinking rationally, you will think irrationally. If you reject aesthetic satisfactions you will fall into sensual satisfactions."[46] Third, Lewis recognizes that there can be an intrinsic good in culture for its own sake. He is not here speaking of moral goodness, but of a goodness that is pleasurable or enjoyable. He explains it this way, "I enjoyed my breakfast this morning, and I think it was a good thing and I do not think it was condemned by God. But I do not think myself a good man for enjoying it."[47] Fourth, Lewis recognized that the "values assumed in literature were seldom those of Christianity."[48] There were, to be sure, values encountered by the reader in literature; but he categorizes most of these as "sub-values." These "sub-values" include a) honor, b) sexual love, c) material prosperity, d) a pantheistic contemplation of nature, as in Wordsworth, e) "*Sehnsucht* awakened by the past, the remote, or the (imagined) supernatural," and f) the liberation of impulses.[49] He makes no defense for (c) and (f), and in calling the others sub-Christian, he does not mean that they possess no value. Being "immediately below the lowest level of spiritual value,"[50] they can provide an avenue up into the higher Christian values. They can also provide a way toward di-

---

44. C. S. Lewis, *Christian Reflections*, 20.

45. Ibid., 20.

46. C. S. Lewis, *Weight of Glory*, 46.

47. C. S. Lewis, *Christian Reflections*, 36.

48. Ibid., 21.

49. Ibid., 21–22.

50. Ibid., 22.

minishing spiritual affection. As Lewis says, "Any road out of Jerusalem must also be a road into Jerusalem."[51] A little later he develops this idea more fully:

> Culture is a storehouse of the best sub-Christian values. These values are in themselves of the soul, not the spirit. But God created the soul. Its values may be expected, therefore, to contain some reflection or antepast of the spiritual values. They will save no man. They resemble the regenerate life only as affection resembles charity, or honour resembles virtue, or the moon the sun. But though 'like is not the same,' it is better than unlike. Imitation may pass into initiation. For some it is a good beginning, for others it is not; culture is not everyone's road into Jerusalem, and for some it is a road out.[52]

Lewis implicitly suggests that culture can play a role in the process of conversion for some, but that there are no guarantees. He suggests two roles that culture might play in the lives of the converted. First, the pre-Christian joys, which might have played a part on the road into Jerusalem, need not to be forsaken at conversion. The pleasures to be found in the suburbs of Jerusalem do not have to be disparaged.[53] For this reason, it is clear that Lewis was not a Gnostic, nor could he be accused of being a strict Platonist. Second, people may engage themselves in glorifying God by doing something that becomes a glory to God in its very offering. Those whose aptitudes lead them to lives of literature, music, fine arts, and scholarship can benefit spiritually by these activities if they are offered to God.[54] The cultural activity itself is not meritorious. It will not be the means of salvation, but, as an act of self-giving, will be evidence of spiritual health. Lewis warns, however, that it is not the cultural activities themselves which are spiritually valuable, but the offering; i.e., "doing it as unto the Lord." In this way, any kind of hierarchy that identifies one type of activity as superior to another is a false hierarchy. Sweeping a room, as an activity offered to God, is as exalted, in that sense, as writing the *Summa Theologica*.

Having said this, Lewis admits to doubts. In his own field of literature, he is aware of a tension that exists between objective and subjec-

51. Ibid.
52. Ibid., 23.
53. Ibid., 24.
54. Ibid., 24.

tive approaches to criticism. On the one hand, if criticism of books is objective, then judgments of the text can also be judged by how fairly they represent that text. On the other hand, if criticism is reduced to subjective judgments, making criticism merely a matter of taste, then all judgments are valid and none significant. Lewis senses the tension between two kinds of good and bad in literature—one objective, and thus moral, the other subjective and without moral implication. He struggles to fit these two approaches "into a consistent philosophy of values," and adds, "but it is one thing to be unable to explain a phenomenon, another to ignore it."[55]

Lewis believed this tension between the subjective and objective was healthy, as long as both were operational. This acceptance of tension led to a development in his literary thinking that would arrive at full stature in his *An Experiment in Criticism*,[56] which he would publish some twenty years after the "Christianity and Culture" article. In this investigation of Lewis's literary criticism and the problem of evil, the question still remains: in what way is culture generally, and literature specifically, a road into Jerusalem, and in what way is it a road out? And what might the implications of this be for subjectivism and the problem of evil? Lewis addresses these matters before the academy rhetorically, developing his argument logically as he builds his case against subjectivism.

## Christianity and Literature

Having considered what Lewis has said about culture, I now turn my attention to what he has written about literature, seeking to understand the larger problem of subjectivism and literary criticism. Lewis published, "Christianity and Literature,"[57] a year before "Christianity and Culture" first appeared. Here Lewis begins by attending to the question of Christianity and literature specifically. He thinks little can be said about the topic, for the rules that govern what might be called "Christian literature" are not much different than rules that govern literature in general. Putting it simply he writes, "I think, Christian

55. Ibid., 35.

56. C. S. Lewis, *Experiment in Criticism*, 61. This will be developed further later in the chapter.

57. C. S. Lewis, *Christian Reflections*. 36.

literature can exist only in the same sense in which Christian cookery might exist. Boiling an egg is the same process whether you are a Christian or a pagan."[58] He wonders if it might be more profitable to explore "what may be called the Christian approach to literature; about the principles, if you will, of Christian literary theory and criticism."[59] Lewis then begins to identify two things that a Christian approach to literature would oppose.

First, the Christian approach would oppose the idea of genius in literature. Here he identifies some "key-words of modern criticism;" these are "*Creative*, with its opposite *derivative*; *spontaneity*, with its opposite *convention*; *freedom*, contrasted with *rules*."[60] Because man's creative endeavor is the work of created beings, Lewis believes, perhaps too strongly, that a Christian approach to literature ought to be derivative, conventional and obedient. He writes, "In the New Testament the art of life itself is an art of imitation: can we, believing this, believe that literature, which must derive from real life, is to aim at being 'creative,' 'original,' and 'spontaneous'?"[61] It appears that Lewis has defined too narrowly a New Testament approach to art generally and a Christian approach to literature specifically. To limit Christian art to that which is imitation is short-sighted. His consignment is either too inflexible, allowing for no other options, or too ambiguous, not clarifying as carefully as he could what it is that he opposes to "creative." If he means by this that he rejects anarchy in art, so be it. If he is trying to rein in an antinomian approach to art that acknowledges no rules whatsoever, then perhaps his position is acceptable. But if he is trying to suggest that the artist must be prevented from doing something unconventional

58. Ibid., 1.

59. Ibid., 3.

60. Ibid., 3.

61. Ibid., 6. Lewis writes, "An author should never conceive himself as bringing into existence beauty or wisdom which did not exist before, but simply and solely as trying to embody in terms of his own art some reflection of eternal Beauty and Wisdom. Our criticism would therefore from the beginning group itself with some existing theories of poetry against others. It would have affinities with the primitive or Homeric theory in which the poet is the mere pensioner of the Muse. It would have affinities with the Platonic doctrine of a transcendent Form partly imitable on earth; and remoter affinities with the Aristotelian doctrine of *mimesis* and the Augustinian doctrine about the imitation of nature and the Ancients. It would be opposed to the theory of genius as, perhaps, generally understood; and above all it would be opposed to the idea that literature is self-expression" (7).

because it is less than a Christian approach to art would permit, I must disagree. Convention, at that point, is a myth. In a strict sense, imitation is never utterly conventional. An individual, "fearfully and wonderfully made" engages in something particular, unique, not having been tried in quite the same way and under the same set of circumstances before. Art may have an imitative quality, but the picture being painted has not been attempted before on this canvas and with the same brush strokes. Furthermore, periods, movements, or schools in art, music and literature are, by their very existence, indications that something new has happened. The new school may have borrowed, copied, even mixed elements from the past to discover and make something new. It may be that Lewis would respond and suggest that the creative ability is itself derivative. But if that is the case, is it not safe to suggest that man made in the image of a Creator could create something unique? If God is Omniscient, human creativity will not produce something outside the realm of what He knows and may in fact be the way in which He chooses to bring new things into existence. Of course, I am not suggesting that man could create as God, *ex nihilo*; but as God can bring something new into existence, could we not expect that man, made in that image, as sub-creator, could also produce works of art that are not limited to mere imitation? Should Lewis respond that all acts of man, as creative acts, will always be acts of imitation, then it would seem that we could expect no progress in the arts whatsoever. His suggestion that a Christian approach to art and literature would be one that was opposed to genius appears to be weak. Lewis makes no argument against subjectivism here.

The second element a Christian approach to literature would oppose, and one that narrows in on Lewis's concern about subjectivism, is that Lewis believes a Christian approach to literature would oppose "the idea that literature is self-expression."[62] He illustrates what he means by "self-expression" as he contrasts the *Confessions* of Rousseau with the *Confessions* of St. Augustine. Rousseau exhibits "his own temperament" as "a kind of absolute," whereas Augustine desires an enlargement of himself, ashamed of the fact that his is "a narrow house too narrow for Thee to enter—Oh, make it wide. It is in ruins—Oh, rebuild it."[63] It is at

62. Ibid., 7.
63. Ibid., 9.

this point that a reader begins to see Lewis's awareness of the effects of subjectivism on literature. The road out of Jerusalem, it appears, may be the road into self, whereas the road into Jerusalem may be the road out of self. At this point Lewis begins to clarify what he thinks a Christian approach to literature ought to include. The importance of such thinking is underscored by Weaver; he writes, "Rhetoric at its truest seeks to perfect men by showing them better versions of themselves."[64]

## An Experiment in Criticism

*An Experiment in Criticism* was one of the last books of literary criticism Lewis would write before his death.[65] The book is an attempt at a new approach to literary critical methodology. Instead of making judgments on books, Lewis wonders if it might be more profitable to make judgments about the way that books are read. He is cautious as he proceeds.

According to George Bailey, a former student, "Lewis had three standard forms of comment on an essay. If the essay was good: 'There is a good deal in what you say.' If the essay was middling 'There is something in what you say.' If the essay was bad: 'There *may* be something in what you say.'"[66] Then Bailey adds that when literary critical judgments were to be made, Lewis would warn, "not with Brogans, please, slippers are in order when you proceed to make a literary point."[67] Lewis sought to tread softly as he guided his readers through his own experiment. He admitted that

> Observation of how men read is a strong basis for judgements on what they read; but judgements on what they read is a flimsy, even a momentary, basis for judgements on their way of read-

---

64. Weaver, *Ethics*, 25.

65. C. S. Lewis, *Experiment in Criticism*. Lewis prepared another book of literary criticism for publication before he died, it was *The Discarded Image*, which had been Lewis's Prolegomena lectures to Medieval and Renaissance literature, a series, as Lewis says in the preface, "given more than once at Oxford" (*Experiment in Criticism*, vii). Though the lectures were edited for publication after *Experiment in Criticism*, all the data suggests that it was work substantially done earlier than the *Experiment*. It can well be said that *An Experiment in Criticism* reflects Lewis's thinking about literary critical theory at the end of his life.

66. Keefe, *Speaker and Teacher*. 81.

67. Ibid.

ing. For the accepted valuation of literary works varies with every change of fashion, but the distinction between attentive and inattentive, obedient and wilful, disinterested and egoistic, modes of reading is permanent; if ever valid, valid everywhere and always."[68]

Thus, the goal of his "experiment" is to discover what he can observe and learn from the way people read books.

He divides readers into two basic categories: the few, or the literary, and the many, or the unliterary. The unliterary tend to read a book only once: and "the sure mark of an unliterary man is that he considers 'I've read it already' to be a conclusive argument against reading a work."[69] On the other hand, the literary will return to certain books over and over again throughout the course of their lives. Lewis explains that the many, the unliterary, tend to read only for the event.[70] Once the plot is known and the conclusion settled, they see no reason to return again to the same book. For the few, the literary, the entire world, which the book has opened up to their senses, keeps drawing them back. They are not dissuaded from returning to the book because they already know its surprises. It is the very nature of the surprises themselves that beckon them to return. It is the enjoyment and exposure to the very quiddity of the world the author has invented, with all of its sensual experience, that draws the literary back again and again.

Lewis clarifies the difference in the reading of the few and the many when he considers how they each look at visual art.[71] "The distinction can hardly be better expressed than by saying that the many *use* art and the few *receive* it."[72] He warns, "We must not let loose our own subjectivity upon the pictures and make them its vehicles. We must begin by laying aside as completely as we can all our own preconceptions, interests, and associations."[73] Of course this is difficult, but it is a discipline

---

68. C. S. Lewis, *Experiment in Criticism*, 106. Lewis writes that "Fashions in literary taste come and go among adults, and every period has its own shibboleths" (C. S. Lewis, *Of Other Worlds*, 40).

69. C. S. Lewis, *Experiment in Criticism*, 2.

70. Ibid., 30, 36–37.

71. Ibid., 14–26.

72. Ibid., 19.

73. Ibid., 18.

worth cultivating. If it is never attempted then we remain provincial. He informs his readers,

> We must use our eyes. We must look and go on looking till we have certainly seen exactly what is there. We sit down before the picture in order to have something done to us, not that we may do things with it. The first demand any work of art makes upon us is surrender. Look. Listen. Receive. Get yourself out of the way.[74]

At this point Lewis has not yet classified the activity of "using" literature as negative. Nor is he ready to say that the activity of receiving literature is good. So far, it is a matter of understanding how those who use art "do not really see the pictures as they are."[75] Lewis writes, "The real objection to that way of enjoying pictures is that you never get beyond yourself."[76] Apart from utilitarian benefits, the art means nothing to the many.

Lewis acknowledges the subtle ways that "using" may interfere with the possibility of gaining a clear grasp of a text. He recognizes complexities and gives his readers a list of possibilities far from exhaustive. Even so, it is a good start at discovering how "using" can affect the way we see. First, he looks at the possible way even scholars may be found among the many.[77] Their former love of literature has atrophied to the point of mere professional concern. Literature still has a place for them, but its purposes are utilitarian and focused primarily on making a living. Second, he considers the status seeker.[78] This is a person "entirely dominated by fashion." He has a desire to be recognized at parties as one on the cutting edge. For the status seeker, literature is a tool that keeps him up on the trends of the moment and connects him with the people whose company matters to him the most. The third, and perhaps most subtle, group of "users" Lewis mentions are the devotees of culture.[79] These are people who expose themselves to a wide range of cultural activities. They are not driven by enjoyment. They have not found pleasure in the activity of reading. Their drive is for "self-improvement."

74. Ibid., 19.
75. Ibid., 21.
76. Ibid.
77. Ibid., 6–7.
78. Ibid., 7–8.
79. Ibid., 8–11.

Here the danger lies in the fact that their efforts fix "the ultimate atten-tion on oneself."[80] This inward attention may lead to the subjectivism which concerns Lewis so deeply; if left undiscovered and unchecked, Lewis warns, this can produce the sophistication of a literary puritan, grown full of "self-examination, the distrust of pleasure, which his fore-bears applied to the spiritual life; and perhaps soon all the intolerance and self-righteousness."[81] Once an interest in "self-improvement" takes over, a person's focus will be turned inward towards perfection. This can breed a kind of pretence, for no one is perfect, but those who think they can approximate some kind of cultured perfection will soon live in de-nial of their own short-comings and may become less patient towards the short-comings of others. Their lives become increasingly more seri-ous, elevated and far removed from the pleasures and enjoyments Lewis suggests are waiting for others who choose to *receive* literature rather than *use* it. He writes,

> Now the true reader reads every work seriously in the sense that he reads it whole-heartedly, makes himself as receptive as he can. But for that very reason he cannot possibly read every work solemnly or gravely. For he will read 'in the same spirit that the author writ.' What is meant lightly he will take lightly; what is meant gravely, gravely. He will 'laugh and shake in Rabelais' easy chair' while he reads Chaucer's *faibliaux* and respond with exquisite frivolity to *The Rape of the Lock*. He will enjoy a kick-shaw as a kickshaw and a tragedy as a tragedy. He will never commit the error of trying to munch whipped cream as if it were venison.[82]

Being a *user* or *receiver* of literature, according to Lewis, is not a mark of education, or social class, or even age. He writes of the house in which a party is taking place downstairs, a party full of status seekers talking of literature when the only real lover of books is the little boy upstairs. Put to bed long hours earlier, but remains awake under his covers, reading *Treasure Island* by flashlight.[83] Again, Lewis has respect

---

80. Ibid., 9.
81. Ibid., 10.
82. Ibid., 11.
83. Ibid., 8.

for complexities in that he recognizes any individual may be a *user* of one type of book and a *receiver* of another.[84]

As one will see throughout "the experiment," Lewis is making a rhetorical case against subjectivism before the academy. Lewis's chief concern is to make judgments not so much of books themselves, but rather of the way they are read. The type of reading he considers good is that which *receives*; it attends to the object rather than *using* the book, making it fit the reader's own subjectivistic purposes. Whenever a book is interpreted in such a way as to suggest that it is a reflection of "real life," Lewis is again concerned that an act of *using* has bubbled up to the surface. He writes that books "are complex and carefully made objects. Attention to the very objects they are is our first step. To value them chiefly for reflections, which they may suggest to us, or for morals, which we may draw from them, is a flagrant instance of 'using' instead of 'receiving.'"[85] He warns that "real life" is never like that which is portrayed in books. "Real life" may be the well from which the author has drawn, but once the story begins to be told the author is adding to it. He selects parts of the story and rejects others contingent upon purposes he brings to the story itself. He shapes and develops according to a plan and breathes into the bare bones of "real life" details the elements that make of it the kind of story he wants to tell. The reader who sees in the book a vision for "real life," a glimpse of morality, or a model for virtue itself, may be tipping his hand. At that point, he has become a *user*. He has ceased to see the book for what it is in itself, and has directed his energies into turning it into what it is not. He is using the book to support some vision of life he holds dear rather than attending to the literary style and purpose of the book, which the author has given. Again, this purpose is never life as it is actually lived apart from books. In the following passage, Lewis observes the limitations of literary modes of expression to capture real life:

> Tragedies omit the clumsy and apparently meaningless bludgeoning of much real misfortune and the prosaic littleness which usually rob real sorrows of their dignity. Comedies ignore the possibility that the marriage of lovers does not always lead to permanent, nor ever to perfect, happiness. Farce excludes pity for its butts in situations where, if they were real, they would

84. Ibid., 13.
85. Ibid., 82–83.

deserve it. None of the three kinds is making a statement about life in general. They are all constructions; things made out of the stuff of real life; additions to life rather than comments on it.[86]

Naturally, the author gives shape to the details in order to tell the story. To receive the story is to be attentive to its shape and style. It is not only what has been said, but also how it is said that flows over the one surrendered to the work. Lewis adds, "Shape is a nonentity apart from the body whose shape it is. But an 'appreciation' of sculpture which ignored the statue's shape in favour of the sculptor's 'view of life' would be self-deception."[87] The danger is obvious: as long as we are returning to a story to find mere confirmation for our point of view, we are not truly reading the story. For, as Lewis writes, "since everything can be a symbol, or an irony, or an ambiguity—we shall easily find what we want."[88] Once a literary work simply becomes a vehicle by which or through which I may say what I want with no disciplined attempt to discover what the author really means, I will find all literature to be simply my ideas channeled through the pen of some other person. I will not be able to do literary criticism because I am too deeply engaged in literary ventriloquism. Subjectivism substitutes the voice of the author for the voice of the reader and objectivity is lost.

The literary life is not to be confused with the spiritual life. It is not the means of soteriological grace. Lewis has already observed, however, that for some it may be a road into Jerusalem and for others a road out. And for pilgrims travelling in either direction, *An Experiment in Criticism* draws the map more clearly. The road into Jerusalem is the road out of self. The road out of Jerusalem is the road that becomes preoccupied with self. Living in denial of the world as it is, it sets out to create a world of his own making. This is a world very small, but then it needs room only for one. Lewis is not be satisfied with a place so confined. In the *Epilogue* to *An Experiment in Criticism*, Lewis, with his "slippers" on, ventures to suggest why, or in what way, the life of literature can address the matter of subjectivism. He explains,

> The nearest I have yet got to an answer is that we seek an enlargement of our being. We want to be more than ourselves.

86. Ibid., 81.
87. Ibid., 84.
88. Ibid., 85.

Each of us by nature sees the whole world from one point of view with a perspective and a selectiveness peculiar to himself. And even when we build disinterested fantasies, they are saturated with, and limited by, our own psychology. To acquiesce in this particularity on the sensuous level—in other words, not to discount perspective—would be lunacy. We should then believe that the railway line really grew narrower as it receded into the distance. But we want to escape the illusions of perspective on higher levels too. We want to see with other eyes, to imagine with other imaginations, to feel with other hearts, as well as with our own.

Literary experience heals the wound, without undermining the privilege of individuality. There are mass emotions which heal the wound; but they destroy the privilege. In them our separate selves are pooled and we sink back into sub-individuality. But in reading great literature I become a thousand men and yet remain myself. Like the night sky in the Greek poem, I see with a myriad eyes, but it is still I who see. Here, as in worship, in love, in moral action, and in knowing, I transcend myself; and am never more myself than when I do.[89]

As this passage reveals, a Christian approach to literature is an approach that allows an individual to grow in his capacity to see objectively, to get oneself out of the way. But subjectivism, the alienation of the individual perspective from objective reality, puts a reader at risk. This weakness cannot be corrected merely through literary interests. He believes that only the grace of God could do that, but certainly literature might be a means of that grace. So too, it would appear that he is saying literature can be used by a subjectivist (whether he is an unbeliever content to remain where he is or a believer disinterested in maturing in his faith) to reinforce and maintain a self-interested, egotistical point of view. Lewis demonstrates rhetorically that the literary life can be an aid to correcting this provincialism. Lewis could not possibly mean that one must be religious to be sophisticated. The Pharisees of the New Testament were very religious, and generally provincial. The non-religious may be enriched by the literary life and may find that its road leads into Jerusalem. Believers may also be enriched and discover that this road leads further into Jerusalem. Here Weaver clarifies the point by warning that "The road away from idolatry remains the same as it did before: it

89. Ibid., 137–38, 140–41.

lies in respect for the struggling dignity of man and for his orientation toward something higher than himself which he has not created."[90]

It is one thing to point out an instance or two where Lewis seems to be concerned with matters related to the problem of evil in his literary criticism. It is quite another thing to suggest that the problem of evil is a matter of such proportion that it occupies a great deal of his thinking when he engages in literary studies. In order to validate the argument of this study, I must cite many examples of instances in which Lewis expresses concerns about subjectivism in criticism; these, together, form a composite revealing the pervasiveness and frequency of Lewis's recurring concern to address rhetorically the dangers of subjectivism. By moving from numerous examples, a good argument seeks a generalized judgment that points to some form of defining features. While a generalization is not an exact representation of a particular thing, it is nevertheless, a valid representation. It may be modified, but it is not likely to be discarded altogether, for it has come to be through observing numerous examples. In this regard, Weaver would point out that "the value of a generalization is that while it leaves out the specific features that are of the individual or of the moment, it expresses features that are general to a class and may be lacking or imperfect in the single instance."[91] Furthermore, a generalization is a kind of definition, and it is to be remembered that arguments based on definition are the most ethical, and therefore the most effective, in making their case. Since Lewis is addressing the academy, he provides a wide spectrum of information for investigation. I am arguing that Lewis wants to make perfectly clear that subjectivism has infected literary criticism, and thus warns against the practice in many works of criticism and rhetoric.

## The Poison of Subjectivism

On February 24, 1943, Lewis delivered the Riddell Memorial Lectures at Durham. These would later be published as *The Abolition of Man*.[92] In the summer of that year, he also published an article titled, "The Poison of Subjectivism,"[93] which shares many of the same ideas as *The*

90. Weaver, *Visions of Order*, 91.
91. Weaver, *Defense of Tradition*, 396.
92. Green and Hooper, *Biography*, 218.
93. *The Poison of Subjectivism* was originally published in *Religion in Life* 12 (Summer

*Abolition of Man. Subjectivism* is a point of view isolated from objective reality. This is "the poison of subjectivism:" it either considers objective reality unknowable, making objects as they are of no importance, or projects onto objects what it wants to find in them. This subjectivist point of view, rather than surrendering to an object, tends to swell in its pseudo-significance. Though neither *The Abolition of Man* nor *The Poison of Subjectivism* is a work of literary criticism, each does address certain presuppositions that can affect the way a critic might approach a text.[94] Lewis believed subjectivism could prevent a critic from seeing what is really offered up by an author in a given text. To disregard the meanings of words as the author intended them, or to neglect content and style, will render the critic blind to the work as it is. He cautions, "What we get may be, in our opinion, a poem; but it will be our own poem not [the author's]."[95]

"The poison of subjectivism" certainly has consequences for literary criticism, but it comes with other dangers as well. It is important to point out once again what it is that Lewis thinks is at stake when subjectivism is unchecked:

> One cause of misery and vice is always present with us in the greed and pride of men, but at certain periods of history this is greatly increased by the temporary prevalence of some false philosophy. Correct thinking will not make good men of bad ones; but a purely theoretical error may remove ordinary checks to evil and deprive good intentions of their natural support. An error of this sort is abroad at present. I am referring to Subjectivism.[96]

Subjectivism has its consequences in the world, and these are likely to be far reaching. Therefore, Lewis was eager to reiterate that literary critics must be aware of the possibilities for evil inherent in certain kinds of critical approaches.

1943); c.f. C. S. Lewis, *Christian Reflections*, xiii, where the essay is reprinted.

94. Ibid., 3. Harry Blamires, commenting on Lewis's literary critical approach, writes, "The impulse to go out of the self, to enter into other men's beliefs, and to be admitted to experience other than our own is what is satisfied by good literature." Blamires continues, "'The great art of criticism is to get oneself out of the way and to let humanity decide,' in contradistinction to the educational fashion for persistently pressing students on their judgment of what they have read" (Blamires, *Literary Criticism*, 351).

95. C. S. Lewis, *Studies in Words*, 3.

96. C. S. Lewis, *Christian Reflections*, 72.

## Reading Between the Lines

Another way Lewis describes subjectivism as it presents itself in literary criticism is the phenomenon he calls, "reading between the lines."[97] Early in his life he developed a suspicion of this approach. As a young boy, he observed how often his father would guard a misunderstanding by claiming to have the ability to "read between the lines."[98] Once the senior Lewis was convinced a truth was hidden or that somebody had a reason to hide it, any attempt to correct his error proved futile. He considered it a matter of cleverness that he could see what others could not.

Lewis's early skepticism of "reading between the lines" was reinforced by his experience as a student of philosophy while an undergraduate. In his autobiography, he writes that the tradition of Benjamin Jowett was still dominant at Oxford, and

> One was brought up to believe that the real meaning of Plato had been misunderstood by Aristotle and widely travestied by the neo-Platonists only to be recovered by the moderns. When recovered, it turned out (most fortunately) that Plato had really all along been an English Hegelian.[99]

It was this same practice of reading between the lines that led Lewis to question some of the work done by the higher critics of Scripture. They would miss the obvious but see the hidden, and Lewis reacted, "These men ask me to believe they can read between the lines of the old texts; the evidence is their obvious inability to read (in any sense worth discussing) the lines themselves. They claim to see fern-seed and can't see an elephant ten yards away in broad daylight."[100]

---

97. C. S. Lewis, *Experiment in Criticism*, 106, 119.

98. Lewis writes, "It was axiomatic to my father (in theory) that nothing was said or done from an obvious motive. Hence he who in real life was the most honourable and impulsive of men, and the easiest victim that any knave or impostor could hope to meet, became a positive Machiavel when he knitted his brows and applied to the behaviour of people he had never seen the spectral and labyrinthine operation which he called 'reading between the lines.' Once embarked upon that, he might make his landfall anywhere in this wide world; and always with unshakeable conviction, 'I see it all'—'I understand it perfectly'—'It is as plain as pike staff'" (C. S. Lewis, *Surprised By Joy*, 121–22; see also 120–16, for more of this tendency which Lewis observed in his father).

99. C. S. Lewis, *Christian Reflections*, 157.

100. Ibid.

The error of "reading between the lines" may be committed in relative innocence. We often forget that the peculiarities of time and place are not universals, and when we forget, it is an easy matter to project onto the text of any work that which is not there. Lewis once reported that a friend of his, a schoolmaster, sought to explain the necessity of consulting the notes in a Milton text. They are necessary, lest the student read into the text ideas remote to Milton but proximate to the student. The schoolmaster then reminded the students that they should also consider how many notes Milton would need if he were to read a modern book.[101] In part, Lewis's attempts to correct this kind of reading between the lines led him to write *The Discarded Image*[102] in order to supply the student of medieval literature some background for bringing to light obscurities which need illumination by the literary historian. Though reading between the lines may begin as an innocent error, it puts the student on the wrong road, and it will keep the student on the wrong road if it is uncorrected. Furthermore, that road can also become the road out of Jerusalem.

## Historicism

Another subjectivist approach Lewis seeks to confront is that which he calls "historicism."[103] He defines it as "the belief that men can, by the use of their natural powers, discover an inner meaning in the historical process."[104] He believed that this whole approach "is an illusion,"[105] a reading into history what the historicist wants to find there. It is making a philosophical presupposition primary and the data of history subordinate to the philosophy by employing a cookie-cutter approach to the

101. C. S. Lewis, *A Preface to Paradise Lost*, 61.

102. C. S. Lewis, *Discarded Image*.

103. C. S. Lewis, *Christian Reflections*, 100–13.

104. C. S. Lewis, *Discarded Image*, 100. Lewis similarly defines historicism as "The belief that by studying the past we can learn not only historical but metahistorical or transcendental truth" (174). Lewis gives a host of examples of "historicism;" he writes, "When Carlyle spoke of history as a 'book of revelations,' he was a Historicist. When Novalls called history 'an evangel' he was a Historicist. When Hegel saw in history the progressive self-manifestation of absolute spirit he was a Historicist. Evolutionism, when it ceases to be simply a theorem in biology and becomes a principle for interpreting the total historical process, is a form of Historicism. Keat's *Hyperion* is the epic historicism" (*Christian Reflections*, 101).

105. C. S. Lewis, *Christian Reflections*, 101.

study of history. Its error is that "we have no notion what stage in the journey we have reached. Are we in Act I or Act V? Are our present diseases those of childhood or senility?"[106] In his inaugural address at Cambridge, he cautioned his readers to remember that the division of history into periods is arbitrary. "Periods are not facts,"[107] he declared. There was a day when Lewis himself had fallen into this error. He was lifted out of it by his friend Owen Barfield, and referred henceforth to this periodizing in his own day as "chronological snobbery."[108] The snobbery consisted in that form of subjectivist thinking that believes without question that what is newest and contemporary must necessarily be best, thereby judging against the past simply because it is the past. Historicists tend to read into history an interpretation of it as if they stood outside of the historical process, forgetting that they cannot interpret a story till they know the whole of it.

Lewis is not seeking to discredit the study of history. He is seeking to invalidate effectively, a subjectivist approach to the study of history which goes to the data with skewed preconceptions. The subjectivist has a tendency to overstate his case and make claims that cannot be validated. It is against these inflated claims that Lewis writes,

> We have not yet read history to the end. There might be no dead wood. If it is a story written by the finger of God, there probably isn't. And if not, how can we suppose that we have seen 'the point' already? No doubt there are things we can say about this story even now. We can say it is an exciting story, or a crowded story, or a story with humorous characters in it. The one thing we must not say is what it means, or what its total pattern is.[109]

Historicism, then, amounts to reading one's point of view into the events of history. In such cases the historicist will find it difficult to correct his subjectivism.

---

106. Ibid., 106.

107. C. S. Lewis, *Selected Literary Essays*, 2.

108. C. S. Lewis, *Surprised By Joy*, 207.

109. C. S. Lewis, *Christian Reflections*, 106.

## *The Anthropological Approach*

Historicism, as Lewis defines it, leads to a type of literary criticism he calls "the anthropological approach."[110] This critical approach provides another example of subjectivism, for this approach is a kind of criticism where the critic seeks to reconstruct from the text the sources he believes produced the work.

G. K. Chesterton's book *The Everlasting Man*[111] provides an illustration of the anthropological approach. He notes that since prehistoric man has left us with no written record, most of our attempts to reconstruct his society and culture are speculative. Chesterton admits that the one thing that can be known about prehistoric man is that he was an artist for his only record approximating a written record is painted on the walls of caves. To discuss the purpose of the paintings is interesting, but such discussions produce only guesses and nothing more. Perhaps these paintings were the work of artists in a communal society, and were merely decorations to entertain the children as they were kept in a cave-nursery while their parents worked for the collective. Others might imagine that the paintings decorated the walls of the cave for purposes of worship and were used for the religious customs of that ancient society. Others still might speculate that they decorated the walls of the man-cave and celebrated the stories of past hunts, keeping alive tribal memories of heroic deeds. Still others might suggest that the pictures represent the pastime recreation of people who spent long winter hours in the cave waiting out the cold and longing for warmer days. Any number of suggestions might be given, but there is no way to check the certainty of the theory when at least nothing so far has permitted verification. Furthermore, the speculation does nothing for the appreciation of the work itself. Trying to apprehend the conditions under which the artist painted will not increase an art critic's grasp of the line quality, the integrity, proportion or clarity of the art. So too, Lewis suggests that attempts to recreate and manufacture imagined histories of how texts came to be written do not necessarily help in the literary critical work itself. If anything, the "anthropological approach" distracts from the understanding of the text; this kind of criticism ends up moving further and further from the text. The critic spends most of

110. C. S. Lewis, *Selected Literary Essays*, 301–11.

111. Chesterton, *Everlasting Man*, 29–39.

his time working on the material produced by speculation.[112] The temptation is still to read into the work what is not there.[113] And if we are reading into the text, it is more than likely that we are reading ourselves into it. This is a rhetoric of deception and potential manipulation. Here again, as with the subjectivist and the historicist, it appears that there is a closing down into self.

Lewis wants criticism to be more objective and text centered. He wants the readers of his criticism to focus on the text—in other words, to focus on *logos*. In an address he gave to a joint meeting of the Classical and English Associations at Oxford, he praised the value of grammar as a kind of corrective to the "anthropological approach." He says:

> There have been critics of Chaucer who perpetuated serious blunders in translation and built up formidable aesthetic superstructures on a purely intuitive, and sometimes erroneous, conception of the author's meaning. But I presume that everyone present agrees that if you are going to read a book at all, it is desirable to be able to tell which words are in the Nominative and which are in the Accusative.[114]

It is clear to Lewis that some speculative errors about the text can be corrected by the text itself. The ancients believed (like Quintilian) that grammar was essential first, then dialectic, then rhetoric. Grammar should tether the critic to the text. The work may be misinterpreted. We may carry our biases to the work and subconsciously rediscover them there. But as long as the text is before us as something other than ourselves, misinterpretations and misconceptions can be corrected. This kind of care with the text may put us on the right road, and we could discover that it is the road into Jerusalem. It is not a guarantee, but it is a place to start.

Three final observations must be made before moving on from the anthropological approach. First, Lewis shares with his readers what he

---

112. Lewis writes that "this type of criticism always takes us away form the actual poem and the individual poet to seek the sources of their power in something earlier and less known" (*Selected Literary Essays*, 306).

113. David Downing observes that one of the inevitable dangers in "source criticism" is that "one's identification of antecedents or influences, however plausible, might simply be wrong." *Planets In Peril*, 121.

114. C. S. Lewis, *Rehabilitations*, 63.

was able to learn by observing how critics approached his work and that of his friends:

> Until you come to be reviewed yourself you would never believe how little of an ordinary review is taken up by criticism in the strict sense: by evaluation, praise, or censure, of the book actually written. Most of it is taken up with imaginary histories of the process by which you wrote it.[115]

These historical reconstructions move the critic away from the text. Consequently he avoids doing work with the text. Lewis observes that this methodology is simply wrong:

> My impression is that in the whole of my experience not one of these guesses has on any one point been right; that the method shows a record of 100 per cent failure. You would expect that by mere chance they would hit as often as they miss. But it is my impression that they do no such thing. I can't remember a single hit. But as I have not kept a careful record my mere impression might be mistaken. What I think I can say with certainty is that they are usually wrong . . . And yet they would often sound—if you didn't know the truth—extremely convincing.[116]

Second, the "anthropological approach," with its imagined history, will do nothing to aid in any helpful criticisms of the text, for as Lewis states regarding this pseudo-history of the text, "the unknown cannot illuminate the known."[117]

Third, he shows in an imaginative way what he thinks of the weaknesses of the "anthropological approach" in the *Chronicles of Narnia*. In *The Magician's Nephew*, Digory and Polly find themselves before

---

115. C. S. Lewis, *Christian Reflections*. 159.

116. Ibid., 159–60. Lewis develops this further in relation to the use of source criticism in the higher critical approaches applied to the Bible. He writes, "The reconstruction of the history of a text, when the text is ancient, sounds very convincing. But one is after all sailing by dead reckoning; the results cannot be checked by fact. In order to decide how reliable the method is, what more could you ask for than to be shown an instance where the same method is at work and we have facts to check it by? Well, that is what I have done. And we find, that when the check is available, the results are either always, or else nearly always, wrong. The 'assured results of modern scholarship,' as to the way in which an old book was written, are 'assured,' we may conclude, only because the men who knew the facts are dead and can't blow the gaff" (Ibid., 160–61). For more on this subject, see C. S. Lewis *Of Other Worlds*, 46–50.

117. C. S. Lewis, *Renaissance Literature*. 11.

Queen Jadis of Charn. The two children have just awakened Jadis from a spell. She is very evil and in time will become the White Witch of *The Lion, The Witch and the Wardrobe*. She begins to concoct an elaborate explanation as to how the children have happened to come to her. After hearing Jadis's explanation which is far from what has actually happened, Polly is unable to contain herself and blurts out, "Why that is bosh from beginning to end."[118] One of Jadis's major flaws is that she is always supposing things to be, which are not. She reads into things what she wants to find in them. Primarily, she projects her own will and desire onto everything. There is no evidence of surrender on her part to any measure of Narnian reality. We know what Lewis thinks. He has allowed Polly to tell us, "why that is bosh from beginning to end." And elsewhere, he has warned that "nonsense draws evil after it."[119] Lewis continues to make his rhetorical case against subjectivism in literary critical studies.

## The Doctrine of the Unchanging Human Heart

Another form of literary criticism that tends towards subjectivism is what Lewis calls "the doctrine of the unchanging human heart."[120] The caution here is to guard against those who might make perceived common features in the nature of man the only grounds for literary judgment. Chesterton's prehistoric man may have been an artist, but that fact is hardly grounds for suggesting that he was not much different than we are today. This approach takes matters held in common among humans throughout the ages as the real stuff of mankind, and the rest—such as culture, gender, ethnicity, social status, and what not—as a thin veneer. Thus, Shakespeare may be performed in any period costuming, for Shakespeare's themes are universal and always contemporary. In his critique of Shakespeare's *Hamlet*, Lewis did not deny that common features, related to a shared humanity, do transcend time and place and can be seen in literary descriptions. He acknowledges,

> I would not cross the room to meet Hamlet. It would never be necessary. He is always where I am. Its true hero is man—haunted man—man with his mind on the frontier of two worlds, man

118. C. S. Lewis, *Magician's Nephew*, 63.
119. C. S. Lewis, *Four Loves*, 40.
120. C. S. Lewis, *Preface to Paradise Lost*, 61–64.

unable either quite to reject or quite to admit the supernatural, man struggling to get something done as man has struggled from the beginning, yet incapable of achievement because of his inability to understand either himself or his fellows or the real quality of the universe which has produced him.[121]

He does not deny that there are shared human features held in common by all men at all times.[122] But that is only half the story. If literary criticism were to stop here, there would be the danger of thinking that one has discovered all he needs to know about any work of literary art simply by drawing on his own experience. If a critic is no different from Shakespeare's Hamlet or Chesterton's prehistoric artist, then he may readily believe that he has license to interpret the worlds of other men from his own armchair. The distinctions between occidental and oriental culture become superficial. The issues that plagued classical culture are nothing more, nor less, than those issues encountered in the daily newspaper. This erroneous viewpoint makes work simple for the critic. He can make judgments about any age and any culture without reading books outside his own time and place and without taking a step outside his own home.

The problem with "the doctrine of the unchanging human heart" is that it is flawed rhetorically, because it presupposes that the world lacks rhetorical diversity. Its proponents are short-sighted, for they fail to see real differences do exist among men and affect their views about the world. They lack vision, for they are unable to distinguish those times, places, and circumstances that define uniqueness and particularity—not to mention interest—to any man, any time, any circumstance or, for that matter, any book. The greatness of man must not only be measured by what seems to be static and unchanging features, but also by the elasticity and mutability of our nature; that is, that we can stretch

---

121. C. S. Lewis, *Prince or the Poem*, 14.

122. Lewis writes, "If we stripped the armour off a medieval knight or the lace off a Caroline courtier, we should find beneath them an anatomy identical with our own. So it is held, if we strip off from Virgil his Roman imperialism, from Sidney his code of honour, from Lucretius his Epicurean philosophy, and from all who have it their religion, we shall find the Unchanging Human Heart, and on this we are to concentrate. I held this theory myself for many years, but I have now abandoned it. I continue, of course, to admit that if you remove from people the things that make them different, what is left must be the same, and that the Human heart will certainly appear as Unchanging if you ignore its changes" (C. S. Lewis, *Preface to Paradise Lost*, 61–62).

to be so different from place to place.[123] To have half an understanding is one thing, to act as if it is the whole understanding is quite another. Such projections onto texts or onto the events of one's own experience leads to that kind of subjectivism which may give birth to evil.

Lewis understands that those who abide by "the doctrine of the unchanging human heart" will project themselves onto whatever text they happen to read. All they need to discover about another can be discerned from within. In *The Pilgrim's Regress*, John, the pilgrim, comes to the home of a hermit, who represents History. With a wise and discerning way about him, the hermit warns the pilgrim about the "stay-at-homes." "They *know* very little," he confides, "They never travel and consequently never learn anything."[124] History explains more fully the problem of the "stay-at-homes." "If they like something in their own village they take it for a thing universal and eternal, though perhaps it was never heard of five miles away; if they dislike something, they say it is a local, backward, provincial convention, though in fact, it may be the law of nations."[125]

In the context of explaining the influence of Augustine's theology on Milton, in a later chapter of *A Preface to Paradise Lost*, Lewis ties together the idea of evil and "the doctrine of the unchanging human heart." He recounts the passage in *The City of God* where Augustine connects the Fall with a loss of understanding.[126] After listing Milton's indebtedness to Augustine he makes his case in this extended passage:

> It is my hope that this short analysis will prevent the reader from ever raising certain questions which have, in my opinion, led critics into blind alleys. We need not ask, 'What is the Apple?' It is an apple, just as Desdemona's handkerchief is a handkerchief. Everything hangs on it, but in itself it is of no importance. We can also dismiss that question which has so much agitated some great critics. 'What is the Fall?' The Fall is simply and solely Disobedience—doing what you have been told not to do: and it results from Pride—from being too big for your own boots, forgetting your place, thinking that you are God. That is what St. Augustine thinks and what (to the best of my knowledge)

123. Lewis quotes Pascal, "On ne montre pas so grandeur pour entre a une extremite, mais bien touchant les deux a lo fois et remplissant tout l'entre-deux" (Ibid., 7).

124. C. S. Lewis, *Pilgrim's Regress*, 145.

125. Ibid., 146.

126. C. S. Lewis, *A Preface To Paradise Lost*, 68.

the Church has always taught; this Milton states in the very first line of the first Book, this all his characters reiterate and vary from every possible point of view throughout the poem as if it were the subject of a fugue. Eve's arguments in favor of eating the Apple are, in themselves, reasonable enough; the answer to them consists simply in the reminder, 'You mustn't. You were told not to.' 'The great moral which reigns in Milton,' said Addison, 'is the most universal and most useful that can be imagined, that Obedience to the will of God makes men happy and that Disobedience makes them miserable.' Dr. Tillyard amazes me by calling this a 'rather vague explanation' (*Milton*, 258). Dull, if you will, or platitudinous, or harsh, or jejune; but how *vague*? Has it not rather the desolating clarity and concreteness of certain classic utterances we remember from the morning of our own lives; 'Bend over'—'Go to bed'—'Write out I *must do as I am told a hundred times*'—'Do not speak with your mouth full.' How are we to account for the fact that great modern scholars have missed what is so dazzlingly simple? I think we must suppose that the real nature of the Fall and the real moral of the poem involve an idea so uninteresting or so intensely disagreeable to them that they have been under a sort of psychological necessity of passing it over and hushing it up. Milton, they feel, must have meant something more than that! And here once again, the doctrine of the unchanging human heart comes into play. If there is no God, then Milton's poem, as interpreted by Addison, has no obvious relation to real life. It is therefore necessary to sweep away the main thing Milton was writing about as a mere historical accident and to fix on quite marginal or subsidiary aspects of his work as the real core. For there can be no serious doubts that Milton meant just what Addison said: neither more, nor less, nor other than that. If you can't be instructed in that, you can't be interested in *Paradise Lost*.[127]

Lewis here attributes to Tillyard the kind of projection onto texts he has identified as "the doctrine of the unchanging human heart." Of course, Lewis himself is engaged in some degree of speculation here. Yet, there is room for other interpretations of Milton and even other interpretations of Tillyard on Milton. He may be wrong about Tillyard. When Tillyard says *vague*, it does not necessarily mean he thought the command to be vague, but perhaps only the reasons God issued the command. If this is what Tillyard was thinking, Lewis might have been too quick to

127. Ibid., 69–70.

judge. Lewis may be wrong about some critics and their interpretations of some texts, but an understanding of Lewis would be flawed if we were to be ignorant of what he thought of subjectivist approaches to literary criticism. The goal here is not an attempt to demonstrate the rightness or wrongness of Lewis's assessment of Tillyard. It is merely to note that Lewis is conscious of the matters related to subjectivism and its implications for human fallenness and evil as he does his work in literary criticism, criticism he addresses to those in the academy.

### The Personal Heresy

Lewis read in E. M. W. Tillyard's critical work on Milton that *Paradise Lost* was "really about the true state of Milton's mind when he wrote it."[128] If this were so, then criticism would not be about the artist's work, but about the artist himself. Literary criticism would be reduced to biography or psychology. This is an approach Lewis found intolerable, because it drew attention away from the work itself, and focused it on the personality of the author. It was simply another subjectivist approach that kept one from the text. Such an action is like describing the size, color and dimensions of a boat long out of view by drawing clues from its wake. The description is suspect. And when this approach is used in literary criticism, the description the critic develops of the author reveals more about the critic's imagination than either the poet or his work. Furthermore, the text remains untouched. Lewis called this "the personal heresy," and wrote about it in an article by that name which first appeared in *Essays and Studies*.[129] Tillyard responded the next year, and Lewis again the year after that. Eventually the discussion between Lewis and Tillyard was developed further and published as *The Personal Heresy: A Controversy*.[130]

Tillyard defined personality as "some mental pattern that makes Keats Keats and not Mr. Smith or Mr. Jones and displaying itself to us

---

128. Tillyard, *Milton*, 201. In the introduction, Tillyard makes a similar comment: "No one reading through *Paradise Lost* with any degree of seriousness can help asking with what the poem as a whole is most truly concerned, what were the feelings and ideas that dominated Milton's mind when he wrote it" (*Milton*, 1).

129. LEWIS, C. S., 1934. The Personal Heresy, *Essays and Studies*. Published by members of the Oxford English Association, Vol. XIX.

130. C. S. Lewis, *Personal Heresy*.

by style."[131] Tillyard derives from this assumption that "style is the poetry,"[132] and adds, "experience shows how directly personality revealed
through style can constitute the major appeal of poetry."[133] Lewis strongly disagrees. He is less concerned with the intricacies of personality and
its effect on the poet's work than with the relationship of the reader
with the poet's work. Of course, this is a rhetorical conviction—the text
(*logos*) matters more than the communicator (*ethos*). Lewis writes, "The
thing presented to us in any poem is not and never can be the personality of the poet."[134] Lewis does make the following concession: "Let it
be granted that I do approach the poet; at least I do it by sharing his
consciousness, not by studying it. I look with his eyes not at him. He
for that moment will be precisely what I do not see; for you can see any
eyes rather than the pair you see with."[135] Developing the idea further,
he adds, "The poet is not a man who asks me to look at *him*; he is a man
who says 'look at that' and points; the more I follow the pointing of his
finger the less I can possibly see of *him*."[136] Finally, Lewis makes the
following judgment: "To see things as the poet sees them I must share
his consciousness and not attend to it; I must look where he looks and
not turn around to face him; I must make of him not a spectacle but
a pair of spectacles."[137] As a scholar of medieval literature, Lewis sees
this is an issue of great importance. He is aware that many texts cannot
claim a single author. Writers of that period would, most often, work
with stories that had already been written. They would retell the story,
embellishing it for whatever reasons they might have had. By the time a
story reaches us, it may have been altered in content and literary style.
Some stories were translated into English from other languages; these
too were often not merely translated but embellished.[138] In such cases,

---

131. Ibid., 50. This is Lewis's summary of Tillyard's point, made on 35.

132. Ibid., 36.

133. Ibid.

134. Ibid., 11.

135. Ibid.

136. Ibid.

137. Ibid., 12.

138. C. S. Lewis, *Renaissance Literature*, 36–38. Lewis writes, "In my opinion all
criticism should be of books, not of authors. But when we are treating the Middle Ages
it often must be, for many of the texts there is no human being who can really be the
author in the full sense" (*Renaissance Literature*, 38).

literary criticism cannot be focused on the personality of the author, for there is no primary author or personality. Lewis raises concerns about this approach because it distracts critics and readers alike from the text itself.[139] Once the personality of the author is made the primary concern for literary judgments, the reader neglects the text. Furthermore, attempts to reconstruct the author's personality from hints within the text will create another example of "reading into the text." Lewis is trying to prevent this from becoming widespread by his warnings in *The Personal Heresy*.

Duffy and Jacobi, commenting on the rhetoric of Weaver highlight all the more the importance of objective value in literary criticism. They comment that "knowledge is not constructed through language but only discovered through it, and then only partly so."[140] Knowledge is an outgrowth of accommodating one's thoughts and ideas to objects, and this must be done in community, that is dialectically through discourse, honing and clarifying one's understanding. If a critic, or reader, cuts himself off from the rhetoric of the text and an actual engagement with an author's words, that reader has seriously injured his opportunity to grow intellectually. Duffy and Jacobi continue, "Language is primarily a tool for the transfer of knowledge—either 'objectively' or 'manipulatively.'"[141] If Duffy and Jacobi are right, then those who engage in the rhetoric of textual analysis without serious attention to the actual texts, are being manipulative. This is a serious blow to those who might commit the "personal heresy" and to their approach to literary criticism.

## A CHALLENGE TO LEWIS'S PERSONAL HERESY

Lewis's concerns regarding "the personal heresy" have been misunderstood. I would like to consider one such case as a means of better understanding what Lewis objects to in his idea of subjectivism. Peter J. Schakel's *Reason and Imagination in C. S. Lewis*[142] is sympathetic to

---

139. Lewis writes that multiple authors (as was often the case with medieval books) combined with "the personal heresy," and "while this often makes criticism of authors impossible it leaves criticism of books untouched. The text before us, however it came into existence, must be allowed to work on us in its own way and must be judged on its own merits" (*Renaissance Literature*, 39).

140. Duffy and Jacobi, *Politics of Rhetoric*, 119.

141. Ibid.

142. Schakel, *Reason and Imagination*.

Lewis and provides some interesting and valuable insight, but it also reveals a significant misunderstanding of Lewis's ideas as he develops them in *The Personal Heresy*. So great is the misunderstanding that Schakel himself engages in "the personal heresy" apparently without realizing it. He seeks to reconstruct from the personality of Lewis and from circumstances in his life a rationale for his literary critical method.

Schakel quotes from Owen Barfield's introduction to *Light on C. S. Lewis*.[143] Barfield had been a friend of Lewis since their days as students at Oxford University. Barfield observes that around the time of Lewis's conversion, he was aware that Lewis, "deliberately ceased to take any interest in himself."[144] Barfield says that he first consciously took note of this in the 1930's, during the time Lewis was engaged in his dialogue with Tillyard over "the personal heresy."[145] While this has been mentioned earlier, it is important here to see how Schakel builds on Barfield's observation. Schakel claims that "A consciousness of self, and of the inevitability of a degree of subjectivity, is necessary to proper understanding even of 'objective' things, and that Lewis' failure to include self in his thinking was an inhibiting factor in his thought and work."[146] He cites Barfield as saying that Lewis deliberately sought to shut down interest in himself as a means of combating pride in his life.[147] While one might agree with Schakel that Lewis sought to guard himself against pride, especially in his academic work as a literary critic, it appears that Schakel has misunderstood Lewis's terminology. Lewis does not deny a place for the subjective as he hones in on a literary text. The fact that something can be understood implies both a knower and a thing to be known. Lewis believed, however, that the subject must conform to the object if a matter is to be grasped. His concerns about subjectivism are based on the dominance of the subject over the object, which either eclipses the object or denies it; in either case, the object becomes unimportant. And in literary criticism this takes the critic away from the text. Unfortunately, Schakel confuses Lewis's concerns about *subjectivism* with a denial of *subjectivity* in the subject-object

143. Gibb, *Light on C. S. Lewis*, ix–xi. Owen Barfield contributed the Introduction to this book.

144. Ibid., xvi (quoted in Schakel, *Reason and Imagination*, 89).

145. Ibid., ix–xi (in Schakel, *Reason and Imagination*, 89).

146. Schakel, *Reason and Imagination*, 89.

147. Ibid., 89.

relationship. Consequently, Schakel believes that this is a characteristic behavior which creates a conflict between the rational and the romantic and severely restricts Lewis as a literary critic. If anything, the conflict between reason and romance (the rational and the imaginative) existed in Lewis long before his conversion to Christianity. Confirmation of this can be found in his autobiography, *Surprised by Joy*, as well as in his allegorical autobiography, *The Pilgrim's Regress: An Allegorical Apology for Christianity, Reason and Romanticism*. In both of these, Lewis clarifies that coming to faith neither created, nor sustained, any conflict between these two halves of his life. If anything, it united them. Schakel seems to think that Lewis's post-conversion disregard for himself made it difficult for him to approach a literary text properly. Such an approach would demand sensitivity for the subject as well as the object and Lewis, according to Schakel, had truncated this process by repressing his feeling side.

Schakel's error is one of equivocation. He confuses Lewis's habits and exercise of spiritual discipline with his sensitivity to literary texts, believing that Lewis's interest in any text as an object comes at the expense of himself as subject. He charges Lewis with creating a "'depersonalized' theory of poetry."[148] It appears that Schakel misreads Lewis when he interprets his personal heresy as an attempt "to concretize the 'objective' and to isolate it from the subjective."[149] Schakel then argues that Lewis has created an ultimately inadequate approach to reading.[150] From a misunderstanding of Barfield's remark about Lewis's disinterest in himself, Schakel has redefined a significant aspect of Lewis's literary critical theory.

Lewis never suggests that the reader or the critic must attempt to approach a text as object by denial of himself as subject or denial of the affective and emotional. He is concerned, instead, that the subject surrenders to the object. He is not suggesting that the subjective is of no consequence. His concern is that the reader engages in what Matthew Arnold described as the necessary and proper approach to the academic disciplines. "The endeavour, in all branches of knowledge,

148. Ibid., 108.
149. Ibid., 115.
150. Ibid.

theology, philosophy, history, art, science—to see the object as in itself it really is."[151]

Schakel does believe that Lewis eventually changed from denying the subjective to affirming the subject's participation with the object in the critical endeavor. What brought about this sudden transformation that released the repressed Lewis and made him able to function more holistically? Schakel gives a rather surprising list of things that led to the change. First, he suggests that Lewis's debate with G. E. M. Anscombe at the Oxford Socratic Club led Lewis to reassess "his earlier heavy reliance upon reason."[152] He indicates that there might have been a movement on Lewis's part away from further apologetic work because of this debate. I will challenge this supposition in the following chapter. Nevertheless, it is important here that Schakel believes this debate began the process of Lewis's softening. Second, he believes that twenty years of hearing Tolkien read from his mythology at weekly Inkling meetings also rekindled Lewis's own imaginative side.[153] It does seem incredible that after reading *Surprised by Joy*, anyone could think Lewis's imaginative side would need to be rekindled. Years of conversation with his friend Owen Barfield on the subject of "consciousness" added a third element that supposedly contributed to a more self-conscious awareness.[154] Fourth, Schakel adds, Lewis's relationship with his wife Joy, helped to break down "the chasm, the sense of exile, the way in which he was less than fully man [the] lack of balance between heart and head."[155] Fifth, the composition of his autobiography, *Surprised By Joy*, finally enabled Lewis to get in touch with the side of himself that

---

151. Arnold, *Essays Literary and Critical*, 249. See also, ibid., 114. Lewis says as much in *Studies in Words*, 326, and in *Experiment in Criticism*, 119.

152. Schakel, *Reason and Imagination*, 149. On page 148, Schakel describes Anscombe at the time of the debate as a "then already well-known and impressive philosopher." This seems to conflict with what Anscombe herself wrote in the introduction to her second volume of collected philosophical papers, where she published the very paper she read at the Socratic Club, and writes that it was "the earliest purely philosophical writing on my part which was published" (Anscombe, *Collected Philosophical Papers of G. E. M. Anscombe, Volume Two*, ix). It is difficult, from Anscombe's remarks, to believe that she had already risen to the stature attributed to her by Schakel.

153. Schakel, *Reason and Imagination*, 150.

154. Ibid., 150–51.

155. Ibid., 151.

had long remained dormant, repressed and unacknowledged.[156] This too seems far-fetched considering the elements of strong feeling evident in *The Pilgrim's Regress*, a book written over twenty years before *Surprised by Joy*. The items listed above, lead Schakel to believe there is a dramatic contrast between the literary critical approach Lewis championed in *The Personal Heresy* and the one he held towards the end of his life when he wrote *An Experiment in Criticism*.[157] Schakel's assessment, though interesting, is largely speculation far from fact.

Nevertheless, there are changes that do appear in Lewis's literary critical approach over the years. I think they reflect "continuity and change in development," a phrase used by David Llewellyn Dodds to describe Charles Williams's poetry.[158] But these are not changes in kind, as Schakel would have his readers believe; they are changes of degree, reflecting development and maturation as Lewis's respect for and understanding of objective value increased.

Schakel does not even mention the significance Lewis attaches to the thought of Samuel Alexander. In his diary, Lewis records that he was reading Alexander's *Space, Time, and Deity* on Saturday, 8 March 1924.[159] He expresses great interest in the way Alexander distinguishes between enjoyment and contemplation. Years later, in *Surprised by Joy*, Lewis would recall the clarity that Alexander's book brought to his own thinking. The theory is simply stated: "When you see a table, you 'enjoy' the act of seeing and 'contemplate' the table."[160] Focusing on the object had for Lewis a sense of subjective participation. Lewis writes of Alexander's distinctions, "I accepted this at once and have ever since regarded it as an indispensable tool of thought."[161] Contrary to Schakel's assertions, Lewis was, in part, guided by this belief when he wrote *The Personal Heresy*, and it was still operational for him when he wrote *Surprised by Joy* twenty years later.

When Lewis published his Riddell Memorial Lectures in 1947 as *The Abolition of Man*, his idea of objectivity did not exclude subjective

---

156. Ibid., 151–60.
157. Ibid., 163.
158. Huttar and Schakel, *Rhetoric of Vision*, 192.
159. C. S. Lewis, *All My Road Before Me*, 301.
160. C. S. Lewis, *Surprised By Joy*, 218.
161. Ibid., 218.

participation. He defined the Tao, as "the doctrine of objective value, the belief that certain attitudes are really true, and others really false, to the kind of thing the universe is and the kind of things we are."[162] He not only asserts that reason should be reflective of reality, he says that sentiments should correspond to reality also. He cites Augustine, who, "defines virtue as *ordo amoris*, the ordinate condition of the affections in which every object is accorded that kind and degree of love which is appropriate to it."[163] He also quotes Metaphysical poet Thomas Traherne, who asks, "Can you be righteous unless you be just in rendering to things their due esteem?"[164] He calls this "ordinate affections" or "just sentiments."[165] This is not the perspective of a person who has extinguished or sacrificed the subjective for some unrealistic pursuit of the objective. Schakel does not mention *The Abolition of Man* in his study. Lewis may have had the capacity to feel more deeply after the death of his wife; one would find no grounds for contesting this. However, this does not prove his inability to be subjectively engaged before his wife died. The passages, mentioned above, from *The Abolition of Man* would also indicate that Lewis certainly thought ordered emotions and subjective responses important be they love, anger or grief. And one can imagine that grief is not the *only* experience that might teach this.

While Lewis prepared his manuscript for the *Oxford History of English Literature, English Literature in the Sixteenth Century Excluding Drama*, he read widely from the works published in Britain throughout that century. As he comments on the books he reads, he does not write as if he is emotionally uninvolved or detached. His theory of literature and literary criticism does not demand that he should. After reading many pieces from that period, he expresses delight.[166] Again, Schakel

162. C. S. Lewis, *Abolition of Man*, 29.

163. Ibid., 26.

164. Ibid.

165. Ibid.

166. C. S. Lewis, 1968. *English Literature in the Sixteenth Century*. From this work many examples could be cited:

1. The humanists, according to Lewis, could not fully appreciate the ancient texts because "they brought to their reading of the ancients certain damaging preconceptions" (26). This of course prevented them from surrendering to the text, seeing the object as it really was and enjoying it.

2. Lewis writes of a passage in Bradshaw, "The passage is funny because it is true to nature, and it is true to nature because Bradshaw keeps his eye on the object" (123).

makes no mention of this work. Lewis's concern about "subjectivist" approaches to literary criticism was not an attempt to deny the role of subjectivity, but rather a reminder that the subjective should surrender to the lead of the literature as it is. Attempts to understand a text in this way may be imperfect, but approximations to understanding are to be preferred over a reading which twists the text into a shape the author never intended and which the text does not merit.

Furthermore, Schakel fails to recognize that Lewis was still advocating the position he set forth in *The Personal Heresy* right up to the end of his life. Another book which Schakel fails to mention is Lewis's *Studies in Medieval and Renaissance Literature*.[167] Walter Hooper, who collected the essays in this book, includes, "The Genesis of a Medieval Book." In his preface, Hooper reveals that this essay was the beginning of a book Lewis started at the end of his life but never finished. Hooper remarks, "This is one of the last pieces he wrote."[168] And here, as strongly as ever, Lewis is warning about "the personal heresy." Lewis turns his attention, in this essay, to Layamon's *Brut*. Though he believes most of the text was by Layamon himself, he does not assume this in his treatment of that text.[169] He writes:

> Who, or how many people, or in what proportions each, made it what it is, is a question I cannot answer. This inability of course frustrates our curiosity as scholars, and it puts out of use our characteristically modern critical habits. There is no question here of finding the single author, totally responsible for his work

Lewis adds that Bradshaw understood what many often forget, that "poetry must please" (123).

3. In another passage he writes, "No art lives by *nature*, only by acts of voluntary attention on the part of human individuals. When these are not made, it ceases to exist" (124).

4. Regarding Philip Sidney's *Astrophil and Stella*, Lewis writes, "Here at last a situation is not merely written about: it is created, presented, so as to compel our imaginations" (329).

5. Later of the *Arcadia*, Lewis observes, "We can almost say of Sidney as Johnson said of Richardson, 'You must read him for the sentiment.'" This is hardly the kind of thing a man of repressed feelings would be likely to say (338). And, "We are meant to feel as an unpurchasable grace that single kiss which Pamela vouchsafes to her lover" (339).

167. C. S. Lewis, *Renaissance Literature*.
168. Ibid., viii.
169. Ibid., 22.

of art, and expressing his unique personality through it. But this frustration is instructive, and it is fortunate that the text which meets us at the very threshold of Middle English poetry should so clearly render the modern approach impossible. If criticism cannot do without the clear separation of one work from another and the clear unity of the individual author with the individual text, then criticism of medieval literature is impossible.[170]

Nearly thirty years had passed since Lewis first published *The Personal Heresy* in *Essays and Studies*, and Lewis obviously had not changed his position.

Schakel himself engages in "the personal heresy" when he develops his criticism of Lewis's work. He wants his readers to believe that Lewis, out of touch with himself, represses his feelings and overemphasizes reason in his life. After experiencing the hard knocks of life, most dramatically the death of his wife, and learning from the patient longsuffering of his friends, Lewis finally changed his literary critical approach at the very end of his life. The evidence shows otherwise. Lewis did not alter this basic literary critical premise, but he did develop it further. Lewis made changes, but they were not the kind of changes Schakel has in mind. At the heart of his literary critical approach throughout was a belief that "within a given story any object, person, or place is neither more nor less nor other than what that story effectively shows it to be."[171] This remained his conviction throughout his literary career. His suspicions of subjectivist approaches to criticism were not the fruit of some kind of psychological repression. They were rather the result of a concern that subjectivism could set one on the road out of Jerusalem. Lewis also believed that this kind of subjectivism, left unchecked, could lend support for an inclination to evil.

## The Place of Psychology in Lewis's Literary Criticism

Lewis is not unaware of issues in psychology pertinent to literature. He is consistent, however, in his desire that psychological issues, particularly as seen by critics, detract as little as possible from the appreciation of literary texts. One may see his concerns about psychology primarily in two ways. First, he does not wish to have psychological theories lead

170. Ibid., 22.
171. Ibid., 40.

either the reader or the critic away from the text. Literary criticism must not become a stage for the professional psychologist to do his work and upstage what the author has provided in the text itself. Second, he is concerned that a critic's own pathology not detract from the text. When the work of the critic is directed towards communicating his feelings, his likes and dislikes about the text at hand, all attention is drawn away from the text and riveted on the critic. Lewis is unsympathetic toward all literary critical approaches that detract from texts themselves, especially those approaches that force the reader to attend to the critic rather than the text.

In an essay Lewis called "Psycho-Analysis and Literary Criticism,"[172] he says that he does not intend "to attack psycho-analysis, but only to contribute to the solution of some frontier problems between psycho-analysis and literary criticism."[173] When a literary critic uses psychology or the psychologist uses literary criticism in order to "infer the pathology of a poet from his work,"[174] undesirable consequences for literary criticism occur. Lewis notes that attention is turned away from the critical question of "why, and how, should we read this?"[175] to the more historical question of "why did he write it?"[176] Lewis points out that the question, "Why did he write it?" is not a question designed to elucidate the author's intention, but actually implies, "impelled by what causes"[177] was he motivated to write it? This sends the critic on a quest for psychological motives and takes him away from the text itself.

Lewis observes that Freud believed all art may be traced to author fantasies, "that is the day-dreams or waking wish-fulfillments of the artist."[178]

> The artist wants 'honour, power, riches, fame and the love of women,' but being unable to get these in the real world, he has to do the best he can by imagining or pretending that he has got them. So far, according to Freud, he does not differ from the rest of us. What makes him an artist is the curious faculty he

172. C. S. Lewis, *Selected Literary Essays*, 286–300.

173. Ibid., 286.

174. Ibid.

175. Ibid.

176. Ibid.

177. Ibid.

178. Ibid.

possesses of 'elaborating his day-dreams, so that they lose that personal note which grates upon strange ears and become enjoyable to others.' As we others also like a good wish-fulfilment dream, we are now ready to pay for the privilege of sharing his. Thus, for the artist, as Freud says, there is a path through fantasy back to reality; by publishing his mere dreams of 'honour, power, riches, fame, and love of women,' he acquires 'honour, power, riches, fame, and the love of women' in reality.[179]

Lewis is quick to point out that Freud assumes all daydreaming to be of a singular kind, "wish-fulfilment" which features the dreamer as the hero of the dreams. Lewis does not deny the type of daydream Freud describes. With "the dreams of success, fame, love and the like—I confess that I am lamentably familiar. I have had dozens of them."[180] But he also admits to another kind of daydream with which he is equally familiar. This second type of daydream, for lack of a better label, could be called a fairy-tale, or fantasy type. He says of this variety that he does not feature himself in them as a hero, a beneficiary of wealth or the favors of women. They are daydreams in which he is not present as a character.

Thus, Lewis, perhaps more robust in his imagination than Freud, describes two types of imaginings in place of the psychologist's one. For, as Lewis writes, "the self is absent from the one and present as a hero in the other."[181] He admits that some wish-fulfillment imaginative work may make its way into published stories. He cites Charlotte Brontë and Anthony Trollope as examples of authors who appear to be engaged in the wish-fulfillment type of daydream.[182] He does not develop this from mere conjecture, building a psychological profile of Trollope from the text, and thus violating his own critical approach. He says that Trollope confesses in his *Autobiography* to some degree of "castle-building" in his novels.[183] Lewis quotes him as saying, "I myself was of course my own hero."[184] Lewis then points out that Trollope adds, not insignificantly, that, "in after years—I have *discovered the hero* of my earlier dreams

179. Ibid., 286–87. Here Lewis is quoting from Freud, *Introductory Lectures*, 314.

180. C. S. Lewis, *Selected Literary Essays*, 287.

181. Ibid., 288.

182. Ibid., 289.

183. Ibid.

184. Ibid. Quoting from Trollope, *An Autobiography*, vol. 1, 57–58.

and have been able to lay my own identity aside."[185] To this Lewis makes the following judgment, that "Where a work of art originated in a self-regarding reverie, it becomes art by ceasing to be what it was."[186] Then Lewis points out, "It is hard to imagine a more radical change than the disappearance of the self who was by hypothesis, the *raison d'être* of the original dream." He continues, "The very root from which the dream grew is severed and the dream planted in a new soil; it is killed as fantasy [wish-fulfillment] before it is raised as art."[187]

Lewis distinguishes these two types of imagination further. The first, which I have called fantasy, he also calls "free," claiming that its active characteristics are those of a free imagination which produces literature that "may be roughly called the fantastic, or mythical or improbable type of literature."[188] He adds that it "passes from the status of dream to that of art by a process which may legitimately be called 'elaboration': "incoherencies are tidied up, banalities removed, private values and associations replaced, proportion, relief, and temperance are introduced."[189] The other type of imaginative activity Lewis calls 'servile.' Its characteristics are wish-fulfillment, gratification and realism.[190] The kind of wishes our imaginations create, either wish-fulfillment as he has described it, or fantasy, can begin to reveal which direction one might be travelling on the road into and out of Jerusalem. The wish-fulfillment type leads deeper into self and farther from Jerusalem. The fantasy type takes one out of self and opens him up to worlds and insights beyond mere provincialism. In addition to these two directional possibilities, he adds elsewhere that these "are two kinds of longing. The one is an *askesis*, a spiritual exercise, the other is a disease."[191]

Lewis also disagrees with Freud's use of symbols as a means to literary critical analysis. Freud believed that there were archetypal symbols, "words, so to speak, of a universal image-language."[192] Lewis notes several of these symbols as used by Freud: "A *House* signifies the human

---

185. C. S. Lewis, *Selected Literary Essays*, 289.

186. Ibid., 290.

187. Ibid.

188. Ibid.

189. Ibid.

190. Ibid.

191. C. S. Lewis, *Of Other Worlds*, 30.

192. C. S. Lewis, *Selected Literary Essays*, 291.

body; *Kings and Queens*, fathers and mothers; *Journeys*, death; *small animals* one's brothers and sisters; *Fruit, Landscapes, Gardens, Blossoms*, the female body or various parts of it."[193] Lewis has no interest in this at all. It is not because he thinks these images are false. He allows that they might have significance for the professional psychologist, but they have "no literary bearing."[194] These symbols, so interpreted and so universalized, are destined to obscure the text from the view of the literary critic who uses them. The method makes all texts opaque. The symbols have decided the outcome of the literary investigation before the critic has set out to do his work. Of this Lewis observes that:

> It is certainly this, and this alone, which brings psycho-analytic symbolism into contact with literary values. It is in this that the sting lies. We do not mind being told that when we enjoy Milton's description of Eden some latent sexual interest is, as a matter of fact, and along with a thousand other things, present in our unconscious. Our quarrel is with the man who says 'You know why you're *really* enjoying this?' or 'Of course you realize what's behind this?' or 'It *all* comes from so-and-so.' What we resent, in fact, is not so much the suggestion that we are interested in the female body as the suggestion that we have no interest in gardens: not what the wiseacre would force upon us, but what he threatens to take away.[195]

The problem of subjectivism resurfaces again in a new form. New walls have been built, leaving literary judgments trapped behind them. And now, compounding the situation, blindness sets in behind these opaque symbols. The critic only gropes along the road to Jerusalem. He can no longer consider which way he might be going or whether there is even a road on which to travel. In this regard, psychological theories become a hindrance to any kind of literary criticism truly interested in grasping a particular text.

There is another way, according to Lewis, that we ought to consider psychological issues when we engage in literary criticism. This is the tendency for the pathology of the critic to negatively affect his ability to do his work. In *Studies in Words*, Lewis observes that his is an age where words have lost their meaning. He calls the process of a word

193. Ibid., 291.
194. Ibid., 292.
195. Ibid., 293.

moving from a term of description to that of evaluation, "verbicide, the murder of a word,"[196] and writes:

> The greatest cause of verbicide is the fact that most people are obviously far more anxious to express their approval and disapproval of things than to describe them. Hence the tendency of words to become less descriptive and more evaluative—useless synonyms for *good* or *bad*. . . . If modern critical usage seems to be initiating a process which might finally make *adolescent* and *contemporary* mere synonyms for *bad* and *good*—and stranger things have happened—we should banish them from our vocabulary.[197]

It is not difficult to find examples of literary or film criticism in the popular press that use descriptive terms in the way described above. The criticism teaches nothing about the book or film in question. Lewis writes, "Indeed we cannot even think about the book under discussion. The critic rivets our attention on himself."[198] We know all of the critic's likes and dislikes. We have become familiar with the things that disturb him; whether they are features of the book or film we could not say, for the article has not taught us enough about the piece to make a judgment. We are curious to know if the critic knows any more about the book or film than we do. Lewis reminds his readers, "The function of criticism, however, is 'to get ourselves out of the way and let humanity decide;' not to discharge our hatred but to expose the grounds for it; not to vilify faults but to diagnose and exhibit them."[199] "Verbicide" occurs by making *contemporary* a term of praise. In what way is something, merely by being up to date, worthy of praise? The word *adolescent* is not a synonym for bad, yet some critics might use it for one. That which is considered adolescent may be perfectly acceptable and expected of a teenager. The word *adult* does not automatically connote a thing's

196. C. S. Lewis, *Studies in Words*, 7.

197. Ibid., 7–8. In *Four Loves*, Lewis notes that "The human mind is generally more eager to praise and dispraise than to describe and define" (*Four Loves*, 21). He continues, "it wants to make every distinction a distinction of value; hence those fatal critics who can never point out the differing quality of two poets without putting them in an order of preference as if they were candidates for a prize" (*Four Loves*, 21).

198. C. S. Lewis, *Studies in Words*, 330.

199. Ibid., 326.

respectability. But when a word is used to judge something without an explanation or reason, it is difficult to take the criticism seriously.[200]

Weaver was certainly aware of Lewis's discussion about "verbicide." He had written a review of *Studies in Words*, the work in which Lewis develops the concept. Weaver goes further than Lewis, however, noting that these terms when they develop significance beyond proportion to any reality supporting them, can affect entire cultures and not merely individuals. Weaver calls these words "god terms" when used to speak of that valued by a culture, whether there is a reality to support the claim or not; he calls them "devil terms" when used to vilify and marginalize. By Weaver's valuation, these terms reflect the pathologies of a culture and extend the evil that is done by unchecked subjectivism.[201]

Lewis warns of the acrimony of some critics, "which produces heat instead of light."[202] In these cases, he recognizes that psychology may have its value for the critic, but

> The strength of our dislike is itself a probable symptom that all is not well within; that some raw place in our psychology has been touched, or else that some personal or partisan motive is secretly at work. If we were simply exercising judgement we should be calmer; less anxious to speak. And if we do speak, we shall almost certainly make fools of ourselves.[203]

---

200. In a humorous passage in "On Three Ways of Writing for Children," appearing in *Of Other Worlds*, Lewis wonders why that which reveals maturation *per se* should be seen as a sign of praise. If childlike and adolescent is seen as negative, simply because these lack the maturity of adulthood, Lewis wonders, "Why should we stop at the adult? Why should not *senile* be equally a term of approval? Why are we not to be congratulated on losing our teeth and hair" (*Of Other Worlds*, 26).

201. Weaver, *Ethics*, 212–29. Weaver's "god terms" include: Progress (212), Fact (213), Science (215), Modern (217) (this is a term that may date Weaver, and could be substituted by the term "Post-modern," which is a "god term" in some quarters and a "devil term" in others), Efficient (217), and—since he was writing for an American audience—American (218). "God terms" do not have to be explained; mere reference to them produces a reverent response from an audience. Weaver's "devil terms" include: Un-American (222), Prejudice (222); others might be added such as Racist, Homophobic, and Anti-abortionist. The characteristic of both kinds of terms is that they produce an emotional response in an audience, without respect for any kind of reality that may or may not support them. These terms are tools of subjectivism and they, with others like them, can cloak any amount of evil.

202. C. S. Lewis, *Experiment in Criticism*, 112.

203. C. S. Lewis, *Studies in Words*, 331.

At this point Lewis advises the would-be critic that if the desire to condemn is especially strong in him, he would be wise to refrain from comment altogether. "The very desire is a danger signal."[204]

Lewis recognizes these tendencies to subjectify. He also believes that human-kind is affected by the ways of pride, self-centeredness, disobedience to God, and the failure to love others properly. Some subjectivity may be a consequence of misjudgment; for instance, one may have lacked a sufficient grasp of the necessary facts to make a proper judgment. One may neglect a point, here or there, necessary for putting all the pieces of the puzzle in place and getting the picture clear and complete. It may be that subjectivism is a consequence of our immaturity. Perhaps developmentally one may not have arrived at that stature where one sees things with the proper age appropriateness. In these ways, a degree of subjectivity does not necessarily signal a moral deficiency: when an error is pointed out and one persists in it, it is another matter; when the deliberate choice is made not to see a thing as it is for fear of what changes one might have to make, the drift into the realm of moral compromise becomes more likely; when circumstances are manipulated and controlled in order to insure that a point of view is accepted and adopted as the platform for one's party, the risks grow graver; and when one seeks only to read books that support a personally held position, or keep as friends those who never challenge judgments, and automatically reject those who do, the risks remain. Lewis acknowledges throughout his work, particularly in his literary criticism, that, "To love and admire anything outside yourself is to take one step away from utter spiritual ruin; though we shall not be well so long as we love and admire anything more than we love and admire God."[205] The road into Jerusalem may also be the road out. Lewis recognizes that literature itself may escort the pilgrim in either direction. In Lewis's critical theory, the way into Jerusalem is the way of the objectivist, the road out, the subjectivist.

---

204. Ibid., 331. He noted, "If we are not careful, criticism may become a mere excuse for taking revenge on books whose smell we dislike by erecting our temperamental antipathies into pseudo-moral judgements" (*Christian Reflections*, 31).

205. C. S. Lewis, *Mere Christianity*, 113.

# Further Considerations

While Lewis is very much concerned to address rhetorically the abuses of subjectivism as these occur in literary criticism, he also makes some positive claims in relationship to literature and "real life." In *An Experiment in Criticism*, Lewis writes that literature can never be like real life. Tragedy in real life will be far more complex than a tragedy in literature or drama can make it. Lewis observes, rightly I think, "If tragedy is taken as a comment on life in the sense that we are meant to conclude from it 'This is the typical or usual, or ultimate, form of human misery,' then tragedy becomes wishful moonshine."[206] Lewis writes:

> The tragedian dare not present the totality of suffering as it usually is He selects from reality just what his art needs; and what it needs is the exceptional. Conversely, to approach someone in real sorrow with these ideas about tragic grandeur, to insinuate that he is now assuming that 'sceptred pall,' would be worse than imbecile: it would be odious.[207]

This is not the same Lewis who wrote *The Problem of Pain*, his horizons have broadened to include greater complexities. Nevertheless he also writes in this same book that he believes, for the literary, "Scenes and characters from books provide them with a sort of iconography by which they interpret or sum up their own experience."[208] In other words, literature assists in understanding "real life" or life as it is really lived. How can this be so? Does this contradict Lewis's other assertions?

To resolve the problem, it might help to look briefly at some of the authors of whom Lewis attributed the capacity to portray something approximating real life. Lewis includes in that description Dante, Shakespeare, Jane Austen and William Morris.[209] Each of these writers approximates real life differently, and yet something similar can be observed in all four. In Dante, Lewis discovered real life in his power to construct many different types of similes[210] and to use different kinds

206. C. S. Lewis, *Experiment in Criticism*, 77.

207. Ibid., 78–79.

208. Ibid., 3.

209. C. S. Lewis, *Selected Literary Essays*, chapters 6, 13 and 16. C. S. Lewis, *Renaissance Literature*, chapters 4 and 5.

210. C. S. Lewis, *Renaissance Literature*, 64–77.

of images[211] so that his portrayals were not bound by a single vision. Shakespeare's capacity is evident in what Lewis calls "variation." He writes: "He wants to see the object from a dozen different angles."[212] In Jane Austen it can be found in her ability to write of "Undeception," that is, the awakening of her heroines from false notions about themselves and about life.[213] Lewis observes this as the turning points in her novels, which she develops in different ways in each one. Finally, in Morris Lewis appreciates the power to generalize on the one hand,[214] and the care he takes not to particularize his imagery on the other.[215] Because Morris tends to universalize his artistic vision of life, he appears, at first glance, to go against the grain of a pattern clearly recognizable in the first three authors mentioned, that pattern of trying to gain perspective beyond one's initial grasp. But Lewis brings Morris into the fold by mentioning: "In Morris there are no conclusions. Balance is attained and immediately lost; everything is always beginning over again: it is a dance not a diagram. It can no more be seized in an epigram, summed up and docketed, than experience itself."[216] The ability of Dante, Shakespeare and Austen to approximate "real life" in their literature is found in their power to look at particular aspects of life through a variety of perspectives. Shakespeare does this through variation, Dante by means of multiplied images, none permanent but each widening the perspective. Austen looks at a particular character through her heroine's fallible eyes until the readers sees that she has gotten it all wrong, for there is more there than was first seen. Morris, though a generalizer, does not allow the generalizations to last for long, and in this way he too gives a vision that approximates reality as it is truly lived. In this way, literature provides a way out of self: it allows the reader an opportunity to break out of a self-centered approach to life, seeing things as they are rather than how one would make or force them to be. When Lewis sees literature extending an individual's vision of life through variation, he is not making a statement about the problem of evil specifically, but he is

211. Ibid., 78–93.
212. Ibid., 75.
213. Ibid., 175–79.
214. Ibid., 220.
215. C. S. Lewis, *Selected Literary Essays*, 221.
216. Ibid., 229.

trying to prevent that subjectivism that can lead to evil, and will likely cause pain if unchecked.

Lewis writes in the *Epilogue* to *An Experiment in Criticism* that he wants an enlargement of himself. He wishes he could see with other eyes. He even wishes that the brutes could write books; he longs to know how the world might present itself to the eye of a mouse or a bee, and to hear how it is perceived by the olfactory sense of a dog. He says, "Reality even seen through the eyes of many is not enough. I will see what others have invented."[217] He sees fiction as a means of extending an appreciation for real life, in both its poverty and richness, as well as its complexity and depth

## Conclusion

Cultures must respond to things as they are. In other words, cultures require a sense of objective value. This is true in literature because it is true to the *Tao*, or the very way of the world. Weaver writes, "Cultures do respond to differences in what nature has provided, such as the sea, or a kind of terrain, or a hot or cold climate, these having the power to initiate imaginative reactions."[218] Thought and word are both elevated by objective value; to speak what is, as best it is known, widens one's vision of the world. Language shapes culture, for description is selective, both exhibiting and limiting what can be known and understood. Weaver writes that 'cultures reflect different regions and varying kinds of historical endowment.'[219] In this regard, however, objectivity, even as it surrenders to things as they are, does not become altogether passive. It is possible for a culture to change its physical environment. Weaver says, "the collective consciousness of the group creates a mode of looking at the world or arrives at some imaginative visual bearing. It 'sees' the world metaphorically according to some felt need of the group, and thus entails an ordering which denotes dissatisfaction with 'things as they are.'"[220] Thus, the ordering of a culture (even when it seeks to change its environment) is a response to objects. So too, dissatisfaction is a response to objects, but it is fed by further objective considerations

217. C. S. Lewis, *Experiment in Criticism*, 140.

218. Weaver, *Visions of Order*, 10.

219. Ibid., 10–11.

220. Ibid., 10.

such as the felt needs of the culture which drive its dissatisfactions; this also is objective. If culture develops out of a response to the environment, i.e., objective reality, thus developing its morality from objective value, then the culture that begins to move towards subjectivism is a culture at risk of destroying itself.

What I have been arguing in this chapter is that Lewis sees in literature and in literary criticism either an opportunity to develop objectivity and perspective, or to withdraw into subjectivism. The critic moves towards a subjectivist position when he moves away from the text and engages in criticism of some imagined text of his own making. Lewis speaks out against several such abuses of this sort. Subjectivism and its false notions, unchecked, can lead to evil. Subjectivism removes from a culture its liberty to grow. Lewis's rhetoric is passionate, for he wills that people experience better. He employs every means to make his point. Fiction may be the best tool in his chest. The reason why he chooses fiction to make his case against subjectivism is the subject of my next chapter.

# 4

## The Rhetorical Aim of Lewis's Fiction
## in Light of a Problem of Evil

## Introduction

IN THIS CHAPTER I ARGUE THAT C. S. LEWIS USES FICTION AS A PRI-
mary means to address the problem of evil as exhibited in subjectivism. Contrary to the view that Lewis's fiction is merely a retreat from
failed efforts as an apologist (a position held by Humphrey Carpenter
in *The Inklings*, Lewis's friend George Sayer in his biography *Jack*, and
A. N. Wilson in *C. S. Lewis: A Biography*),[1] I will show that Lewis recognizes the significance of using fiction as a literary form of rhetoric,
one that serves a pervasive purpose which apologetic discourse cannot.
Many scholars have come to believe that Lewis lost his ability to speak
or write in a way that reflected philosophical sophistication; in other
words, he became woefully behind the times and out of step with the
current philosophical discussion of his day. It appears, however, that
other explanations better account for the complexities surrounding
his use of fiction throughout his life, particularly during his last fifteen
years. I will consider Lewis's own claim that the 'imaginative man' in
him is older and more continually operative throughout his life. Clearly,
Lewis acknowledges in his autobiography what he describes as a rift
between his reason and his imagination—at least the part of his imagination fed by romantic longing, which defines much of his literary interests. Nevertheless, his conversion to Christianity goes far to repair
the apparent contradictions, and much of his interest in using fiction

---

1. Carpenter, *Inklings*, 216–17; Sayer, *Jack*, 186–87; Wilson, *Biography*, 211, 213,
214–15, 218, 220, 225. More details below in footnote 4.

serves as a means to address the evil he fears is latent in subjectivism. Furthermore, I will provide background which suggests that Lewis chooses the mode in order to describe most effectively suprasensibles—intangibles beyond empirical demonstration—making it possible to address concerns about the potentially corrosive effects of subjectivism. Lewis also observes that narrative enables him to "smuggle theology" into the minds of the unsuspecting. However, this inclination raises an important question yet to be considered by Lewis scholars: Did Lewis violate convictions he espouses in *The Abolition of Man* when he chides the authors of an English grammar text for using their book to smuggle pseudo-philosophy into the minds of unsuspecting students? I will assert that Lewis has rhetorical designs that justify his actions. Finally, I will make some concluding observations supporting the argument that narrative is the supreme method Lewis employs to address that aspect of the problem of evil encountered in subjectivism.

## Lewis's Reasons for Writing Fiction

The discovery of meaning is an imaginative endeavor. Lewis knew this, and therefore used fiction as a way to persuade his readers to consider the questions of evil in a fresh light. He saw that evil, as well as the subjectivism that supported it, provided the exigence for a rhetorical situation. An audience may, or may not, be responsive to a mere discursive attempt to address the problem of evil. There may be obstacles to the reader's reception of the Christian resolution to the problem. Therefore, Lewis used fiction to eliminate the barriers keeping his audience from faith. Lewis believed that it was possible to make some sense of evil, suffering, and death, but that transcendent purposes lying behind these things may not always be so clear. Infinite and eternal intentions, if they exist, are likely to be misunderstood from the perspective of space and time. While propositions and dialectical discussions, in general, may be helpful in sharpening an understanding of what can be known, when it comes to the meaning and significance of evil and suffering, perhaps understanding will best be extended imaginatively. An attributive interpretation of the facts of evil and suffering would deem them incompatible with God's goodness and omnipotence. Nevertheless, the facts themselves do not necessarily denote this incompatibility.

Furthermore, feelings of pity or anger and indignation can affect how one interprets facts. But what authority do these feelings have in themselves? Lewis writes,

> If I regard this pity and indignation simply as subjective experiences of my own with no validity beyond their strength at the moment (which next moment will change), I can hardly use them as standards whereby to arraign the creation. On the contrary, they become strong arguments against God just in so far as I take them to be transcendent illumination to which creation must conform or be condemned. They are arguments against God only if they are themselves the voice of God. The more Shelleyan, the more Promethean my revolt, the more surely it claims divine sanction.[2]

Feelings come and go. They may be congruous to the circumstances of one's life, but can they be trusted hermeneutically? Lewis writes, "No. Not in so far as we feel these things, but in so far as we claim to be right in feeling them;" in other words, there must be something objective that allows for the judgment that these feelings are right, or good, or true. "In so far as we are sure that these standards have an empire *de jure* over all possible worlds, so far, and so far only, do they become grounds for disbelief—and at the same moment, for belief."[3] Despite this avowal, Lewis clearly believed that the emotional constraint to belief needed to be addressed. This is exactly what he does in his fiction.

Does the fact of suffering disallow the existence of God, or at least of the Christian God, who is both good and omnipotent? Is such a conclusion the only one that might be drawn from the existence of suffering in the world? Could other possibilities be considered, and if so, what would they look like? These are questions Lewis addresses in his fiction. Because Lewis himself wrestled so strongly with the problem of evil, it stands to reason that his fiction reflects his concerns. If his fiction plays a significant role in his approach to evil, in what way is it helpful?

Lewis does not merely write fiction simply to resolve thorny issues surrounding the problem of evil; even so, matters related to the problem of evil do keep coming into his books, indicating that such concerns were on his mind. Before examining Lewis's use of fiction,

2. C. S. Lewis, *God in the Dock*, 171.
3. Ibid., 171.

I will counter the argument that Lewis retreats into the realm of non-discursive language to compensate for his failed apologetics.

## Lewis's Fiction Was Not a Retreat

Some have suggested that Lewis turned to fiction only after an embarrassing encounter in a debate with the philosopher Elizabeth Anscombe at the Oxford Socratic Club, February 2nd, 1948.[4] Those who claim this say that Lewis lost the debate because he lacked sufficient philosophical depth, relative to contemporary discussions in philosophy, and could no longer be taken seriously as a Christian Apologist. His methods were limited and archaic, critics assert. Furthermore, some have suggested that Lewis's interest in fiction following this debate signaled a kind of retreat to ground where arguments could be neither pressed nor challenged. In point of fact, the evidence suggests that the Anscombe debate had a lesser effect on Lewis's work as an apologist than has been supposed. He actually published no fewer than thirty-four essays in Christian apologetics after the debate,[5] and Anscombe herself played

4. In his biography of Lewis, George Sayer observes that "the debate had been a humiliating experience, but perhaps it was ultimately good for him. In the past he had been far too proud of his logical ability. Now, he was humbled." Later, Sayer reports, "'I can never write another book of that sort,' he said to me of *Miracles*. And he never did" (Sayer, *Jack*, 187). Humphrey Carpenter writes, "Lewis had learnt his lesson: for after this he wrote no further books of Christian Apologetics for ten years." The apologetic book Carpenter has in mind is *Reflections on the Psalms*: "It was notably quieter in tone and did not attempt any further intellectual proofs of theism or Christianity" (Carpenter, *Inklings*, 217). A. N. Wilson, in his biography of Lewis, intimates no less than five times that it was the Anscombe debate that brought an end to Lewis's life as an apologist. See Wilson, *Biography*, 214–15, 218, 220, 225, 236.

5. The book *The World's Last Night*, a collection of published essays that Lewis himself gathered from various periodicals, was published in 1960. Every essay in the book (seven in all) was written after the Anscombe debate. Here is a book of Christian Apologetics, intentionally made available by Lewis, discrediting the suggestion that the debate signaled the end of his apologetic endeavors. Two books of essays in apologetics were gathered and edited by Walter Hooper after Lewis's death. A survey of the dates when the individual essays were published is also revealing. In *God in the Dock*, twenty-nine of the essays were published before the debate, while twenty of the essays were published after. The title essay published in *God in the Dock*, written shortly after the debate, was originally titled, *Difficulties in Presenting the Christian Faith to Modern Unbelievers*, and first appeared in *Lumen Vitae* 3 (September, 1948) 421–26. In this essay, Lewis is instructing others on the fine points of engaging in apologetic work with unbelievers. It is hardly the kind of thing one would expect from someone devastated in debate and questioning his suitability as an apologist. In *Christian Reflections*, four-

down the hyperbole which has attached itself to this single evening at the Socratic Club.[6] While it may indicate that a falsehood repeated enough times may be mistaken for a fact, the Anscombe debate could hardly be grounds for proving that Lewis's interest in fiction was increased by his failure as an apologist. If this is so, then what might his reasons have been for writing fiction?

---

teen essays are included; of these, seven were originally published after the Anscombe debate. All told, from these three collections, thirty-six of the essays were written before the Anscombe debate and thirty-four after. Nearly fifty percent of the essays Lewis wrote in Christian Apologetics came after 2 February 1948.

6. Anscombe, *Collected Papers*, 2:ix–x. Also see chapter 21, "A Reply to Mr. C. S. Lewis's Argument that 'Naturalism' is Self-Refuting," where the paper Anscombe presented to the Socratic Club is reproduced. It is not the intent of this study to develop the intricacies of the Anscombe-Lewis debate; I am simply concerned to argue that whatever the content of the debate or Lewis's response to Anscombe, there is not sufficient grounds to claim that the debate signaled either the end of Lewis's apologetic work, or a retreat to fiction. Even so, a brief summary of the issues involved might be helpful for the reader. Lewis writes in the first edition of *Miracles*, "We may in fact state it as a rule that *no thought is valid if it can be fully explained as the result of irrational causes*" (C. S. Lewis, *Miracles*, 27). Anscombe, a Christian, also had her doubts about the Naturalist's assumptions; nevertheless, she questioned the strength of Lewis's argument at this point. She summarizes her own position, "I do not think that there is sufficiently good reason for maintaining the 'Naturalist' hypothesis about human behaviour and thought. But someone who does maintain it cannot be refuted as you [Lewis] try to refute him, by saying it is inconsistent to maintain it and to believe that human reasoning is valid and that human reasoning sometimes produces human opinion" (Anscombe, *Collected Papers*, 2:231). Lewis concedes the point, and later writes in response to Anscombe, "I admit that *valid* was a bad word for what I meant; *veridical* (or *verific* or *veriferous*) would have been better" (Anscombe, *Collected Papers*, 2:231). Lewis made adjustments to the chapter thirteen years later in the second edition published in 1960 as a Fontana Paperback. The delay hardly supports the idea that Lewis was deeply concerned about the matter. Also, the fact that he worked on a later edition of *Miracles* does not support the idea that he thought his contribution to Christian apologetics was complete. Anscombe indicates that she was not fully satisfied with the changes, but she believed them an improvement over his earlier edition and thought they were signs of Lewis's "honesty and seriousness" (Anscombe, *Collected Papers*, x). For a fair treatment of the matter, attention should be given to Christopher Mitchell's article on the Anscombe-Lewis debate in *Seven: An Anglo-American Literary Review*, vol. 14, 1997. It is also useful to note that after the debate with Anscombe, Lewis stayed on as President of the Socratic Club for several years, until he accepted his position at Cambridge University.

### Finding Concord Between Reason and Romance

Lewis published *The Pilgrim's Regress* in 1933. It was his first book to come to print after his conversion to Christianity. The book was subtitled *An Allegorical Apology for Christianity Reason and Romance.* As the subtitle indicates, he believed early on that fiction could be a vehicle for work in apologetics and in clarifying the claims of the Christian faith. In Lewis's critical work on Charles Williams's Arthurian poetry, he mentions that the "first problem of life" is the reconciliation of intellect, or reason, with poetry, or romance.[7] This "first problem" was a lifelong concern for Lewis. It is also a difficulty when considering the problem of evil and suffering, since the issue is made more complex by the fact that it is both something one seeks to understand and something one feels. Mere intellectual attempts at attaining the reconciliation of reason with romance do not prove satisfactory when one is under the weight of suffering. The complaint of the sufferer, as valid as those complaints might be, is often so clouded by feeling that reasoned attempts to understand evil and suffering seem trivial and offensive. Sometimes it is wisest to "weep with those who weep." As problems related to understanding persist and apologists must continue to attempt understanding, Christians must make a space for the contribution of fiction to the discussion. To the degree that it can provide some kind of *supposal* satisfying for the intellect, as well as some glimpse of meaning and significance for the heart, its contribution can be helpful.

---

7. C. S. Lewis, *Arthurian Torso*. In the course of this work, Lewis turns his attention to Williams's poem, *The Coming of Galahad*. To explain the poem, Lewis draws on Book V of Wordsworth's *Prelude*. There, Wordsworth tells of meeting, in a dream, a Bedouin who is carrying a stone and a shell: "the stone was 'Euclid's elements' and the shell was something of more worth: a shell full of prophetic sound. The Bedouin, in fact, is carrying Intellect and Poetry" (Wordsworth, *Prelude*, 167). In Williams's poem, Lewis suggests that Williams is attempting to fit the stone in the shell. It could be suggested that throughout his life, Lewis himself was engaged in this endeavor. The reconciliation of Intellect, or reason, with poetry, or romance, is of paramount importance to him. This is also true in attempting to understand issues related to the problem of evil. Suffice it to say that in wrestling with the problem of evil Lewis sought to develop an approach that was both reasoned and romantic.

## MEDITATION IN A TOOL SHED

In *Meditation in a Tool Shed*,[8] Lewis writes about an experience he once had while entering his tool shed. At first he describes noticing a beam of sunlight shining through a crack in the roof. As he looks at the beam, he becomes aware of little dust particles floating about, illumined by a bright ray from the sun. After a moment, he re-positions himself so that he is actually standing in the beam; looking up along the beam, his entire perspective changes. In that brightness, the rest of the tool shed seems to disappear. Looking along and through the beam, he sees the blinding light of the sun some ninety-three million miles away. Lewis is marked by this experience and sees from it that there are at least two ways to look at any experience: one, to stand as an outsider and examine it, the other, to stand inside the experience and "look along." This essay brings to mind the passage in his autobiography where he recalls reading Samuel Alexander's *Space, Time and Deity*.[9] It is Alexander who provides Lewis with the vocabulary to sort out the differences between these two ways of seeing. Borrowing from Alexander, Lewis uses the words *contemplation* and *enjoyment*. To see a thing as an object is to look at it or to *contemplate* it. To have the experience of looking along is no longer to *contemplate*, but to *enjoy*. Lewis writes, "I accepted this distinction at once and have ever regarded it as an indispensable tool of thought."[10] One's attempts to understand anything more thoroughly, especially the problem of evil, will be enhanced by one's effort to look both *at* as well as *along*. Lewis was given to this kind of approach early in his academic career. Therefore, the use of story as a means of exploration and understanding can be understood, not as a place of retreat for the defeated apologist, but as part of the entire schema of his design as an author.

8. C. S. Lewis, *God in the Dock*, 240–44.

9. C. S. Lewis, *Surprised By Joy*, 212–18. Further details concerning the impression Alexander's work left on the young Lewis can be found in his published journal *All My Road Before Me*. Lewis mentions that he actually started reading Alexander on Saturday, March 8, 1924 (*All My Road Before Me*, 301). On Wednesday, May 12, 1926, Lewis reports that while teaching a class at Lady Margaret Hall, he was explaining Alexander's concepts of *Enjoyment* and *Contemplation* (*All My Road Before Me*, 394). On Sunday, May 30, 1926, Lewis recalls that he went to Hertford College to hear Alexander lecture (*All My Road Before Me*, 403–4).

10. C. S. Lewis, *Surprised By Joy*, 218.

Before his conversion, Lewis used poetry as a way to wrestle with issues related to the problem of evil.[11] As an atheist, he was little concerned either to prove the existence of God or justify his acts in the world. Still, he believed that the language of fiction and poetry was useful for addressing matters related to the problem of evil and suffering.[12] Furthermore, shortly before his conversion, he continued to use poetry as a means to solve that "first problem of life." In a poem entitled *Reason*,[13] Lewis writes of the conflict within him, the struggle between reason ("the maid") and imagination ("the mother"). By these classifications, Lewis appears to propose a hierarchy in which the maid serves the mother. The imaginative side of Lewis is the dominant side. It is not imagination at the expense of reason, but reason as the servant of the imagination:

> Oh who will reconcile in me both maid and mother,
> Who will make a concord of depth and height?
> Who make imaginations dim exploring touch
> Ever report the same as intellectual sight?
> Then I could truly say, and not deceive,
> Then wholly say, that I BELIEVE.[14]

One may doubt that such a hierarchy between reason and imagination actually exists; nevertheless, Lewis is right in believing that it is necessary that these two be in some kind of concord if meaning and under-

11. Lewis, in a letter to his friend Arthur Greeves, describes the theme of his first book of poetry, *Spirits in Bondage*, that it "is mainly strung around the idea that I mentioned to you before that nature is wholly diabolical and malevolent and that God, if he exists, is outside of and in opposition to the cosmic arrangements" (C. S. Lewis, *They Stand Together*, 230).

12. C. S. Lewis, *Narrative Poems. Dymer* was originally published in 1926. Dymer, the main character of the poem, contemplates difficult circumstances facing him and says of the gods,
. . . and I suppose
They, they up there, the old contriving powers,
They knew it all the time – for someone knows
And waits and watches till we pluck the flowers,
Then Leaps. (Canto V, 48)
And later in the same poem, Lewis writes,
A man must crouch to face
Infinite malice. . . . (Canto V, 14, 49)

13. C. S. Lewis, *Poems*, 95.

14. Ibid.

standing are to grow. (This idea will be further developed throughout this chapter.) It is also clear from this poem that he believes faith to be supported by the contributions that imagination can make to understanding. Suffice it to say, here, that Lewis's interest in fiction has nothing to do with the Anscombe debate or any other disappointments. It is, for him, no place of retreat. In a letter from 1955, he writes,

> The imaginative man in me is older, more continuously operative, and in that sense, more basic than either the religious writer or the critic. It was he who made me first attempt (with little success) to be a poet. It was he who, in response to the poetry of others, made me a critic, and in defence of that response, sometimes a critical controversialist. It was he who after my conversion led me to embody my religious belief in symbolical or mythopeic forms, ranging from *Screwtape* to a kind of theologised science fiction. And it was of course he who has brought me, in the last few years to write the series of Narnian stories for children. . . .[15]

## At Times Fiction Is the Rhetorician's Best Tool

Lewis sees other important virtues in the use of fiction to accomplish his rhetorical purposes surrounding the problem of evil. He distinguishes two impulses of the imaginative writer. One is the author's impulse to please, what rhetoricians call *delectare*. The other is what he calls the man's impulse to instruct, which the rhetoricians call *docere*.[16] The imaginative vision delighted him, and he felt compelled to describe it in such a way that others might also *see* and take delight.[17] His description of it will have a specific form. As he writes, "It is easy to forget that the man who writes a good love sonnet needs not only to be enamoured of a woman, but also to be enamoured of the sonnet."[18] Lewis noticed that

15. C. S. Lewis, *Letters of C. S. Lewis*, 260. Lewis is also free to acknowledge, "People often express their deepest thought, speculations, desires, etc. in a story" (*Letters of C. S. Lewis*, 261). And to a young girl, he writes, "I enjoy writing fiction more than anything else, wouldn't anyone?" (C. S. Lewis, *Letters to Children*, 95).

16. C. S. Lewis, *Of Other Worlds*, 35.

17. Lewis writes, "There are usually two reasons for writing an imaginative work, which may be called the author's reason and the man's. If only one of these is present, then, so far as I'm concerned, the book will not be written. If the first is lacking, it can't; if the second is lacking it shouldn't" (*Of Other Worlds*, 35).

18. C. S. Lewis, *Preface to Paradise Lost*, 3.

his own stories, particularly his fantasies, began with pictures or images. Soon, "These images sorted themselves into events (i.e., became a story)."[19] These events, which constitute the story, sent the author looking for a form.

Lewis recognizes that form is intrinsic to what the author wants to say and how he will say it, just "as the hardness of the stone pleases the sculptor or the difficulty of the sonnet delights the sonneteer."[20] The form acts as a kind of vehicle delivering what the author sees or imagines in such a way that the reader might see and also take delight. But Lewis believes certain inhibitions can stand sentry over the heart, like a dragon that refuses to let anything pass. Even so, it is not unusual to observe that a story told in a book or movie can produce laughter or tears, anticipation or suspense, delight or fear, because the observer has surrendered to the power of the narrative itself. The reader's own judgments, for good or for ill, are at rest. The concern to judge or condemn or even to praise is dormant. For the moment, the story holds sway; it is a subtle form of rhetoric. The reader has stepped into the beam and is looking along. Lewis notes this process in his own life when he writes of fantasy,

> I thought I saw how stories of this kind could steal past a certain inhibition which had paralysed much of my own religion in childhood. Why did one feel it so hard to feel as one was told one ought to feel about God or the sufferings of Christ? I thought the chief reason was that one was told one ought to. An obligation to feel can freeze feelings, and reverence itself did harm. The whole subject was associated with lowered voices; almost as if it were something medical. But supposing that by casting all these things into an imaginary world, stripping them of their stained glass and Sunday school associations, one could make them for the first time appear in their real potency? Could one not thus steal past those watchful dragons? I thought one could.[21]

19. C. S. Lewis, *Of Other Worlds*, 36.

20. Ibid., 37.

21. Ibid. Lewis recalls in his autobiography that such processes were, in fact, operant in his own life before his conversion. He writes, "I came far nearer to feeling this [joy, reverence, delight] about Norse gods whom I disbelieved in than I had ever done about the true God while I believed. Sometimes I can almost think that I was sent back to the false gods there to acquire some capacity for worship against the day when the true God should recall me to himself" (*Surprised By Joy*, 77).

If the subjectivist has projected his ideas onto his world, he is unlikely to receive messages from that world which may check his self-centeredness. Here, the persuasive power of fictional rhetoric is able to do what discursive language cannot. When the subjectivist comes to a work of fiction, it may be that he is less threatened and, with his guard down, may surrender to the story itself and thus receive a message from "outside." Furthermore, through fiction Lewis could cast some of his characters as subjectivists, revealing consequences which might result from such a point of view. In this way, fiction appeals directly to the senses and indirectly to the emotions.

By reading mythologies in his youth, Lewis developed a desire for divine things (at least the divine things of the mythical world). Such literature whet his appetite for a kind of truth beyond mere reason. The stories appealed to his senses, providing him with an experience that taught him reverence. According to Lewis, good fiction awakens in the reader a desire for other worlds.[22] One can break out of the limits of his own particularities and see farther than he has seen before. The formulas and systems of philosophers and theologians, as helpful as they may be, are never enough in themselves to convey fully the complexity and significance of the world in which one lives. Of course, the stories cannot reveal anything like a full picture either. Nevertheless, none expects such things from fiction; whereas often one may be deceived to think that the most recent philosophical or scientific explanation resolves once and for all some thorny question. Fiction makes no such pretense, but as an imaginative exercise it may open one's eyes to possibilities yet to be explored. The Psalmist's words have the ring of truth about them when he directs his readers to "taste and see that the Lord is good."[23] Fiction provides a mode of interaction akin to tasting and seeing, and thus was useful to Lewis as a means of looking at the problem of evil.

---

22. Lewis also observes, "To construct plausible and moving 'other worlds' you must draw on the only real 'other world' we know, that of the spirit" (*Of Other Worlds*, 12). (see also, C. S. Lewis, ed., *Essays Presented to Charles Williams*, 98.). Tolkien notes that "fantasy, the making or glimpsing of Other-worlds, was the heart of the desire of Faerie" (*Essays Presented to Charles Williams*, 63.).

23. Ps 34:8 (NASB).

## Is There a Contradiction in Lewis?

When Lewis uses fiction to "steal past those watchful dragons," is he violating his own convictions? While he makes a case for the power of stories to convey something of the transcendent, and while this might be helpful in an investigation of evil, it also raises a significant question which other Lewis scholars do not discuss. In a letter he writes to an acquaintance shortly after the publication of his first science fiction novel, *Out of the Silent Planet*, Lewis notes,

> You will be both grieved and amused to hear that out of about 60 reviews only 2 showed any knowledge that my idea of the fall of the Bent One was anything but an invention of my own. But if there was someone with a richer talent and more leisure I think that this great ignorance might be a help to the evange-lisation of England; any amount of theology can now be smug-gled into people's minds under cover of romance without their knowing it.[24]

If fiction allows the author to smuggle theology into the mind of the un-suspecting reader, is that not manipulative? The problem compounds. In Lewis's *The Abolition of Man*, he takes to task two authors he refers to as *Gaius* and *Titius*, who, in their grammar book (simply called by Lewis, *The Green Book*) seek to smuggle their subjectivist philosophy into the minds of unsuspecting schoolboys. He writes:

> I must point out that it is a philosophical and not a literary posi-tion. In filling their book with it they have been unjust to the parent or headmaster who buys it and who had got the work of amateur philosophers where he expected the work of profes-sional grammarians. A man would be annoyed if his son re-turned from the dentist with his teeth untouched and his head crammed with the dentist's obiter dicta on bimetallism or the Baconian theory.[25]

Lewis is offended by the actions of these authors, but seems to have no objection to his own practice. It is possible Lewis was unaware of this contradiction. The letter to the acquaintance, unlike the books pub-lished during his lifetime, was written and perhaps forgotten. If this is so, Lewis may have been inconsistent but not intentionally dishonest,

---

24. C. S. Lewis, *Letters*, 167.
25. C. S. Lewis, *Abolition of Man*, 23.

simply forgetting the conflict. But this suggestion cannot stand for long. During the very decade he wrote *The Abolition of Man*, he also published his essay *Christian Apologetics*, in which he writes, "We must attack the enemy's line of communication. What we want is not more little books about Christianity, but more little books by Christians on other subjects—with their Christianity latent."[26] It is quite clear that Lewis is advocating for Christians a form of rhetoric that he condemned when employed by grammarians. However, it could be that Lewis did not so much mind the tactic as much as he was concerned about the content promoted by those who use it. Instead of receiving the grammar they have paid for, parents and headmasters end up with philosophy; but the main problem is that they have purchased faulty philosophy. Further support for this may be found in the fact that Lewis, in *The Abolition of Man*, does not expect an educator to be morally neutral. But he suspects that *Gaius* and *Titius* may have missed what he senses to be the educational need of the day:

> The task of the modern educator is not to cut down jungles but to irrigate deserts. The right defence against false sentiments is to inculcate just sentiments. By starving the sensibility of our pupils we only make them easier prey to the propagandist when he comes. For famished nature will be avenged and a hard heart is no infallible protection against a soft-head.[27]

Given that Lewis's fiction has a relationship to his consideration of the problem of evil, it might be useful to note that, for Lewis, the "irrigation of deserts" and the work of inculcating "just sentiments" will certainly involve story.[28] If a person is not inclined to see how evil and

26. C. S. Lewis, *God in the Dock*, 93.

27. C. S. Lewis, *Abolition of Man*. 24.

28. Lewis expresses this belief in several places. "It seems to me appropriate, almost inevitable, that when that great Imagination which in the beginning, for Its own delight and for the delight of men and angels and (in their proper mode) of beasts, had invented and formed the whole world of Nature, submitted to express Itself in human speech, that speech should sometimes be poetry. For poetry too is a little incarnation, giving body to what had been before invisible and inaudible" (*Reflections on the Psalms*, 5). In a lengthy passage, Lewis explains how he believes imaginative writing sets about this task, "Poetry most often communicates emotions, not directly, but by creating imaginatively the grounds for those emotions. It therefore communicates something more than emotion; only by means of that something more does it communicate the emotion at all. . . . This, which is eminently true of poetry, is true of all imaginative writing. One of the first things we have to say to a beginner who has brought us his MS

human suffering might be reconcilable with the concept of a good and omnipotent God by way of his reason, he may begin to understand by means of his imagination. Lewis clearly believes in the power of non-discursive writing to persuade, even when the reason is on guard, and he is intentional in his use of fiction as a rhetorical tool. While one can observe the practice explicitly in his fiction, it is also implicitly evident in his use of illustration and figurative language in his non-fiction. He is aware that emotional wounds might exist in his readers, making them critical beyond that which could be considered reasonable. He warns that in literary criticism it is wise not to critique a literary work against which we find in ourselves a strong reaction. "The strength of our dislike is itself a probable symptom that all is not well within."[29] Lewis writes that there is a particular type of literature that makes him uncomfortable. He sees that this literature, which is innocent enough in itself, reveals what he suspects is a flaw in his own character.[30] If flaws, weaknesses, or emotional reactions exist that cause us to react against types of literature, races of people, economic classes, or political parties, might it be equally possible that reactions to religion, religious people, or even God could also be partly motivated by emotion more

---

is, 'avoid telling us that something was "mysterious" or "loathsome" or "awe-inspiring" or "voluptuous." Do you think your readers will believe you just because you say so? You must go quite a different way to work. By direct description, by metaphor and simile, by secretly evoking powerful associations, by offering the right stimuli to our nerves (in the right degree and the right order), and by the very beat and vowel melody and length and brevity of your sentences, you must bring it about that we, the readers, not you, exclaim "how mysterious!" or "loathsome" or whatever it is. Let me taste for myself, and you'll have no need to tell me how I should react to the flavour'" (*Studies in Words*, 317–18). Finally, Lewis observes, "The poet's route to our emotions lies through our imaginations" (*Studies in Words*, 319).

29. C. S. Lewis, *Studies in Words*, 331. Lewis also notes that it is dangerous for a reviewer to write literary reviews or criticisms about works he hates. "Hatred obscures all distinctions" (C. S. Lewis, *Of Other Worlds*, 60).

30. Lewis both warns and confesses, "Do not criticize what you have no taste for without great caution. And above all, do not ever criticize what you simply can't stand. I will lay my cards on the table. I have long since discovered my own private *phobia*, the thing I can't bear in literature, the thing which makes me profoundly uncomfort-able, is the representation of anything like a quasi love affair between two children. It embarrasses and nauseates me . . . my reaction is unreasonable: such child-loves quite certainly occur in real life and I can give no reason why they should not be represented in art. If they touch the scar of some early *trauma* in me, that is my misfortune" (C. S Lewis, *Of Other Worlds*, 72).

than reason? Lewis certainly thinks so. It is necessary to acknowledge that some who doubt God, because of the problem of evil and suffering, may perhaps be more emotional than rational. They may hold a subjectivist stance, such as the kinds Lewis embraced in his early days. Imagination may be the best way to pierce a guarded heart, when mere dialectic maneuverings cannot calm emotional storms. It is unlikely that rational arguments will convince a person who is burdened with a yoke of bitterness. But a story of forgiveness may go further, as Lewis knew. No explanations are likely to fill the empty spaces left in the life of one bereaved, but a story that elicits formerly unwept tears may provide a first step in the process of seeing things as they are so that one may begin grieving and perhaps, in a strange way, attain some comfort. It could be that a person who questions God's existence or goodness may encounter in story ways in which the goodness of God and his omnipotence can be understood to be compatible with pain and suffering. Lewis believes that stories are sometimes the best way to express what should be said. Therefore story has significance for understanding the problem of evil and that dimension of it Lewis calls subjectivism.

## The Limits of Definition

The limits of definition provide the ground for another virtue Lewis sees in using fiction to accomplish his rhetorical ends. Since (as it has been noted) the word *definition* literally means *of the finite*, then a thing must be defined by its limitations and its function.[31] To be properly defined, it must be small enough to wrap words around. If this is so, then the question comes to mind, "How is one to define God?" If He is infinite, then He stands outside the category of strict definition. What can be said here of His person can also be said of His actions. All understanding is approximate, and one must constantly be seeking better and better approximations.[32] This does not mean Lewis thinks God cannot be talked

---

31. C. S. Lewis, *Pilgrim's Regress*, 149. Lewis writes, "We define a thing by its perfection." He recognizes that he stands in a long tradition when he sees definition in this way. Citing Aristotle's Politics, 1254a, he writes, "We feel no difficulty when Aristotle says, 'We must study what is *natural (phusei)* in specimens which are *in their natural condition (kata phusin)*, not those which have been damaged'" (C. S. Lewis, *Studies in Words*, 45).

32. Lewis calls God the "Bright Blur" in *Letters to Malcolm*, 110. Later he writes, "Almost everyday furnishes us with so to speak, 'bearings' on the Bright Blur. It be-

about discursively, but that he does not believe He can be talked about purely propositionally. This being the case, Lewis believes it is necessary to use figurative language when speaking about God. This has a broader application. He writes, "All language about things other than physical objects is necessarily metaphorical."[33]

Philosopher Janet Soskice asserts, in *Metaphor and Religious Language*, that the theological realist has the right to make metaphorical claims. This can be done apart from attempts to prove the existence of God, and without expectations that the metaphors Christians use to speak about God should be accepted as having "a special validity." She says of her own purposes, "Our concern is with conceptual possibility rather than proof, and with a demonstration that we may justly claim to speak about God without claiming to define him, and to do so by means of metaphor."[34] In a similar way, Lewis's use of metaphor, as well as fiction, is designed to present possibilities for his readers as to how God and His work in the universe might be understood in regard to their significance and meaning.

Lewis writes about two types of metaphors, what he calls *the master's metaphor* and *the pupil's metaphor*.[35] The master's metaphor is "the metaphor we invent to teach by;" it "is freely chosen; it is one among many possible modes of expression; it does not at all hinder, and only very slightly helps, the thought of its maker."[36] The antecedent idea of which the metaphor is an explanation is independent of the metaphor itself. The master chooses this particular metaphor; he might have chosen several others. Biblical metaphors could be seen as master's metaphors, and if so, they must not be seen as definitive or unchanging remarks on the subject for which they are used. The teacher's thought is "independent of the metaphors [he] employ[s] in so far as these meta-

---

comes brighter but less blurry" (*Letters to Malcom*, 119).

33. C. S. Lewis, *Weight of Glory*, 102. Lewis begins this paragraph: "We are invited to restate our belief in a form free from metaphor and symbol. The reason we don't is that we can't. We can, if you like, say 'God entered history' instead of saying 'God came down to earth.' But of course 'entered' is just as metaphorical as 'came down.' You have only substituted horizontal or undefined movement for vertical movement. We can make our language duller; we cannot make it less metaphorical" (*Weight of Glory*, 101–2).

34. Soskice, *Religious Language*, 148.

35. See C. S. Lewis, *Selected Literary Essays*, 255.

36. Ibid., 255.

phors are optional: that is in so far as we are able to have the same idea without them."[37] On the other hand, the pupil's metaphor is "the metaphor from which we learn." In this sense, it "is not chosen at all; it is the unique expression of a meaning that we cannot have on any other terms; it dominates completely the thought of the recipient; his truth cannot rise above the truth of the original metaphor."[38] In this case, thought is not independent of the metaphor. The pupil's metaphor is at present the only way a particular idea can be thought about or expressed. Lewis explains that "Where the metaphor is our only method of reaching a given idea at all, there our thinking is limited by the metaphor so long as we retain the metaphor; and when the metaphor becomes fossilized, our 'thinking' is not thinking at all."[39]

A sure word may be considered to be that word which is axiomatic. Further understanding revolves around the sure word, and that understanding will likely have to be adjusted, at times, to accommodate the new information. The process itself can be painful. Robert Browning writes, "Welcome each rebuff that turns earth's smoothness rough."[40] One might think one has a clear enough understanding of a matter. One's earth is smooth and spherical. But in fact, the earth is not a perfect sphere. It has geography, texture, peaks and valleys. One must welcome those "rebuffs" that remind him of this if he would see with clarity. The difficulties and perplexities of life, the struggles and suffering, can bring with them some degree of fresh sight. The atheist must consider that if there is no God, why, in a crisis, should he expect things to be better than what he is experiencing? The theist must ask in a crisis what it is that he does not yet understand about God whereby he cannot reconcile his present experience with his current understanding of Him. In both cases, growth may follow, and this growth is likely to have an imaginative element to it.

The best definitions will be those which can account for the greatest degree of complexity. Even so, in a world of mutability, complexities are likely to compound further. To think well, adjustments must constantly be made. Lewis observes, "Change is never complete, and change never

37. Ibid.
38. Ibid.
39. Ibid.
40. Browning, "Rabbi ben Ezra," 305.

ceases. Nothing is ever quite finished with; it may always begin over again." Furthermore, he notes, "Nothing is ever quite new; it is always somehow anticipated or prepared for. A seamless, formless continuity-in-mutability is the mode of our life."[41] The foregoing comment is from the inaugural address Lewis gave at Cambridge University when he was elected to the Chair of Medieval and Renaissance Literature. The context of his comment sheds further light on this discussion. He explains that drawing hard lines to separate *periods* in literary history is unwise, for such lines may be mistaken for facts. He observes, "There is nothing in history that quite corresponds to a coastline or a watershed in geography."[42] Even so, he makes this concession:

> We cannot hold together huge masses of particulars without putting into them some kind of structure. Still less can we arrange a term's work or draw up a lecture list. Thus we are driven back upon periods. All divisions will falsify our material to some extent; the best one can hope is to choose those which will falsify it least.[43]

The tension between generalizing and particularizing here becomes apparent. The value of fiction can be seen, in part, for its capacity to supply particular instances. Its claims are unpretentious. It provides a reader with a case in point. And when fiction provides an instance of a subjectivist, somebody struggling with suffering or someone in a position to confront evil, it does not universalize the event. The story seeks to work out the circumstances of this particular person, and in that way gives the reader an opportunity to interpret his own experience at that level. Descriptions are possible, but they are not pressed or deemed permanent. Consequently, though judgments may be made in a fictional work, they must be made honestly, with the recognition that they may have to be altered. Even when a judgment is correct by and large, it will not be entirely correct. Certainly, the future horizon unfolding in the story will reveal more yet to be considered. Fiction, because it is not expected to give hard definitions, is less likely to tempt the reader into thinking its world is complete or fully understood. Fiction is able to describe without eliminating all the ambiguities. In fact, often it is at

---

41. C. S. Lewis, *Selected Literary Essays*, 2.

42. Ibid., 3.

43. Ibid., 4.

rest with a degree of ambiguity. All stories begin with a kind of "once upon a time." The telling of the story begins by breaking into a world already functioning. Seldom are the origins of that made-up world ever described. Enough detail is given that the reader might make sense of the story, enough to capture the significance and meaning of what is going to happen in the telling of the tale. Here again, fiction is helpful in wrestling with some of the elements encountered in the problem of evil and suffering. Since a last word will inevitably elude the reader, and since life has its ambiguities and complexities, it is possible to capture enough in a story to satisfy the reader for the time being. Lewis allows his readers to struggle with these issues. His fiction overcomes the problems of definition, particularly as they are related to God and His work in the world. The story must not be confused with an overt apologetic; even so, it can provide a useful and pervasive means for making some sense of a world where evil and its subjectivist support are present.

## Transposition

Lewis sees other benefits in his use of fiction to achieve his rhetorical goals. He believes that the use of fiction is not merely a desirable compliment to non-fiction, but a necessary one. Certainly fiction does not always communicate truth in a way that supplies the reader with facts and knowledge about those facts, but, as has been suggested, it may open the door to truths not yet understood. However, there is more to be considered here. Lewis writes, "Heaven is, by nature, outside our experience, but all intelligible descriptions must be of things within our experience."[44] The process whereby one might translate suprasensibles into the world of sense he calls *transposition*. If God exists and acts in ways not immediately accessible to his creatures, how might his intentions be made clear? How does the greater transpose itself into the lesser? Since Lewis has rhetorical interests to compel his readers toward truth, then this is an important matter to him whenever he is considering questions related to the problem of evil. How can the ways and intentions of God be justified to man in light of the limits of human understanding? It would be premature to assume that judgments concerning the goodness of God or cruelty could be substantiated and conclusively determined in moments of crisis. While one's focus is riveted on the

44. C. S. Lewis, *Weight of Glory*, 29.

present, painful experience, it may be next to impossible to understand any transcendent idioms that would enable an individual to make sense of that suffering. Attempts to clarify a greater meaning or significance of the trial at hand must be structured to fit the limitations of the one incapacitated by those circumstances. This is the problem of transposition, and one can fairly apply Lewis's arguments along these lines. The limits caused by the sufferer may affect his understanding of God or His goodness. The sufferer may see the facts but miss their meaning. A Christian in such a crisis may find some comfort in meditating on the Passion of Christ, but he will recognize the Passion as non-fiction rather than fiction. In a similar way, the unbeliever may find some comfort in reading a story with elements similar to the Passion of Christ. He may not mark the similarities at a first read, but the elements of the story, a story such as the death and resurrection of Aslan (as Lewis develops it in *The Narnian Chronicles*) may reach the unbelieving sufferer in a way that a book on apologetics could not.

Lewis observes that dogs do not understand what a pointing finger signifies. Rather than directing their attention to the thing signified, they sniff at the finger.[45] This underscores the difficulty of the greater communicating itself to the understanding of the lesser. Therefore, any revelation of divine intention will have to be communication in a way both accessible and comprehensible to the receptor of that message. Due to the difficulties of this communication, incredulity would appear to be, if not justifiable, at least understandable.[46] Perhaps then it is only

45. Ibid., 88.

46. Lewis writes, "If we have really been visited by a revelation from beyond Nature, is it not very strange that an Apocalypse can furnish heaven with nothing more than selections from terrestrial experience (crowns, thrones, and music), that devotion can find no language but that of human lovers, and that the rite whereby Christians enact a mystical union should turn out to be only the old, familiar act of eating and drinking?" (C. S. Lewis, *Weight of Glory*, 74). In Lewis's *The Silver Chair*, a company of three are sent by the Lion Aslan (The Christ figure of the Narnian Chronicles) to rescue Prince Rilian. He is held under a spell by a green witch, the Queen of the underground world. The prince is rescued and the party, in the process of making their escape from the underground world are confronted by the witch. She seeks to cast a new spell on the four of them by means of various enchantments. As she does this, she queries them about the land of Narnia of which they speak so often. One of the party tries to describe the sun. Since there is no sun in Underworld, he is reduced to saying it is like the lamp which hangs over their heads in the cavern where they are held. The captives try to describe Aslan the lion. Since there are no lions in Underworld, the attempt seems feeble as one member of the rescue party explains that a lion is like a giant cat with

by faith that these suprasensibles can be understood. An individual who is seeking to be objective, but who does not possess faith, would probably assert that if transcendent realities exist there would be some difficulty in accommodating language to account for both their existence and their intentions. For instance, if lines were used on paper to explain the realities of sky, earth, sea, trees, birds, animals and the world of men, experience with these real things would cause, by comparison, the lines on paper to appear weak, feeble, obsolete. The realities cause the pictures nearly to vanish, but "only as pencil lines vanish from the real landscape, not as a candle flame that is put out but as a candle flame which becomes invisible because someone has pulled up the blind, thrown open the shutters, and let in the blaze of the sun."[47] The pilgrim John, in Lewis's *The Pilgrim's Regress*, learns that story itself, with its elements of myth and metaphor, is God's invention. It is through his fiction that Lewis focuses the attention of his readers that they might see in story a kind of veil under which God is able to appear to men in

---

a mane—not a mane like a horse—one that looks more like a judge's wig. The humor of the passage underscores the difficulty of transposition. C. S. Lewis, *Silver Chair*, 152–57. Similar difficulties are developed throughout Lewis's fiction. In *The Great Divorce*, glorified men and women come out of heaven to speak to shades who have been brought up from hell to the threshold of heaven. As the glorified beings speak of eternal realities, the shades find what is spoken to be incomprehensible. So too, in *Till We Have Faces*, Psyche finds it impossible to communicate to Orual in a manner Orual will find understandable. She cannot see that the god Cupid is real or comprehend that he might be good. In *Surprised by Joy* (pp. 223, 227), Lewis says that prior to his conversion to Christianity he did not believe he could know God personally any more than Hamlet could know Shakespeare. He revisits this image and finds it helpful after all. Hamlet as a character in the play could never break out of the play to get to know the author, but Shakespeare the author could write himself into the play as a character Shakespeare and thus make the introduction possible. Lewis believes this provided a useful analogy for the Incarnation. It may be helpful, but it is not free of problems. Here again the complexities surrounding the idea of *Transposition* are at play. One can wonder what might happen at Ellsinore if Shakespeare appeared suddenly. Amidst so many strange goings on at court (the unexpected death of the king; the immediate marriage of the queen to the king's brother, the crown passing to the king's brother rather than to the crown prince, Hamlet, the reports circulating around the court that the old king's ghost has been seen at court and has spoken to Hamlet, the perceived madness in the behavior of the prince), how would the courtiers respond to an individual who happened to show up wearing Elizabethan tights and claiming to be Shakespeare the author of a play in which all others in that world are merely characters of his own invention? The analogy could be taken further than Lewis takes it, yielding a richer understanding of the difficulties inherent in *Transposition*.

47. C. S. Lewis, *Weight of Glory*, 86.

ways the creature might begin to understand. For as Lewis has God say to his character John, "For this end I made your senses and for this end your imagination, that you might see My face and live."[48]

## Saving the Appearances

There are still other benefits Lewis sees in using fiction to address the problem of evil and subjectivism. In *The Discarded Image*, Lewis explains that the medieval world-view or model of the universe was developed from a few guiding principles. First, it was believed that nature was mutable, but that the heavens were in a state of immutability. It was observed that within the realm of nature, "Things happen in the same way not perfectly nor invariably but 'on the whole' or for the most part."[49] It was not until the supernova of 1572 that belief in the immutability of the heavens began to be seriously questioned.[50] Second, in the Middle Ages great trust was placed in what was passed along in manuscripts; what had been written carried significant authority.[51] Third, since manuscripts at times conflicted, the scholar saw his task, in part, as one that required him to put together all the bits into a coherent system.[52] What emerged was the Medieval Model of the Universe,

48. C. S. Lewis, *Pilgrim's Regress*, 125.

49. Lewis continues by observing that contrasted with the world of nature, "the world studied by astronomy seemed quite different. No nova had yet been observed. So far as he [the man of the middle ages] could find out, the celestial bodies were permanent; they neither came into existence nor passed away. And the more you studied them, the more perfectly regular their movements seemed to be. Apparently, then, the universe was divided into two regions. The lower region of change and irregularity he called the Nature (*phusis*). The upper he called sky (*ouranos*)" ( *Discarded Image*, 4). In light of this Lewis observes in a footnote on the same page. "The great nova in Cassiopeia of Nov. 1572 was a most important event for the history of thought." (see Johnson, *Astronomical Thought*, 154).

50. C. S. Lewis, *Discarded Image*, 4.

51. Lewis notes, "If their culture is regarded as a response to environment, then the elements in that environment to which it responded most vigorously were manuscripts." Later, Lewis contrasts his own time with the medieval and observes that "In our own society, most knowledge depends, in the last resort, on observation. But the Middle Ages depended predominantly on books. Though literacy was of course far rarer than now, reading was in one way a more important ingredient of the total culture" (*Discarded Image*, 5).

52. Here again, Lewis notes, "At his most characteristic, medieval man was not a dreamer nor a wanderer. He was an organiser, a codifier, a builder of systems" (*Discarded Image*, 10). And later he adds that since books (as authoritative) must be

a model that "was not totally and confidently abandoned till the end of the seventeenth century."[53] The fact that the Model was abandoned reveals that it was fictitious; nevertheless, it was helpful in enabling people of the period to understand, as best they might, the world and their place in it.

According to Lewis, the Medieval Model preserved two additional principles of theory construction. The first was drawn from the writings of Simplicius and was common enough to be included in Milton's Paradise Lost. It was known as "saving the appearances" (σῷζειν τα φαινομενα).[54] The concept stipulated that "a scientific theory must 'save' or 'preserve' the appearances, the phenomena, it deals with, in the sense of getting them all in, doing justice to them."[55] In other words, good theories were intended to avoid subjectivism by providing an understanding of the objective world, as best they might. Theories were not seen as last words about reality; they were merely approximations. The aim of a theorist was to pursue more accurate approximations. The standard of evaluation was proximity to reality, which is proximity to the one thing against which the theory could be measured for accuracy. Second, the theories that were considered better were those that saved the appearances with the fewest number of assumptions.[56] These theories, Lewis observes, are never statements of fact,[57] but rather *supposals*. The theorist suggests a possible way that the data might be accounted for coherently. Of course, newer, less complicated *supposals* would replace earlier ones; and new data would certainly require modifications in the overall Model. Lewis points out that the Model was recognized to be provisional.[58] It is important, here, to note that the Model was a fiction, albeit a very helpful one. "Every Model is a construct of answered

---

true, contradictions were merely apparent contradictions; and "All the apparent contradictions must be harmonized. A Model must be built, which will get everything in without a clash; and it can do this only by becoming intricate, by mediating its unity through a great and finely ordered, multiplicity" (*Discarded Image*, 11).

53. C. S. Lewis, *Discarded Image*, 13.

54. Ibid., 14–15. This is from Simplicius's commentary on the Aristotelian *DeCaelo*. See also Milton's *Paradise Lost*, VIII, 82.

55. C. S. Lewis, *Discarded Image*, 14.

56. This is with respect to Occam's Law of Parsimony. C. S. Lewis, *Discarded Image*, 15.

57. Ibid.

58. Ibid., 16.

questions. The expert is engaged either in raising new questions or in giving answers to old ones." Therefore, "When he is doing the first, the old, agreed Model is of no interest to him; when he is doing the second, he is beginning the operation which will finally destroy the old Model altogether."[59] The entire endeavor reflected a theory about theories, and gave life to "the great Medieval labour of harmonisation and syncretism."[60] The Model as a whole was a work of art. Lewis goes so far as to suggest that it was "perhaps, after all, the greatest work of art the Middle Ages produced. Of course it was not a mere fantasy. It was intended to cover, and up to a point did cover, the facts as they knew them."[61]

In a very interesting section of *The Discarded Image*, Lewis posits that Galileo provoked controversy not because he challenged the conventions of Geocentrism, but because he set forth his theory of Heliocentrism not as a *supposal*, but as a fact.[62] This estimation of

59. Ibid., 18.

60. C. S. Lewis, *Renaissance Literature*, 57.

61. Ibid., 63. Similarly, in *The Discarded Image* he notes that these old models are reminders that "No Model is a catalogue of ultimate realities, and none is a mere fantasy" (222). This has its applications for every age. All ages have their Models of the Universe and it is good to be reminded that, as helpful as they may be, they are simply models.

62. Lewis writes, "The real reason why Copernicus raised no ripple and Galileo raised a storm, may well be that whereas the one offered a new supposal about celestial motions, the other insisted on treating this supposal as fact. If so, the real revolution consisted not in a new theory of the heavens but in a 'new theory of the nature of theory'" (*Discarded Image*, 16). Lewis is quoting from Barfield, *Saving the Appearances*, 51. Barfield develops these ideas much further. He notes, "The Greek and Medieval astronomers were not at all disturbed by the facts that the same appearances could be saved by two or more quite different hypotheses . . . All that mattered was, which was the simplest and most convenient for practical purposes; for neither of them had any essential part in truth or knowledge" (*Saving Appearances*, 49). He continues, "Actually, the *hypothesis* that the earth revolves round the sun is at least as old as the third century B. C., when it was advanced by Aristarchus of Samos, and he was neither the only, nor probably the first astronomer to think of it. Copernicus himself knew this" (*Saving Appearances*, 50). Then Barfield presses the point further by observing, "It was this, this novel idea that the Copernican (and therefore any other) hypothesis might not be a hypothesis at all but the ultimate truth, that was almost enough in itself to constitute the 'scientific revolution' of which Professor Butterfield has written: 'It outshines everything since the rise of Christianity and reduces the Renaissance and Reformation to the rank of mere episode,' mere internal displacements, within the system of medieval Christendom. When many men hear that the church told Galileo that he might teach Copernicanism as a hypothesis which saved all the celestial phenomena satisfactorily, but 'not as being the truth,' he laughs. But this was really how Ptolemaic astronomy

human capability was regarded as inflated. Though his theory of the universe was Heliocentric, his theory of theories was Galileocentric. In a way, he put himself at the centre of his universe, demanding that all turn to his conception of it, irrespective of what more might eventually be known and what understanding might have to be modified or further amplified. Lewis emphasizes that such an approach could not prevent Galileo from falling into a form of subjectivism. While he was certainly informed by the objective universe, he could not anticipate the contribution that Kepler would eventually make. In fact, the Earth did not orbit the Sun in a circle, but an ellipsis. Galileo's theory was better than those that preceded his, but it was still incomplete. He did not have the final word about the universe. The Medieval Model, while certainly not the last word on the universe, was decidedly so.

Lewis reminds us that Medieval man saw himself as "anthropoperipheral;" furthermore, he asserts, "We are creatures of the Margin."[63] The Medieval Model was not man-centered but God-centered. He could be known, but He was past finding out. Knowledge of Him as He exhibited Himself in the world could increase, but it could not be completely realized. Man was on the outside looking in; not in actual fact, for place, in relationship to the omnipresent, is a much more difficult concept than that. But by way of *supposal* the Medieval Model was far less pretentious about man's place in the universe. The medieval man was less tempted to take his point of view so seriously.[64] But, even as he considered him-

---

had been taught! In its actual place in history it was not a casuistical quibble; it was a refusal (unjustified it may be) to allow the introduction of a new theory of the nature of theory; namely, that, if a hypothesis saves all the appearances, it is identical with truth" (*Saving Appearances*, 50–51). Here Barfield supports this position by citing Aquinas in the *Summa*, Ia. Qu. 32. a.I and 2, and Ptolemy in the *Almagest*, Bk. III, chap. 6. ii an div; Bk. XIII, chaps. Ii.

63. C. S. Lewis, *Discarded Image*, 58.

64. This Lewis affirms when he writes, "Medieval and nineteenth century man agreed that their present was no very admirable age; not to be compared (said one) with the glory that was, not to be compared (said the other) with the glory that is still to come. The odd thing is that the first view seems to have bred on the whole a more cheerful temper. Historically as well as cosmically, medieval man stood at the foot of a stairway; looking up, he felt delight. The backward, like the upward, glance exhilarated him with a majestic spectacle, and humility was rewarded with the pleasures of admiration. And thanks to his deficiency in the sense of period, that packed and gorgeous past was far more immediate to him than the dark and bestial past could every be to a Lecky or a Wells. It differed from the present only by being better. Hector was like any other knight, only braver. The saints looked down on one's spiritual life, the kings,

self on the outside looking in, he did not feel himself shut out. His look was not the look of one abandoned. It was more the gaze of one sitting on the perimeter of the dance floor at a ball. There was joy to be had and the expectancy that each, in his turn, would become a part of the dance. In Lewis's own language, it is "Further up and further in."[65]

Discussion of the Medieval Model of learning is significant for the debate about the problem of evil. All models for understanding evil and suffering are, like the Medieval Model, simply models. To embrace the model as a last word on the matter leads to a form of subjectivism, for it is no longer responsive to the complexities inherent in the problem. Models are helpful, but must be seen to be temporary. Furthermore, no philosophical or theological model should be given a degree of regard beyond what is proper to it. The insights they provide are relative only to what might be known in any given moment. In a sense, they are a kind of fiction, and each in turn will have to be discarded or modified to *save the appearances*. Knowing this will not minimize the pain of any given moment, but failure to recognize it can extend pain and suffering beyond what may be necessary. And since these models are also, in their way, fictions, they remind one that other significant insights provided by other forms of fiction may be just as useful in helping others to endure suffering. Each, in its way, may address issues related to the problem of evil, and each, in its way, makes a contribution to understanding. But again, none of these contributions is permanent or comprehensive. Perhaps the fact that Lewis explores such matters in his fiction reveals not only that the concern about problem of evil is pervasive in his writing, but also that his attempts to get all around the problem is, in its way, uniquely helpful.

In his fiction, Lewis is conscious that he is endeavoring to produce something like a *supposal*, a fanciful look at certain kinds of tensions set in another world and capable of providing for his readers a fresh way of seeing.[66] In this way, his fiction does not function as allegory, *per se*; for

---

sages, and warriors on one's secular life, the great lovers of old on one's own amours, to foster, encourage, and instruct. There were friends, ancestors, patrons in every age. One had one's place, however modest, in a great succession; one need be neither proud nor lonely" (C. S. Lewis, *Discarded Image*, 185).

65. C. S. Lewis, *Last Battle*, 153ff.

66. Lewis uses the word *suppose* often enough. When he intends to clarify a point he has made by an illustration or word picture, he will often use the word *suppose* at the

the most part, Lewis is not seeking to be as overt as that. It is a mistake to read Lewis as if his fantasies or science fiction are allegorical, to treat the characters and events as if they are always representing something else or trying to cloak real meanings that must be discovered beneath the story itself. He even cautions against reading allegory as if its treasures are cryptic and must be somehow deciphered. This sort of reading misses what the artist is seeking to produce with that literary form. "We ought not to be thinking, 'This green valley, where the shepherd boy is singing, represents humility;' we ought to be discovering, as we read, that humility is like that green valley."[67] It is by these images that one seeks to make sense of *real life*.

It could also be said that no consideration of the problem of evil is likely to progress as far as it might without developing in some way along these lines. In the use of models, images, and supposals, fiction is helpful as long as it is constantly implied that these things are not real life, that they only provide a means by which real life might be better understood. Again, allegories, and supposals are works of art, and as works of art or images they must always become *discarded images*. It is important to remember that fictions are less likely to deceive than scientific models or other models of thought. People do not generally mistake a story for reality; the same cannot be said as quickly about a scientific or philosophical model. The supposals are designed to create images that have enough substance to "save the appearances." For the literary, Lewis observes, "Scenes and characters from books provide them with a sort of iconography by which they interpret or sum up their own experience."[68] It is Lewis's ability to create meaningful sup-

---

beginning of his discussion. In a letter he wrote to a child who had inquired about his Narnian Chronicles, he is explicit. "You are mistaken when you think that everything in the books 'represents' something in the world. Things do that in Pilgrim's Progress but I am not writing in that way. I did not say to myself 'let us represent Jesus as He really is in our world by a Lion in Narnia:' I said 'let us suppose that there were a land like Narnia and that the Son of God, as He became a Man in our world, became a lion there, and then imagine what would happen.' If you think about it, you will see it is quite a different thing" (*Letters to Children*, 44–45). For more on this, see also 92–93 in a letter dated 8 June 1960.

67. C. S. Lewis, *Selected Literary Essays*, 149.

68. C. S. Lewis, *Experiment in Criticism*, 3.

posals that Austin Farrer sees as one of his greatest strengths. He writes of Lewis that "his real power was not proof, it was depiction."[69]

## Reality Is Iconoclastic

Descriptions of God and His activities require, by their very nature, modification and reshaping. Moreover, Lewis writes, "you can't have a good description of anything so vague."[70] But what does he mean by vague? He clarifies the point: "If [God] exists at all, He is the most concrete thing there is. . . . He is unspeakable not by being indefinite but by being too definite for the unavoidable vagueness of language."[71] In Lewis's mind, God is "the Naked Other, imageless (though our imagination salutes it with a hundred images), unknown, undefined, desired."[72] If this is so, a growing understanding of God and His ways will require fresh images, and certainly the acquisition of images comes with a degree of risk. In a given moment, a matter which has long been perplexing may suddenly become clear. An image emerges, but if it is held too tenaciously, this once helpful image runs the risk of competing against the acquisition of a growing understanding. It ceases to be a mere image and becomes an idol. Lewis's long-time friend Owen Barfield explains, "Idolatry may be defined as the valuing of images or representations in the wrong way and for the wrong reasons; and an *idol*, is an image so valued." He continues by adding, "More particularly, idolatry is the effective tendency to abstract the sense-content from the whole representation and seek that for its own sake, transmuting the admired image into a desired object."[73] Lewis writes, "Reality is iconoclastic."[74] God is always knocking down the walls of the temples built for Him because He wants to give more of Himself.[75] Lewis observes, "Since every earthly

---

69. Farrer, *Brink of Mystery*, 46.

70. C. S. Lewis, *Letters to Malcolm*, 110.

71. C. S. Lewis, *Miracles*, 93.

72. C. S. Lewis, *Surprised By Joy*, 209.

73. Barfield, *Saving The Appearances*, 110–11.

74. Though this idea runs through all of Lewis's writing—both pre-Christian and Christian—it is stated explicitly in two sources: *A Grief Observed*, 56 and 60, written shortly after his wife's death, and more explicitly in the last book Lewis prepared for publication, a book of worship and devotion, entitled *Letters to Malcolm*, 109–10.

75. Lewis writes in his autobiography that he was aware of a deep longing that, in some ways, possessed him. This longing was, for him, a matter of fact. He was, however,

good is only an image, therefore the breaking of that image 'doesn't matter;' it is only an image."[76] This is not to suggest that the breaking of the image does not matter at all. It merely affirms that it does not matter ultimately. The idol-breaking process may be accompanied by pain and suffering, and the degree of suffering will be commensurate with the value attributed to the idol. God may allow the pain of a moment because He desires that more of Him should be known.

Following his wife's death, Lewis struggled to make sense of his grief, writing that "images, I must suppose, have their use or they would not have been so popular."[77] What then is the value of images? There are, it would appear, many, and at least two have already been mentioned. First, as Lewis suggests, they allow the reader to see God's face and live.[78] The story is the veil, according to Lewis, by which the character of God might become visible, as rustling leaves or a flying kite are indicators of the presence of wind. Of course, to see something of God's character manifest in stories or events assumes that there is something equally present in the character of the one reading the story which enables him to see. Lewis is aware of the ethos of his audience, and the constraints

---

uncertain as to the object of this desire. In his youth, he thought he had found the object in Norse Mythology, and was pre-occupied in pursuing all he could find in it. This desire, which he called "joy," set him to "building" a temple for the God of his imagination. As Lewis tells it, "finally I woke from building the temple to find that the God had flown" (*Surprised By Joy*, 165). As Lewis reflects back on this experience he adds, "The very nature of joy makes nonsense of our common distinction between having and wanting there, to have is to want and to want is to have. Thus, the very moment when I longed to be so stabbed again, was itself again such a stabbing. The desirable which once alighted on Valhalla was now alighted on a particular moment of my own past; and I would not recognize him there because, being an idolater and a formalist, I insisted that he ought to appear in the temple I had built for him; not knowing that he cares only for temples building and not at all for temples built" (*Surprised By Joy* 166–67). In *A Grief Observed*, Lewis echoes this sentiment. "Images of the holy easily become holy images—sacrosanct. My idea of God is not a divine idea. It has to be shattered time after time. He shatters it Himself. He is the great iconoclast. Could we not almost say that this shattering is one of the marks of His presence. The Incarnation is the supreme example; it leaves all previous ideas of the Messiah in ruins. And most are 'offended' by the iconoclasm; and blessed are those who are not" (*Surprised By Joy*, 55–56).

76. C. S. Lewis, *Arthurian Torso*, 181.

77. C. S. Lewis, *A Grief Observed*, 55.

78. C. S. Lewis, *Pilgrim's Regress*, 125.

posed by their ethos, for skeptics may well remain as unconvinced as Orual is when Psyche seeks desperately to show her Cupid's palace.[79]

Additionally, as I have already noted, images allow for an extension of the known into that which is not yet known. This is of vital importance when wrestling with the idea of evil. It may be suggested that senseless evil is enough to conclude that God cannot possibly exist. Certainly it is fair to struggle with doubts during a crisis. The Scriptures themselves dignify honest doubt in the life of a struggler. Job gives voice to an anguished soul, as do the imprecatory Psalms and the book of Habakkuk. Thomas's questioning doubts are, without exception, met with significant and profound answers. It is necessary to be honest in one's doubts. As the seventeenth-century, metaphysical poet John Donne writes,

> . . . doubt wisely.
> In a strange way to stand inquiring right,
> Is not to stray; to sleep or run wrong is.[80]

The passage of time (with its grieving and tears), and the prospects of eternal life (with all of its light and hope) become something like a large canvas on which the discordant brush stroke might be understood, or a tapestry within which an apparent errant thread might make sense. However, to call the horrible events of life senseless evil, to suggest that no sense may ever be made from them, is to press a point too far.[81] In the midst of his own struggles, Lewis suggests that belief in a bad God is too anthropomorphic:

79. C. S. Lewis, *Till We Have Faces*, 115–26. Much later in the novel, Orual will see that the deficiency is all on her side. She will ask, "How can they [the gods] meet us face to face till we have faces?" 294. She realizes after repeated demands of the gods that they should give account of themselves to her, that she is the one who must change in the end. And change she does, albeit not without pain and heartache. Before she dies, she records these words in her book of complaints against the gods: "I ended my first book with the words no answer. I know now, Lord, why you utter no answer. You are yourself the answer. Before your face questions die away. What other answer would suffice?" (308).

80. Donne, *Selected Poetry*, 176.

81. In C. S. Lewis, *Great Divorce*. George MacDonald's character instructs Lewis's character on this very point. "They say of some temporal suffering. 'No future bliss can make up for it.' Not knowing that Heaven, once attained, will work backwards and turn even that agony into a glory. And of some sinful pleasure they say 'Let me but have this and, I'll take the consequences:' little dreaming how damnation will spread back into their past and contaminate the pleasure of the sin. Both processes begin even before Death" (62).

When you come to think of it, it is far more anthropomorphic than picturing Him as a grave old king with a long beard. That image is a Jungian archetype. It links God with all the wise old kings in the fairy-tales, with prophets, sages, magicians. Though it is (formally) the picture of a man, it suggests something more than humanity. At the very least it gets in the idea of something older than yourself, something that knows more, something you can't fathom. It preserves mystery, therefore room for hope. Therefore room for a dread or awe that needn't be mere fear of mischief from a spiritual potentate.[82]

Suffering may make anger understandable, but it does not give license to irrationality. To charge that some circumstance cannot possibly be rationalized demands more from the one who makes the charge than he possesses. If tragic events themselves can occur quickly, as an utter shock, then resolutions to those tragedies may come equally quickly and unexpectedly. It is fair, in a given moment, to say, "It is difficult to see how anything good could come from this." It is overstated to say, "Nothing could ever make sense of this." Furthermore, if reality is meaningless, why should one bother to trouble himself thinking about anything at all? In such a world, there would be no problem of evil and suffering, and complaints against God, as well as doubts of His existence, would all be nonsense.[83] Nevertheless, images may make it possible to imagine how sense can be made out of tragedy, and without this kind of effort the dangers of subjectivism may set in; projection on the world is likely to take precedence over objective reality itself.

While it may be clear that images can, in fact, be helpful in wrestling with the problem of evil, it is not yet clear how this applies specifically to fiction. What is the unique value of a story, and in what way is it useful for discussing this topic? While it possesses the strengths of an image, a story can also do more. It pulls together in its narrative circumstances that create tension and crises. Furthermore, it places its characters at the heart of these circumstances in order to reveal their courage and fortitude or their failure and recovery from failure. This provides an example for *mimesis*, fortifying the reader with both resolve

82. C. S. Lewis, *A Grief Observed*, 27–28.

83. In C. S. Lewis. *Till We Have Faces*, Orual says, "'The gods are real, and viler than the vilest men.' 'Or else,' said Psyche, 'they are real gods but don't really do these things. Or even—mightn't it be—they do these things and the things are not what they seem to be?'" (71).

and hope for the day when he might face his own particular crisis in a given time and place.

Lewis explains a third way in which images that are developed in fiction might have value. He does this in an essay in which he explores Dante's use of similes. He writes, "Every idea presented to the mind, as in a figure, repeats the subject in a slightly different way and suggests further and further applications of it."[84] The scenes in a story add perspective to the reader's understanding. A novelist can create images like those caught in a video camera. The reader is enabled to get all around the circumstances of the story and to see it from several different angles. This is often something even a person's experience of a given moment does not allow. In grief or crisis, rational arguments concerning evil may seem unconvincing. On the other hand, while no actual crisis may be current in the life of the reader, he may still find himself thoroughly engaged in the events of a book (unable to put it down). He has a vicarious experience that extends his understanding, perhaps preparing himself for a day when pain may be his portion. The storyteller's art and his use of images are not directed towards proving anything, and yet the story may become more convincing than attempted proofs because it satisfactorily imparts to the reader a meaning which transcends mere circumstance. It breaks the reader out of his subjectivism.[85]

The fourth way in which images might be valued has to do with the nature of definitions. All definitions should be approached as working definitions. Systems and formulas in philosophy or theology are tentative, yet the system of formalized thought is likely to bring with it a temptation to accept it as a last word on a given matter. An honest look at God will be encouraged by the use of images. Philosopher Austin Farrer observes, "Those who have found God, still have God to find, every morning when they go to pray, and every evening when they come to repent."[86] It is not a God of the Calvinist, the Wesleyan, the Papist, or the Anglican but the God of the personal encounter on this day and in these circumstances that Lewis seeks to know and understand.

---

84. C. S. Lewis, *Renaissance Literature*, 74.

85. C. S. Lewis, *Of Other Worlds*, 37. Lewis thought that the vigilance which stands sentry, guarding access to the emotions, could be penetrated by story, and through that, understanding and the significance of transcendence could be grasped.

86. Farrer, *Brink of Mystery*, 140.

Fifth, images have value as works of art. In *The Discarded Image*, Lewis notes that the Medieval Model of the universe, long after it was discarded in favor of other models, still had value as a work of art.[87] Of course, a portion of its value rests in the way it reminds future generations that their own models of the universe are all equally tentative and will one day be discarded. The Medieval Model, as Lewis observes, "was not a mere fantasy. It was intended to cover, and up to a point did cover, the facts as they knew them."[88] The creative work of the contributors to that model revealed not merely their genius but also their craftsmanship. As art, these models required skill and humility in the making. In the same way, no matter how much pleasure they bring, or popularity they enjoy, all images will, given time, have to be discarded.

In *Living by Fiction*, the Christian author Annie Dillard asks, "Can fiction interpret the world?"[89] She then observes, "we are missing a whole class of investigators: those who interpret the raw universe in terms of meaning."[90] By "raw universe" she means "all that we experience, all things cultural and natural, all of the universe that is known, given, made, and changing: the world, and they that dwell therein."[91] Dillard suggests that this interpretation of the "raw world" is something done by schizophrenics, superstitious people, pantheists, some scientists, prophets and the founders of religions, theologians, metaphysical philosophers, and artists. And Dillard believes artists are best at interpreting the raw data of the world.[92]

Since Dillard is herself a literary artist and poet, it is tempting to think her words might be self-serving, but she does open an interesting window. In many ways, her concerns echo Lewis's own. The scientist can illuminate what a thing is and how it is different from other things; he can atomize the parts of a whole and explain how they function in relation to other parts, and in that way describe what each part contributes and means in relation to another part. The scientist may even tell what one organism means in relation to its function with other or-

---

87. C. S. Lewis, *Renaissance Literature*, 62.

88. Ibid., 62.

89. Dillard, *Living By Fiction*, 145.

90. Ibid.

91. Ibid.

92. Ibid., 146.

ganisms. It would seem that individuals could only discover the meaning of particular things in relation to other things as they examine the
universe. Things mean nothing in isolation from other things. Though
it is possible to say that pain hurts all by itself, I cannot say whether
that pain is good or bad all by itself, for it can only be understood in
relationship to other things. A cut made by a scalpel hurts whether or
not the cut comes by accident or by a surgeon. The proximity to judging whether the cut designates healing (done by a surgeon) or trouble
(done by accident) is contingent on seeing the relationship between the
cut and its source. If the surgeon understands far more than the patient (and it is to be expected that he does), the meaning of the incision
may never be fully understood by the patient. And if it is a veterinarian
who has administered the incision on a dog, it would be impossible for
the dog to comprehend the intentions behind the cut. But how does a
physician explain his intentions regarding a medical procedure to his
patient? The patient cannot generally grasp the technical explanations
and procedures which it took years for the doctor to acquire and perfect. Most often, any attempt by a doctor to explain to a patient what
he intends to do in surgery is preceded with the phrase, "It is like this.
. . ." What follows is a simile, metaphor, or some other type of figurative language. In this sense, Dillard and Lewis may be right: artists (or
in this case the artistic part of the physician) may be most helpful in
bringing to light difficult concepts. A fiction is used to explain the truth
and extend the patient's understanding. For certainly the procedure is
not exactly what the doctor has described to his patient but only ap-
proximately like it. This does not invalidate the benefits of technical
language, which has its place. Lewis goes on to explain that figurative
language is not merely employed by the artist, but is, in fact, the most
common way that communication is done. "The very essence of our life
as conscious beings, all day and every day, consists of something which
cannot be communicated except by hints, similes and metaphors and
the use of those emotions (themselves not very important) which are
pointers to it."[93] The literary artist who uses imagination must mediate
what he will say through fiction, and he does not merely engage in an

93. C. S. Lewis, *Christian Reflections*, 177.

extravagance. He has much to teach us about the way meaning must be communicated.[94]

This imaginative use of language is often less pretentious than language used by the technician. The artist, or the artistic part of any individual, is least likely to forget that beyond an image is that which transcends the image itself. William Morris says he was an idle singer whose "murmuring rhyme / beats with light wing against an ivory gate."[95] Perhaps this speaks truth to all who would seek to recognize that we

---

94. It is of interest to note Lewis's clear sense of the development of the philosophy of literary art in the west. As a not unrelated aside, it might be proper to spell this out here. In his *English Literature in the Sixteenth Century Excluding Drama*, part of *The Oxford History of English Literature*, Lewis writes, "The defence of poetry will not be rightly understood unless we keep two facts carefully in mind." 1) "It is a defence not of poetry as against prose, but of fiction as against fact. What is in question is not man's right to sing but his right to feign, to 'make things up.'" 2) "Europe became conscious of fiction as an activity distinct from history on the one hand and from lying on the other" (318–19). "It was of course Plato who opened up this debate, and he made two very different contributions to it" 1) "On the one hand, in the *Ion and the Phaedrus*, he stated in an extreme form the doctrine of inspiration. He denied that poetry was art. It was produced in a divine alienation of mind by men who did not know what they were doing" (319). In this sense, those so moved, and guided by the muse, were merely channels for the deity, and produced what might be akin to Lewis's explanation of *Transposition*, the greater is descanted into the lesser and through it into the world. 2) "On the other hand, in the *Republic* he condemned poetry along with all other 'mimetic' or representational arts. This condemnation was two sided" (319). a) "In part it is directed (and so indeed is his theory of inspiration) against the old error, still dangerous when Plutarch wrote, or mistaking art for science and treating Homer as an encyclopaedia. To that extent it was a real advance" (319). b) "In part it was metaphysical. Nature, the phenomenal worlds, is in Plato's dualism a copy of the real and supersensuous world. Dialectic leads us up from unreal Nature to her real original. But the arts which imitate Nature lead us down, further away from reality to 'the copy of the copy'" (319). In this sense, Reality is iconoclastic. "The Platonic theory of inspiration was passed along via Politian (in the *Nutricia*), Facino (*De Furore Poetico*), Scaliger, Tasso, Spenser and Milton are agreed, and Horace's rationalism is ignored" (322). "Two different answers were given to Plato, which may roughly be called the Aristotelian and the Neo-Platonic." 1) Aristotle: "Poetry, he maintained, does not copy the particulars of nature; it disengages and represents her general characteristics . . . it reveals the universal" (319). 2) Neo-Platonic: "far later and more gradually, arose from prolonged reflection on sacred iconography; even, it would appear, from reflection on a single sacred image." a) Thus, the Neo-platonic created images. . . . b) Philostratus, in the *De Vita Apollonii*, vi, xix writes of the images: "Imagination made them and she is a better artist than imitation; for where the one carves only what she has seen, the other carves what she has not seen" (320).

95. C. S. Lewis, *Selected Literary Essays*, 224 (citing, *The Earthly Paradise*, Introductory Verses, 1.24, I).

brush against understanding like a moth brushing its wings against the light of a window.

## Conclusion

Lewis uses fiction, in part, as a means to discuss the problem of evil. It is a literary mode that makes it possible to say things he can not say better by some other written means. Contrary to those who say Lewis's foray into fiction was the result of a defeat by Anscombe at the Oxford Socratic club, he wrestled with the problem of evil and suffering and was aware of the particular benefits imaginative literature could bring to the discussion. He sought to marshal those benefits in order to persuade his audience and encourage them to faith.

The ways in which imaginative endeavors may be useful in wrestling with the problem of pain are also the ways in which imaginative endeavors are helpful in any enterprise. Finite attempts to look at deep matters, from the poet's ponderings to the scientist's hypothesizing, will benefit from the use of the imagination. Of course, the use of the imagination, as it crystallizes into fiction, is no guarantee that truth will be discovered or that an imaginative hypothesis will be proved. Like all things human, the imagination runs the risk of going awry. Even so, advances are unlikely without it. So how is it possible to engage in the imaginative enterprise in a way that is helpful? It must be remembered that the imagination does not provide facts; it is not in its nature to do so. It can look at 'fanciless fact' in fresh ways. The question could be asked: Does the use of fiction guarantee philosophical accuracy? But the question may not be fair, for it makes demands on fiction which even scientific or logical speculation cannot supply. Scientific investigations are modified through further research. And, though there are rules to logic as there are rules to the game of chess, knowledge of the rules is no guarantee that a player will win every time he sits down at the board to play. One's skill, the application of the rules, and the skills of one's opponent all help determine who will win the game. Yet the game cannot even be played without the rules. The imagination benefits inquiry. Lewis knew this and used the imagination to serve his rhetorical aims to instruct as well as to please.

If an atheist suggests that a loving and powerful God cannot exist because some horrible incident has occurred, his judgments may be both premature and myopic. The incident, no matter how horrifying, is insufficient in itself to sustain the broad generalization. Does this mean that an atheist is incapable of getting anything right? Does this mean that a Christian will seldom be wrong? Does this mean that a person with religious convictions is incapable of misunderstanding? Certainly atheists can modify their positions and change; Lewis did. And it is equally clear that religious people can be condescending and stubborn; the Pharisees in the New Testament were. All are capable of behavior which falls beneath the expectations of others and, more surprisingly, beneath one's own expectations as well. It is at this point that the use of fiction can allow one to see oneself in a clearer light, for when one reads of the characters in books, one reads something of oneself reflected back. One can become aware of his limitations and therefore become less pretentious in his judgments. For both the atheist and the Christian, this can be an asset in wrestling with the problem of evil and suffering.

At the end of *An Experiment in Criticism*, Lewis asks,

> What then is the good of—what is even the defence for—occupying our hearts with stories of what never happened and entering vicariously into feelings which we should try to avoid having in our own person? Or of fixing our inner eye earnestly on things that can never exist—on Dante's earthly paradise, Thetis rising from the sea to comfort Achilles, Chaucer's or Spenser's Lady Nature, or the Mariner's skeleton ship?[96]

He answers,

> The man who is contented to be only himself, and therefore less a self, is in prison. My own eyes are not enough for me, I will see through those of others. Reality, even seen through the eyes of many, is not enough. I will see what others have invented. Even the eyes of all humanity are not enough. I regret that the brutes cannot write books. Very gladly would I learn what face things present to a mouse or a bee; more gladly still would I perceive the olfactory world charged with all the information and emotion it carries for a dog. Literary experience heals the wound, without undermining the privilege, of individuality . . . in reading great literature I become a thousand men and yet remain myself. Like the night sky in the Greek poem, I see with a myriad eyes, but it is still I who see. Here, as in worship, in

---

96. C. S. Lewis, *Experiment in Criticism*, 137.

> love, in moral action, and in knowing, I transcend myself; and
> am never more myself than when I do.[97]

Lewis is not offering literature as a panacea for the problem of evil, but rather as a means to opening one's eyes.

The Materialist's aims—to show that the problem of evil is sufficient to disprove God's existence—can be appreciated for their simplicity; however, they fail to *save the appearances*. In another age, it was not so much the problem of evil as it was the issue of evil. Evil existed—there was no doubt of that—but how or in what way might it be reconciled with omnipotence and goodness? Supposals followed. The naturalists' failure will be manifest in time, because their equation—omnipotence + goodness + evil = no God—is tantamount to a last word supported with little. Supernaturalists, in general, and some of those of the Christian category, were more cautious. Though they believed they were faced with the issue of evil, they also believed that resolutions would be found. They took their lead from the Scriptures, which were filled with stories of people like Job, Habakkuk and Jeremiah. They were familiar with accounts of Israel's bondage in Egypt and their later captivity in Babylon. Christians worshipped the Incarnate Deity who suffered and died on a cross and rose again. Their history was that of a fledgling Church which grew in the teeth of persecutions. Their doctrines, though built on a solid core of beliefs, revealed a history of changing supposals and adjusted paradigms, as reflected by their councils and creeds, which made them applicable in a plethora of cultural settings. It was their faith that made them tenacious, even though they were familiar with the issue of evil. They were not without struggles, nor did they lose hope. Lewis, who counted himself among that number, provided the Church with fresh supposals in his fiction. They were not the first, nor will they be the last; but they do stand in a long tradition of helpful images, works of art which affirm, with Viktor Frankl, "If there is a meaning in life at all then there must be a meaning in suffering."[98] Lewis's fiction was designed to provide the kinds of images that take readers "further up and further in,"[99] forsaking the confines of subjectivism and opening up to a larger understanding of suffering in the world.

97. Ibid., 140–41.
98. Frankl, *Search for Meaning*, 88.
99. C. S. Lewis, *Last Battle*, 153ff.

# 5

# Literary Analysis

## Introduction

C. S. LEWIS'S LITERARY CHARACTERS ARE NEVER NEUTRAL: THEY EITHER move towards the good (that is, the real) or they move away from it. They may repent and experience transformation, but they are always in transition, and their very souls are in the balance. It is part of Lewis's rhetorical design that it should be so, for he is appealing to his readers to consider their own moral state. As Lewis scholar David Downing observes, "Lewis believed that every moral choice humans make moves them one step closer to heaven or to hell."[1] This is particularly notice-able in Lewis's evil characters; furthermore, it is remarkable how those engaged in Lewis scholarship see common characteristics manifest in these particular characters. This can, of course, be attributed both to his clarity of style as well as his unified sense of what is at stake in the diminishing of one's character. Feminist critic and Lewis scholar Kath Filmer, [who is often sympathetic to Lewis,] says, "Lewis depicts evil or unredeemed characters as self-centred and selfish, and arms them with a variety of excuses by which they attempt to veil the truth about themselves."[2] These excuses are cloaked in subjectivism and lead to a diminishing of the self, ironically producing the opposite of what the characters set out to achieve. Downing sees five common traits running through Lewis's evil characters. First they have a tendency to set aside morality for the sake of utility. Second they disregard for the sanctity of both animal and human life. Third, they are "progressives" who "find

1. Downing, *Planets in Peril*, 83.
2. Filmer, *Mask and Mirror*, 37.

little value in history, tradition or the classics. Fourth they prefer the scientific, artificial, and industrial over the simple and natural. Fifth they use language to conceal and distort reality rather than reveal it."[3] Each of these tendencies reveals the fact that Lewis uses the rhetoric of fiction to addresses issues related to subjectivism. One could say that Lewis's evil characters espouse a rhetoric of subjectivism, and his good characters, by contrast, employ a rhetoric of objectivism.

In this chapter I analyze four imaginative works written by Lewis which support my argument that he is seeking rhetorically to make the case that evil develops when subjectivism is unchecked by the objective world. The works are as follows: *Dymer* (published in 1926); *Out of the Silent Planet* (published in 1938); *The Great Divorce* (published in 1945); and *The Magician's Nephew* (published in 1955). When characters are unresponsive to the way of the Tao of their world, they will tend to become evil in the process of time. By contrast, those characters who do respond to the world as it is, and not merely as they would have it be, may suffer, but nevertheless will develop and mature positively. I am choosing only four books from which to make this point. Admittedly, the list of works is selective; even so, I argue that these four works contain examples of motifs that appear in a variety of ways in Lewis. I will also show that Lewis's argument is not limited to his post-conversion literature. The conflict between objectivist concerns versus subjectivist appears in his pre-Christian literary craft, as well (though there it is not nearly as developed as it later comes to be). I have selected these particular works because they represent four consecutive decades of Lewis's life. Such a choice is necessary to show that his interest in subjectivism was not something peculiar to his later work, thus further supporting the argument made in the last chapter. Each work also contains contrasting good and evil characters, making the distinctions more pronounced and clear. I will reference other works by Lewis when his rhetorical use of similar motifs highlights and clarifies my argument.

Four motifs appear in the works mentioned above, which exhibit subjectivism and make Lewis's case rhetorically. These motifs include the following: escape versus rebellion, as in *Dymer*; surrender to the natural world (in a way that cultivates humility, wonder, and awe) versus the attempt to control nature (for one's own selfish interest) as in *Out of*

3. Downing, *Planets in Peril*, 84.

*the Silent Planet*; the paradox that he who gives his life finds it and he who keeps his life loses it, as in the case of *The Great Divorce*; and lastly, surrender and self-giving to benefit others versus self-importance and manipulation at the expense of others, as in *The Magician's Nephew*.

## Richard Weaver and "The Last Metaphysical Right"

Before analyzing Lewis's fiction, a consideration of his values, in light of Weaver, is in order. There is no culture without an order of human values, or, as Richard Weaver writes, "Culture is a creation in the world, and it must obey certain fundamental conditions of existence."[4] Though culture may be understood in a variety of ways, from Matthew Arnold's "high culture," to John Bodley's culture as social heritage, Weaver here speaks of culture as the "collective consciousness."[5] In this way, cultures, at their best, seek to accommodate themselves to what may be collectively understood about the world. They seek, or should seek, to be expressions of what Lewis calls the *Tao*, or the doctrine of objective value. Thus, Lewis can write rhetorically that all cultures embrace an image of the world which, if it will be true and just in rendering to things their due, must, in time, become a "discarded image." This image is similar to what Weaver calls a "metaphysical image," a vision of the universe which is believed to be true and by which a culture understands itself. Weaver writes, "The nature and proper end of man are central to any discussion not only of whether a certain culture is weakening, but also whether such a culture is worth preserving."[6] It could be argued that no "metaphysical image" is ultimate. In time it will need to be discarded. It could be further argued that to the degree this image is embraced by cultures or individuals without any of the necessary suppleness, allowing it to be modified properly (in other words, that it no longer adequately defines the world in which it is held), it is equal to subjectivism and may give occasion to the rise of evil in that culture. In such cases, the culture becomes an end in itself and not a means toward understanding man's place in a larger universe.

The end of any given thing and the purpose towards which it serves cannot be discovered in isolation from other things, for an understand-

4. Weaver, *Visions of Order*, 9.
5. Ibid., 10.
6. Ibid., 4.

ing of any given thing must be found with respect for the place of other
things in the world as well. Otherwise, civilizations and cultures are
reduced to anarchies or tyrannies, depending on how power happens
to be distributed. If the values necessary for a culture to succeed must
be found outside of itself—in other words, if culture is a means and not
an end of existence—then, as Weaver asserts, that culture will have a
sense of awe. He writes, "Look beneath the surface of the most brilliant
cultures of history, and you will find a hunger and wonderment, reaching even to a kind of melancholia."[7] These cultures are alive with a sense
of humility and curiosity in a world seen as much larger than they are;
an interest in knowing and an awareness that much is yet unknown
produces positive results for such cultures. A corollary would be that
cultures tending to ossify have lost that sense of wonder, becoming ends
in themselves and no longer looking outwards toward the transcendent.
In such cases, both cultures and individuals become self-referential. In
this regard, Weaver notes, "How obvious here is the extinction of the
idea of mission."[8] Consequently, the worship of comfort and self absorption prevails and, as Weaver observes, "absorption in ease is one of
the most reliable signs of present or impending decay."[9] Furthermore,
Weaver suggests that "addiction to comfort unfits us for survival."[10]

Weaver writes that evil flows "from a falsified picture of the world
which . . . results in an inability to interpret current happenings."[11] He
believes that "the last metaphysical right" comes from a sense of "the
right of personal property."[12] This concept may seem odd, at first,
but Weaver means something significant by it, and what he says will
prove useful for interpreting subjectivism and evil in Lewis's fiction.
Since "virtue is a state of character concerned with choice, it flourishes
only in the area of volition."[13] The owner of private property has the
responsibility either to extract his living from that property (as in the
case of farmland) or work hard to keep it up that it might maintain

---

7. Ibid., 10.
8. Weaver, *Ideas*, 116.
9. Ibid., 117.
10. Ibid., 118.
11. Ibid., 129.
12. Ibid., 131.
13. Ibid., 137.

its usefulness for shelter and comfort (as in the case of a domicile). Its obligations prevent the landowner from living merely in the present. He has to learn from the lessons of the past and think about the future; this "calls for the exercise of reason and imagination."[14] He has to bear the responsibility for his success or failure. His choices are validated or invalidated by the inexorable nature of the objective world in which he finds himself. Thus, the rational life, mixed with the imaginative and applied to choices, contributes to the development of character; failure to respond in this way may lead to the diminishing of character. While all of the implications of this which concern Weaver are interesting in their own right, it is sufficient to note for the purposes of this study that moral health is found in the accommodation of one's thoughts and actions to the world as it is. Moreover, evil is found when one is either unresponsive to the demands of the objective world or seeks to manipulate that world to sustain whatever falsehoods that serve one's subjectivist purposes. In this chapter, I use Weaver to provide a way to examine the actions of Lewis's fictional characters, based on their willingness or unwillingness to accommodate themselves to the worlds in which they find themselves—that is, to accommodate themselves to "the last metaphysical right." Characters develop positively who make and continue to make these adjustments, while characters decline morally who fail in this regard. Furthermore, evil characters employ a rhetoric of subjectivism, that is they use language to deny objective reality—what Weaver references in "the last metaphysical right"—in order to project their self-referential and utilitarian interests and control others to advance themselves. Meanwhile, Lewis's good characters engage in a rhetoric of objectivity, which leads to humility, and opens them up to a world full of wonder. I will use Weaver (as described above) for critical analysis of the four Lewis texts.

## Dymer

In his critical work on Lewis's poetry, literary critic and Lewis scholar Don King observes that during the early twenties Lewis was composing an autobiography in verse. He wrote three poems about former teachers; one of these was about Robert Capron, the headmaster at the boarding school to which Lewis was sent immediately after his mother died. In

14. Ibid., 139.

Lewis's autobiography, Capron is "Oldie" in the chapter titled "Belsen," after the Nazi concentration camp. In the Lewis family papers, Warren Lewis writes of him, that "By secluding himself from all who were not under his dominion, [he] had reached such a degree of tyranny that the kindest verdict I can pass on him, is . . . that he was not quite sane."[15] C. S. Lewis's poem about Capron speaks similarly; he writes, "for at his gate no neighbour went in."[16] Capron's lunacy, which bordered on evil, was marked by projection; he kept the objective world from breaking in and correcting his own misconceptions of it. Something like this can be seen in the evil characters in *Dymer*, a poem Lewis was writing at the same time he wrote the Capron piece.

Unfortunately, *Dymer* (1926) is often neglected, and yet rightly does King observe that "those who have studied the poem closely find much to admire."[17] Owen Barfield, Lewis's life-long friend, also notes, "It is practically the only place where the voice of the earlier Lewis [pre-conversion to Christ] . . . is heard speaking not through the memory of the later Lewis but one could say in his own person."[18] George Sayer comments on the poem that it is "the most ambitious and important of C. S. Lewis poems."[19] He also says that what characterizes much of Lewis's early work is an escape from guilt which depends "upon some union with nature."[20] It is interesting to point out that here one sees hints of the Weaverian concept of property as "the last metaphysical right" coming to light, for nature itself leads out of self and into the larger world with all of its demands and responsibilities. Furthermore, Sayer claims that the "main subject of *Dymer* . . . is without doubt the tempta-tion of fantasies,"[21] and these fantasies are what Lewis calls "Christiana Dreams."[22] He took the name from Christina Pontifex, a character in Samuel Butler's novel *Erwhon*. These dreams speak of the awakening of sexual desire and fantasy at adolescence. Sayer says that the poem

15. King, *C. S. Lewis, Poet*, 98.

16. Ibid., 99.

17. Ibid., 109.

18. Ibid. Quoting from "C. S. Lewis," an address given at Wheaton College, October 16, 1964.

19. Sayer, "C. S. Lewis's 'Dymer,'" 94.

20. Ibid., 96.

21. Ibid., 97.

22. C. S. Lewis, *Narrative Poems*, 4. Also, Sayer, "C. S. Lewis's 'Dymer,'" 97.

was written in "a state of angry revolt against that spell."[23] However, it is difficult to believe that this is the case, since the poem was written over the period of a decade, and one can hardly imagine that Lewis maintained this anger towards adolescent disappointments for such a sustained period of time. Although these matters are brought into the story, Lewis's rhetorical interests lie elsewhere.

In *Dymer* the idea of escape from subjectivism is most likely the main theme of the poem, which Lewis develops by contrasting the ideas of escape verses rebellion. While Lewis is opposed to the use of literature as a means of escaping from the disappointments of this world—in other words, as a kind of drug to anesthetize one's sorrows—he holds similar convictions as Professor Tolkien, whose essay *On Fairy Stories* informs readers not to confuse "the Escape of the Prisoner with the Flight of the Deserter."[24] The deserter runs from his circumstances out of cowardice, whereas the prisoner seeks to leave his confinement for a larger world. Furthermore, the distinction is for Lewis of such importance that he says, "The one is an *askesis*, a spiritual exercise, and the other is a disease."[25] In at least one of his works, Lewis defines a rebel by comparing his actions to the revolt of branches against the tree.[26] Such a rebellion cannot ultimately succeed. This is the way the term is being used here; it is a subjectivist's revolt, merely destructive, not tending toward anything objective and serving no transcendent ends. The means are autonomous. Dymer, representing "escape," leaves a tyrannical city in search of something more real and satisfying. He is contrasted with another character named Bran, who represents the subjectivist's position. Bran seeks only to destroy. He is anarchistic, looking for no transcendent reference point beyond himself. In the introduction to the second edition, Lewis declares his clear intention of contrasting these two, "For it seemed to me that two opposite forces in man tended equally to revolt." Lewis says of the first, Dymer, "The one criticizes and at need defies civilization because it is not good enough." Dymer will discover a universe outside the city more real and satisfying to the longings of his heart. The city represents for him an image in need of

23. Sayer, "C. S. Lewis's 'Dymer,'" 97.
24. C. S. Lewis, *Essays to Charles Williams*, 76.
25. C. S. Lewis, *Of Other Worlds*, 30.
26. C. S. Lewis, *Abolition of Man*, 56.

discarding in the hopes of discovering something larger and more appropriate. "The other stabs it from below and behind because it is too good for total baseness to endure."[27] This second form of rebellion is exhibited in Bran. His destructive interests are not motivated by any form of a larger ideal. His rebellion is self-referential.

There is a further contrast in the poem, as well; it is the contrast between Dymer, who longs for the real wherever it may lead him, and the Magician of Cantos VI and VII. The Magician has chosen to do whatever he may to block out the real world in favor of a world of dreams. Employing a rhetoric of subjectivism, he nearly convinces Dymer to do the same. The contrast between these two, as will be shown, also highlights the difference between that form of subjectivism leading to evil and that kind of objectivist position that leads to development and growth.

## Canto I

In the first Canto of the poem, Lewis introduces the reader to Dymer as a young inhabitant of a city which has become a tyrannical place. It is the utopian ideal of the Plato's *Republic*, and Lewis is explicit about this in verse 4. The Platonists have built this city, forcing their ideas into brick and mortar: "They laid / The strong foundations, torturing into stone / Each bubble that the Academy had blown."[28] Their ideal is the mould into which they have poured their world in order to make it fit their wishes. By indicating the incongruities of bubbles forced into stone, Lewis makes his rhetorical claims clear and reveals the nonsense of such endeavors to his readers: theories of the universe are *not* the universe, any more than theology is God. These theories and theologies may represent the best thoughts one may have of a given tract of reality, but they are not to be confused for last words. When they are pressed onto the universe, making it what its proponents must have it be, clear sight is lost and evil may take centre stage. It is not a coincidence that in verse 2, the inhabitants scornfully label their world, "The Perfect City;" the emphasis is on the pretence it has become.

Lewis marks for his readers the unnaturalness of the City and its intentions, describing in verse 7 the affect on Dymer:

27. C. S. Lewis, *Narrative Poems*, x.
28. Ibid., 8.

For nineteen years they worked upon his soul,
Refining, chipping, moulding and adorning.
Then came the moment that undid the whole—
The ripple of rude life without a warning,
It came in lecture-time one April morning—
Alas who ever learned to censor the spring days?[29]

One is struck by the fact that though the "conditioners" and planners of the city seek to indoctrinate Dymer to their vision of life, though they work for nineteen years "refining, chipping, moulding" him to be what they want him to be, one moment of real life overturns all the falsehoods of their subjectivist rhetoric. Lewis's underscores this fact by placing Dymer in a lecture hall, enduring further indoctrination, when he notices the spring day outside the window. Verse 8 develops the image of the real world breaking in on the pseudo-world of "The City:" as a breeze from outside reaches his cheek, a brown bird perches on the sill outside the window, and Dymer is stirred. The images are particularized, seemingly insignificant things, but real and therefore great contrasts to what is represented by "The City." He laughs out loud—a proper response to the real he sees, as compared with the spectral classroom and its lecture. The teacher seeks to silence him. Here is a situation in which Lewis is making his case rhetorically: the subjectivist position is personified by the City, and the lecturer as its representative who tries to prevent both a true vision of the universe and a proper response to that universe when it is encountered. Dymer, in an act inconsistent with the real world which is breaking in on him but consistent with his youth and the disappointment of nineteen years of indoctrination, strikes the lecturer dead and leaves the city. The description of his departure is found in verse 13: "Down the white street and past the gate and forth / Beyond the wall he came to grassy places."[30] The street of the city is colorless and unreal, whereas the image of "grassy places" suggests greenness, nature, life, and growth. The realness of the grass is an image Lewis uses later in his book *The Great Divorce*, when shades from Hell, given a chance to come to the threshold of Heaven, cannot accommodate themselves to the solid and real grass they find there, for they are not of a substance capable of bending it beneath their feet. The

29. Ibid., 8–9.
30. Ibid., 10.

image "beyond the wall" has significance also in light of Lewis's earlier publication, *Spirits in Bondage: A Cycle of Lyrics*, where he writes:

> I catch a sight of lands beyond the wall,
> I see a strange god's face.
>
> And some day this will work upon me so
> I shall arise and leave both friends and home
> And over many lands a pilgrim go
> Through alien woods and foam,
>
> Seeking the last steep edges of the earth
> Whence I may leap into that gulf of light
> Wherein, before my narrowing Self had birth,
> Part of me lived aright.[31]

The escape from boundaries, in search of something to which his desire calls, is also evident in the first work of fiction Lewis published after his conversion, *The Pilgrim's Regress*. Having gained a vision of a distant island, John breaks out of the constricted world he finds himself in and goes through the wall into a real wood and onto the road which makes him a pilgrim and wanderer.

In his *Preface*, written for the 1950 edition of *Dymer*, Lewis explains that Dymer's life is meant to capture the 'extreme' anarchism that characterized that period of his life.[32] Sayer is surprised by this confession of Lewis and writes, "I know nothing in any of his letters of the period to suggest that he was really by temperament 'an extreme anarchist.'"[33] It would appear that the evidence lies with Sayer's assessment. Lewis makes no mention of that tendency toward "extreme anarchy" in the letters of the time. This gives credence to the importance Barfield places on *Dymer* as a means of gaining access to Lewis's voice apart from intruding commentary by the mature Lewis. At times Lewis

---

31. C. S. Lewis, *Spirits in Bondage*, 86–87. It is also interesting to note Lewis's use of contrast between "white roads" leading out to a wider world, "Where the gods unseen in their valleys green are glad at the ends of earth And fear no morrow to bring them sorrow, nor night to quench their mirth" (*Spirits in Bondage*, xxxiv). "The Roads" (*Spirits in Bondage*, 92). Similar images of escape from restricted cloistered environments into a world more real and distant are scattered throughout *Spirits in Bondage*.

32. C. S. Lewis, *Narrative Poems*, 3.

33. Sayer, "C. S. Lewis's 'Dymer,'" 99.

tends to exaggerate his past in order to shape his rhetorical ends and outcomes.[34]

Dymer hears music and, following it, finds that it leads him to embrace emotions otherwise long suppressed by the unrealities of the City. The music is emblematic of a real world so different from the world he has left. It feeds his imagination and caters to his sense of wonder, long stifled by the machinations of the Platonists. Lewis observes:

> That music could have crumbled proud belief
> With doubt . . .
> And turn the young man's feet to pilgrimage—
> So sharp it was, so sure a path it found,
> Soulward with stabbing wounds of bitter sound.[35]

Soulward speaks of that which revives Dymer's soul, awakening it all the more from the deadening indoctrinations of the City. The objective world enlivens real life, whereas the false world of the City had stifled his soul. His path takes him through a wood where he eventually finds a manor house or castle, which he enters and finds empty.

## Canto II

Canto II tells of the adventures Dymer has in the castle. At several points, the contrasts are played out between subjectivism and Dymer's growing surrender to reality. After he enters the castle, he is startled by a mirror (verse 5); thinking he is confronted by a challenger, he sets himself up for a fight, only to discover he has misperceived reality. Once he recognizes himself in the mirror, he smiles before it, "wondering like a child." Here, Lewis posits "wonder" as a proper response when one finds things as they truly are, as opposed to a lack of wonder when one forces an image. In verse 10, Dymer looks again into the mirror:

> Till suddenly he started with surprise,
> Catching, by chance, his own familiar eyes,
> Fevered, yet still the same, without their share
> Of bravery, undeceived and watching there.[36]

34. A particular example that comes to mind is one mentioned by his brother Major W. H. Lewis who takes exception to Lewis's description, in *Surprised by Joy*, of his life at Malvern College. W. H. Lewis, memoir in *Letters*, 4–5.

35. C. S. Lewis, *Narrative Poems*, 13. Verse 24.

36. Ibid., 18. Verse 10.

Though Dymer has seen himself once in this mirror, Lewis makes the point rhetorically that one look at an object will not be enough to plumb its depths. The real world in which Dymer now finds himself demands more from him. He sees himself "still the same," and yet, "undeceived," notices depths which have escaped him in the past; he is less brave than he has first assumed. After a while, he leaves the mirror to continue his exploration of the house. Lewis frames Dymer's search of the house with the observation, "The boy went on . . . manly playing at manhood,"[37] thus suggesting that the hero of the poem still lacks what it is he must become. He is developing into his mature or real self, becoming more real as he surrenders to things as they actually are. This is a situation not unlike that of *The Great Divorce*, in which the shades from Hell either accept reality as they find it and in the end become solid, or reject the realities of Heaven and remain undeveloped. As the poem's plot continues, Dymer enters a chamber in the night and discovers "the breathing body of a girl," Overcome with selfish desire, he sleeps with her. Here Lewis hints at the evil which is to come from this act, noting that the night is evil, for it has "sent the young wolves thirsting after blood."[38]

## Cantos III and IV

In Canto III, Dymer awakens from his night of rapture, wondering where he is and what has happened the night before. He leaves the castle only to discover that "Out of the unscythed grass the nettle grew."[39] The green grass, which had once symbolized his escape from the City into the spring, now has sprouted nettles. He suddenly recognizes the evil of his act: he failed even to learn the name of the maiden; his carnal rapture was not about a relationship between two people with all of its objective complexities, but was the mere satisfying of appetite without respect for this other person. He begins to feel guilty, a sign also of objective value, and a quality which escapes the subjectivist, and returns to the manor in order to find the young woman. To his dismay, he only finds an immense old hag there. He tries desperately to enter the castle again in order to find the young woman, who is now becoming his idealized beloved; unfortunately, every entrance is blocked and bared by the hag.

37. Ibid., 19. Verse 12.
38. Ibid., 24–25. Verses 32–23.
39. Ibid., 28. Verse 8.

He is initially filled with bravado, vowing to rescue the maiden, but in the end his courage fails him. He begs the hag to let him enter, and she strikes Dymer, wounding him on his heart. Defeated, Dymer stagers away from the castle and wanders into the wood thinking about his beloved. Sayer observes that "Much of the rest of the poem is the story of his quest for her, for a being of whose nature he knows very little."[40]

In Canto IV, the contrast between Dymer and Bran begins. Dymer endures a horrible storm in the wood. When calm is restored, he is surprised to discover a man wounded, moaning and blinded, lying near death. Dymer tries to comfort him, and then asks to hear his story. The man says that he once lived in "The Perfect City," where all had been well until the day that a rebel named Dymer "at one blow brought ruin on us all."[41] Dymer is shocked, for the wounded man projects onto him motives that were not his. Still, he listens quietly to the man's tale, the wounded man's blindness guarding Dymer's identity. The obvious incongruities between the man's tale, which makes Dymer out to be a mere rebel, and reality, set the stage for the introduction of Bran, an actual rebel, who calls others to join him in the destruction of the City, shouting out Dymer's name as a rallying cry.[42] Bran is a subjectivist with no objective value to guide him. He does not have anyone's welfare in mind but his own, nor does he look beyond himself for some transcendent source of moral guidance. He is truly an anarchist: "And at his heels a hundred murderers ran, / With prisoners now, clamouring to take and try them / And burn them, wedge their nails up, crucify them."[43] Lewis shows the mindlessness of the rebellion and the subjectivist rhetoric of its leader, who "with maddening words dethrones the mind of men." The motivation of these rebels is nothing more than "doom and strong delusion."[44] Dymer is told, "Wherever the most shame / Was done the doer called on Dymer's name."[45] The dying man explains that Bran's tyrannies were such that he would even turn on his own, and that he himself was a victim of Bran's violence. The man wishes he had health

40. Sayer, "C. S. Lewis's 'Dymer,'" 103.
41. C. S. Lewis, *Narrative Poems*, 40. Verse 16.
42. Ibid., 42. Verse 24.
43. Ibid., 43–44. Verse 28.
44. Ibid., 44. Verse 29.
45. Ibid., 44. Verse 30.

and that Dymer were at hand so he could avenge the harm he has suffered. Dymer stays by his side till he dies, again, unrecognized due to the fallen man's blindness. Here, Lewis clearly contrasts Dymer's flight with Bran's destruction of the "City." Dymer seeks escape into the real, while Bran tries to assert his will and destroy. Bran is clearly portrayed as evil. He is a precursor to the more developed villains in Lewis's mature work. He is a subjectivist who uses any means to force his own will on the world around him.

## Canto V

As this Canto begins, Dymer is dumbfounded by all he has seen and heard. He rushes further into the wood in an attempt to escape the horrors behind him, but he does not gain any kind of solace for his grief. At this point, Lewis begins to insert into the narrative descriptions of the land and the foliage, the skies and stars and sea. It would appear that Lewis is drawing another contrast between the consequences of the evil actions of Bran, the subjectivist, and the power of the real world to soothe Dymer's sorrows. Eventually, Dymer falls asleep near a calming brook, only to have a horrid dream. The power of the nightmare is only broken when Dymer awakens into the real world once again, where "over him the scroll of stars unfurled."[46] Here, too, Lewis seems to be making the point that the subjectivity of the dream must itself yield, in its proper time, to the real world. And while the dream looms large in its power to cause fear, a single sight of the real world, with stars and sky, shakes Dymer free of the false and restores him.

When he has awakened, he longs for the woman who brought comfort to him the night before. This stirs up in him a long complaint against the gods, which continues for nearly one third of the Canto. The complaint is consistent with the kind of anger Lewis himself claims to have had around the time of the poem's composition, a time of pre-Christian angst directed at God. Dymer's cry at the end of his long complaint is this: "Great God, take back your world."[47] This complaint comes from the mouth of one who the reader sees is tending to get things wrong, whose life is in the process of accommodating itself to reality. Although Lewis was not yet a Christian when he wrote this poem, there

46. Ibid., 47. Verse 7.
47. Ibid., 50. Verse 15.

is an uncanny sense that Dymer's complaint against God is not proper or right. It is likely Lewis considers the complaint to be similar to that of Prometheus, and he has nothing in mind related to the Christian God at all. Nevertheless, it is a curious feature that the complaint, unlike those found in other myths, is against God and not *the gods*.

Wandering again along a path that takes him through woods and over a mountain Dymer comes to a place where he sleeps. This time his dream he is more reassuring. In it, he hears a lark that

> Sang out of heaven, 'The world will never end,'
> Sang from the gates of heaven, 'Will never end.'
> Sang till it seemed there was no other thing
> But bright space and one voice set there to sing.[48]

In this dream, Dymer is wooed by the lark to look at something so large and compelling it eclipses from view all other things. It is set apart and distinct from the ever changing and mutable world in which he has found himself by virtue of its immutability and "never ending" qualities. Lewis begins the next two verses with the words "It seemed," and here he sets out to interpret the song of the lark for his readers, thus making his aims very clear. The lark has sang, "I AM;" Lewis writes, "whence flows the justice that men call Divine."[49] Sayer observes, "He is rescued by contact with complete and integrated, God-made creatures, whom he can accept as they really are."[50] But as he awakes, Dymer believes that what he heard was only a mere bird piping, and attributes to this experience no transcendent significance. The Canto ends as Dymer takes to his pilgrim road once again.

## Cantos VI and VII

Though complex, Cantos VI and VII are by far the most significant in uncovering the poem's statement against subjectivism, which is embedded in the struggle between the evil antagonist and the hero. Dymer starts out fresh in Canto VI, awakened to what he suspects is the truth of his world. He says, "Pack up the dreams and let the life begin."[51] In

---

48. Ibid., 53. Verse 27.
49. Ibid., 53. Verse 28.
50. Sayer, "C. S. Lewis's 'Dymer,'" 106.
51. C. S. Lewis, *Narrative Poems*, 55. Verse 2.

the next verse he notices the spring again, thus tying this part of his quest with his original act of stepping out of the City. It is with jarring shock that Dymer then hears the firing of a gun. When he rushes off to investigate the source of the shooting, he comes to another house, partly hidden behind a "yew hedge." It is a house with a clock tower but "a clock that had no hands and told no hour."[52] In other words, it is a useless clock unless Dymer is stepping into a place where the time of the objective world is of no real consequence. This is a foretelling of what he is to find in the house, for its master, a magician who traffics in dreams, dwells in a world out of time. On his arrival at the house, the magician asks if Dymer has heard his gun, announcing without remorse that it was he who has killed the lark. Dymer is horrified at the news and lets his sorrow be known, to which the magician announces that the singing of these birds "interrupt my dreams."[53] Regarding this section of the poem, Sayer underscores what the reader has discerned, that "everything about the Master [of the house] is evil." [54]The magician has denied the claims of "The Last Metaphysical Right" and all it represents about allegiance to objective value; he has chosen the world of pseudo-reality in pursuit of dreams. Here Lewis draws a sharp contrast between Dymer's escape into the real world and this new antagonist's escape from it. Lewis's references to magic and magicians will be discussed later in this chapter, in context with *The Magician's Nephew*. Suffice it to say that Lewis himself, once tempted by the occult, has little use for it here.

The magician feeds his newly arrived guest and then Dymer, nearly fallen under some sort of a spell, drowsily tells of all his experiences up to that point. The magician has no interest in the parts of the story about Bran; he only wants to hear of the young woman in the castle. As Walsh notes, "The magician has no interest in the visible world except as an entrance into the invisible."[55] The subjectivist magician tells Dymer that he can teach him the art of dreaming so that he will be able to have the woman whenever he wants her. At this moment a sharp disagreement breaks out. Dymer, more alert, says: "'Dreams?'

52. Ibid., 56. Verse 5.

53. Ibid., 57. Verse 10.

54. Sayer, "C. S. Lewis's 'Dymer,'" 108.

55. Walsh, *Literary Legacy*, 47.

I have had my dream too long. I thought / The sun rose for my sake."[56] Now the difference between Dymer's quest for objective value and the magician's subjectivist's commitments are brought into focus. The rhetoric of subjectivism values control over others to further its own narcissistic interests. Therefore, the magician seeks to persuade Dymer that his real interests lie not in a realm inhabited by an actual woman but rather the dream world where he can have control over the circumstances, thus insuring that he will meet the woman whenever he chooses. This idea is confusing to Dymer, but in a weakened moment the magician has baited his trap and nearly caught his prey: "The Master smiled. 'You are in haste! / For broken dreams the cure is, Dream again / And deeper.'"[57] Dymer, still sorrowing over the report of Bran and the rebellion he inspired, asks the magician if these dreams can wipe out "blood-guiltiness" and "undo what's done amiss, and bid the thing that has been be no more?"[58] Dymer is willing to do whatever will help him ease his sorrows. The pain is real, and the dreams are not, but Dymer will be persuaded by the rhetoric of subjectivism if it serves his utility. The magician takes full advantage of this opportunity to say that such things, as Dymer longs for, can only be found in dreams:

> In dreams the fool is free from scorning voices.
> Grey-headed whores are virgin there again.
> . . . There the stain
> Of oldest sins—how do the good words go?—
> Though they were scarlet, shall be white as snow."[59]

This is a denial of "the last metaphysical right," for here there is a denial of reality manifest when the magician discounts Dymer's guilt, suggesting that it is merely a dream, having no source in the objective world. The magician's rhetoric of subjectivism is manipulative as he denies reality once again.

Dymer, nearly persuaded by the magician's rhetoric, comes again to his senses by thoughts of his beloved. He would remain in the waking world if he knew he might possibly see her again. He would muster whatever "courage" was necessary if he was assured of his goal. At the

---

56. C. S. Lewis, *Narrative Poems*, 61. Verse 23.

57. Ibid., 61. Verse 24.

58. Ibid., 61. Verse 25.

59. Ibid., 61–63. Verse 26.

mere mention of courage, the magician discounts the benefits of virtue and that kind of character necessary to live in the objective world. He seeks to prevent Dymer from developing those benefits inherent in the real world of "the last metaphysical right." Dymer succumbs to the persistent rhetoric of the magician, who has prepared a sleeping potion for him. Just before he falls into the power of the dreaming spell, he says to the magician, "Oh, lies, all lies . . . Why did you kill the lark?"[60] As sleep overtakes him, Dymer recognizes that the magician's rhetoric is wrong as he gets in touch with the objective world and remembers the senseless killing of the lark.

As Canto VII begins, Dymer drifts off into the dreams concocted by the magician's spell. It is in this moment that Lewis explicitly reveals the magician's evil intentions: "He laughed out loud / Only once: then looked round him, hushed and cowed."[61] Like a man having something to hide, he gloats at the spell under which he has put the guest in his house, but only as he first looks around to see that no watching eye observes his deed. His reactions indicate two things: first, his action has clearly violated an objective value; second, he has done wrong knowingly, and therefore his act against Dymer is an evil act. While Dymer sleeps, the magician, "like a dog returning to his vomit,"[62] returns to his bookshelves which are full of the tools of his necromancy:

> . . . such grubs are bred
> From minds that lose the spirit and seek instead
> For spirits in the dust of dead men's error,
> Buying the joys of dream with dreamland terror.[63]

In calling his treasures "grubs," Lewis not only projects a low value on these books but also attributes to the magician that quality of life that feeds on grubs. He is a "lost soul;"[64] not willing to be content within his own misery, he must destroy others as well. The magician is a prototype of the Lewisian villain, a precursor to the ghosts in *The Great Divorce*, and Weston as the "Unman" in *Perelandra*. He has lost his humanity in denying the inexorable claims of objective value. Or, as Lewis will

60. Ibid., 64. Verse 36.
61. Ibid., 65. Verse 3.
62. Ibid., 66. Verse 7.
63. Ibid., 67. Verse 8.
64. Ibid., 68. Verse 9.

later write in *The Abolition of Man*, "Stepping outside the *Tao*, they have stepped into the void."[65] The magician is not satisfied with his own condition but must ensnare others as well, and it would appear that Dymer, as he dreams, has been caught in the magician's web.

With all of this working against him, Dymer stirs from his dream, and waking, he cries out one word, "Water!"[66] It is mere thirst that breaks the dream-spell, a longing for something real and objective that brings Dymer to his senses. He drinks one glass and asks immediately for another, emphasizing the point of how simple the illusions of subjectivism can be diminished. As he drinks, Dymer chides the magician, saying his land of dreams is "all lies!" and that the magic is "all accursed."[67] He tells the magician that it was wrong to send him to the world of dreams, for "I sought a living spirit and found instead / Bogies and wraiths."[68] The explicit image makes the contrast very clear: Lewis's design is to reveal to his reader's that the artificial world of the subjectivist should not be preferred over the real. Dymer speaks with the rhetoric of objectivism, and his message is a clear call to attend to the inexorable demands of reality.

The magician, experienced at ignoring reality and unmoved by Dymer's chiding—simply asks to hear about the dream. What motivates the magician to make such a request? He may be seeking to woo Dymer back into the world from which he has just escaped, or he may be so caught up in the falseness that any report from the dream world is now more highly valued by him than its rivals. Again, like a dog returning to its vomit, the magician grovels for whatever grubs will satisfy his palate. Oddly enough, in a manner incongruous with his contempt for the magician, Dymer complies and begins to tell the story of his dream. Of course, his story is necessary for the continuance of the narrative, but it is an awkward moment, nonetheless. Lewis supplies no reason why Dymer would grant the magician's request. Even so, Dymer tells his story. He speaks of a bear that enters into the wood of his dream. Perhaps it is a precursor to the bear Mr. Bultitude, who appears in *That Hideous Strength*. In that novel the bear underscores the power of

65. C. S. Lewis, *Abolition of Man*, 77.

66. C. S. Lewis, *Narrative Poems*, 67. Verse. 11.

67. Ibid., 67. Verse 11.

68. Ibid., 68. Verse 12.

nature to break the spell of subjectivism, represented by the "scientism" of the N.I.C.E.. The bear's purpose, which is to speak of nature and the real world breaking into the false, is made evident from the way he comes into the dream, "Whispering of Eden-fields long lost by man."[69] Still, Dymer chides the magician, discounting the appearance of both bear and wood: "Do you think I could not see / That beasts and wood were nothing else but me?"[70] Though it does suggest something of the natural world breaking in on him, Dymer only sees the falsehood of the magician's dream world. The reader will recall that as Dymer fell under the magician's spell, he longed for the real rather than the artificial. The bear and wood are there, but, as Dymer reflects back on this, he knows it was nothing more than projection, a subjectivistic manufacture, because "I was making everything I saw, / Too sweet, far too well fitted to desire / To be a living thing."[71] Dymer desperately wants the world as it is, with all of its risks and dangers, more than a world that is false to the thing the universe truly is and was meant to be.

Again, whether he is addicted to the dream world or merely desiring to ensnare Dymer in another trap, the magician asks if Dymer found his lady in the dream. After affirming that she was there, the magician asks, "Was she not fair?" Then he adds, "Almost a living soul."[72] By these remarks he seeks to persuade Dymer to prefer the unreal to the real. The insistence of the magician to coax Dymer into this world of the unreal, all done in the context of spells and magic, is a motif similar to the one Lewis employs nearly thirty years later in *The Silver Chair*. There, a Green Witch attempts to ensnare Prince Rilian of Narnia, Eustace Scrubb, Jill Poole, and Puddelglum the Marshwiggle into a world of her making in order to control them. By remembering the real over against the Witch's artificial world, as painful as that should prove to be, the company is able at last to break the enchantment.[73] No more effective than the Green Witch, the magician fails, too. Dymer sees through the

69. Ibid., 69. Verse 16.
70. Ibid., 69. Verse 17.
71. Ibid., 69. Verse 18.
72. Ibid., 70. Verse 20.

73. C. S. Lewis, *Silver Chair*. It is there that Lewis reminds his readers how the real world, even with its pains, can restore one from the falsehoods of the subjectivists. He writes, "There is nothing like a good shock of pain for dissolving certain kinds of magic" (*Silver Chair*, 154).

magician's manipulative rhetoric and refuses to take the subjectivist's route. He objects to the magician's world of dreams, noting,

> But every part
> Was what I made it—all that I had dreamed—
> No more, no less: the mirror of my heart,
> Such things as boyhood feigns beneath the smart
> Of solitude and spring. I was deceived.[74]

The mirror recalls the earlier mirror of Canto II, a clear reminder of self-projection. As Dymer continues to recount his story for the magician, he speaks of the lady's words to him: "Her sweetness drew/ A veil before my eyes."[75] She seeks to woo by saying that "the shadow-lands of earth" were really only loved in desire for the world of the dream. She contrasts the subjectivist's world for that of the objective world, claiming that the real world is only a substitute for the dream. She tells Dymer that he has at last come to his home and she begins to worship him. It is at this point that Dymer asks the moral question that brings the matter of good and evil into the arena of this subjectivism: "Is it not wrong / That men's delusions should be made so strong?"[76] The temptation to succumb to the dream is strong in him, but a moment comes when the spell is at last broken. Though he has been "nearly wrecked," he notes,

> She went too fast. Soft to my arms she came.
> The robe slipped from her shoulder. The smooth breast
> Was bare against my own. She shone like flame
> Before me in the dusk, all love, all shame—
> Faugh!—and it was myself.[77]

In realizing the truth that the woman in his dream is nothing but his own projection, Dymer breaks free of the spell once and for all, and asks for water. Here, Lewis begins to tie the various parts of the poem together. The woman in the dream is of his own manufacture, not unlike the "The Perfect City" is the manufacture of the Platonists; they had "tortured bubbles into stone." It was necessary for Dymer to escape the unreality of both worlds. Reality is iconoclastic. Something as simple

---

74. C. S. Lewis, *Narrative Poems*, 70. Verse 20.

75. Ibid., 70. Verse 21.

76. Ibid., 71. Verse 23.

77. Ibid., 71. Verse 25.

as spring awakened him from the one world, and now something as simple as water awakens him from the other.

The magician tells Dymer he must leave his house, for Dymer has nearly destroyed the illusions by speaking to his host about things as they are, rather than as the magician would have them be. As Dymer begins to leave the house, the magician raises his gun and shoots him. The events at the magician's house begin with the slaughter of the lark, the destruction of that which threatens his dream world; in the end the magician shoots Dymer because his developing commitments to objective value are a threat to the subjectivism of the magician. He will have his way, and his uncorrected falsehoods will sustain him in his evil acts, both against the lark, representing nature, and Dymer, representing humanity. One can see the emerging ideas Lewis later develops in *The Abolition of Man*, where he asserts, "The power of Man to make himself what he pleases means, as we have seen, the power of some men to make other men what *they* please."[78] The magician has failed, once again, to respect "the last metaphysical right." He has no valuation for others, only himself. Weaver would say he lacks piety, or justice. He is incapable of rendering to others their due.

> Piety is a discipline of the will through respect. It admits the right to exist of things larger than the ego, of things different of the ego. And before we can bring harmony back into the world where everything seems now to meet 'in mere oppugnancy,' we shall have to regard with the spirit of piety three things: nature, our neighbors—by which I mean all people—and the past.[79]

What Weaver demands is beyond the capacity of the likes of the magician, for, lacking respect for objective value, he has no sense of piety or obligation.

## Cantos VIII and IX

In his wounded state, Dymer is ever more sensitive to the objective world. He notices "the wind along the hedges," and "the quarter striking from a neighbouring tower."[80] It is not merely the hedge, but the observation of the unseen wind animating its leaves. While it is not

78. C. S. Lewis, *Abolition of Man*, 72.

79. Weaver, *Ideas*, 172.

80. C. S. Lewis, *Narrative Poems*, 75. Verse 3.

visible, the wind is more real than the things he has encountered in the two preceding cantos. It is not merely that Dymer notices the clock; he also notices the detail that it strikes the quarter of the hour. He has escaped the dreams of the magician's house, whose faceless clock has no hands and whose world is out of beat with the objective world, to discover clocks whose time is measured and precise. As he travels on with "thundering pain," the fog from the magician's house clears, and he sees the clouds break and the night sky "Spacious with sudden stars."[81] These are real stars in a wide, wide sky, unlike the stifling make-believe world of the dreams. Though wounded, he has escaped.

In this real world, he is surprised to discover that he has come upon the woman after whom he has been seeking. He asks if she is "The loved one, the long lost," and staring at her, asks "Truly?" She replies, "Truly indeed."[82] This again establishes the reality of the world where Dymer finds himself, and contrasting it with the one from which he has come. Still he has his doubts, and wants to be sure she is not "one more phantom to beguile." The reality of this experience is marked by the fact that the clock's bell "Tolled out another quarter."[83] Dymer asks that she leave him, for he suspects that she is a god who cannot understand all he has suffered. She corrects him and says, "The gods themselves know pain, the eternal forms." She has "looked into their eyes," so she is, in fact, familiar with pain and suffering.[84] He wants to know if it is the gods who have called him out of the City, and, if so, has he sinned by following them. It would appear that he is asking if the rebellion that followed his departure from the City is to be counted against him. He does not give her time to answer before he asks what is to him a more important question: "Must things of dust / Guess their own way in the dark?" To which she answers, "They must."[85] Dymer responds in wrath, wanting to know why she has come "in human shape, in sweet disguise / Wooing me, lurking for me in my path / . . . snared me with shows of love—and all was lies." The answer is difficult for Dymer, for the goddess says, "our kind must come to all / If bidden, but in the shape for

81. Ibid., 76. Verse 4.
82. Ibid., 76. Verse 6.
83. Ibid., 76–77. Verse 7.
84. Ibid., 77. Verse 9.
85. Ibid., 78. Verse 12.

which they call."[86] She eventually tells him that he must now "Go forth; the journey is not ended yet." The purpose for Dymer's journey is now revealed by the goddess. She says that he has already seen himself dead and "on the bier" many times before, that in fact Dymer has slain himself every hour. It is an enigma, but as Dymer turns to question the goddess further, she is gone.[87] In a passage that greatly prefigures Lewis's mature work, Dymer reflects the truth that there have been many former Dymers. Yet life's experiences have lain to rest each Dymer for one who was yet emerging. He speculates about his own pilgrimage:

> There was a Dymer once who worked and played
> About the City; I slough him off and ran.
> There was a Dymer in the forest glade
> Ranting alone, skulking the fates of man.
> I cast him also, and a third began
> And he too died. But I am none of those.
> Is there another still to die . . . Who knows?[88]

Again, "Reality is Iconoclastic." Dymer's life is becoming more true and authentic; he is in the process of emerging as he is continually defined and redefined, becoming shaped by his world and his experience. The final word has not been uttered about him, as it cannot be uttered about any man. As Walter Hooper acknowledges when Helen Joy Davidman visited Lewis for the Christmas holidays in 1952, Lewis wrote in her copy of *The Great Divorce* the following words: "There are three images in my mind which I must continually forsake and replace by better ones: the false image of God, the false image of my neighbours, and the false image of myself. C. S. Lewis 30 December 1952 (from an unwritten chapter on Iconoclasm)."[89] Even though this chapter was yet unwritten, it would appear that it was, in some ways, anticipated by this Canto in *Dymer*. As Canto VIII ends, Dymer struggles to get to a "belfried place," and passing through an old gate finds himself in a cemetery.

In Canto IX, Dymer meets the sentry of that place who is guarding against the intrusion of a monster. The sentry tells Dymer the tale of this particular beast's origin, and, to his surprise, Dymer discovers that

---

86. Ibid., 78. Verse 13.

87. Ibid., 80. Verses 19–20.

88. Ibid., 81. Verse 24.

89. Hooper, *Companion Guide*, 61.

it is the product of the night he lay with the woman in the castle. For some reason which Lewis never fully provides, Dymer decides that he must either slay the beast or be slain by it.[90] As the dawn breaks and the beast arrives, Dymer sees that the region is "a ruinous land."[91] He faces the beast and it kills Dymer in an instant; but in that very moment "came the rising sun," and with it the "ruinous land" sprouts forth vegetation and the brute becomes a god.[92] Thus ends the story of Dymer. In his *Preface* to the 1950 edition of the poem, Lewis says of Dymer, "Hunger and shock of real danger bring him to his senses and he at last accepts reality."[93]

## A Concluding Word about Dymer

Dymer grows by accepting what Richard Weaver calls the "The Last Metaphysical Right;" in other words, he accommodates himself to objective value. He chooses to redress his wrongs and accepts his fate by facing the monster whose very existence is the result of Dymer's indulgent fantasies. The non-Christian Lewis has Dymer atone for his own sins. There is nothing related to the Vicarious Atonement in this book, but the choice to face reality, even if such a choice reveals flaws of character, is presented as a likely aid to set one on a right road. In his introduction to *The Great Divorce*, Lewis notes that when one sets out on a wrong road, there is no making it the right road any more than wrong figures can lead to a right sum. The only way to begin the process of fixing the error is to acknowledge the mistake and go back where it can be set it right. "Evil can be undone, but it cannot 'develop' into good."[94]

In relation to the argument of this study, we can see that Lewis's objectivist interests, though not as developed as they eventually come to be, are obviously present in this very early work. It can also be seen that his evil characters are subjectivists, self-referential and indifferent to objective value. The fact that Lewis held this position, and sets it forth rhetorically in poetic form, indicates that he is a person open to

90. C. S. Lewis, *Narrative Poems*, 86. Verse 15.
91. Ibid., 89. Verse 24.
92. Ibid., 90–91. Verses 30–35.
93. Ibid., 4.
94. C. S. Lewis, *Great Divorce*, vi.

development in his own thinking. While his autobiography makes this obvious, the adjustment to objective value begins to clarify the reasons behind these changes. Biographical details may explain the "what" but his objectivist commitments explain the "why." Furthermore, Lewis's awareness that character and the risk of good and evil are in the balance—as he displays in his literary characters—heightens the seriousness of Lewis's commitment. Expressions of evil in his characters are strung like beads along this common thread of subjectivism, providing a sense of the pervasiveness of this theme.

It is also fair to suggest that some Christian themes can be seen to emerge in the early Lewis. Three things indicate how this may be so. First, Lewis himself says that shortly before his conversion to Christianity his friends Hugo Dyson and J. R. R. Tolkien had a late-night discussion with him. He recounts the event in a letter to his friend Arthur Greeves:

> Now what Dyson and Tolkien showed me was this: that if I met the idea of sacrifice in a Pagan story I didn't mind it at all: again, that if I met the idea of god sacrificing himself to himself (cf. the quotation opposite the title page of *Dymer*) I liked it very much and was mysteriously moved by it: again, that the idea of the dying and reviving god (Balder, Adonis, Bacchus) similarly moved me provided I met it anywhere *except* the Gospels. The reason was that in Pagan stories I was prepared to feel the myth as profound and suggestive of meanings beyond my grasp even tho' I could not say in cold prose "what it meant." Now the story of Christ is simply a true myth: a myth working on us in the same way as the others, but with this tremendous difference that it *really happened*: and one must be content to accept it in the same way, remembering that it is God's myth where the others are men's myths: i.e., the Pagan stories are God expressing Himself through the minds of poets, using such images as He found there, while Christianity is God expressing Himself through what we call "real things." Therefore it is *true*, not in the sense of being a "description" of God (that no finite mind could take in) but in the sense of being the way in which God chooses to (or can) appear to our faculties.[95]

---

95. C. S. Lewis, *Letters of C. S. Lewis: Revised*, 288–89.

It is clear from this that Lewis believed the Christian story could be seen to be present in the early pre-Christian myths.[96] Second, in *The Great Divorce*, George MacDonald's character says that Heaven and Hell are retrospective, for each works backward to transform what has gone on before. Something of Heaven or Hell will be seen to be evident in all of life's experience in the end, "The good man's past begins to change so that his forgiven sins and remembered sorrows take on the quality of Heaven: the bad man's past already conforms to his badness and is filled with dreariness."[97] Third, in *Mere* Christianity, Lewis notes, "If you are a Christian you do not have to believe that all the other religions are simply wrong all through."[98] Equally, it should not be supposed that everything in the pre-Christian Lewis must be over-shadowed or discounted by the writings of the converted Lewis. There is much at play in Lewis's early work that anticipates the themes of his later material, and this is principally seen in his objectivist commitments. These commitments are also at play in Lewis's early Science Fiction.

## Out of the Silent Planet

*Out of the Silent Planet* (1938) is the first of three works in Science Fiction Lewis published in his life-time. The three books are a sort of trilogy by virtue of the fact that the hero, Elwin Ransom, appears in each of the books. The first two books have Ransom travelling to two other planets. The first, *Out of the Silent Planet*, is situated on Mars or Malacandra; the second, on Venus or Perelandra. *Out of the Silent Planet* allows a context for Lewis to further his warning against subjectivism. Ransom (and Lewis) engages in a rhetoric of objectivism, whereas, the antagonist, a physicist named Weston, employs the rhetoric of subjectivism. Weston seeks to control nature and shape it to his own whims and predilections. Ransom, on the other hand, seeks to surrender to the world in which he finds himself, thus cultivating a sense of humility, wonder, and awe.

The plot of the book is simple enough, and a basic understanding of the plot is necessary to make critical judgments about the book and

96. C. S. Lewis, *Mere Christianity*, II, 1, 29.
97. C. S. Lewis, *Great Divorce*, 64.
98. C. S. Lewis, *Mere Christianity*, II, 1, 29.

Lewis's intentions for the story. Ransom is kidnapped by Weston and his accomplice, an entrepreneur and opportunist named Devine. The motive for the abduction lies in the fact that Weston and Devine have made an earlier trip to Malacandra and fear that on their return they may have to sacrifice a human to what they have perceived to be the hostile native species of that world. Ransom is taken due to his expendability. The clearly subjectivistic sentiments of the two abductors is distinguished early on in the book. Their self-interested designs leave little sympathy for an overarching, objective, moral law. The motives of Weston and Devine are more clearly stated by Lewis when, in commenting about his own works, Lewis declares that *Out of the Silent Planet*

> 'is an attack, if not on scientists, yet on something which might be called "scientism"—a certain outlook on the world which is casually connected with the popularization of the sciences, though it is much less common among real scientists than among their readers. It is, in a word, the belief that the supreme moral end is the perpetuation of our own species, and that this is to be pursued even if, in the process of being fitted for survival, our species has to be stripped of all those things for which we value it—of pity, of happiness and of freedom.[99]

The scientist and the opportunist seek to colonize outer space so that they might project their utilitarian designs onto other worlds.

Upon reaching Malacandra, however, Ransom manages to escape and finds himself befriended by one of the indigenous species. In time, Ransom discovers that there are three different kinds of rational species on Mars: the first, are the hrossa—the poets of the planet; next, the seroni—the intelligentsia; and last, the pfifltriggi—the engineers and craftsmen-artisans. Over a period of months, Ransom has positive encounters with all three groups and finds that they are unfallen and good. He first lives among the hrossa, and is befriended by one named Hyoi. Being a philologist, Ransom learns the language quickly, and with the power to communicate, he opens himself up to the history, culture, and ways of the Malacandrians. After many months, Weston and Devine come upon the village of the hrossa, where Ransom has been living, and shoot Hyoi. It is at this time that Ransom is told he has been sent for by the Oyarsa, the ruling archangel of Mars. Weston and

99. C. S. Lewis, *Of Other Worlds*, 76–77.

Devine are also brought to the Oyarsa and their purposes are discerned, after which time they are sent back to earth. This short summary does little to convey the wonder of the book A. N. Wilson described as "Unput-downable,"[100] nevertheless, it is necessary to provide background and context for the book's interpretive themes.

*Out of the Silent Planet*, has been described as "a book in which the author is firing on all cylinders,"[101] a "blend of literary originality and religious truth."[102] This assessment is significant in light of the fact that the critic, Wilson, is not always sympathetic to Lewis. Yet, as he explains, it is a book where "the theology does not wage war on the story,"[103] and he believes that it allows Lewis to be classed with writers such as Dante and Milton, though on a less grand scale.[104] Additionally, Downing writes that *"Out of the Silent Planet* is written with all of Lewis's convictions, with his whole world view in the background."[105] The fact that so much of Lewis's thought comes through in the book increases its value as an example of Lewis's best literary rhetoric as it relates to subjectivism.

Nevertheless, Downing sees a flaw in the book: Lewis's bad characters seem under developed.[106] This is a view shared by Doris Myers, who writes that "It might be argued that in making Ransom so unmistakably good and his captors so evil, Lewis has eliminated moral complexity from the story."[107] On the other hand, I argue that contrasting these characters as he does is Lewis's way to highlight, with a rhetorician's commitment to clarity, the conflict between the rhetoric of subjectivism (in the case of Devine, and particularly Weston) and the rhetoric of objectivism (in the case of Ransom). Similarly, through the portrayal of evil characters there appears to be an implicit critique of dark social forces, as Myers observes:

> Thus within the framework of the given Wellsian narrative Lewis communicates his philosophical disagreement with so-

100. Wilson, *Biography*, 154.
101. Ibid.,
102. Ibid., 156.
103. Ibid., 155.
104. Ibid.
105. Downing, *Planets in Peril*, 36.
106. Ibid., 84.
107. Myers, *C. S. Lewis in Context*, 43.

cial Darwinism, with the modern social scientist's common assumption that economics is destiny, with the modern pride in technology. This depiction of the moral dimensions of scientific advancement is one of the tasks that science fiction, among all forms of literature, is uniquely qualified to accomplish, and Lewis's work helped to push the genre in that direction.[108]

However, while I would agree with Myers that Lewis is engaged in communicating a point of view, his primary concern is not fundamentally against social Darwinism, social science, or technology. Lewis is trying to get to something more foundational—he is attacking the *Poison of Subjectivism*, which is at the root of all philosophies that support and sustain evil practices. He is trying to refute the rhetoric of subjectivism as it appears in all of its social manifestations.

The narrative seems to have a connection with Lewis's life, also, according to some critics. Downing quotes Chad Walsh, explaining that Ransom's "one besetting sin is anxiety."[109] Then Downing continues for several pages to explain that Ransom's "time spent in this quirky sort of paradise [Malacandra] has begun the process of healing his childhood complex of fears."[110] Connecting Ransom's fears with Lewis's own childhood fears, Downing hits the target but is still far from the mark. Ransom does not simply reflect the young Lewis; the narrative is not an allegory. Certainly there are moments of anxiety in Ransom's character. But these can be better understood as evidence of his humanity in light of his abduction by Weston and Devine, as well as his being taken to another planet. Thus fears can be expected to occur in Ransom's character, especially in light of his circumstances. Here, Myers does a better job of emphasizing that the characteristic most visible in Ransom is his sense of wonder in light of the Malacandrian environment, where everything is so strange and different. In fact, what the careful reader is bound to be impressed with is the sense of awe that comes over Ransom. As he begins to describe this world, so new to him, the reader marks the contrast between the antagonists who seek only to possess and control to satisfy selfish, and subjectivist, desires, verses Ransom, the protagonist who has fallen under the spell of Malacandra and allowed that planet

108. Ibid., 47.

109. Downing, *Planets in Peril*, 104.

110. Ibid., 107. See also 104–7, for multiple references to Ransom's anxieties and fears.

to take possession of him. Ransom's objectivist interests are clear as he seeks to express not only explicit descriptions, but also indirectly to engage the rhetoric of objectification, appealing to the external world to make his points. In this sense, he is most like Lewis himself.

It is not long before Ransom finds himself comfortable in an environment that remains hostile to his antagonists. Lewis critic Lionel Adey observes, "By a nice irony, the philologist Ransom can adapt to life on Malacandra as the scientists cannot."[111] Adey's observation that Ransom's skill as a philologist makes Ransom's adjustment to his Martian environment is not wasted. At first Ransom cannot make things out as clearly as he would like. Lewis says of Ransom's initial experience, "Moreover, he knew nothing yet well enough to see it: you cannot see things till you know what they are."[112] Facility with language opens Ransom up to the larger world. He is able to adapt himself to Malacandrian community life: thereby, to gain a vocabulary by which to process his experience; thereby, to gain perspective of the objective world from which he can begin to appreciate the world as it is and grow in the rhetoric of objectivity. Far from the fears and anxieties that Downing notes, Ransom reveals strength of character and that kind of security which allows him his role as an explainer of things as they are. Furthermore, the text says of Ransom's experience on this strange planet that "Moreover, he knew nothing yet well enough to see it: you cannot see things till you know what they are."[113] Earlier it was mentioned that Downing sees the evil characters as underdeveloped, leaving the book flawed, and that Myers notes the good and bad characters as too simplistic to be useful in any kind of developed moralistic way. While I do agree that these characters are relatively simple, I would argue that Lewis designed them that way precisely because of the moral he was seeking to draw, and this moral was part of his clear and deliberate rhetorical aim. Lewis says explicitly that he intentionally made the characters in *Out of the Silent Planet* simple. Speaking of this book, Lewis writes,

> Every good writer knows that the more unusual the scenes and events of his story are, the slighter, the more ordinary, the more typical his persons should be. Hence Guliver is a common place

111. Adey, *Writer, Dreamer, and Mentor*, 122.

112. C. S. Lewis, *Out of the Silent Planet*, 42.

113. Ibid.

little man and Alice a common place little girl. If they had been more remarkable they would have wrecked their books. The Ancient Mariner himself is a very ordinary man. To tell how odd things struck odd people is to have an oddity too much: he who sees strange sights must not himself be strange. He ought to be as nearly as possible Everyman or Anyman.[114]

Unquestionably, Lewis turned to the use of Science Fiction because he himself seeks to engage in the rhetoric of objectivism. He wrote in this mode to show the complexity and largess of the world of story, as well as the world that transcends it. He sought to awaken in his reading audience a desire for these other worlds, and ultimately, for the only other world one can know, the supernatural.[115]

Lewis's descriptions, mediated through the thoughts of the protagonist, reveal in Ransom a sense of awe as he develops in response to the objective world. By contrast, Weston sees nothing in Malacandra beyond its utility, and he slowly shrivels into what is described in Perelandra as the "Unman."[116] He is from that same class of men and women Lewis's readers meet in The Great Divorce, those from Hell who, having denied "the last metaphysical right" and rejecting reality, lose their own humanity. They exemplify the process of "the abolition of man."

Weston projects onto Malacandra his vision for that planet without respect for the wishes of its citizenry. His interests are self-serving and for control. Weaver sheds light on such a character as Weston when he writes, "The nature and proper end of man are central to any discussion not only of whether a certain culture is weakening, but also whether such a culture is worth preserving."[117] Here is an irony: Weston projects his civilization onto Malacandra. He would destroy Martian culture in order to extend his own. He has lost the capacity to see if his culture is worth preserving, holding to the assumption that his culture is automatically the best. His colonialism is rooted in subjectivism, and it this subjectivism that allows him license to do evil to others. Furthermore, he has lost the capacity for true evaluation because he has lost all tran-

114. C. S. Lewis, Of Other Worlds, 64–65.

115. This is in large part, the theme of Lewis's essay "On Stories" in Of Other Worlds, 3–21.

116. C. S. Lewis, Perelandra, chapter 9.

117. Weaver, Visions of Order, 4.

scendent standards of evaluation as they might be known by reasonable men and women.

Weston lacks the capacity to define. When asked by the Oyarsa, "What do you mean by man?"[118] Weston is unable to give a clear answer. The Oyarsa responds, "I see now how the lord of the silent world has bent you. There are laws that all *hnau* [rational and properly reasoning creatures] know of pity and straight dealing and shame and the like, and one of these is love of kindred."[119] Because Weston has become so bent toward himself, the Oyarsa says to him, "You have the mind of an animal."[120] Weston is already on the slope, sliding towards becoming the "Unman." Furthermore, the Oyarsa asks Weston, "Let me see if there is anything in your mind besides fear and death and desire."[121] Whatever the quality of the rhetoric of subjectivism, one can see through this statement what motivates the messenger. Weston's fears drive him; he is too insecure to live in the universe on any other terms but his own. Desire also consumes him; it is a taking, exploiting desire without promise of satiation and without a moral compass. He has no self governance. He has loosed himself from the tether of objective value. As Weaver describes this loss of reason and emotion, without which humanity atrophies, his description reveals all that is absent in Weston:

> Rationality is an indispensable part to be sure, yet humanity includes emotionality, or the capacity to feel and suffer, to know pleasure, and it includes the capacity for aesthetic satisfaction, and what can only be suggested, a yearning to be in relation with something infinite. This last is his religious passion, or his aspiration to feel significant and to have a sense of belonging in a world that is productive of much frustration. These at least are the properties of humanity.[122]

What is clear from *Out of the Silent Planet* is the warning Lewis presents through his bad characters—evil sustains itself through subjectivism.

118. C. S. Lewis, *Out of the Silent Planet*, 138.

119. Ibid.

120. Ibid., 134.

121. Ibid.

122. Weaver, *Language is Sermonic*, 1352.

## *The Great Divorce*

British fantasy critic Colin Manlove writes that Lewis's *The Great Divorce* (1945) is an "often beautifully imagined book,"[123] while others, such as Lewis scholar and critic Donald Glover, believe that Lewis's rhetorical vision in *The Great Divorce* fails. Manlove observes that it is "the shortest and most clearly didactic of Lewis's fiction."[124] This didactic nature detracts from any success the book might have had, for "the tone of the book is that of instruction rather than self-transcendent enlightenment," and it is little more than "a lecture illustrated by examples."[125] It fails to captivate interest; it "is not a debate because the argument is all on one side, and as a consequence it fails to hold our imaginative interest and must rely on a rational engagement which comes close to being dry at times."[126] While there is something in what Glover says, for the book is clearly neither a novel nor a polemic in theology, it is nevertheless a work of imaginative theology, cleverly set forth by means of literary vignettes to make sense of the Christian doctrines of Heaven and Hell. In contrast with Glover's assessment, Chad Walsh observes, "Lewis, with his stern Christian orthodoxy, found a way to solve the dilemma [of the finality between Hell and Heaven] that is esthetically and morally satisfying, whatever theological problems it may pose."[127]

Walsh rightly observes that Lewis has borrowed from Dante's *Divine Comedy* in the creation of *The Great Divorce*.[128] While Lewis's work is a Satire, and it was certainly never his intention to write anything as grand as the *Comedy*, the influence of that work is clearly evident. As Dante appears as a character in his work, so Lewis is a primary character in the *Divorce*; as Dante is guided by Virgil and later Beatrice, so Lewis is guided by George MacDonald; as the discussion between Dante and his guides make up the interpretive structure of the *Comedy*, so too the ongoing conversation between Lewis and MacDonald provides the interpretive direction for the *Divorce*; as Hell and Heaven are the background of Dante, so they are for Lewis. Here the similarities

123. Manlove, *Literary Achievement*, 97.

124. Glover, *Art of Enchantment*, 129.

125. Ibid., 130.

126. Ibid.

127. Walsh, *Literary Legacy*, 71.

128. Ibid., 69–70.

fade, for Dante uses actual people and particularizes the images in his work, while Lewis's characters are made from generalized circumstances (though in that way each individual character may apply to a wider audience). Walsh also notes that on occasion the dialogue turns to "long-winded" moralizing and suffers tediousness for doing so. Even though these weaknesses are apparent in the book, Walsh still thinks it is the best approximation to Dante written in the twentieth-century. [129] It should also be noted that Lewis probably borrowed from Augustine. Lewis was certainly very familiar with his works. And when Lewis's good characters become more solid and real and his evil characters become diminished, something from the thought of Augustine comes into focus. In fact, there is a curious passage in *The City of God* that sounds very much like background material for *The Great Divorce*. Augustine writes, "Man did not so fall away as to become absolutely nothing; but being turned towards himself, his being became more contracted than it was when he clave to Him, Who supremely is." Augustine notes the consequences of this turn toward self: "Accordingly, to exist in himself, that is, to be his own satisfaction after abandoning God, is not quite to become a nonentity, but to approximate that."[130]

## Background

In *The Great Divorce*, the reader finds Lewis speaking rhetorically in order to challenge his readers to consider the consequences of their good and bad choices. At stake in the book is the interplay between the subjectivist's positions of "man as the measure of all things" and the opening of oneself to a larger world of objective reality and inexorable objective value. As a character in the story, Lewis finds himself in Hell. Manlove suggests that his role as narrator of the story is "to forfeit any moral purity he might otherwise wrongly have seemed to have."[131] If Lewis is himself a character counted among the damned, his judgments become less condescending (he looks down on no one since he is speaking as an insider) and more compelling. Manlove further suggests, "The whole book could be said to be a portrayal in various modes

---

129. Ibid., 79–80.

130. Augustine, *City of God*, 13.

131. Manlove, *Literary Achievement*, 116.

of the differences between Hell and Heaven."[132] Hell is characterized by a sprawling city whose central buildings are grey, dilapidated and empty. The city's emptiness is due to the fact that everyone is moving to the suburbs, not because space within the city is at a premium, but because nobody can tolerate anyone else for very long. As Kilby notes, "The same selfishness which has taken them to hell has continued its work of isolation until some are many light years from the centre."[133] Flight from this city is reminiscent of Dymer's flight from "The Perfect City," only here the flight is the first hint of subjectivism; the individual asserts his will over others and in doing so becomes very isolated and removed from the kinds of relationships that can check and balance the encroachments of evil. Lewis finds himself in a bus queue, eventually boarding a bus that takes him to the threshold of Heaven. He introduces the passengers one by one through a clever device which itself emphasizes once again the horrors of self-centeredness and its resultant isolation. As fights break out periodically during the bus trip, each one of the passengers is jumbled about and Lewis finds himself sitting next to a different character. He describes each in tragic detail, clearly describing their flaws without noticing his own until the bus reaches the threshold of Heaven. In that moment, light from Heaven illumines the inside of the bus; Lewis, looking down the aisle and seeing a mirror at the end of the bus, recognizes that he, too, qualifies to be counted among the hideous passengers.[134]

On exiting the bus, all of the passengers discover how unsuited they are for Heaven. While Hell is a city, Heaven, at least that portion of it exhibited in the book, is country "with grass, trees, birds, rivers

---

132. Ibid., 99.

133. Kilby, *Christian World*, 45.

134. This use of reflection, by means of a mirror, or a pool of water, is a common motif in Lewis. It occurs to characters caught in the balance and in need of making a choice that will be either destructive or beneficial. It can be found in *Dymer*; it is used when Eustace, *In the Voyage of the Dawn Treader*, becomes a dragon and first notices in a reflection pond the kind of person he has been all his life; it is used when Orual, in *Till We Have Faces*, looks into a pool of water to discover that she is *Ungit* (who symbolizes all that she hates most); it is in a similar way used of Lucy in *The Voyage of the Dawn Treader*, when she is tempted to say a spell in a magic book that will make her beautiful beyond the lot of mortals and the book, like a mirror, reflects back to her what it will make of her.

and hills."[135] What each discovers in that very real place is that he or she is nothing more than a shade or ghost. Each lacks noteworthy substance. This is made clear by the fact that the ghosts are so insubstantial they cannot even bend the grass beneath their feet. Nor can they pick flowers, for the stems are harder than wood or iron, like diamonds. Something about these ghosts makes them unable to accommodate themselves to Heaven. Manlove notes, "The true sin is the orientation towards self—self advancement and self-protection—that underlies the evasion of reality."[136] In other words, their subjectivism has turned devilish. Even so, each ghost is greeted by someone from within Heaven who will hopefully help make the transaction out of self and into a larger world. The heavenly beings engage the ghosts rhetorically by confronting them with something in their lives which the ghosts would prefer to keep in place of God. Lewis's own rhetorical vision is seen in these dialogues, too. Since his characters are generalized, it is easy enough for the reader to see much of himself in any given character. In this way, Lewis is challenging his readers. The ghosts are given an opportunity to renounce their particular idiosyncrasies in order to accept God's grace and forgiveness, become solid, and enter into Heaven. Yet throughout the entire book only one ghost chooses to be made whole. Lewis's character is greeted by his guide, the Scottish author George MacDonald, whose books had been such a source of inspiration to him. Clearly Lewis would like to persuade his readers to look afresh at their own lives; and MacDonald becomes the means through whom this rhetorical point is made, for he acts as narrator, explaining what is at stake in each ghost's encounter with one of the solid people. If the characters from Hell are to enter Heaven, their hope lies in their responses to "The Last Metaphysical Right," that is to the hardness of the real world, where they may surrender to things as they actually are and thereby grow solid and real.

## Sarah Smith and Frank the Tragedian

Near the end of the book, Lewis notices a great lady—solid, whole, glorious, one whom Lewis was tempted to worship. Her retinue is travelling in pageant from the heart of Heaven, obviously coming to the threshold

135. Manlove, *Literary Achievement*, 99.
136. Ibid., 108.

of that place in order to speak with one of the ghosts. In awe, Lewis asks his guide who she might be. MacDonald is quick to answer, "It's someone ye'll have never have heard of. Her name on earth was Sarah Smith and she lived at Golders Green."[137] The name is simple enough and the place is common enough, but it is clear that this woman has been gloriously rewarded for her faithfulness on earth. She has come to rescue, if she might, her very proud husband. The contrasts between them are notable. She is real; he is a ghost. She is great and solid; he is a midget, diminutive and ethereal. She has no pretence, and he is full of it. Lewis asks MacDonald if she is a person of importance. He says that she is, but mentions that importance is not measured in Heaven the same way as it is on earth. Lewis also asks about those who follow her, wondering if they are her family. MacDonald acknowledges that all who have come in contact with her become her family. She has had plenty of the quality of motherhood to bestow nurturing and grace on all who have come into her presence. "Those on whom it fell," MacDonald says, "went back to their natural parents loving them more. Few men looked on her without becoming, in a certain fashion, her lovers. But it was the kind of love that made them not less true, but truer, to their own wives."[138] MacDonald says that all nature around her has derived benefit from her. "Every beast and bird that came near her had its place in her love. In her they became themselves."[139] She stands in sharp contrast to the subjectivism of the Magician in *Dymer*, who kills a lark for disturbing his dreams. Having opened herself up to experience the abundance of real life, Sarah Smith is now teeming with it. She is a giver, and all stand to benefit from her. While many critics have appreciated the richness of this characterization, certainly not all have. For instance, Kath Filmer says, interestingly enough, that Lewis has identified strengths in Sarah Smith that connect her with a medieval ideal of chaste love. Lewis may value in her a kind of fertile mother-image and nature-goddess, but "he neglects any intellectual virtue in his female characters," and Sarah Smith is a case in point.[140] Filmer may be right in assuming from Lewis's language and description that his "Metaphysical Image" is "not so much

137. C. S. Lewis, *Great Divorce*, 109.

138. Ibid., 110.

139. Ibid., 110.

140. Filmer, *Mask and Mirror*, 94.

biblical as medieval," and that Sarah Smith is "The lady of Courtly love tradition."[141] Filmer wonders if Lewis's characterization is of much use, "Since, the exclusive identification of the spiritually whole, psychologically individuated woman with total domesticity is far from probable."[142] While Filmer's concern seems valid enough in one way, it is difficult to believe that this character has no rhetorical value for Lewis. Certainly a book written in the 1940s will lack some accommodation to the culture of the twenty-first century. It may also be valid to point out that a book written by a person of one gender is unlikely to accurately portray a person of another. But there will always be some disqualifiers, for doing justice to everyone's experience requires that everyone's experience be the same. It is important to ascertain if a character—whether from Jane Austen, Shakespeare, Edmund Spenser, or, for that matter, from any author of any age—can still speak to this present culture. If not, then a kind of cultural subjectivism may be present, making it impossible to learn from any age or culture other than one's own, and that is a precarious position in which to find oneself. In spite of the flaws of Sarah Smith as a character (or any of Lewis's characters), she still has a value in rhetorical instruction, and Sarah Smith's influence is largely due to the contrast she plays to her husband.

Sarah Smith is greeted not by one, but two phantoms. One is a tall ghost, "a seedy" tragic actor, and the other is a dwarf. It looks as if the tragedian has the dwarf on a chain, like an organ grinder dragging a monkey.[143] In time it becomes clear that it is the midget ghost that Sarah Smith has come to rescue. The tragedian merely represents the pretence of the dwarf. His character has lived in denial of the inexorable demands of objective value, and has shriveled up to nearly nothing. He seems to be incapable of seeing things as they are, though there are moments of hope. As Sarah Smith greets the dwarf, she gives him a kiss and the dwarf becomes a little more visible.[144] He refuses to answer her himself, however, and yanks the chain of the tragedian whenever a response is necessary. This seems to indicate that the ghost has so identified himself with the falsehood and pretence that there is very little of the real still

141. Ibid., 94–95.
142. Ibid., 94.
143. C. S. Lewis, *Great Divorce*, 111.
144. Ibid., 112.

remaining in him. There is an instance when the dwarf, whose name is Frank, actually recognizes Sarah Smith. Here it appears that Frank starts to grow more man-like.[145] In that moment, Lewis presents the exigency of the rhetorical situation in such a way that clarifies for the reader that Frank may move closer to wholeness if he responds to the objective world; yet, the opportunity is diminished when he disregards it in order to maintain his subjectivist stance. Lewis is subtly persuading his readers to attend to objective values. The dwarf, speaking through the tragedian, assumes that Sarah Smith has been miserable in Heaven without him. It is an indication of his sense of self importance; he is deflated when he discovers that she has been fulfilled in his absence. At one point, the dwarf and the tragedian speak in unison, but not to the lady; they speak to each other, so that it cannot be missed that the tragedian is nothing more that a subjectivist self-projection, rather than an integrated person.[146] The rhetoric is narcissistic as the tragedian gives off theatrical airs throughout the dialogue, further hints of his pretence. He plays to the hilt the ways in which he was hurt by Sarah Smith during their earthly life, making it clear that whatever case he might have had against her, he has not let it go. He is not a forgiver, and he is practiced at holding a grudge.

The tragedian begins to lecture the lady about the nature of love. It is a ridiculous posture for him to take. The reader is too familiar with the tragic-comedic appearances of the other ghosts who have appeared in the book up till now. Furthermore, Sarah Smith is so solid and real that her splendor makes further nonsense of anything spectral that the ghost might say on the nature of love. Nevertheless, he strikes a pose and begins to speak about love. He stops suddenly only to begin over again in a voice "a few notes deeper." He asks about love, "Do you know the meaning of the word?"[147] Here Sarah Smith marks that on earth the examples fell far short of real love because "what we called love down there was mostly the craving to be loved. In the main I loved you for my own sake; because I needed you."[148] The tragedian is not very happy at the revelation that she does not need him anymore. She has found real

---

145. Ibid., 113.
146. Ibid., 114.
147. Ibid., 116.
148. Ibid.

love in Heaven; she is not looking to him for her fulfillment and, consequently, she can now love better than before. "We shall have no *need* for one another now: we can begin to love truly."[149] The dwarf is nearly evaporated by this statement. He has developed a tyrannical posture of the need to be needed, and thus he has a need to control every situation. He has used this posture as a means to manipulate others by his "hurt" feelings. He never recovers, and in the end he virtually disappears, lost. Unable to accommodate himself to reality, unable to release any misconceptions he might have to do so, he chooses damnation rather than life on some other terms than his own.

There is an irony in this passage. Without thought of herself, Sarah Smith gives her energy and resources away and is made whole by it. She is followed by throngs of those she has uplifted and encouraged. By contrast, the ghost longs to be noticed; he is the consummate actor looking for an audience. He wants others to notice him, to value him, to acknowledge his importance. The rhetoric of his subjectivist ways have lost all persuasive power and produce an effect opposite from the ghosts self-centered desire. He is diminished by his self importance. Because he will not surrender himself to the claims objective value make upon him, he comes to the place where he no longer has a self to give. Such it is with Lewis's evil characters. This is further evident in *The Magician's Nephew*.

## *The Magician's Nephew*

While *The Magician's Nephew* (1955) is the sixth book Lewis wrote in his seven book collection called *The Chronicles of Narnia*, it is actually the first book in the historic chronology of that world, for it contains the creation of Narnia. Nevertheless, there has been some debate as to its main thrust or theme. Manlove says that "growth" is the ruling "metaphor"[150] that one must keep in mind to properly interpret *The Magician's Nephew*. It is possible to observe within the story growth in relation to magic, evil, the creation and development of Narnia, and moral development in some of its characters. Glover, on the other hand, says, "At its most basic level, the book is concerned with the difference between magic

149. Ibid. This idea of love is one Lewis also develops in *Four Loves*, 10–15, and 62–63.

150. Manlove, *Literary Achievement*, 174

and creativity."[151] Jadis, Queen of Charn (the eventual White Witch of *The Lion, the Witch and the Wardrobe*) and Uncle Andrew use magic in the book to gain power and ascendancy. By contrast, creativity is in the power of Aslan, the Christ figure of the books, and he uses it to grant life to others. Walsh believes that within the book, "The one serious theme is the nature of good and evil."[152] Queen Jadis represents evil, and as Walsh observes, "It is not that she is filled with evil. She *is* evil."[153] In contrast, Kathryn Ann Lindskoog writes that the main theme of the book is power: "The characters in *The Magician's Nephew* moved from weakness to power—or at least tried to do so." Lindskoog further says that they do so because "anyone with spunk wants power."[154] Furthermore, Professor Doris T. Myers writes, "The major issue of *The Magician's Nephew* . . . is the relationship between illicit knowledge and the control of Nature."[155] She also writes many times over that the book feels "middle-aged," and that "On a more personal level, the book allows Lewis to go back to the time when he was a child," to revisit with nostalgia the world in which he grew up, as well as revisit the circumstances surrounding the death of his mother.[156] While each of the authors above sees something of the vision of *The Magician's Nephew*, none of them has as full a picture as they might of Lewis's rhetorical purpose for the book.

Certainly all of the above can be found in the book, but when one considers the theme in light of Lewis's corpus, it becomes clear that it is primarily about subjectivism and the evil that comes from it, as well as the character traits that emerge from choices made with respect to objective value. The argument of the book may be best seen if it is unpackaged thematically. While the book has many important characters, the primary ones include Uncle Andrew, otherwise known as "the Magician;" his alter-ego Jadis, Queen of Charn, also the White Witch of Narnia; and Digory, the "Nephew," also Professor Kirke of *The Lion, the Witch and the Wardrobe*. Certainly other characters could be highlighted to underscore the theme more deeply. Other good characters

---

151. Glover, *Art of Enchantment*, 173.

152. Walsh, *Literary Legacy*, 134.

153. Ibid., 136.

154. Lindskoog, *Journey into Narnia*.

155. Myers, *C. S. Lewis in Context*, 167.

156. Ibid., 166–67.

include Polly, (Digory's friend), The Cabby Frank and his wife Helen (who become the first King and Queen of Narnia) and Aunt Letty and Digory's mother—all characters who support the idea that good may come from acts of surrender to objective value.

## The Magician

The first time Digory Kirke mentions Uncle Andrew to his new neighbor, Polly Plummer, he says that his Uncle is mad. Digory has left his home in the country to live in London with his old bachelor Uncle and his old maid Aunt Letty. As his father has had to go to India, the Aunt has volunteered to watch over him and his dying mother. The two children happen, by accident, into Uncle Andrew's attic study, and it is on this occasion the reader first gets a glimpse at the mysterious Uncle, who enters the room "like a pantomime demon coming up out of a trapdoor."[157] The comparison with a demon is clearly intentional and makes Lewis's rhetorical case concerning Uncle Andrew's character very clear. Uncle Andrew tricks Polly into touching a yellow ring made from the dust of Atlantis, sending her out of her world and into another, or as he says, "a world that could only be reached by Magic."[158] It is here that Uncle Andrew's role as a magician is revealed, and that something of Lewis's views of magic must be understood.

As a medievalist, Lewis had written rather clearly about the nature of magic, or at least how the art of magic was understood in the sixteenth century. In his contribution to the *Oxford History of English Literature*, Lewis writes that the literary historian "is not concerned with those ideas in his period which have since proved fruitful, but with those which seemed important at the time." In this regard his is a difficult task, for "He must even try to forget his knowledge of what comes after, and see the egg as if he did not know that it was going to become a bird."[159] For example, although today magic and astrology might be lumped together, Lewis writes that they were seen in opposition during the Middle Ages. "The magician asserts human omnipotence; the astrologer, human impotence."[160] The astrologer is a "determinist,"

157. C. S. Lewis, *Magician's Nephew*, 18.
158. Ibid., 25.
159. C. S. Lewis, *English Literature*, 4–5.
160. Ibid., 6.

whereas the magician seeks to assert his will over nature. It was believed by Campanella (1568–1639) that the senses were "more certain than intellectual knowledge," and since the sentient was shared by man and beast, perhaps there was a way to awaken the "sleeping sense" of the brutes. "If we and Nature are all one, there must be some nearer way of controlling her than by mechanics; some direct way, 'as when one man commandeth another who is in his power.'"[161]

Lewis links the magician's desire to control with the interest of the new science that was developing under the efforts of Sir Francis Bacon, for the scientist and the magician shared similar aims.[162] As Lewis explains, the sixteenth-century revival of interest in magic created an atmosphere in which "*magia* far from being an anomaly in that age, falls into its place among other dreams of power which then haunted the European mind."[163] Lewis explicitly states that "most obviously it falls into place beside the thought of Bacon," for "Bacon and the magicians have the closest possible affinity. Both seek knowledge for the sake of power." In a text that seems to echo the interests of Uncle Andrew, and Jadis Queen of Charn, Lewis writes that magicians, as well as the sixteenth-century scientist, "move in a grandiose dream of days when Man shall have been raised to the performance of 'all things possible.'"[164] Lewis also writes that Bacon thought the aim of magic was a noble one. In the Middle Ages there was a doctrine of man whereby he saw himself on a particular rung of a hierarchy which included Nature and man's obligations to it. The power sought by the magicians and scientists of that era placed man above his hierarchical responsibilities, and objective value was less likely to guide him.[165] To put it in terms familiar to Weaver, the magician failed to respect "the last metaphysical right." He had no sense of obligation to property as an object signaling either objective value or morality. His interest to control for personal gain put him at risk to deduce an end in himself. Lewis warns against this kind of philosophy in *The Abolition of Man*. He says, "For the wise men of old the cardinal problem had been how to conform the soul to reality,

161. Ibid.
162. Ibid., 13–14.
163. Ibid., 13.
164. Ibid., 13–14.
165. Ibid., 14.

and the solution had been knowledge, self-discipline, and virtue. For magic and applied science alike the problem is how to subdue reality to the wishes of men."[166]

In effect, Uncle Andrew has stepped away from the *Tao*, and as a consequence his humanity is diminished. He has no sense of self-giving; he is a manipulator whose design is self-aggrandizement at the expense of others. Lewis establishes this point by means of numerous demonstrations throughout the book. Uncle Andrew maintains inappropriate ambiguity in his own morality.[167] He claims to be above the rules that would govern "little boys—and servants—and women—and even people in general." He declares to Digory, "Men like me, who possess hidden wisdom, are freed from common rules just as we are cut off from common pleasures. Ours, my boy, is a high and lonely destiny."[168] His cowardice sends others into harms way, as it does with Polly, but he is not willing to take risks himself; in this way he demonstrates his lack of regard for the welfare of others.[169] This fact is developed further in that he blackmails Digory to go to the other world where he has sent Polly in order to retrieve her. If Digory refuses, Polly will be lost forever.[170] In this way, Uncle Andrew demonstrates how evil he has become. Lewis gives ongoing examples to establish the lapses in Uncle Andrew's character. Time after time he chooses to act contrary to objective value, doing to others things he would not have wanted done to him. He takes advantage of Digory's scruples knowingly; he is calculating and clever about getting others to do his bidding. Throughout the book, Lewis makes it clear that Uncle Andrew is a closet alcoholic. He has taken advantage of Aunt Letty's resources, stealing from her for a period of thirty years.[171] He is cruel to animals,[172] and therefore very much like the magician in *Dymer*, who shoots the lark because it disturbs his dreams; likewise, Uncle Andrew longs numerous times to have a gun in Narnia that he might shoot Aslan.[173] Given the opportunity, he would

166. C. S. Lewis, *Abolition of Man*, 88.
167. C. S. Lewis, *Magician's Nephew*, 22.
168. Ibid., 23.
169. Ibid., 20–30.
170. Ibid., 28.
171. Ibid., 75.
172. Ibid., 26.
173. Ibid., 96, 101–2, 103.

destroy anything that might stand in his way to assert his will over the world. This is seen in direct contrast with Aslan, who in the creation of Narnia is the giver of life.[174] Uncle Andrew blames others for his sins and short-comings.[175] He is narcissistic.[176] He thinks he can win the heart of the Witch by his charms, and worse, he wants to do so because he alone values her.[177] He misinterprets data, reading into it that which will be to his own advantage. He will not surrender to objective reality.[178] "Like the Witch, he was dreadfully practical."[179] Finally, he "suppresses the truth in his unrighteousness;" rather than acknowledge the power of Aslan and His claims upon him, Digory at first refuses to see and hear things as they are, until at last he can neither see nor hear.[180] His refusal to accept the universe as it is, and his attempts to project his own self-interests in order to shape his world, causes him to be reduced in a way similar to the ghosts in *The Great Divorce*. And like Weston in *Perelandra*, he has become an "unman."

## The Magician's Alter Ego: Jadis Queen of Charn

Polly and Andrew find themselves in another world, a world of suspended animation. They enter into a great hall filled with people who, in their suspended state, appear to be reduced to mere images. The faces of the people are solemn and grave. One particular figure of a woman attracts their attention for her beauty, her severity, and her size. There is a bell in the centre of the hall, and carved in a stone pillar is this inscription:

> *Make your choice, adventurous Stranger;*
> *Strike the bell and bide the danger,*
> *Or wonder, till it drives you mad,*
> *What would have followed if you had.*[181]

The inscription refers to the consequences of ringing the bell. It is a call to the exercise of choice. To leave it alone is to avoid the dangers it refer-

---

174. Ibid., 108–9.
175. Ibid., 90.
176. Ibid., 117
177. Ibid., 73.
178. Ibid., 118–19.
179. Ibid., 116.
180. Ibid., 117–18.
181. Ibid., 50.

ences, while to strike it may put the children in the place of the beautiful Pandora. Certainly the circumstances themselves mark the potential for evil, should one step away from the objective value implied. Digory is tempted by the inscription, and he and Polly argue about whether they ought to strike the bell. She simply wants to leave. But in an unthinking rush of anger, and much against Polly's will, Digory yields to the temptation. Like the fall of man itself, the sound of the bell seems small, at first; yet rather than dissipating, it increases to a deafening crescendo. Lewis's rhetorical designs are as clear as the ringing of the bell itself; he shows that evil—as significant as the overwhelming peal of the bell—can be aroused. In a moment, the children discover that they have awakened the beautiful but severe woman statue.

This woman is Jadis, Queen of Charn. Several things are apparent about her right away. First, she ignores Polly completely, assuming that Digory is the one who has the power between the two children. Her character is such that she only seems to notice those who are useful to her interests. She warns the children that the palace of the great hall is about to collapse on them, and grabbing them with her powerful grasp makes escape from her impossible.[182] It is clear that she is only saving them because she sees them as her own means of escape. She questions the children about the powerful magician who sent them, assuming that he has sent delegates to bring her back as his queen. She interprets their presence in her world in a way that projects onto the facts whatever it is she wants. She is, like Uncle Andrew and all of the villains of Lewis's invention, a subjectivist. She will make the facts fit her interpretation of them. She will not accommodate herself to the world as it is. And as to her interpretations, Polly says, "Why, it's bosh from beginning to end." Lewis's rhetorical judgments regarding this character are clear.[183]

The queen has done more than merely project her interpretation on the facts as they are; she has also asserted her will on the world that is crumbling before the children's eyes. She tells bits and pieces of her story, shading the details so that she will appear in a good light. Unfortunately, the details are so horrible that the children see clearly that the Witch is self-deceived. She explains that there had been a war in Charn between her and her sister and that she had sacrificed great numbers of her army

182. Ibid., 55.
183. Ibid., 63.

until she was defeated by the forces of the opposition. It was then that she spoke "the deplorable word," a magic word that she had learned at a great price. It gave her the power, when spoken, to wipe out every living being in her world but herself alone.[184] Pertaining to this passage, Myers says the "deplorable word" is "obviously a counterpart of the atom bomb." She may be right, but it is not obviously so, for the witch, having destroyed the world, still remains alive and escapes the destruction, something that would not have happened had her use of the "word" been exactly like the bomb. I think the idea of subjectivism works better in describing what has happened. For the sake of her selfish ambition, and with a desire to maintain herself, even at her world's expense, she has uttered the "word." This position is further supported by the text as Digory expresses his horror: "But the people?" The Witch wonders as to what Digory can have in mind and asks, "What people, boy?" Polly answers, "All the ordinary people . . . who'd never done you any harm. And the women, and the children, and the animals." The Witch speaks condescendingly to Digory, ignoring Polly, "Don't you understand.... They were all *my* people. What else were they there for but to do my will?"[185] She then explains that being a great Queen allows her to do some things that might be wrong for others, "The weight of the world is on our shoulders. We must be freed from all rules. Ours is a high and lonely destiny."[186] She utters the exact same words Uncle Andrew has already spoken to Digory after he had sent Polly's disappearance into the other world; the subjectivist justification which they both employ, with its corresponding rhetoric, seems to amplify their wickedness. Jadis has forsaken "the last metaphysical right," and with it any sense of responsibility to others. As Weaver explains, "piety accepts the substance of other beings."[187] Yet, she has none of the chivalry that was evident in the best of kings and queens of old. Here again, Weaver's insight is relevant:

> Chivalry was a most practical expression of the basic brotherhood of man. But to have enough imagination to see other lives and enough piety to realize that their existence is a part of be-

184. Ibid., 60–61.

185. Ibid., 61.

186. Ibid.

187. Weaver, *Ideas*, 175.

neficent creation is the very foundation of human community. There appear to be two types to whom this kind of charity is unthinkable: the barbarian, who would destroy what is different because it is different, and the neurotic, who always reaches out for control of others, probably because his own integration has been lost. However that may be, the shortsightedness which will not grant substance to other people or other personalities is just that intolerance which finds different less worthy.[188]

Jadis, like all of Lewis's evil characters, operates with the rhetoric of subjectivism, motivated by either barbarianism, or insecurity, or both.

Jadis's attitude is not unique among those characters in Lewis who are either evil or at risk of becoming evil. A case in point may be found in a short story titled *The Shoddy Lands*. Lewis has a daydream about a woman named Peggy who grows very large, while the things in her world grow distorted and out of focus; they become shoddy lands, shoddy sky, shoddy woods, shoddy trees, shoddy grass and shoddy people. The only things that remain in focus for Peggy are those things that are of im-mediate use to her—things such as cut flowers, sandy beaches without oceans, an occasional man's face or an occasional woman's outfit. She seems to know nothing about the objective world, nor does she seem to care about its claims upon her. Before the daydream is over, Lewis hears the voice of Peggy's fiancé knocking, calling to Peggy desperately to be allowed into her world. She makes no room for him. Then Lewis hears another "voice at whose sound my bones turned to water: 'Child, child, child, let me in before the night comes.'"[189]

This particular motif may also be found in *The Voyage of the Dawn Treader*. Lucy is in a magician's house, looking through a very large book in the hopes of discovering a certain spell. As she searches through the book, she runs across "*An infallible spell to make beautiful her that uttereth it beyond the lot of mortals.*" She is even given opportunity to watch what will happen if she might say the words of this particular spell: it is all flattery to the ego; she becomes the center of the world, and for her beauty wars are fought, kingdoms are laid waste, and the world nearly destroyed so that she can have her way. It is very close to a pronouncement of the "deplorable word." She is only restrained from saying the spell by a vision of Aslan, whose inexorable growl brings

188. Ibid., 175–76.
189. C. S. Lewis, *Of Other Worlds*, 105.

Lucy back to the demands of objective value and prevents her from going down the path of Jadis.[190]

As the Kingdom of Charn crumbles, Jadis says to Digory and Polly, "Now let's be going." The children are surprised at this, and even more so when they learn of her intention to take over their world. Despite their efforts, they cannot prevent her from entering and bringing havoc to the streets of London. Eventually, Digory is able to get her out of London, accompanied by a cabby named Frank, his horse Strawberry, Uncle Andrew, Jadis and Polly. They all find themselves at the dawn of a new world, which happens to be Narnia. Even here, Jadis sets her sights on conquest, no matter what it may cost the new Narnians in order for her to achieve power. She will, in time, be able to make it "always winter in Narnia but never Christmas."[191] She is a supreme example of Lewis's evil characters. As Filmer writes, "Theologically, his position seems to be that the Fall essentially consisted of the assertion of the self over God." Furthermore, "Those beings who are enslaved to the self seek to dominate and control others to the point of absorbing their wills and personalities."[192]

## The Magician's Nephew: Digory

Because of the significant role of Digory's character in the book, much of who he is and what he does has been seen as backdrop against the character development of the evil Uncle Andrew and Queen Jadis. Nevertheless, Digory's moment of failure takes place—as has been mentioned—when he rings the bell in the "Hall of Images," in the crumbling palace of Charn. He has to admit that this act ultimately makes him responsible as the one who introduces evil into Narnia at the moment of its creation. While *The Magician's Nephew* is a children's book, Digory is not necessarily a simple character. When Uncle Andrew sends Polly off into another world, Digory does not have to deliberate as to whether or not he will go after her. He is courageous. Nevertheless, he makes a foolish mistake when he intemperately rings the bell that awakens Jadis because he cannot control his curiosity. He again demonstrates courage

---

190. C. S. Lewis, *Voyage of the Dawn Treader*, 127–28.

191. C. S. Lewis, *Lion, the Witch and the Wardrobe*, 14, 32–33.

192. Filmer, *Mask and Mirror*, 29.

when he takes risks to remove the Queen from London. But his biggest challenge comes late in the book.

The adventures which make up the story of *The Magician's Nephew* are, for Digory, mere canvas compared to the more pressing concern he has for the health of his dying mother. At one point he overhears his Aunt Letty say that if his mother might have some fruit from another world, perhaps she could be cured of her disease.[193] The comment sets Digory to thinking that he might, by virtue of his use of the magic rings, explore other worlds until he finds a cure for his mother. Lewis uses Digory's concern for his mother and his power of the rings to set the stage for his biggest temptation. As has been mentioned, Weaver observes that, "Virtue is a state of character concerned with choice, it flourishes only in the area of volition."[194] Digory is given an opportunity to set right the evil he has done. After Aslan creates Narnia, Digory musters up the courage to approach the Lion to ask if he would do something to heal his mother. Aslan confronts Digory with the errors he has committed at Charn, and then he tells him of a tree, far away, whose apples have the power to prevent the Witch from gaining control of Narnia. Digory must go and bring one of the apples from the tree; therein is his temptation, for as the apple can preserve Narnia, it can also save his mother. In a very moving passage, Digory stands head bowed and teary-eyed before Aslan, wrestling with the interior struggle. He looks up into the Lion's face to see a tear in his eyes as well.[195] In light of Lewis's experience with the death of his mother, the passage suggests that perhaps Lewis was revisiting the experience in his memory as he wrote. Aslan's tears give Digory a sense of courage and commitment as he sets out on his task.

Digory arrives at a walled garden, within which grows the tree, to find an inscription on the gate, written on gold with silver letters. It is reminiscent of the inscription carved in the stone pillar by the bell in the hall of Charn. This time, Digory follows the instructions exactly. To his shock he finds that the Witch is also at the garden, eating the apples in order to gain immortality for herself. She tempts Digory to do the same, but his obedience, and his willingness to sacrifice personal

---

193. C. S. Lewis, *Magician's Nephew*, 81.

194. Weaver, *Ideas Have Consequences*, 137.

195. C. S. Lewis, *Magician's Nephew*, 131.

desires for the sake of others, allows him to escape becoming like the Witch and Uncle Andrew. By forming a proper response to his situation, Digory respects "the last metaphysical right," or objective value. In the end Narnia is able to ward off the encroachment of the Witch for hundreds of years, and Aslan heals Digory's mother.

## Conclusions

I have argued in this chapter that Lewis's villains are subjectivists. They seek to press personal advantage without respect for objective value or the property of others, and they do so by bringing pain to others and peril to themselves. The results are evil. Lewis's rhetorical concern for objective value and his warnings against subjectivism are highlighted by Richard Weaver's objectivist commitments as he develops them in his ideas of property as "the last metaphysical right." These pervasive objectivist commitments in Lewis unify his poetry, fiction and non-fiction. In the end, when his villains step away from objective value, they do so at the loss of their own humanity. On the other hand, his heroes, in conformity to reality, grow through struggle to develop in character and solidity.

# 6

# Conclusions

## Summary of the Argument

I HAVE ARGUED THAT A CENTRAL UNIFYING ELEMENT IN C. S. LEWIS'S work may be attributed to his desire to understand and argue rhetorically for objective reality, or objects as they really are. Consequently, he challenges his readers to conform to objective value in a way that is intellectually, emotionally, and psychologically appropriate. I have also argued that to move away from Lewis's doctrine of objective value is to move towards subjectivism, which is unresponsive to the way that things are. Subjectivism is not necessarily evil, but unchecked it may become the dangerous support for evil. Lewis's concerns about the insipid nature of subjectivism and its inclination toward evil leads him to account for the problem in virtually all of the modes in which he writes. This is particularly notable in the development of his literary characters; ideally, background material on subjectivism and objectivism, when considered, helps the reader make sense of Lewis's literary figures. I argue that Lewis believes that a subjectivist may be set straight again by an honest response to things as they are, as best one might know them. And here, rhetorical theorist Richard Weaver's work provides a means for evaluating Lewis's thought in select ways. For example, Weaver's ideas on the validity of various types of arguments allows for fair judgments of Lewis's *The Abolition of Man*. Ultimately, Lewis's objectivist commitments should motivate his readers to dig more deeply even when it comes to understanding Lewis's own work.

In chapter 2, I have shown that Lewis's biographical details, as best as they might be understood and organized into interpretive clusters, are also an important part of this study. Lewis was concerned about the problem of evil from his earliest childhood days, and the pathos of his disappointing situation had much in it to drive him far from the Sunday school faith of those early years. His return to faith in his early thirties led him to examine the *logos* of the arguments both for and against Christianity. He was convinced of the reasonableness of his faith, and he set about in this period of his life to present Christianity apologetically to the masses. Foremost, the death of his wife forced him to look more deeply still at the arguments for Christianity, which had sustained him up to that point. Lewis's rhetorical voice is given credence because of all he was forced to process, and, speaking honestly about his loss, he gained increased creditability. His objectivist beliefs made it possible for him to grow and adjust to life as he encountered it.

In chapter 3, I have shown that Lewis's strong commitment to objectivity, his awareness that evil can emerge from subjectivism, and his widespread concern for his readers' situations, all led him to account for this problem in light of the practice of literary criticism. Lewis exposes many of the literary critical practices that subjectify literature so that one may read into a text whatever one is predisposed to find there. I argue that Lewis's criticism of these practices further indicates his concern about subjectivism as a problem of evil, and that the idea is pervasive in the Lewis corpus, especially regarding the characters in his fictional works.

Lewis's reasons for using fiction are significant to the topic of this study. Some have suggested that failure to keep abreast of the complex philosophical issues of his day caused Lewis to abandon Christian apologetics for fiction; but in chapter four, I argue that fiction was a significant portion of his literary output all along. Furthermore, Lewis's rhetorical interests were served by his fiction in ways that allowed him to creatively address issues which would otherwise be limited by the use of non-fiction.

Also, in chapter 5 I have asserted that an analysis of four particular literary texts—each from a different decade of Lewis's life—reveals the motivations of evil characters in contrast to the motives of good characters. In Lewis's pre-Christian narrative poem *Dymer*, I have shown that the protagonist Dymer is strikingly different in relation to the antagonists Bran and the Magician. Dymer's development occurs as he adjusts his thought and action in a way congruous with objective reality. On the other hand, his antagonists seek to modify reality to fit their wishes. The former results in positive, though at times painful, development, while the latter leads to the diminishing of self and to evil. In the analysis of *Out of the Silent Planet*, I have shown that the protagonist Ransom, responsive to things as they are, grows with a sense of awe and wonder; whereas, his antagonist Weston projects his own will onto the natural order of things in an attempt to control his environment. Lewis makes it evident that the subjectivism of Weston leads to the destruction of his own soul, and Ransom's positive responses, informed by objective value, results in his mental, emotional, and relational health. In exploring the characters of *The Great Divorce*, a similar insight has been offered, for those who surrender to the inexorable claims of objective value mature to wholeness, while those who do not, choosing instead the path of subjectivism, become evil and are reduced to nothing. This phenomenon is further explored in Lewis's *The Magician's Nephew*. The character Digory makes a grievous error when he chooses that which is contrary to good sense, but redeems himself and grows when he responds to his circumstances with humility, accepting things as they are, not as he would have them to be. Digory is contrasted with his Uncle Andrew and Queen Jadis of Charn. These two characters, also subjectivists, display that kind of evil which develops due to a lack of response to objective value. Other literary works by Lewis also support the claim that Lewis's evil characters are driven by subjectivism. I simply seek to cite several representative examples over a four-decade span to support the claim that the idea of subjectivism, and its connection with evil, is significant and pervasive in Lewis's writing. Therefore his rhetorical interest is to set forth the problem in various ways, particularly in his fiction.

## Areas for Further Study

While this study has demonstrated its argument according to the paths described above, it would appear that many other interesting areas of possible inquiry necessarily had to be ignored which may be useful for future study and development. A lengthier analysis of a wider range of Lewis's evil characters would effectively show how Lewis nuances the concept of evil, emerging through subjectivism. Furthermore, the discussion of *Dymer* has brought forth the richness of some of Lewis's pre-Christian work. There has been very little done thus far in relation to the continuity of thought between Lewis's pre-Christian thinking and his more mature thought. Hence, it is an area worthy of study for several reasons. First, there can be a tendency among some secular and Christian circles, to look doubtfully, and sometimes condescendingly, at each other's world views. Nevertheless, a large body of material may be held in common by both camps who are making critical judgments of one another. As an adult convert to Christianity, Lewis had much of the foundation of his thought well in place prior to his conversion: his training in logic and discursive thought, his background in classical languages and literature, and his familiarity with English language and literature. It is difficult to believe that all his thinking was jettisoned at the time he became a Christian, leaving him to start over again. Certainly modifications to the foundations of his thought were necessary, but modifications are inevitable for anyone who is truly growing and developing intellectually. Lewis provides a rich source of study to discover where lines may or may not be drawn in the distinction between Christian and non-Christian thought. It is reasonable to suppose that differences between the two groups may be less drastic than one might suspect. Of course, the issues related to supernaturalism versus materialism would be a real divide. Even so, much thought related to traditionalist versus progressive, conservative versus liberal, or bourgeois versus proletarian, tends to find its way into the streams of both secular and religious thought. Since there is much in Lewis's early thinking (recorded in his published poetry, his journal, numerous letters, and even in the bits of *The Allegory of Love* which were completed before his conversion) that survives into adulthood, he would be an interesting source of study along these lines. His work may even enhance a developing respect among those whose world views conflict, as well as provide a wide range of topics to be discussed in forums that generate a kind of collegiality, while at the same time reducing suspicion.

## Further Benefits of the Study

Lewis's life was complex, and a lifetime of pain and reflection led to his looking at the matter of evil and suffering from many angles. The evidence for this is particularly notable because Lewis allowed the discussion of evil and its related themes to work its way into all of his expressive modes. I would not call this a preoccupation or an obsession, on his part, but because evil was an unavoidable fact of his world, thoughts regarding it were unavoidably present in his work. Because he wrote honestly about the world in which he lived, he necessarily had to account for evil. And because he took his faith seriously, he had to reconcile evil and suffering with the existence of a good and all-powerful God. Also, since the worlds he made up in his fiction were to have coherence and value for the world in which he lived, those works of fiction had to have dangers from evil, pain, and suffering. Additionally the characters he created, by necessity had to encounter evil in their worlds and face the realities of evil and weakness in their own natures.

In those places where modifications in his thinking about evil can be observed, the changes reveal a breaking down and revising of old conceptions; but Lewis's thinking does not start all over again. His tendency is to modify and add to what has come before. This is itself reminiscent of what he writes about the medieval man, who was constantly seeking to enlarge his model of the universe so that he could fit more and more into it. While Lewis's approach has its flaws, it also has value for anyone who might read Lewis with an open mind. The process evident in his growth contains value in itself. He develops before his readers a growing and dynamic vision of reality—a rhetoric for life. Still Lewis's work does not allow for a final conclusion. His insights come with the rhetorical challenge to his readers to go "Further up and further in." To claim that any single grasp of the matter has achieved the weight of a last word for Lewis would be false. If God is to be seen as vindicated in light of the problem of evil and suffering, it presupposes that He will need to be understood by His creatures over and over again. Perhaps this is why Lewis made so much of the struggle of good and evil in his fiction. Likewise, perhaps it is why the struggle of good and evil is common to most fiction. No one expects permanent resolutions from a story. We long to see the tensions of a particular story resolved in a particular way so that from the story we might have hope. It does the reader well to see that the subjectivist motivations of evil characters prevent them from opening up to a larger understanding of their world. It is also helpful to discover that good characters find hope in opening up to a world larger than their speculation about it at any given time. They also find that kind of humility which is the by-product of wonder and awe.

Furthermore, Lewis seems to guard against universalizing; he moves away from it not because he does not believe in the possibility of universal truths, but because he believes that no mortal mind is capable of such comprehension or competent to communicate such things to others. He is content in the end with *supposals* and particular instances. How might the problem of evil and suffering work out in the kind of situation described in a particular story? If evil existed in a world like *Narnia*, made by a good creator, how might things come to a coherent conclusion? In one of the Narnia books, Aslan tells Lucy that he exists in her world too, and adds, "This was the very reason why you were brought to Narnia, that by knowing me here for a little, you may know me better there."[1] Perhaps it might equally be said that understanding some degree of resolution to the problem of evil as it is developed in a story might also translate into real life experience. To know how resolutions work in a story might open a reader's eyes to how resolutions manifest themselves day to day.

Lewis does not work through the issues related to evil and suffering only once. Time after time, over and over, volume after volume, story after story, he comes at it first from this direction and then from that. For example, in *The Narnian Chronicles*, it is worked out for Digory as he struggles to reconcile himself with the grief he feels in light of the imminent death of his mother. It is worked out further when he discovers that Aslan's tears have matched his own. It is worked out again for Digory when he discovers Aslan's way for dealing with the evil that has come into Narnia through Queen Jadis. It is worked out for Edmund after he gets himself in a mess with the White Witch, betraying his own siblings in the process. He cannot rescue himself. Aslan must rescue him in a way unique to Edmund's situation, in a way not presupposed by the characters in the story. At first sight, it is a surprise that Aslan would die to set Edmund free from the consequences of his evil acts. And yet the surprise is followed by the reader's concession: "Yes that is how Aslan might have been expected to act. I just never thought of it." Perhaps it is something *like* that for each of us. It is worked out for Lucy and High King Peter, Mr. Tumnus and the Beavers. It is worked out for Caspian, Reepicheep, and Prince Rilian. It is seen again in the particular instance of Eustace's undragoning. Likewise, it is worked out through Ransom's battle against the Unman in order to save Perelandra from a Fall like that which has occurred on the "Silent Planet." It is worked out through Mark Studdock's battle with ambition and Queen Orual's

---

1. C. S. Lewis, *Voyage of the Dawn Treader*, 188.

complaint against the gods. In fact, all of Lewis's fictional rhetoric serves to prove that one picture will not do, and that one image is too small to reveal something so grand as God's purpose for and method of dealing with evil and suffering.

The problem of keeping faith in light of the existence of evil has unique complexities which were familiar to Lewis. How can the finite confidently judge the intentions of the Infinite? How does one of limited understanding grasp the rationale of the Omniscient? Certainly there may seem to be contradictions, ambiguities, and paradoxes. Should these not be expected? If God exists, then we can imagine that there will be mystery surrounding some of His activities. Even so, we must exert effort to understand as much as can be understood. Although Lewis is to be commended to the degree he tries to work his way through these thorny issues, there are places where his attempts to explain evil produced nonsense. That, too, should be expected. And it should come as a warning to those who over-idealize his capabilities. Lewis was, like any man, capable of errors in judgment. But if every one is capable of misjudgment, then we must take care not to silence any voice too quickly. For just as there are those who would over-idealize Lewis, so there are those who would quickly dismiss him. He was both serious and public about his faith, and thus his public opinions drew criticism. In some cases I think he welcomed it; for criticisms that brought to light actual deficiencies in his arguments pressed him toward the truth. But those criticisms that were nothing more than an attack on the man did not contribute constructively to the discussion. Lewis seems to have enjoyed noble opposition. He would challenge ideas in the hopes of advance. If he was proven wrong, so be it; objections were clarified and truth or right opinion was the victor. On this point, I have been impressed by the absence of *ad hominems* in his writing. He could be bold and confident, and perhaps some found that offensive, but there is little evidence of actual discourtesy in him. In this way, his debating and discursive reasoning provide examples of fair rhetorical play, and that is a helpful model. Its lessons are useful for any discussion. When we consider the problem of evil and suffering (whether we consider our own experience or the experiences of others), we are simply considering data. And that data must be interpreted. Interpretations represent the following: 1) They may be right. (Does anyone have the confidence that he can be completely right about his speculations on any issue, let alone the problem of evil? Certainly one may believe he knows enough to be convinced one way or another, but what mere mortal would suggest that complete success, all the time, could be achieved?) 2) They may be wrong; or 3) They may be partially right, and thus partially wrong. In the end, Lewis is to be valued, not for what he cannot give, but for what he can give. He enlivens discussion through fresh examples and illustrations, and sets his readers on a good path.

Lewis does not consider the problem of evil apart from honesty about his own failures and proclivities to go wrong. There is little sign of subjectivism in him. Furthermore, for him, evil is not merely an issue for theological or philosophical discussion, nor is it a topic that gives him license to blame God or others for the majority of problems that he faces. His approach is more "homey" than that. He wrestles with issues while maintaining an honesty and humility that will not allow him to forget his own shortcomings. This is also a helpful example, useful for coping not only with the intellectual idea of suffering and evil, but also with the failures and disappointments of day-to-day life. He writes, "We learn, on the one hand, that we cannot trust ourselves even in our best moments, and, on the other, that we need not despair even in our worst, for our failures are forgiven."[2]

## A Final Word

All academic studies must end in some degree of doubt. There is always something left out. Limitations of time and space have necessitated that such is the case in this investigation. Lewis's skill has made me wish I could simply say to readers, "Oh but you should read him for yourself! I know you will benefit from the experience." I have enjoyed his work so much, and his books have opened doors for me on hundreds of others. The most difficult part of this process has been for me to learn how to read him more critically. It is like asking someone to look critically on a familiar landscape that has brought years of pleasure. And yet, the greatest benefit from the whole process of writing this book has come from the cultivating a critical eye. The effort to develop new angles of vision—or better, to widen the one I had—has allowed me to see things in the familiar landscape I would have otherwise missed. As a result, my appreciation of Lewis has not diminished, but my focus has become

2. C. S. Lewis, *Mere Christianity*, 81.

clearer. During the time of his greatest test of faith, Lewis wrote, "I want God not my idea of God." It is a fitting desire to prefer what is real. Like Lewis, I have cultivated the discipline to pursue the objective over the subjective. Therefore, this study has been an endeavor to *know* C. S. Lewis better than I did before. I have learned to want Lewis, not my idea of him, and the result has been professionally and personally transforming.

# Permissions

The author and publisher wish to thank the following for the material included in this edition.

*The Abolition of Man: Or, Reflections on Education, with Special Reference to the Teaching of English in the Upper Forms of Schools.* Extracts by C. S. Lewis, copyright © C. S. Lewis Pte. Ltd. 1947. Reprinted by permission.

*The Allegory of Love: A Study in Medieval Tradition.* Extracts by C. S. Lewis, copyright © C. S. Lewis Pte. Ltd. 1936. Reprinted by permission.

*All My Road Before Me: The Diary of C. S. Lewis, 1922–1927.* Extracts by C. S. Lewis, copyright © C. S. Lewis Pte. Ltd. 1991. Reprinted by permission.

*Arthurian Torso: Containing the Posthumous Fragment "The Figure of Arthur" by Charles Williams and a Commentary on the Arthur Poems of Charles Williams by C. S. Lewis.* Extracts by C. S. Lewis, copyright © C. S. Lewis Pte. Ltd. 1948. Reprinted by permission.

*Boxen: The Imaginary World of the Young C. S. Lewis.* Extracts by C. S. Lewis, copyright © C. S. Lewis Pte. Ltd. 1985. Reprinted by permission.

*Christian Reflections.* Extracts by C. S. Lewis, copyright © C. S. Lewis Pte. Ltd. 1967. Reprinted by permission.

*C. S. Lewis: Letters to Children.* Extracts by C. S. Lewis, copyright © C. S. Lewis Pte. Ltd. 1985. Reprinted by permission.

*The Collected Poems of C. S. Lewis.* Extracts by C. S. Lewis, copyright © C. S. Lewis Pte. Ltd. 1994. Reprinted by permission.

*The Dark Tower and Other Stories.* Extracts by C. S. Lewis, copyright © C. S. Lewis Pte. Ltd. 1977. Reprinted by permission.

*The Discarded Image: An Introduction to Medieval and Renaissance Literature.* Extracts by C. S. Lewis, copyright © C. S. Lewis Pte. Ltd. 1964. Reprinted by permission.

*Dymer.* Extracts by C. S. Lewis, copyright © C. S. Lewis Pte. Ltd. 1926. Reprinted by permission.

*English Literature in the Sixteenth Century, Excluding Drama.* Extracts by C. S. Lewis copyright © C. S. Lewis Pte. Ltd. 1954. Reprinted by permission.

*Essays Presented to Charles Williams.* Extracts by C. S. Lewis, copyright © C. S. Lewis Pte. Ltd. 1974. Reprinted by permission.

*An Experiment in Criticism.* Extracts by C. S. Lewis, copyright © C. S. Lewis Pte. Ltd. 1961. Reprinted by permission.

*The Four Loves.* Extracts by C. S. Lewis, copyright © C. S. Lewis Pte. Ltd. 1960. Reprinted by permission.

*God in the Dock: Essays on Theology and Ethics.* Extracts by C. S. Lewis, copyright © C. S. Lewis Pte. Ltd. 1970. Reprinted by permission.

*The Great Divorce.* Extracts by C. S. Lewis copyright © C. S. Lewis Pte. Ltd. 1945. Reprinted by permission.

*A Grief Observed.* Extracts by C. S. Lewis, copyright © C. S. Lewis Pte. Ltd. 1961. Reprinted by permission.

*Hamlet: The Prince or the Poem?* Extracts by C. S. Lewis, copyright © C. S. Lewis Pte. Ltd. 1976. Reprinted by permission.

*The Horse and His Boy.* Extracts by C. S. Lewis, copyright © C. S. Lewis Pte. Ltd. 1954. Reprinted by permission.

*The Last Battle.* Extracts by C. S. Lewis copyright © C. S. Lewis Pte. Ltd. 1956. Reprinted by permission.

*Letters to an American Lady.* Extracts by C. S. Lewis, copyright © C. S. Lewis Pte. Ltd. 1967. Reprinted by permission.

*Letters of C. S. Lewis.* Extracts by C. S. Lewis, copyright © C. S. Lewis Pte. Ltd. 1966. Reprinted by permission.

*Letters, C. S. Lewis—Don Giovanni Calabria: A Study in Friendship.* Extracts by C. S. Lewis, translated and edited by Martin Moynihan, copyright © C. S. Lewis Pte. Ltd. 1988. Reprinted by permission.

*C. S. Lewis: Letters to Children.* Extracts by C. S. Lewis, copyright © C. S. Lewis Pte. Ltd. 1985. Reprinted by permission.

*Letters to Malcolm: Chiefly on Prayer.* Extracts by C. S. Lewis, copyright © C. S. Lewis Pte. Ltd. 1964. Reprinted by permission.

*The Lion, the Witch and the Wardrobe.* Extracts by C. S. Lewis, copyright © C. S. Lewis Pte. Ltd. 1950. Reprinted by permission.

*The Magician's Nephew.* Extracts by C. S. Lewis, copyright © C. S. Lewis Pte. Ltd. 1955. Reprinted by permission.

*Mere Christianity.* Extracts by C. S. Lewis, copyright © C. S. Lewis Pte. Ltd. 1952. Reprinted by permission.

*Miracles: A Preliminary Study.* Extracts by C. S. Lewis, copyright © C. S. Lewis Pte. Ltd. 1945. Reprinted by permission.

*Narrative Poems.* Extracts by C. S. Lewis, copyright © C. S. Lewis Pte. Ltd. 1969. Reprinted by permission.

*Of Other Worlds.* Extracts by C. S. Lewis, copyright © C. S. Lewis Pte. Ltd. 1966. Reprinted by permission.

*Out of the Silent Planet.* Extracts by C. S. Lewis, copyright © C. S. Lewis Pte. Ltd. 1938. Reprinted by permission.

*Perelandra.* Extracts by C. S. Lewis, copyright © C. S. Lewis Pte. Ltd. 1943. Reprinted by permission.

*The Personal Heresy: A Controversy.* Extracts by C. S. Lewis, copyright © C. S. Lewis Pte. Ltd. 1939. Reprinted by permission.

*The Pilgrim's Regress: An Allegorical Apology for Christianity, Reason and Romanticism.* Extracts by C. S. Lewis, copyright © C. S. Lewis Pte. Ltd. 1933. Reprinted by permission.

*Poems.* Extracts by C. S. Lewis, copyright © C. S. Lewis Pte. Ltd. 1965. Reprinted by permission.

*A Preface to Paradise Lost.* Extracts by C. S. Lewis, copyright © C. S. Lewis Pte. Ltd. 1942. Reprinted by permission.

# Bibliography

## Primary Sources

Lewis, C. S. *The Abolition of Man: Or, Reflections on Education, with Special Reference to the Teaching of English in the Upper Forms of Schools.* New York: Macmillan, 1947.

———. *The Allegory of Love: A Study in Medieval Tradition.* Oxford: Oxford University Press, 1936.

———. *All My Road Before Me: The Diary of C. S. Lewis, 1922–1927.* Edited by Walter Hooper. New York: Harcourt, 1991.

———. *Arthurian Torso: Containing the Posthumous Fragment "The Figure of Arthur" by Charles Williams and a Commentary on the Arthur Poems of Charles Williams by C. S. Lewis.* London: Oxford University Press, 1948.

———. *Boxen: The Imaginary World of the Young C. S. Lewis.* Edited by Walter Hooper. New York: Harcourt, 1985.

———. *Christian Reflections.* Edited by Walter Hooper. Grand Rapids: Eerdmans, 1967.

———. "Christianity and Culture." *Theology: A Monthly Review* 40:237 (March 1940) 166–79.

———. *C. S. Lewis: Letters to Children.* Edited by Lyle Dorsett and Marjorie Lamp Mead. New York: Macmillan, 1985.

———. *The Collected Poems of C. S. Lewis.* Edited by Walter Hooper. London: Fount, 1994.

———. *The Dark Tower and Other Stories.* Edited by Walter Hooper. New York: Harcourt, 1977.

———. *The Discarded Image: An Introduction to Medieval and Renaissance Literature.* Cambridge: Cambridge University Press, 1964.

——— [Clive Hamilton, pseud.]. *Dymer.* London: Dent, 1926.

———. *English Literature in the Sixteenth Century, Excluding Drama.* Vol. 3, *The Oxford History of English Literature.* Oxford: Clarendon, 1954.

———, editor. *Essays Presented to Charles Williams.* Grand Rapids: Eerdmans, 1974.

———. *An Experiment in Criticism.* Cambridge: Cambridge University Press, 1961.

———. *The Four Loves.* New York: Harcourt, 1960.

———. *God in the Dock: Essays on Theology and Ethics.* Edited by Walter Hooper. Grand Rapids: Eerdmans, 1970.

———. *The Great Divorce: A Dream.* London: Bless, 1945.

——— [N. W. Clerk, pseud.]. *A Grief Observed.* New York: Faber, 1961.

———. *Hamlet: The Prince or the Poem?* Norwood, PA: Norwood, 1976.

———. *The Horse and His Boy*. New York: Macmillan, 1954.

———. *The Last Battle A Story for Children*. New York: Harcourt, 1956.

———. *Letters to an American Lady*. Edited by Clyde Kilby. Grand Rapids: Eerdmans, 1967.

———. *Letters of C. S. Lewis*. Edited and with a memoir by W. H. Lewis. New York: Harcourt, 1966.

———. *Letters of C. S. Lewis: Revised and Enlarged Edition*. Edited and with a memoir by W. H. Lewis. Revised edition edited by Walter Hooper. San Diego: A Harvest Original, 1993

———. *Letters, C. S. Lewis—Don Giovanni Calabria: A Study in Friendship*. Translated and edited by Martin Moynihan. Ann Arbor: Servant, 1988.

———. *C. S. Lewis: Letters to Children*. Edited by Lyle W. Dorsett and Marjorie Lamp Mead. New York: Macmillan, 1985.

———. *Letters to Malcolm: Chiefly on Prayer*. London: Bles, 1964.

———. *The Lion, the Witch and the Wardrobe: A Story for Children*. New York: Macmillan, 1950.

———. *The Magician's Nephew*. New York: Macmillan, 1955.

———. *Mere Christianity: A Revised and Amplified Edition With a New Introduction of the Three Books: Broadcast Talks, Christian Behavior and Beyond Personality*. New York: Macmillan, 1952.

———. *Miracles: A Preliminary Study*. London: Bles, 1945.

———. *Narrative Poems*. Edited by Walter Hooper. London: Bles, 1969.

———. *Of Other Worlds*. Edited by Walter Hooper. New York: Harcourt, 1966.

———. *Out of the Silent Planet*. Oxford: John Lane, 1938.

———. *Perelandra*. Oxford: John Lane, 1943.

———, and E. M. W. Tillyard. *The Personal Heresy: A Controversy*. Oxford: Oxford University Press, 1939.

———. *The Pilgrim's Regress: An Allegorical Apology for Christianity, Reason and Romanticism*. London: Dent, 1933.

———. *Poems*. Edited by Walter Hooper. New York: Harcourt, 1965.

———. *A Preface to Paradise Lost*. Oxford: Oxford University Press, 1942.

———. *Present Concerns: Essays by C. S. Lewis*. Edited by Walter Hooper. New York: Harcourt, 1986.

———. *Prince Caspian*. New York: Macmillan, 1951.

———. *The Problem of Pain*. London: Bles, 1940.

———. *Reflections on the Psalms*. New York: Harcourt, 1958.

———. *Rehabilitations and Other Essays*. London: Oxford University Press, 1939.

———. *The Screwtape Letters*. London: Bles, 1942.

———. *Screwtape Proposes a Toast and Other Pieces*. Edited by Walter Hooper. London: Fontana, 1965.

———. *Selected Literary Essays*. Edited by Walter Hooper. Cambridge: Cambridge University Press, 1969.

———. *The Silver Chair*. New York: Macmillan, 1954.

———. *Spenser's Images of Life*. Edited by Alistair Fowler. Cambridge: Cambridge University Press, 1967.

——— [Clive Hamiltion, pseud.]. *Spirits in Bondage: A Cycle of Lyrics*. London: Heinemann, 1919.

———. *Studies in Medieval and Renaissance Literature.* Edited by Walter Hooper. Cambridge: Cambridge University Press, 1966.

———. *Studies in Words.* 2nd ed. Cambridge: Cambridge University Press, 1967.

———. *Surprised by Joy: The Shape of My Early Life.* London: Bles, 1955.

———. *That Hideous Strength: A Modern Fairytale for Grownups.* Oxford: Lane, 1945.

———. *They Asked for a Paper: Papers and Addresses.* London: Bles, 1962.

———. *They Stand Together: The Letters of C. S. Lewis to Arthur Greeves,* 1914–1963. Edited by Walter Hooper. London: Collins, 1979.

———. *Till We Have Faces: A Myth Retold.* New York: Harcourt, 1957.

———. *The Voyage of the Dawn Treader.* New York: Macmillan, 1952.

———. *The Weight of Glory and Other Addresses.* New York: Macmillan, 1949.

———. *The World's Last Night and Other Essays.* New York: Harcourt, 1960.

## Books Edited or with a Preface by C. S. Lewis

Athanasius. *The Incarnation of the Word of God: Being the Treatise of St. Athanasius "De Incarnatione Verbi Dei" Newly Translated into English by A Religious of C. S. M. V. S. Th.* With an Introduction by C. S. Lewis. London: Bles, 1944.

Bentley, Eric. *The Cult of the Superman: A Study in the Idea of Heroism in Carlyle and Nietzsche, with Notes on Other Hero-Worshippers of Modern Times.* With an Appreciation by C. S. Lewis. New York: Macmillan, 1954.

Brook, G. L., editor. *Selections from Layamon's Brut.* With an Introduction by C. S. Lewis. Oxford: Oxford University Press, 1963.

Davidman, Joy. *Smoke on the Mountain: An Interpretation of the Ten Commandments.* Foreword by C. S. Lewis. Philadelphia: Westminster, 1954.

Farrer, Austin. *A Faith of Our Own.* With a Preface by C. S. Lewis. Cleveland: World, 1960.

Harding, D. E. *The Hierarchy of Heaven and Earth: A New Diagram of Man in the Universe.* With a Preface by C. S. Lewis. New York: Harper, 1952.

MacDonald, George. *George MacDonald: An Anthology.* Edited by C. S. Lewis. London: Bles, 1946.

Phillips, J. B. *Letters to Young Churches: A Translation of the New Testament Epistles.* With an Introduction by C. S. Lewis. New York: Macmillan, 1954.

Sandhurst, B. G. *How Heathen is Britain?* Preface by C. S. Lewis. London: Collins, 1946.

## Secondary Sources

Abanes, Richard. *Harry Potter, Narnia, and the Lord of the Rings.* Eugene, OR: Harvest, 2005.

Adams, Marilyn McCord. *Horrendous Evils and the God of Goodness.* Ithaca: Cornell University Press. 1999.

———, and Robert Merrihew Adams, editors. *The Problem of Evil.* Oxford: Oxford University Press, 1994.

Adey, Lionel. *C. S. Lewis: Writer, Dreamer, and Mentor.* Grand Rapids: Eerdmans, 1998.

————. *C. S. Lewis's "Great War" With Owen Barfield*. University of Victoria, British Colombia: ELS, 1978.

Adler, Mortimer. *Great Ideas from the Great Books*. New York: Washington Times, 1961.

Aeschliman, Michael D. *The Restitution of Man: C. S. Lewis and the Case Against Scientism*. Grand Rapids: Eerdmans, 1983.

Ahern, M. B. *The Problem of Evil*. London: Routledge and Kegan Paul, 1971.

Anscombe, G. E. M. *The Collected Papers of G. E. M. Anscombe*. Vol. 2, *Metaphysics and the Philosophy of Mind*. Minneapolis: University of Minnesota Press, 1981.

Anselm. *Proslogion*. Translated by S. N. Deane. Chicago: Open Court, 1974.

Aquinas, Thomas. *The Summa Theologica*. Translated by Fathers of the English Dominican Province. Great Books of the Western World 19–20. Revised by Daniel J. Sullivan. Chicago: Encyclopedia Britannica, 1952.

Aritstotle. *Nicomachean Ethics*. Great Books of the Western World 9. Chicago: Encyclopedia Brittanica, 1952.

Arnold, Matthew. *Culture and Anarchy*. Edited with an introduction by J. Dover Wilson. Cambridge: Cambridge University Press, 1990.

————. *Essays Literary and Critical*. London: J. M. Dent, 1914.

————. *Matthew Arnold*. In *Allott*, edited by Miriam and Robert H. Super. Oxford Authors Series. Oxford: Oxford University Press, 1986.

————. *Matthew Arnold's Essays in Criticism: First and Second Series*. Everyman's Library. London: Dent, 1964.

Arnott, Anne. *The Secret Country of C. S. Lewis*. London: Hodder and Stoughton, 1974.

Arthur, Sarah. *Walking Through the Wardrobe; A Devotional Quest Into The Lion the Witch and the Wardrobe*. Wheaton, IL: Tyndale, 2005.

Atkinson, Bruce E. "From Facelessness to Divine Identity: An Analysis of C. S. Lewis's 'Till We Have Faces.'" *The Lamp-Post of the Southern California C. S. Lewis Society: A Journal for Lewis Studies* 15 (1991) 21–30.

Attenbourough, Richard, Director. *Shadowlands*. Screenplay by William Nicholson. Savoy Pictures, 1993.

Augustine. *The City of God*. Translated by Marcus Dods. Great Books of the Western World 18. Chicago: Encyclopedia Britannica, 1952.

————. *The Confessions*. Translated by E. B. Pusey. Great Books of the Western World 18. Chicago: Encyclopedia Britannica, 1952.

————. *The Enchiridion*. In *A Select Library of the Nicene and Post-Nicene Fathers of the Christian Church*. Vol. 3, edited by Philip Schaff. Grand Rapids: Eerdmans, 1988.

Ayer, A. J. *Language Truth and Logic*. London: Penguin, 1990.

Baehr, Ted, and James Baehr. *Narnia Beckons: C. S. Lewis's the Lion the Witch and the Wardrobe and Beyond*. Nashville: Broadman and Holman, 2005.

Bafield, Owen. "A Visit to Beatrice." *Seven: An Anglo American Literary Review* 9 (1988) 15–18.

————. *Owen Barfield on C. S. Lewis*. Edited by G. B. Tennyson. Middletown, CT: Wesleyan University Press, 1989.

————. *Saving the Appearances: A Study in Idolatry*. New York: Harcourt Brace Jovanovich, 1965.

Barry, Peter. *Beginning Theory: An Introduction to Literary and Cultural Theory.* Manchester: Manchester University Press, 1995.

Bassham, Gregory, and Jerry L. Walls, editors. *The Chronicles of Narnia and Philosophy: The Lion, the Witch and the Wardrobe.* Chicago and La Salle, IL: Open Court, 2005.

Batstone, Patricia. *In Debt to C. S. Lewis.* Dunkeswell, Devon, England: Cottage, 1999.

Bauerlein, Mark. *Literary Criticism: An Autopsy.* Philadelphia: University of Pennsylvania Press, 1997.

Beahm, George. *Passport to Narnia: A Newcomer's Guide.* Charlottesville: Hampton Roads, 2005.

Bechtel, Paul. "C. S. Lewis Apostle of Joy." *The Christian Reader* 16:4 (1978) 3–8.

Bell, James Stuart, Carrie Pyykkonen, and Linda Washington. *Inside the Lion, the Witch and the Wardrobe: Myths, Mysteries, and Magic from The Chronicles of Narnia.* New York: St. Martin's Griffin, 2005.

Bennett, Andrew, and Nicholas Royle. *Introduction to Literature, Criticism, and Theory.* 2nd ed. Harlow: Pearson Education, 1999.

Bennett, J. A. W. "The Humane Medievalist: An Inaugural Address." In *Critical Essays on C. S. Lewis*, edited by George Watson. Aldershot, England: Scolar, 1992.

Benson, Bruce Ellis. "The End of the Fantastic Dream: Testifying to the Truth in the "Post" Condition." *Christian Scholar's Review* 30 (2000) 145–61.

———. "Postmodernity." In *Evangelical Dictionary of Christian Education*, edited by Michael Anthony. Grand Rapids: Baker, 2001.

Benson, Thomas W., and Michael H. Prosser, editors. *Readings in Classical Rhetoric.* Bloomington: Indiana University Press, 1972.

Berger, Peter L. *A Rumour of Angels: Modern Society and the Rediscovery of the Supernatural.* Harmondsworth, Middlesex, England: Penguin, 1971.

Betjeman, John. *A Continual Dew: A Little Book of Bourgeois Verse.* London: Murray, 1977.

Beum, Robert, and James W. Sire. *Papers on Literature: Models and Methods.* New York: Holt, Rinehart and Winston, 1970.

Beversluis, John. *C. S. Lewis and the Search for Rational Religion.* Grand Rapids: Eerdmans, 1985.

Bizzell, Pattricia, and Bruce Herzberg, editors. *The Rhetorical Tradition: Readings form Classical Times to the Present.* 2nd ed. Boston: Bedford/St. Martin's, 2001.

Blamires, Harry. "Against the Stream: C. S. Lewis and the Literary Scene (The Inaugural C. S. Lewis Memorial Lecture, 8th October 1982)." *Journal of the Irish Christian Study Center* 1 (1983) 11–22.

Blamires, Harry. *A History of Literary Criticism.* New York: St. Martin's, 1991.

Bloom, Harold, editor. *Modern Fantasy Writers.* New York: Chelsea, 1995.

Boethius. *The Consolation of Philosophy.* Translated by V. E. Watts. London: Penguin, 1969.

Booth, Wayne. *The Rhetoric of Fiction.* Chicago: University of Chicago Press, 1961.

Bramlett, F, C. Perry, and Ronald W. Higdon. *Touring C. S. Lewis' Ireland and England.* Macon, GA: Smyth and Helways, 1998.

Bramlette, Perry. *C. S. Lewis: Life at the Center.* Macon, GA: Peake Road, 1996.

Brand, Paul, and Philip Yancey. *Pain: The Gift Nobody Wants.* New York: HarperCollins, 1993.

Bray, Gerald. *Biblical Interpretation: Past & Present.* Downers Grove: InterVarsity, 1996.

Brent, Doug. *Reading As Rhetorical Invention: Knowledge, Persuasion, and the Teaching of Research-Based Writing.* Urbana, IL: National Council of Teachers of English, 1992.

Bresland, Ronald W. *The Backward Glance: C. S. Lewis and Ireland.* Belfast: Institute of Irish Studies, 1999.

————. *Travel with C. S. Lewis.* Leominster: Day One, 2006.

Bressler, Charles E. *Literary Criticism: An Introduction to Theory and Practice.* 3rd ed. Upper Saddle River, NJ: Prentice Hall, 2003.

Corbett, Edward P. J., editor. *Rhetorical Analysis of Literary Works.* New York: Oxford University Press, 1969.

Brew, Kelli. "Facing the Truth on the Road to Salvation: An Analysis of 'That Hideous Strength' and 'Till We Have Faces.'" *The Lamp-Post of the Southern California C. S. Lewis Society: A Literary Review of Lewis Studies* 22 (1998) 10–12.

Brown, Devin. *Inside Narnia: A Guide to Exploring The Lion the Witch and the Wardrobe.* Grand Rapids: Baker, 2005.

Browning, Robert. "Rabbi ben Ezra." In *Robert Browning: A Critical Edition of the Major Works.* Oxford: Oxford University Press, 1997.

————. *The Ring and the Book: With an Introduction by Edward Dowden and Four Facsimiles.* London: Oxford University Press, 1912.

Bruner, Kurt, and Jim Ware. *Finding God in the Land of Narnia.* Wheaton: Salt River, 2005.

Brunsdale, Mitzi. *Dorothy L. Sayers: Solving the Mystery of Wickedness.* New York: Berg, 1990.

Buechner, Frederick. *Wishful Thinking: A Theological ABC.* New York: Harper & Row, 1973.

Burson, Scott R., and Jerry R. Walls. *C. S. Lewis and Francis Schaeffer: Lessons for a New Century from the Most Influential Apologists of Our Time.* Downers Grove: InterVarsity, 1998.

Calvin, John. *Institutes of the Christian Religion.* 2 vols. Translated by Ford Lewis Battles. Philadelphia: Westminster, 1960.

Cantor, Norman F. *Inventing the Middle Ages: The lives, Works, and Ideas of the Great Medievalists of the Twentieth Century.* Cambridge: Lutterworth, 1992.

Carnell, Corbin Scott. *Bright Shadow of Reality: C. S. Lewis and the Feeling Intellect.* Grand Rapids: Eerdmans, 1974.

Carpenter, Humphrey. *The Inklings: C. S. Lewis, J. R. R. Tolkien, Charles Williams, and Their Friends.* Boston: Houghton Mifflin, 1979.

————. *Tolkien: A Biography.* Boston: Houghton Mifflin, 1977.

Carson, D. A. *The Gagging of God: Christianity Confronts Pluralism.* Grand Rapids: Zondervan, 1966.

Charles, J. Daryl. "Permanent Things." *Christian Reflections: A Series in Faith and Ethics. Inklings of Glory.* The Center for Christian Ethics at Baylor University (2004) 54–58.

Chesterton, G. K. *Heretics*. In *The Collected Works of G. K. Chesterton*. Vol. 1, edited with an introduction and notes by David Dooley. San Francisco: Ignatius, 1986.

———. *Orthodoxy*. In *The Collected Works of G. K. Chesterton*. Vol. 1, edited with an inroduction and notes by David Dooley. San Francisco: Ignatius, 1986.

———. *The Everlasting Man*. London: Hodder and Stoughton, 1947.

———. *Tremendous Trifles*. New York: Sheed and Ward, 1955.

Christensen, Michael J. *C. S. Lewis on Scripture: His Thoughts on the Nature of Biblical Inspiration, The Role of Revelation and the Question of Inerrancy*. Waco: Word, 1979.

Christopher, Joe R. *C. S. Lewis*. Boston: Twayne, 1987.

———, and Joan Ostling. *C. S. Lewis: An Annotated Checklist of Writings About Him and His Works*. Kent: Kent State University Press, 1973.

Cochrane, Charles Norris. *Christianity and Classical Culture: A Study of Thought and Action from Augustus to Augustine*. Oxford: Clarendon, 1940.

Colbert, David. *The Magical Worlds of Narnia: The Symbols, Myths, and Fascinating Facts Behind the Chronicles*. New York: Berkley, 2005.

Como, James, editor. *C. S. Lewis at the Breakfast Table and Other Reminiscences*. New York: Macmillan, 1979.

———, editor. *Remembering C. S. Lewis: Recollections of Those Who Knew Him*. San Francisco: Ignatius, 2005.

———. *Branches to Heaven: The Geniuses of C. S. Lewis*. Dallas: Spence, 1998.

Cording, Ruth James. *C. S. Lewis: A Celebration of His Early Life*. Nashville: Broadman and Holman, 2000.

Coren, Michael. *The Man Who Created Narnia: The Story of C. S. Lewis*. Grand Rapids: Eerdmans, 1994.

Cunningham, David S. *Faithful Persuasion: In Aid of a Rhetoric of Christian Theology*. Notre Dame: University of Notre Dame Press, 1990.

Cunningham, Richard B. *C. S. Lewis: Defender of the Faith*. Philadelphia: Westminster, 1967.

Daniel, Jerry L. "The Taste of the Pineapple: A Basis for Literary Criticism." In *The Taste of the Pineapple: Essays on C. S. Lewis as Reader, Critic, and Imaginative Writer*, edited by Bruce L. Edwards. Bowling Green, OH: Bowling Green State University Popular Press, 1998.

Dante. *The Divine Comedy*. In *Great Books of the Western World*. Vol. 21, translated by Charles Eliot Norton. Chicago: Encyclopedia Britannica, 1952.

Davis, Stephen T., editor. *Encountering Evil: Live Options in Theodicy*. Edinburgh: T. & T. Clark, 1994.

Dearborn, Kerry L. "The Baptized Imagination." In *Inklings of Glory*, 11–20. Christian Reflections: A Series in Faith and Ethics. Waco, TX: The Center for Christian Ethics at Baylor University, 2004.

Derrick, Christopher, et al. *G.K. Chesterton and C. S. Lewis: The Riddle of Joy*. Grand Rapids: Eerdmans, 1989.

———. *C. S. Lewis and the Church of Rome*. San Francisco: Ignatius, 1981.

Derrida, Jacques, 1978. *Writing and Difference*. Chicago: University of Chicago Press, 1978.

Dillard, Annie. *Living by Fiction*. New York: Harper and Row, 1988.

Ditchfield, Christian. *A Family Guide to the Lion, the Witch and the Wardrobe.* Wheaton, IL: Crossway, 2005.

Donne, John. *Selected Poetry.* In *The Signet Classic Poetry Series,* edited by Marius Bewley. New York: The New American Library, 1966.

Dorsett, Lyle W. *And God Came In: The Extraordinary Story of Joy Davidman, Her Life and Marriage to C. S. Lewis.* New York: Macmillan, 1983.

———. C. S. Lewis and Evangelism: A Survey of Useful Books. *Evangelism* 1:4 (1987) 3–8.

———. *Seeking the Secret Place: The Spiritual Formation of C. S. Lewis.* Grand Rapids: Brazos, 2004.

Dostoevsky, Fyodor. *The Brothers Karamazov.* Translated by Constance Garnett. Great Books of the Western World 52. Chicago: Encyclopedia Britannica, 1952.

Doty, William G. *Mythography: The Study of Myths and Rituals.* Tuscaloosa: University of Alabama Press, 1986.

Downing, David C. *Into the Region of Awe: Mysticism in C. S. Lewis.* Downers Grove: InterVarsity, 2005.

———. *Into the Wardrobe: C. S. Lewis and the Narnia Chronicles.* San Francisco: Jossey-Bass, 2005.

———. *Planets in Peril: A Critical Study of C. S. Lewis's Ransom Trilogy.* Amherst: University of Massachusetts Press, 1992.

Du Boulay, Shirley. *A Biography of Bede Griffiths: Beyond the Darkness.* New York: Doubleday, 1988.

Duffy, Bernard K., and Martin Jacobi, editors. *The Politics of Rhetoric: Richard M. Weaver and the Conservative Tradition.* Westport: Greenwood, 1993.

Duncan, John Ryan. *The Magic Never Ends: The Life and Work of C. S. Lewis.* Nashville: W, 2001.

Duriez, Colin. "C.S. Lewis and the Evangelicals." *Christian Librarian: The Journal and Yearbook of the Librarians' Christian Fellowship* 22 (1998) 11–31.

———. *The C. S. Lewis Handbook: A Comprehensive Guide to His Life, Thought, and Writings.* Grand Rapids: Baker, 1990.

———. *Tolkien and C. S. Lewis: The Gift of Friendship.* Mahwah, NJ: Hidden Spring, 2003.

Eagleton, Terry. *Literary Theory: An Introduction.* 2nd ed. Minneapolis: University of Minnesota Press, 1996.

Edwards, Bruce. *A Rhetoric of Reading: C.S. Lewis's Defense of Western Literacy.* Provo: Center for the Study of Christian Values in Literature, 1986.

———. *Further Up & Further In: Understanding C. S. Lewis's The Lion the Witch and the Wardrobe.* Nashville: Broadman and Holman, 2005.

———. *Not a Tame Lion: Unveil Narnia Through the Eyes of Lucy, Peter, and Other Characters Created by C. S. Lewis.* Wheaton: Tyndale, 2005.

———, editor. *The Taste of the Pineapple: Essays on C. S. Lewis As Reader, Critic, and Imaginative Writer.* Bowling Green: Bowling Green State University Popular Press, 1988.

Edwards, Michael. "C. S. Lewis: Imagining Heaven (The Eighth C. S. Lewis Memorial Lecture, 15th February, 1991)". *Journal of the Irish Christian Study Centre* 5 (1994) 16–33.

Erickson, Millard J. *Truth or Consequences: the Promise & Perils of Postmodernism.* Downers Grove: InterVarsity, 2001.

Fadiman, Clifton, editor. *Living Philosophies: The Reflections of Some Eminent Men and Women of Our Time.* New York: Doubleday, 1990.

Farrer, Austin. *Finite and Infinite: A Philosophical Essay.* Westminster: Dacre, 1943

———. *Love Almighty and Ills Unlimited.* London: Collins/Fontana, 1966.

———. *The Brink of Mystery.* Edited by Charles Conti. London: SPCK, 1976.

———. *The Glass of Vision.* Westminster: Dacre, 1958.

———. "The Christian Apologist." In *Light on C. S. Lewis,* edited by Jocelyn Gibb. New York: Harcourt, Brace and World, 1965.

Feinberg, John S. *The Many Faces of Evil: Theological Systems and the Problem of Evil.* Grand Rapids: Zondervan, 1994.

Ferguson, John. *The Place of Suffering.* Cambridge: James Clarke, 1972.

Fetherston, Patience. "C. S. Lewis on Rationalism: (Unpublished Notes)." *Seven: An Anglo-American Literary Review* 9 (1988) 87–89.

Fiddes, Paul. S. *The Creative Suffering of God.* Oxford: Clarendon, 1992.

Filmer-Davies, Kath. *Towards a 'Good Death': The Fantasy Fiction of C. S. Lewis and the Experience of Reading.* New Lambton, Australia: Nimrod, 1998.

Filmer, Kath. "The Polemic Image: The Role of Metaphor and Symbol in the Fiction of C. S. Lewis." *Seven: An Anglo-American Literary Review* 7 (1986) 61–76.

Filmer, Kath. *The Fiction of C. S. Lewis: Mask and Mirror.* New York: St. Martin's, 1993.

Fish, Stanley. *The Trouble with Principle.* Cambridge: Harvard University Press, 1999.

Fleischer, Leonore. *Shadowlands: A Novel.* New York: Signet, 1993.

Ford, Paul F. *Companion to Narnia.* New York: Macmillan, 1986.

Frankl, Viktor. *Man's Search for Meaning.* New York: Washington Square, 1985.

Freud, Sigmund. *A General Introduction to Psycho-Analysis (1915–17).* Great Books of the Western World 54. Chicago: Encyclopedia Britannica, 1952.

Fuller, Edmund, Clyde S. Kilby, Russell Kirk, John W. Montgomery, and Chad Walsh. *Myth Allegory and the Gospel: An Interpretation of J. R. R. Tolkien/ C. S. Lewis/ G. K. Chesterton/ Charles Williams.* Minneapolis: Bethany, 1974.

Gallagher, Susan V., and Roger Lundin. *Literature Through the Eyes of Faith.* San Francisco: Harper & Row, 1989.

Gardner, Helen. "Clive Staples Lewis, 1898–1963." *Proceedings of the British Academy* 51 (1965) 417–28.

Geivett, Douglas R. *Evil and the Evidence for God: The Challenge of John Hick's Theodicy: Afterword by John Hick.* Philadelphia: Temple University Press, 1993.

Gibb, Jocelyn, editor. *Light on C. S. Lewis.* New York: Harcourt, Brace, and World, 1965.

Gibbs, Lee W. *The Middle Way: Voices of Anglicanism.* Cincinnati: Forward Movement, 1991.

Gibson, Evan K. *C. S. Lewis: Spinner of Tales: A Guide to His Fiction.* Washington DC: Christian University Press, 1980.

Gilbert, Douglas, and Clyde Kilby. *C. S. Lewis: Images of His World.* Grand Rapids: Eerdmans, 1973.

Gilchrist, K. James. "Second Lieutenant Lewis." *Seven: An Anglo-American Literary Review* 17 (2000) 61–78.

———. *A Morning After: C. S. Lewis and WW I.* New York: Peter Lang, 2004.

Gilley, Sheridan. "A Prophet Neither in Ireland Nor in England. (The Third C. S. Lewis Memorial Lecture, 25th October, 1985)." *Journal of the Irish Christian Study Centre* 3 (1986) 1–10.

Glaspey, Terry W. *Not a Tame Lion: The Spiritual Legacy of C. S. Lewis.* Nashville: Cumberland, 1996.

Glover, Donald E. *C. S. Lewis and the Art of Enchantment.* Athens: Ohio University Press, 1981.

Goffar, Janine. *C. S. Lewis Index: Rumours from the Sculptor's Mill.* Riverside: La Sierra University Press, 1995.

Gormley, Beatrice. *C. S. Lewis: Christian and Storyteller.* Grand Rapids: Eerdmans, 1998.

Grahame, Kenneth. *The Wind in the Willows.* London: Methuen, 1940.

Gray, William. *C. S. Lewis.* Plymouth, United Kingdom: Northcote, 1998.

Green, Roger Lancelyn, and Walter Hooper. *C. S. Lewis: A Biography.* New York: Harcourt, Brace and Jovanovich, 1974.

———. *Into Other Worlds: Space-Flight in Fiction, from Lucian to Lewis.* Grand Rapids: Eerdmans, 1973.

Gresham, Douglas. *Jack's Life: The Life Story of C. S. Lewis.* Nashville: Broadman and Holman, 2005.

———. *Lenten Lands: My Childhood with Joy Davidman and C. S. Lewis.* New York: Macmillan, 1988.

Griffin, William. *C. S. Lewis: Spirituality for Mere Christians.* New York: Crossroad, 1998.

———. *Clive Staples Lewis: A Dramatic Life.* San Francisco: Harper and Row, 1986.

Hannay, Margaret P. "Provocative Generalizations: *The Allegory of Love* in Retrospect." *Seven: An Anglo-American Literary Review* 7 (1986) 41–60.

———. *C. S. Lewis.* New York: Ungar, 1981.

Harries, Richard. *C. S. Lewis: The Man and His God.* Wilton: Morehouse-Barlow, 1987.

Hart, Dabney Adams. *Through the Open Door: A New Look at C. S. Lewis.* Nashville: Express Media, 1994.

Hastings, Adrian. *A History of English Christianity 1920–1990.* London: SCM, 2001.

Hauser, Gerard A. *Introduction to Rhetorical Theory.* Prospect Heights: Waveland, 1991.

Hebblewaite, B. L. *The Problems of Theology.* Cambridge: Cambridge University Press, 1980.

Heck, Joel D. *Irrigating Deserts: C. S. Lewis on Education.* Saint Louis: Concordia, 2005.

Helm, Paul, editor. *Objective Knowledge: A Christian Perspective.* Leicester: Inter-Varsity, 1987.

Hick, John, editor. *The Existence of God: Readings Selected, Edited, and Furnished with an Introductory Essay by John Hick.* New York: Macmillan, 1964.

———. *Evil and the Love of God.* London: Macmillan, 1966.

———. *Philosophy of Religion.* Englewood Cliffs: Prentice-Hall, 1963.

Hilder, Monika B. "The Foolish Weakness in C. S. Lewis's Cosmic Trilogy: A Feminine Heroic." *Seven: An Anglo-American Literary Review* 19 (2002) 77–90.

Hillegas, Mark R., editor. *Shadows of Imagination: The Fantasies of C. S. Lewis, J. R. R. Tolkien, and Charles Williams*. Carbondale and Edwardsville: Southern Illinois University Press, 1979.

Hillier, Bevis. *Young Betjeman*. London: Sphere, 1989.

Holman, C. Hugh, and William Harmon. *A Handbook to Literature*. 6th ed. New York: Macmillan, 1992.

Holmer, Paul L. *C. S. Lewis: The Shape of His Faith and Thought*. New York: Harper and Row, 1976.

Hooper, Walter. *C. S. Lewis: A Companion & Guide*. London: HarperCollins, 1996.

———. *Past Watchful Dragons: The Narnian Chronicles of C. S. Lewis*. New York: Collier, 1979.

Howard-Snyder, Daniel, editor. *The Evidential Argument from Evil*. Bloomington: Indiana University Press, 1996.

Howard, Thomas. *The Achievement of C. S. Lewis: A Reading of His Fiction*. Wheaton: Harold Shaw, 1980.

———. *C. S. Lewis Man of Letters: A Reading of His Fiction*. San Francisco: Ignatius, 1987.

———. *Narnia and Beyond: A Guide to the Fiction of C. S. Lewis*. San Francisco: Ignatius, 2006.

Hume, David. *Dialogues Concerning Natural Religion*. Edited by Henry D. Aiken. New York: Hafner, 1948.

———. *An Inquiry Concerning Human Understanding*. Great Books of the Western World 35. Chicago: Encyclopedia Britannica, 1952.

Hutchins, Robert M, and Mortimer Adler, editors. *The Great Ideas Today*. Chicago: Encyclopedia Britannica, 1968.

Huttar, Charles, editor. *Imagination and the Spirit: Essays in Literature and the Christian Faith Presented to Clyde S. Kilby*. Grand Rapids: Eerdmans, 1971.

———, and Peter J. Schakel, editors. *The Rhetoric of Vision: Essays on Charles Williams*. London: Associated University Presses, 1996.

Jacobs, Alan. *The Narnian: The Life and Imagination of C. S. Lewis*. San Francisco: Harper Collins, 2005.

———. "The Values of Literary Study: Deconstruction and Other Developments." *Christian Scholar's Review* 16:4 (1987) 373–83.

James, William. *The Principles of Psychology*. Great Books of the Western World 53. Chicago: Encyclopedia Brittanica, 1952.

Jeffrey, David Lyle. "Structuralism, Deconstructionism, and Ideology." *Christian Scholar's Review* 17:4 (1988) 436–48.

Joad, C. E. M. *God and Evil*. London: Faber and Faber, 1942.

———. *The Recovery of Belief: A Restatement of Christian Philosophy*. London: Faber and Faber, 1952.

Johnson, F. R. *Astronomical Thought in Renaissance England*. Baltimore: Johns Hopkins University Press, 1937.

Julian of Norwich. *A Revelation of Divine Love*. Rev. ed. Edited by Marion Glasscoe. Exeter: University of Exeter Press, 1996.

Karkainan, Paul A. *Narnia Explored*. Old Tappan: Revell, 1979.

Keefe, Carolyn, editor. *C. S. Lewis: Speaker & Teacher.* Grand Rapids: Zondervan, 1971.

Kilby, Clyde S. *The Christian World of C. S. Lewis.* Grand Rapids: Eerdmans, 1964.

———. *Images of Salvation in the Fiction of C. S. Lewis.* Wheaton: Shaw, 1978.

———, and Marjorie Lamp Mead. *Brothers and Friends: The Diaries of Major Warren Hamilton Lewis.* San Francisco: Harper and Row, 1988.

King, Don. *C. S. Lewis, Poet: The Legacy of His Poetic Impulse.* Kent: Kent State University Press, 2001.

Knight, Gareth. *The Magical World of the Inklings: J. R. R. Tolkien, C. S. Lewis, Charles Williams, Owen Barfield.* Longmead, England: Element, 1990.

Kopp, Heather, with David Kopp. *Roar.* Sisters, OR: Multnomah, 2005.

Kreeft, Peter. "Lewis and the Two Roads to God." In *The World and I: A Chronicle of Our Changing Era,* 354–62. Washington DC: Washington Times, 1987.

———. *Between Heaven and Hell: A Dialog Somewhere Beyond Death with John F. Kennedy, C. S. Lewis & Aldous Huxley.* Downers Grove: InterVarsity, 1982.

———. *C. S. Lewis for the Third Millennium: Six Essays on the Abolition of Man.* San Francisco: Ignatius, 1994.

———. *C. S. Lewis: A Critical Essay.* Grand Rapids: Eerdmans, 1969.

———. *Ecumenical Jihad: Ecumenism and the Culture War.* San Francisco: Ignatius, 1996.

———. *The Shadow-Lands of C. S. Lewis: The Man Behind the Movie.* San Francisco: Ignatius, 1994.

Kushner, Harold S. *When Bad Things Happen to Good People.* New York: Schocken, 1981.

Kvang, Jonathan L. *The Problem of Hell.* New York: Oxford University Press, 1993.

Lawlor, John, editor. *Patterns of Love and Courtesy: Essays in Memory of C. S. Lewis.* London: Arnold, 1966.

Lawlor, John. *C. S. Lewis: Memories and Reflections.* Dallas: Spence, 1998.

Leibniz, G. W. *Theodicy: Essays on the Goodness of God the Freedom of Man and the Origin of Evil.* Translated by E. M. Huggard. Edited with an introduction by Austin Farrer. La Salle, IL: Open Court, 1996.

Lessel, Thomas M. "The Legacy of C. S. Lewis and the Prospect of Religious Rhetoric." *The Journal of Communication and Religion* 27:1 (2004) 117–37.

Lindskoog, Kathryn Ann. *C. S. Lewis: Mere Christian.* Glendale: Gospel Light, 1973.

———. *The C. S. Lewis Hoax.* Portland: Multnomah, 1988.

———. *Finding the Landlord: A Guidebook to C. S. Lewis's Pilgrim's Regress.* Chicago: Cornerstone, 1995.

———. *Journey into Narnia.* Pasadena, CA: Hope, 1998.

———. *Light in the Shadowlands: Protecting the Real C. S. Lewis.* Sisters, OR: Questar, 1994.

———. *The Lion of Judah in Never Never Land: The Theology of C. S. Lewis Expressed in His Fantasies for Children.* Grand Rapids: Eerdmans, 1973.

———. "The Poetic Finale of the Pilgrim's Regress." *The Lamp-Post of the Southern California C. S. Lewis Society: A Literary Review of Lewis Studies* 22:1 (1998) 6–9.

Lindsley, Art. *C. S. Lewis's Case for Christ: Insights from Reason, Imagination and Faith.* Downers Grove, IL: InterVarsity, 2005.

Lindvall, Terry. *Surprised by Laughter: The Comic World of C. S. Lewis.* Nashville: Nelson, 1996.

Lowenberg, Susan. *C. S. Lewis: A Reference Guide, 1972–1978.* Grand Rapids: Eerdmans, 1993.

Lundin, Roger. *The Culture of Interpretation: Christian Faith and the Postmodern World.* Grand Rapids: Eerdmans, 1993.

Lunsford, Andrea A., and John J. Ruszkiewicz. *Everything's an Argument.* Boston: Bedford/St. Martin's, 1999.

MacDonald, George. *Phantastes: A Faerie Romance for Men and Women.* London: Fifield, 1905.

———. Preface to *Letters From Hell: Given in English,* by L. W. J. S. London: Bentley, 1985.

Mackie, J. L. *The Miracle of Theism: Arguments for and against the Existence of God.* Oxford: Clarendon, 1982.

Macky, Peter W. "Appeasing the Gods in C. S. Lewis's 'Till We Have Faces.'" *Seven: An Anglo-American Literary Review* 7 (1986) 77–90.

Manlove, C. N. *C. S. Lewis: His Literary Achievement.* New York: St. Martin's, 1987.

———. *Modern Fantasy: Five Studies.* London: Cambridge University Press, 1975.

———. "'The Lion' at 50." *Seven: An Anglo-American Literary Review* 17 (2000) 19–26.

Markos, Louis. *Lewis Agonistes: How C. S. Lewis Can Train Us to Wrestle With the Modern and Postmodern World.* Nashville: Broadman and Holman, 2003.

Martin, Thomas L., editor. *Reading the Classics With C. S. Lewis.* Grand Rapids: Baker, 2000.

Martindale, Wayne, and Jerry Root, editors. *The Quotable Lewis.* Wheaton: Tyndale, 1989.

———, editor. *Journey to the Celestial City: Glimpses of Heaven from Great Literary Classics.* Chicago: Moody, 1995.

Mascal, E. L. *The Christian Universe.* New York: Morehouse-Barlow, 1966.

Meilaender, Gilbert. *The Taste for the Other: The Social and Ethical Thought of C. S. Lewis.* Grand Rapids: Eerdmans, 1978.

Menuge, Angus, editor. *C. S. Lewis: Lightbearer in the Shadowlands.* Westchester: Crossway, 1997.

Mesle, C. Robert. *John Hick's Theodicy: A Process Humanist Critique: With a Response by John Hick.* London: Macmillan, 1991.

Mills, David, editor. *The Pilgrim's Guide: C. S. Lewis and the Art of Witness.* Grand Rapids: Eerdmans, 1998.

Milward, Peter. *A Challenge to C. S. Lewis.* Madison, WI: Fairleigh Dickinson University Press, 1995.

Milton, John. *Paradise Lost.* Great Books of the Western World 32. Chicago: Encyclopedia Britannica, 1952.

Mitchell, Basil. *Faith and Criticism.* Oxford: Clarendon, 1994.

———. *How to Play Theological Ping Pong: Essays on Faith and Reason.* Edited by William J. Abraham and Robert W. Prevost. Grand Rapids: Eerdmans, 1990.

———. *The Justification of Religious Belief.* London: Macmillan, 1978.

Montgomery, John Warwick. *History & Christianity.* Downers Grove, IL: InterVarsity, 1974.

Moynihan, Martin. "C. S. Lewis and T. D. Weldon." *Seven: An Anglo-American Literary Review* 5 (1984) 101–5.

———. "The Latin Letters of C. S. Lewis to Don Giovanni Calabria." *Seven: An Anglo-American Literary Review* 6 (1985) 7–22.

———. *The Latin Letters of C. S. Lewis: To Don Giovanni Calabria of Verona and to Members of His Congregation, 1947 to 1961.* Westchester: Crossway, 1987.

Mueller, Steven P. *Not a Tame God: Christ in the Writings of C. S. Lewis.* Saint Louis: Concordia, 2002.

Mulia, Hendra G. "C. S. Lewis's Concept of Myth: An Answer to Linguistic Philosophers." *Stulos Theological Journal* 1 (1993) 49–65.

Murrin, Michael. "The Dialectic of Multiple Worlds: An Analysis of C. S. Lewis's Narnia Stories." *Seven: An Anglo-American Literary Review* 3 (1982) 93–112.

Musacchio, George. *C. S. Lewis: Man & Writer: Essays and Reviews.* Belton, TX: University of Mary Hardin-Baylor, 1994.

———. "Fiction in 'A Grief Observed.'" *Seven: An Anglo-American Literary Review* 8 (1987) 73–83.

Myers-Shaffer, Christina. *The Principles of Literature: A Guide for Readers & Writers.* Hauppauge, NY: Barron's Educational Series, 2000.

Myers, Doris T. *Bareface: A Guide to C. S. Lewis's Last Novel.* Columbia: University of Missouri Press, 2004.

———. "Browsing the Glome Library." *Seven: An Anglo-American Literary Review* 19 (2002) 63–76.

———. *C. S. Lewis in Context.* Kent, OH: Kent State University Press, 1994.

Newsom, William Chad. *Talking of Dragons: The Children's Books of J. R. R. Tolkien and C. S. Lewis.* Ross-shire: Christian Focus, 2005.

Nicholson, William. *Shadowlands.* New York: Plume, 1991.

Noll, Mark A. "C. S. Lewis's 'Mere Christianity' (the Book and the Ideal) at the Start of the Twenty-First Century." *Seven: An Anglo-American Literary Review* 19 (2002) 31–44.

Nuttall, A. D. "Jack the Giant-Killer." *Seven: An Anglo-American Literary Review* 5 (1984) 84–100.

Okiyama, Steve. "'Till We Have Faces': A Review." *The Lamp-Post of the Southern California C. S. Lewis Society: A Journal for Lewis Studies* 15 (1991) 15–20.

Otto, Rudolph. *The Idea of the Holy: An Inquiry into the Non-Rational Factor in the Idea of the Divine and Its Relation to the Rational.* Translated by John W. Harvey. London: Oxford University Press, 1925.

Oury, Scot. "'The Thing Itself': C. S. Lewis and the Value of Something Other." In *The Longing for a Form: Essays on the Fiction of C. S. Lewis*, edited by Peter Schakel. Grand Rapids: Baker, 1979.

Pascal, Blaise, 1952. *Pensees.* Translated by W. F. Trotter. Great Books of the Western World 33. Chicago: Encyclopedia Britannica, 1952.

Patrick, James. *The Magdalen Metaphysicals: Idealism and Orthodoxy at Oxford, 1901–1925.* Macon, GA: Mercer University Press, 1985.

Payne, Leanne. *Real Presence: The Christian World View of C. S. Lewis as Incarnational Reality.* Wheaton, IL: Crossway, 1988.

Peters, John. *C. S. Lewis: The Man and His Achievement.* Exeter, England: Paternoster, 1985.

Peters, Thomas C. *Simply C. S. Lewis: A Beginner's Guide to His Life and Works.* Wheaton, IL: Crossway, 1997.

Phillips, J. B. *The Ring of Truth: A Translator's Testimony.* New York: Macmillan, 1967.

Pittenger, W. Norman. "A Critique of C. S. Lewis." *Christian Century* 75:1 (1958) 1104–7.

Plantinga, Alvin. *God, Freedom, and Evil.* Grand Rapids: Eerdmans, 1991.

Plato. *The Dialogues of Plato.* Great Books of the Western World 7. Chicago: Encyclopedia Britannica, 1952.

Poe, Harry Lee, and Rebecca Whitten Poe, editors. *C. S. Lewis Remembered: Collected Reflections of Students, Friends & Colleagues.* Grand Rapids: Zondervan, 2006.

Polkinghorne, John. *Science and Theology: An Introduction.* Minneapolis: Fortress, 1998.

Preston, Robert. "'Ideas Have Consequences' Fifty Years Later." In *Steps Toward Restoration: The Consequences of Richard Weaver's Ideas*, edited by Ted J. Smith III. Wilmington, DE: Intercollegiate Studies Institute, 1998.

Price, Geoffrey. "Review Article: Scientism and the Flight from Reality." *Seven: An Anglo-American Literary Review* 7 (1986) 117–26.

Prothero, James. "On Lewis Worship and Lewis Bashing: Text and Subtext in A.N. Wilson's 'C.S. Lewis: A Biography.'" *The Lamp-Post of the Southern California C.S. Lewis Society: A Journal for Lewis Studies* 15:4 (1991) 8–17.

———. "What are We to Make of C. S. Lewis?: C. S. Lewis and the Literary Landscape of the 20th Century." *The Lamp-Post of the Southern California C. S. Lewis Society: A Journal for Lewis Studies* 15:1 (1991) 3–14.

Ptomely. *The Almagest.* Translated by R. Catesby Taliafero. Great Books of the Western World 16. Chicago: Encyclopedia Britannica, 1952.

Purtill, Richard L. *C. S. Lewis's Case for the Christian Faith.* San Francisco: Harper and Row, 1981.

Quintilian, Marcus Fabius. *On the Teaching of Speaking and Writing: Translations from Books One, Two, and Ten of the Institutio oratoria.* Edited by James J. Murphy. Carbondale: Southern Illinois University Press, 1987.

Reed, Gerard. *C. S. Lewis and the Bright Shadow of Holiness.* Kansas City: Beacon Hill, 1999.

Reilly, R. J. *Romantic Religion: A Study of Barfield, Lewis, Williams, and Tolkien.* Athens: University of Georgia Press, 1971.

Reppert, Victor. *C. S. Lewis's Dangerous Idea: A Philosophical Defense of Lewis's Argument from Reason.* Downers Grove: Inter Varsity, 2003.

Richards, I. A. *The Philosophy of Rhetoric.* London: Oxford University Press, 1964.

Richter, David H. *Falling Into Theory: Conflicting Views on Reading Literature.* Boston: Bedford Books of St. Martin's, 1994.

Ridler, Anne, editor. *Charles Williams: The Image of the City and Other Essays.* Selected by Anne Ridler with a critical introduction. London: Oxford University Press, 1958.

Roberts, Edgar V. *Writing Themes About Literature.* 4th ed. Englewood Cliffs: Prentice-Hall, 1977.

Rogers, Jonathan. *The World According to Narnia: Christian Meaning in C. S. Lewis's Beloved Chronicles.* New York: Warner Faith, 2005.

Root, Jerry. "Following that Bright Blur." *Christian History Magazine* 4:3 (1985) 27, 35.

———. "Narnia: What Must God Be Like?" *Focus on the Family* 22:12 (1998) 4.

———. "The Man Who Created Narnia." *Focus on the Family* 22:12 (1998) 2–3.

———. "Tools Inadequate and Incomplete: C. S. Lewis and the Great Religions." *Mission and Ministry: The Magazine of Trinity Episcopal School for Ministry* 11:4 and 12:1 (1998) 50–53.

———. "Lewis, Clive Staples (1898–1963)." In *Evangelical Dictionary of Christian Education*, edited by Michael Anthony, 425–26. Grand Rapids: Baker, 2001.

Sammons, Martha C. *A Guide Through C. S. Lewis' Space Trilogy.* Westchester: Cornerstone, 1980.

———. *A Guide Through Narnia.* Wheaton: Shaw, 1979.

———. *A Guide Through Narnia: Revised and Expanded Edition.* Vancouver, British Columbia: Regent College Publishing, 2004.

Sangster, Paul. *Doctor Sangster.* London: Epworth, 1962.

Sayer, George. "C. S. Lewis's 'Dymer.'" *Seven: An Anglo-American Literary Review* 1 (1980) 94–116.

———. *Jack: C. S. Lewis and His Times.* London: Macmillan, 1988.

Sayers, Dorothy L. *Creed or Chaos?* Manchester: Sophia Institute, 1974.

Schakel, Peter J. "Irrigating Deserts with Moral Imagination." In *Inklings of Glory*, 21–29. Christian Reflections: A Series in Faith and Ethics. Waco: Center for Christian Ethics at Baylor University, 2004.

———, editor. *The Longing for a Form: Essays on the Fiction of C. S. Lewis.* Grand Rapids: Baker, 1979.

———. "Seeing and Knowing: The Epistemology of C. S. Lewis's 'Till We Have Faces.'" *Seven: An Anglo-American Literary Review* 4 (1983) 84–97.

———. *Reason and Imagination in C. S. Lewis: A Study of Till We Have Faces.* Grand Rapids: Eerdmans, 1984.

———, and Charles A. Huttar, editors. *Word and Story in C. S. Lewis.* Columbia, Missouri: University of Missouri Press, 1991.

Schofield, Stephen, editor. *In Search of C. S. Lewis.* South Plainfield: Bridge, 1983.

Schwarz, Hans. *Evil: A Historical and Theological Perspective.* Translated by Mark W. Worthing. Minneapolis: Fortress, 1995.

Scotchie, Joseph. *Barbarian in the Saddle: An Intellectual Biography of Richard M. Weaver.* New Brunswick: Transaction, 1997.

Shakespeare, William, *Henry V*. Ware, Hertfordshire, England: Wordsworth Limited Editions, 1994.

Sibley, Brian. *C. S. Lewis Through the Shadowlands.* Old Tappen: Revell, 1994.

———. *Shadowlands: The Story of C. S. Lewis and Joy Davidman.* London: Hodder and Stoughton, 1985.

———. *The Land of Narnia: Brian Sibley Explores the World of C. S. Lewis.* New York: HarperCollins Juvenile, 1990.

Sims, John A. *Missionaries to the Skeptics. Christian Apologists for the Twentieth Century: C. S. Lewis, Edward John Carnell, and Reinhold Niebuhr.* Macon: Mercer University Press, 1995.

Smith, Robert Houston. *Patches of Godlight: The Pattern of Thought of C. S. Lewis.* Athens: University of Georgia Press, 1981.

Smith, Ted J. III, editor. *Steps Towards Restoration: The Consequences of Richard Weaver's Ideas*. Wilmington: Intercollegiate Studies Institute, 1998.

Soper, David Wesley. *These Found the Way: Thirteen Converts to Protestant Christianity*. Philadelphia: Westminster, 1951.

Soskice, Janet Martin. *Metaphor and Religious Language*. Oxford: Clarendon, 1987.

Sproul, R. C. *Surprised by Suffering*. Wheaton: Tyndale, 1989

Swift, Catherine. *C. S. Lewis*. Minneapolis: Bethany, 1989.

Swinburne, Richard. *Miracles*. New York: Macmillan, 1989.

———. *The Coherence of Theism*. Oxford: Clarendon, 1993.

Sykes, John D. Jr. "The Gospel in Tolkien, Lewis, and Sayers." In *Inklings of Glory*, 88–93. Christian Reflections: A Series in Faith and Ethics. Waco: Center for Christian Ethics at Baylor University, 2004.

Tada, Joni Eareckson, and Steve Estes. *When God Weeps: Why Our Sufferings Matter to the Almighty*. Grand Rapids: Zondervan, 1997.

Tadie, Andrew A., and Michael H. Macdonald, editors. *Permanent Things: Toward the Recovery of a More Human Scale at the End of the Twentieth Century*. Grand Rapids: Eerdmans, 1995.

Talbott, Thomas. "C. S. Lewis and the Problem of Evil." *Christian Scholar's Review* 17 (1987) 36–51.

Taliaferro, Charles. "A Hundred Years With the Giants and the Gods: Christians and Twentieth Century Philosophy." *Christian Scholar's Review* 29 (2000) 695–712.

———. "The Co-Inherence." *Christian Scholar's Review* 18 (1989) 333–45.

Taylor, D. J. "What is Truth?: An Open Letter to Kathleen Nott." *Seven: An Anglo-American Literary Review* 4 (1983) 10–13.

Thorson, Stephen. "'Knowledge' in C. S. Lewis's Post-Conversion Thought: His Epistemological Method." *Seven: An Anglo-American Literary Review* 9 (1988) 91–116.

Tillyard, E. M. W. *Milton*. Harmondsworth, England: Penguin, 1968.

———. *Poetry and Its Background: Illustrated by Five Poems* 1470–1870. 6th impression. London: Chatto and Windus, 1961.

———. *The Elizabethan World Picture*. New York: Vintage, 1972.

Tolkien, J. R. R. *Farmer Giles of Ham*. Boston: Houghton Mifflin, 1978.

———. *Smith of Wootton Major*. London: George Allen & Unwin, 1967.

———. *The Fellowship of the Ring: Being the First Part of the Lord of the Rings*. With a new foreword by the author. New York: Ballantine, 1974.

———. *The Hobbit or There and Back Again*. Boston: Houghton Mifflin, 1966.

———. *The Letters of J. R. R. Tolkien*. Selected and edited by Humphrey Carpenter, with the assistance of Christopher Tolkien. Boston: Houghton Mifflin, 1981.

———. *The Return of the King: Being the Third Part of the Lord of the Rings*. With a new foreword by the author. New York: Ballantine, 1973

———. *The Two Towers: Being the Second Part of the Lord of the Rings*. With a new foreword by the author. New York: Ballantine, 1974.

———. *Tree and Leaf*. London: Unwin, 1964.

Trollope, Anthony. *An Autobiography*. 2 vols. Edited by H. M. Trollope. London: Blackwood, 1883.

Trueblood, D. Elton. "Intellectual Integrity." *Faculty Dialogue: Journal of the Institute for Christian Leadership* 2 (1985) 45–60.

————. *While It Is Day: An Autobiography*. New York: Harper and Row, 1974.

Turner, Charles, editor. *Chosen Vessels: Portraits of Ten Outstanding Men*. Ann Arbor: Servant, 1985.

Underhill, Evelyn. *The Letters of Evelyn Underhill*. Edited by Charles Williams. London: Longmans, Green, 1956.

Urang, Gunnar. *Shadows of Heaven: Religion and Fantasy in the Writing of C. S. Lewis, Charles Williams, and J. R. R. Tolkien*. Philadelphia: Pilgrim, 1971.

Vanauken, Sheldon. *A Severe Mercy*. New York: Harper and Row, 1977.

Vander Elst, Philip. *Thinkers of Our Time: C. S. Lewis*. London: Claridge, 1996.

Vanhoozer, Kevin J. *First Theology: God, Scripture & Hermeneutics*. Downers Grove: InterVarsity, 2002.

Vardy, Peter. *The Puzzle of Evil*. Glasgow: Fount, 1992.

Vaus, Will. *Mere Theology: A Guide to the Thought of C. S. Lewis*. Foreword by Douglas Gresham. Downers Grove: InterVarsity, 2004.

Velaverde, Robert. *The Lion, the Witch and the Bible: Good and Evil in the Classic Tales of C. S. Lewis*. Colorado Springs: NavPress, 2005.

Voltaire. *Candide: Or Optimism*. Hertfordshire, England: Wordsworth Classics, 1993.

Von Balthasar, Hans Urs. *Dare We Hope "That All Men Be Saved"? With a Short Discourse on Hell*. Translated by Dr. David Kipp and Rev. Lothar Krauth. San Francisco: Ignatius, 1988.

Von Hugel, Baron Friedrich. *Selected Letters 1896–1924*. Edited with a memoir by Bernard Holland. London: Dent, 1928.

Wagner, Richard. *C. S. Lewis and Narnia for Dummies*. Hoboken: Wiley, 2005.

Waldock, A. J. A. *Paradise Lost and Its Critics*. Gloucester: Peter Smith, 1959.

Walhout, Clarence, and Leland Ryken, editors. *Contemporary Literary Theory: A Christian Appraisal*. Grand Rapids: Eerdmans.

Walker, Andrew, and James Patrick, editors. *A Christian for All Christians: Essays in Honor of C. S. Lewis*. London: Hodder and Stoughton, 1990.

Walsh, Chad. "C. S. Lewis: Critic, Creator and Cult Figure." *Seven: An Anglo-American Literary Review* 2 (1981) 60–80.

————. *C. S. Lewis: Apostle to the Skeptics*. New York: Macmillan, 1949.

————. *Chad Walsh Reviews C. S. Lewis: With a Memoir by Damaris Walsh McGuire*. Altadena: Mythopoeic, 1998.

————. *The Literary Legacy of C. S. Lewis*. New York: Harcourt Brace Jovanovich, 1979.

————. *The Visionary Christian: 131 Readings Selected and Edited by Chad Walsh*. New York: Macmillan, 1981.

Ward, Keith. *God, Faith and the New Millennium: Christian Belief in an Age of Science*. Oxford: One World, 1998.

————. *Religion and Creation*. Oxford, Clarendon, 1996.

Ward, Patricia A. "Worldly Readers and Writerly Texts." *Christian Scholar's Review* 17 (1988) 425–35.

Watson, George, editor. *Critical Essays on C. S. Lewis*. Critical Thought Series 1. Aldershot, England: Scolar, 1992.

Weatherhead, Leslie D. *Why Do Men Suffer?* London: SCM, 1935.

Weaver, Richard M. In *Defense of Tradition: Collected Shorter Writings of Richard M. Weaver,* 1929–1963, edited with an introduction by Ted J. Smith III. Indianapolis: Liberty Fund, 2000.

———. *Ideas Have Consequences.* Chicago: University of Chicago Press, 1948. Midway Reprint, 1976.

———. "Language is Sermonic." In *The Rhetorical Tradition: Readings from the Classical Times to the Present,* edited by Patricia Bizzell and Bruce Herzberg, 1351–60. Boston: Bedford/St. Martin's, 2001.

———. *The Ethics of Rhetoric.* Davis: Hermagoras, 1985.

———. *Visions of Order: The Cultural Crisis of Our Time.* Wilmington: Intercollegiate Studies Institute, 1995.

Wellman, Sam. *C. S. Lewis: Author of Mere Christianity.* Philadelphia: Chelsea, 1999.

White, William Luther. *The Image of Man in C. S. Lewis.* Nashville: Abingdon, 1969.

Williams, Charles. *The Descent of the Dove.* Grand Rapids: Eerdmans, 1974.

———. *The Figure of Beatrice.* London: Faber and Faber, 1943.

———. *The Image of the City: Essays by Charles Williams.* Edited by Anne Ridler. London: Oxford University Press, 1958.

Williams, Donald T. *Inklings of Reality: Essays Toward a Christian Philosophy of Letters.* Toccoa Falls: Toccoa Falls College Press, 1996.

———. *Mere Humanity: G. K. Chesterton, C. S. Lewis, and J. R. R. Tolkien on the Human Condition.* Nashville: Broadman and Holmann, 2006.

Williams, Thomas. *The Heart of the Chronicles of Narnia: Knowing God Here by Finding Him There.* Nashville: Nelson, 2005.

Willis, John Randolph. *Pleasures Forevermore: The Theology of C. S. Lewis.* Chicago: Loyola University Press, 1983.

Wilson, A. N. *C. S. Lewis: A Biography.* London: Collins, 1991.

Wordsworth, William. *The Prelude: A Parallel Text.* Edited by J. C. Maxwell. Reprint, London: Penguin, 1986.

Yandell, Keith E. "Evangelical Thought." *Christian Scholar's Review* 14 (1988) 341–46.

# Index

Addison, Joseph, 127
Adey, Lionel, 217
Adler, Mortimer, 11, 26
  *Great Ideas*, 11
Aeschliman, Michael, 98
agnostics, 16–17
Alexander, Samuel, 134, 154
allegory, 6, 174–75
Amis, Kingsley, 99
animal pain. *See* pain.
Anscombe, G. E. M., 133, 152, 153,
  156, 184
"The anthropological approach,"
  121–24
apologetics, 61, 150–51, 154, 167
Aquinas, Thomas, 12, 65
  *Summa Theologica*, 105
argument, types of
  Authority and Testimony, xix,
    28, 32
  Cause and Effect, or Circum-
    stance, xix, 27–28
  Definition, xix
  Genus, 27
  Similitude, xix, 27, 70–71
Aristotle, xv, 39, 118, 163n
  *Ethics*, 39
  *Politics*, 163n
Arnold, Matthew, 132, 189
art, 107, 108, 110, 121, 138
Aslan, 168, 231–32, 235, 236, 244
astronomy, 170n
atheism, xx, 15n 90, 101, 185
Atlantis, 50

Attenbourough, Richard, 89n
Austen, Jane, 145, 146, 225
*Aut Deus aut malus momo*, 33
Augustine, 6–7, 108, 126, 135, 221
  *The City of God*, 126, 221
  *Confessions*, 6, 108
authority, 33ff, 42
Authority and Testimony, xix

Bacon, Sir Francis, 230
Bailey, George, 109
Barfield, Owen, 5–6, 88, 120,
  131–33, 172, 176, 192, 196
Beatrice, 86–87, 92, 220
beauty, 107n
Bennett, J. A. W., 2
Bible, 101, 123n
Blamires, Harry, 99, 117n
Bodley, John, 189
Booth, Wayne, xiv
Bran, 193, 194, 199, 202, 240
  as evil, 200
  as subjectivist, 199
Brent, Doug, xiv
British Broadcasting Company
  (B. B. C.), 60
Brontë, Charlotte, 139
Browning, Robert, 165
Bultitude, Mr., 205
Bunyan, John, 34
Butler, Samuel, 192

Cabby Frank and his wife Helen,
  229, 236

Cambridge University, xviii, xxi, 2,
    120, 166
Campenella, 230
capitalism, 96
Capron, Robert, 191–92
Carnell, Corbin Scott, 3
Carpenter, Humphrey, xxi, 149,
    152n
    *The Inklings*, 149
cause and effect, or circumstance,
    xix, 27
Chaucer, Geoffrey, xiin, xiii, 112,
    122, 185
checks and balances, 32, 45, 222
Chesterton, G. K., 58, 121, 125
    *The Everlasting Man*, 121
Chretien de Troyes, 6–7
Christ, 76, 90, 158, 212
    The Passion, 168
Christian apologist, 58
Christian/Christianity, xx, 5, 25,
    47, 49, 55, 58, 60, 61, 64, 150,
    184, 200–201, 212, 213, 240
    and art, 107, 108
    and culture, 100–106
    and literature, 106–7, 115
Christopher, Joe, 62
"chronological snobbery," 120
the church, 43
The City (in *Dymer*), 194–95, 199,
    202, 207, 209, 222
Coleridge, Samuel Taylor, 29
Communion of the Saints, 92
Community, 33, 42ff.
Como, James, xi–xii, 62, 63
    *Branches to Heaven*, xiin
conscience, 16, 23
contemplation, 155
courtly love, 225
creativity, 107

*CSL: The Bulletin of the New York
    C. S. Lewis Society*, 96
culture, 26, 48, 95–98, 100–106,
    124, 147, 148, 170n 189–90,
    218, 225
Cunningham, David, xiv
Cunningham, Richard, 61

dance, 62
Daniel, Jerry L., 96, 99
Dante, xiin xiii, 86–87, 92, 145,
    146, 180, 185, 215. 220–21
    *The Divine Comedy*, 86, 220
    *The Vita Nuova*, 86
death, 49–50, 56, 59, 60, 150
definition, xix, 8, 17, 19, 27, 116,
    163, 165, 166, 180
deplorable word, the, 234, 235
dialectic, xv, xix, xx, 26, 27, 33, 46,
    69
Dillard, Annie, 181–82
disobedience, 127
Dodds, David Llewellyn, 134
Donne, John, 178
doubt, 89–90, 246
Downing, David, 2, 122, 186, 188n
    215, 216, 217
Duffy, Bernard, 27, 130
Durham University, 29, 116
Dyson, Hugo, 212

*The Eagle and Child*, 86
Eagleton, Terry, xiii
    discursive theory, xiii
    *Literary Theory*, xiiin
    Rhetoric, xiii
Edwards, Bruce, xiv, 96–97
enjoyment, 155
escape, 193, 198, 200, 202
eschatology, xiv
*Essays and Studies*, 128

ethnicity, 124

evil, xvi, xvii, xxi, 1, 14, 20, 25, 37,
44, 46–50, 56, 60, 64, 66,
73, 84–85, 93, 96, 99, 126,
137, 147, 150, 154–55, 160,
167, 170, 178, 186–87, 188,
190–91, 198, 200–01, 211–12,
215, 216, 222, 235–36, 239,
241, 242–43, 245–46

*Exigence*, 47, 63, 94, 150, 226
Defined, 47

*ex nihilo*, 108

experience, 33, 38ff, 42

*Experiment in Criticism*, xiii, 106,
109–116, 118n

facts, xix, 26, 35, 65, 68

faith, 33, 39, 41ff, 50, 90

Farrar, Austin, xi, 77–78, 79n 176n
180

Fall, the, 36, 126.

fiction, 148, 149–51, 157, 159–62,
166–67, 174, 181–82, 184, 186

fideism, 89

Filmer, Kath, 187, 224–25, 236

Florence, Italy, 86

forensics, 64

Frank the Tragedian, 223, 225–27

Frankl, Victor, 186

free will, 66–67, 73–75, 76

Freud, 138–39

futility, 58–59

Galileo, 172–73

gender, 124

Genesis, 14

geocentrism, 172

Gibb, Jocelyn, 5n 77n

Gilchrist, James K., 56

Glover, Donald, 3, 220, 227

gnostic, 102, 105

God, 19, 24, 25, 37, 44, 50, 53–56,
59, 64, 82, 84, 90–91, 93, 101,
104, 120, 144, 151, 158, 162,
164, 167, 169, 173, 176–79,
180, 184, 200–01, 212, 220,
223, 236, 243, 246, 247
as Creator, 66–68, 72, 108
as Cosmic Sadist, 93
existence of God, 151, 156, 163,
178, 186, 245
glory, 87
goodness, 65, 69–72, 73, 77, 150,
162, 163, 243
grace, 83
immanence, 87
justice, 74, 82–83
love, 69–72, 83, 184
omnipotence, 65–68, 76, 77, 150,
163, 184, 243
omniscience, 83, 108, 245
self-existent, 72
transcendence, 87
Trinity, 66

grammar, 122

Green, Roger Lancelyn, 50n 86n
89n 116n

*The Green Book*, 29, 31, 160

Green Witch, The, 206n

Greeves, Arthur, 156n 212

*A Grief Observed*, xx, 15, 44, 84, 89,
90–92, 93

Griffiths, Dom Bede, 56

Habakkuk, 44n

*Hamlet*, 124, 125

Hannay, Margaret, 3

Harding, D. E., 21

Hauser, Gerard A., 47

heaven, 195, 198, 213, 220, 222–24,
226

Hegelian, 118
heliocentrism, 172–73
hell, 195, 198, 213, 220, 222–23
Herbert, George, 58
historicism, 119–20, 121
history, 119–20, 126
Hitler, Adolpf, 103
Hooper, Walter, 50 n. 60n 86n 89n
    116n 136, 152n 210
hope, 53
hrossa, 214
human freedom, xviii, 66
Hume, David, 38n
humility, 39 ff. 188, 191, 213, 246
Hyoi, 214

*The Idea of the University*, 102
ideas, xix
idolatry, 48, 115, 176
ignorance, 16
images, 176–80, 189
imagination, 6, 138–40, 149–50,
    156–57, 182–83, 184, 191
immanence, 87
Incarnation, 101
Inklings, xxi, 86
Inner Ring, The, 42–43
intelligibility, xviii
invention, 63n

Jacobi, Martin, 27, 130
Jadis, Queen of Charn (*See* White
    Witch), 228, 230, 233,
    235–36, 241, 244
James, William, 37
Jenkin, A. K. Hamilton, 99
Jerusalem, 105–06, 109, 114–15,
    119, 122, 137, 140, 144
Job, 44n 84–85, 178
Johnson, Samuel, 136n
Jonah, 44n

Jowett, Benjamin, 118
Julian of Norwich, 87n

Keefe, Carolyn, 109n
Kepler, Johannes, 173
Ketley, Martin, 29
Kilby, Clyde, 61, 98, 222
King, Alec, 29
King, Don, 191–92
Kirke, Digory (also Professor Kirke),
    123, 228, 231–34, 236–37,
    238, 241, 244
knowledge, xix

language, 18, 47, 130, 164
"language is sermonic," 27, 60, 69n
Law[s] of Nature, 24, 34
Layamon, 136
Lewis, C. S.
    as apologist, xi, xxi, 61, 62,
        152–53
    as atheist, xx, 156
    boarding school, "Belsen," 52–54
    books and essays
        *The Abolition of Man*, xx, 1,
            8, 10, 22n 26, 28–32, 39,
            116–17, 134–35, 150, 160–61,
            193n 205, 208, 218, 230, 231n
            239
        *The Allegory of Love*, 6, 242
        *All My Road before Me*, 134,
            155n
        *The Arthurian Torso*, 42n 86,
            88n 91n 154n 177n
        *Christian Reflections*, 16, 17n
            18n 22n 33n 34n 35n 36n
            38n 41n 58n 100n 101n 104n
            106, 117n 118n 119n 120n
            123n 144n 152n 182n
        "Christian Apologetics," 161

"Christianity and Culture," 103, 106

"Christianity and Literature," 106

"De Futilitate," 58

"Difficulties in Presenting the Christian Faith to Modern Unbelievers," 152n

*The Discarded Image*, xii, 12n 33n 39, 40n 119, 170, 171n 172, 173n 174n 181

*Dymer*, 156n 188, 191–213, 222

*English Literature in the Sixteenth Century*, xiiin 135, 229

*Essays Presented to Charles Williams*, 84n 88n 159n 183n 193n

*An Experiment in Criticism*, xiii, 106, 109–16, 118n 134, 143n 145, 147, 175n 185

*The Four Loves*, 56n 124n 227n

*George MacDonald: An Anthology*, 41n

*God in the Dock*, 10n 11n 33n 35n 38n 57n 82n 151n 152n 155n 161n

*The Great Divorce*, 22n 169n 178n 188–89, 195, 198, 204, 211, 213, 218, 220–27, 232, 241

*A Grief Observed*, xx, 15, 44, 84, 89, 90–92, 93, 176n 177n 179n

"Hamlet: The Prince or the Poem?" 125n

"The Humanitarian Theory of Punishment," 82–83.

"The Inner Ring," 42.

"The Language of Religion," 18–21.

*The Last Battle*, 174n 186n

*Letters*, 5, 51n 52n 53n 54n 57n 71n 85n 89n 157n 160n 197n 212n

*Letters to an American Lady*, 24n

*Letters to Children*, 42n 157n 175n

*Letters to Malcolm*, 10n 87n 163n 164n 176n

*The Lion, the Witch and the Wardrobe*, 124, 228, 236n

*The Magician's Nephew*, 123, 124n 188–89, 202, 227–38, 241

"Meditation in a Tool Shed," 155

"Membership," 43

*Mere Christianity*, 14n 17n 24n 33n 34n 40, 41n 90, 144n 213, 246

*Miracles*, 12, 13n 14n 24n 35n 81, 82n 152n 176n

*Narrative Poems*, 156n 192n 194n 196n 197n 199n 201n 203n 205n 207n 208n 211n

*Of Other Worlds*, 123n 140n 157n 158n 159n 162n 180n 193n 214, 218n 235n

"On Learning in War-time," 59

"On Three Ways of Writing for Children," 143n

*Out of the Silent Planet*, 160, 188, 189, 213–19, 241

*Perelandra*, 3, 23n 204, 218n

*The Personal Heresy*, 128, 134, 136–37

*The Pilgrim's Regress*, 126, 132, 134, 154, 163n 170n 177n 196

*Poems*, 88n 156n 169

"The Poison of Subjectivism," xvii, xx, 1, 22n 116–17, 216

Lewis, C. S. (*continued*)
  *A Preface to Paradise Lost*, 8,
    23n 38n 119, 124n 125n 126n
    157n
  *The Problem of Pain*, xx, 44,
    55n 61–75, 76n 77, 79, 80, 82,
    83–84, 145
  *Reflections on the Psalms*, 15,
    42n 85, 152n 161n
  *Rehabilitations*, 122n
  *Screwtape Letters*, 157
  *Screwtape Proposes a Toast*, 13n
  *Selected Literary Essays*, 33n
    34n 120n 121n 122n 138n
    139n 140n 145n 146n 164n
    166, 175n
  "The Shoddy Lands," 235
  *The Silver Chair*, 168n 169n
    183n 206
  *Spirits in Bondage*, 156n 196
  *Studies in Medieval and Renais-
    sance Literature*, 123n 129n
    130n 136, 145, 172n 180n
    181, n
  *Studies in Words*, xviii, 23n
    26, 117n 136, 141, 143, 162n
    163n
  *Surprised by Joy*, 15n 23n 17n
    34n 39n 50n 51n 53n 54n
    56n 57n 58n 83n 99, 118n
    120n 132–34, 155n 158n
    169n 176n 177n 197n
  *That Hideous Strength*, 3, 22n
    32, 43, 205
  *They Stand Together*, 156n
  *Till We Have Faces*, 6, 15n 179n
  *The Voyage of the Dawn Tread-
    er*, 222n 235, 236n 244n
  *The Weight of Glory*, 34n 42n
    43n 59n 103n 104n 164n 167n
    168n 169n 178n
  *The World's Last Night*, 152n
  boyhood home: Little Lea, 51
  brother: Warren Hamilton Lewis,
    50–51, 52, 54, 197n
  childlike, xvi
  childhood, 50–56
  as a Christian, xx, 49, 50, 64, 242
  conversion to Christianity, xx,
    149, 158n 241
  deformity of thumbs, 51–52
  emotion of, xv–xvi
  father: Albert Lewis, 50, 118
  as fiction writer, xxi, xxii, 2, 32,
    184, 189, 196, 220, 238, 240,
    241, 243
  humility of, xvi
  as imaginative, 79, 149, 157, 220
  joy (as desire), 3, 54
  knowledge of Language: *Greek*;
    *Latin*; *Anglo-Saxon*; *French*;
    *German*; *Italian*; *Icelandic*; xvi
  as literary critic, 99, 106, 109,
    116, 132, 134
  longing, 3
  as a Medievalist, 229
  mother: Flora Hamilton Lewis,
    50, 52, 191
  as objectivist, xvii, xx, 1, 7, 8, 10,
    75, 83–84, 99
  one in the many, 2–3
  pessimism, 51, 54
  as Platonist, 5
  as poet, 192, 238
  as popular writer, xxi
  Preface to D. E. Harding's *The
    Hierarchy of Heaven and
    Earth*, 21
  public school, 54–56
  quest for a unifying element, 2–4
  Riddell Memorial Lectures, 29,
    116, 134

as science fiction writer, 2, 213, 218

self-centeredness, 55

supposals, xxi

rhetoric, xi, xxii

as rhetorician, xiff, xx, xxi, 8, 64, 68–69, 71, 73–74, 76–78, 82, 84, 93–94, 104, 115–16, 124, 149, 157, 162, 167, 187–89, 193, 196–97, 217, 221, 228, 233, 240–41

Lewis, Joy Davidman, xxi, 6, 89–90, 210

death of, xxi, 89–90

*Light on C. S. Lewis*, 131

Lindskoog, Kathryn Ann, 228

literary critic, 22–23, 95, 131

literary criticism, xxi, 98, 100–144, 145, 162, 240

"The anthropological approach," 121–24

"the doctrine of the unchanging human heart," 124–28

"historicism," 119–20, 121

"The personal heresy," 128–37

"Psycho-Analysis and Literary Criticism," 138

"reading between the lines," 53, 118–19

literary judgment, 98

literary theory, 107

literature and "real life," 145–47

love, 55–56, 225–27

Lucretius, 52

Lucy, 235–36, 244

Lydgate, xiii

MacDonald, George, 41

as a character in *The Great Divorce*, 213, 220, 223–24

MacDonald, Michael H., 3

Magdalen College, Oxford, 58, 60

magic, 229–232

The Magician in *Dymer*, 201–8, 224, 240

as subjectivist, 202–3

his subjectivism supports his evil intentions, 204, 207

Malacandra, or Mars, 213–14, 216–18

Malvern College, 197n

Manlove, Colin, 220, 221, 223

Marion E. Wade Center at Wheaton College, Wheaton, Illinois, xii, 98

Mark Studdock, 244

materialist, 12–13, 101, 186

metaphor, 164, 169.

master's metaphor, 164

pupil's metaphor, 164–65

The Metaphysical Dream, xix, 100

metaphysics, 12, 21

methodology, xvii ff, 109, 123

Medieval and Renaissance Literature, xxi

medieval model of the universe, 170–71, 174, 181

Middle Ages, xii, xviii, 170, 229

Milton, John, 88, 119, 126–27, 141, 171n 215

Mitchell, Basil, 93

modern criticism, 107

Modern Language Association, xiv

moral compromise, 25

moral decline, 25

moral failure, 17, 36

morality, 14, 24, 37, 113, 148

moral law, 15–16, 23, 34

Morris, William, 62, 145–46, 183

Myers, Doris, 215–17, 228, 234

myth, 169, 212

mythology, 22, 177n

*The Narnian Chronicles*, 123, 168, 175n 227, 244
Narnia, 232, 236–38, 244
natural evil, 63, 78–82
nature, 76, 170
neo-Platonists, 118
Nero, 103
Newman, John Henry, 102–3
New Testament, 101, 107, 115
N.I.C.E., 206
nominalism, xviii, 7
Norse mythology, 177n

obedience, 33, 39, 41–42, 126–27, 237
the object itself, 4
objective, 6, 11, 21, 24, 28ff, 83, 106, 113, 147, 169, 188, 198
objective morality, 14
objective reality, 13–14, 24, 57, 64, 72, 82, 85, 89–90, 97–98, 115, 171, 179, 191, 208, 217, 221, 235, 239
the objective text/objectivity of texts, 95–96, 98, 106
objective truth, 99
objective value, xviii, xxii, 4, 29–30, 31, 97–99, 104, 134–35, 148, 189, 198, 204, 211–12, 219, 221, 225, 231, 233, 238, 239
objectivist; objectivism, xvii, xx, xxi, 1, 7–8, 11, 20, 30, 32, 46, 49, 56, 57, 60, 75, 83–84, 93, 95, 98, 194, 217, 239–40
objectivity, 7, 10, 32, 39, 45, 66–67, 83–84, 95, 114, 239
Of truth, 8–9, 15, 24ff
Occam's Law of Parsimony, 171n
ontology, xiv, 12
opinion, 11
Orual, 178, 244

Oury, Scott, 3–4
Oxford Socratic Club, xi, 133, 152–53, 184
Oxford University, xviii, xxi, 2, 58, 86, 88, 118, 122
  St. Mary's, 59, 103
Oxford University Press, 86, 88
Oyarsa, 214–15, 219

pain, 59–60, 63, 70–71, 73, 84–85, 93, 177, 182, 238, 242–43
  animal pain, 72, 73–78
Pandora, 233
*Paradise Lost,* 88, 128
Pascal, 126
*pathos,* 94, 240
"Penal Blindness," 23–25
Perelandra, or Venus, 213, 218, 232, 244
persuasion, xv
  classical modes of appeal
    *ethos,* 85, 89, 93, 94, 129, 177–78
    *logos,* 79, 122, 129, 240
    *pathos,* xv, 94, 240
pessimism, 51, 54
Peters, John, 61
Pfifltriggi, 214
Pharisees, 115
Plato, 4–5, 118, 194
  *The Republic,* 194
Platonism/Platonist, 4–5, 105, 194, 197, 207
Plummer, Polly, 123–24, 229, 231–34
poetic language, 18–19
poetry, xv
"The Poison of Subjectivism," 116–17
Poland, 103
Polkinghorne, John, 79n 80

Poole, Jill, 206
possible worlds, 67–68
pre-historic man, 121, 125
Preston, Robert, xviii
pride, 40, 41, 126, 144
Prince Caspian, 44
Prince Rilian, 206, 244
probability, 27
the problem of evil, 25, 44–45, 47,
    53, 56, 65–72, 74, 82, 83, 84,
    93, 94, 106, 116, 146, 150–51,
    154–57, 159, 161, 163, 167,
    174, 179, 184–85, 186, 240,
    243, 246
Psalms, xvi. 15, 44n
psyche, 178
psychology, 101, 115, 137–144
Puddleglum the Marshwiggle, 206

Quintilian, xi, 122

Rabelais, 112
Ransom, Elwin, 213–14, 215, 216,
    217, 218, 241, 244
rationality, 35
"reading between lines," 53, 118–19
realism, xviii
reality, 37, 50, 58, 94, 145, 147, 171,
    179, 185, 187–88, 197, 202,
    205, 209, 211–12, 230–31,
    238–39, 243.
*Reality is Iconoclastic*, 94, 176–84,
    207, 210.
reason, 13, 20, 33, 35ff 41, 42. 191
    not mere cerebral bio-
    chemistry, 13
realists, xviii
Reepicheep, 244
relativism, xviii, 9, 99
Revelation, 34

rhetoric, xii–xiii, xvi, xviii, 1,
    19–20, 26–27, 35, 42, 47–49,
    56, 60–62, 64, 84, 94, 98–99,
    104, 109, 115, 124–25, 130,
    148, 158–59, 188, 203, 217,
    239, 241, 243
  of deception, 122
  delectare, 157
  docere, 157
  of fiction, 188
  of narcissism, 226
  of object, 21
  of objectivism, 188, 191, 205,
    213, 215
  of reading, 97
  of subject, 21
  of subjectivism, 188, 191, 194,
    195, 203, 213, 215–16, 219,
    227, 235
Richards, I. A., 101
Rome, 103
Rousseau, 108

Satan, 75, 79
saving the appearances, 170–76, 186
Sayer, George, xxi, 44, 149, 192,
    196, 199, 201–2
  *Jack*, 149, 152n
Schakel, Peter, 5–7, 130–37
  *Reason and Imagination*, 6n 130
science, 181, 184
science fiction, 32, 157, 175, 218
scientific language, 18–19
scientism, 214
Scripture, 79, 101, 104, 118, 178
Scrubb, Eustace, 206
*Sehnsucht*, 104
self-deception, 1
self-improvement, 111–12
self-justification, 17

self-referential, 191, 194, 211, 223
senses, 38
September 28, 1931, 60
Seroni, 214
severe mercies, 72
*Shadowlands,* 89
Shakespeare, 124–25, 145–46, 169n
    225
Sidney, Philip, 125n 136
    *Arcadia,* 136n
    *Astrophil and Stella,* 136n
Similitude, xix, 27
Simplicius, 171
Sims, John, 63, 89, 90
sin, 41, 223
Smith, Robert Houston, 4–5
Smith, Sarah, 223–27
Smith, Ted J. III, xviii
social Darwinism, 216
sorrow, 60
Soskice, Janet, 164
soteriology, 114
soul-making, 73–75
Spenser, Edmund, 185, 225
subjective, xvii, 6, 21, 90, 106, 135,
    188
subjectivism, xvi–xvii, xviii, xx–xxii,
    7, 10, 15, 17, 20, 31, 35, 40,
    45–46, 48, 52–53, 55, 64, 65,
    74, 94, 96–98, 100, 106, 109,
    112, 113, 114–17, 120, 124,
    126, 128, 130–31, 137, 141,
    143–44, 147–48, 150, 159, 163,
    167, 170–71, 173, 179–80, 186,
    188, 189–90, 191, 193–94,
    197, 199–200, 202–3, 205–8,
    211, 215, 219, 224, 226, 239,
    240–41, 246
    defined, xvii

supports evil, xvii, xxi, 1–2, 187–
    88, 194, 200, 211–12, 216,
    219, 222, 227, 233, 238, 239
subjectivist criticism, 95, 100
subjectivistic rhetoric, xvi, 20, 74,
    188, 191, 194, 195
suffering, 20, 25, 46, 47, 49, 56, 60,
    63, 70–71, 73, 77–78, 85, 93–
    94, 150, 154, 156, 174, 177–
    79, 184, 242–43, 245, 246
supernaturalism, 13, 242
supposals, xxi, 154, 171–76, 186,
    244
symbols, 17, 22 140–41

*Tabula rasa,* 37
Tadie, Andrew H., 3
Tao (as "the doctrine of objective
    value"), 8n 29ff. 135, 147,
    188, 189, 205, 231
teleology, xiv
theodicy, 77
theology, 36, 37, 79, 103
*This also is Thou; neither is this
    Thou,* 87–88, 88–89, 91
Tillyard, E. M. W., 5, 126–29
Tolkien, J. R. R., xxi, 133, 159n 193,
    212
    *On Fairy Stories,* 193
*Topoi,* 63, 242
Traherne, Thomas, 135
transcendence, xiv, 87
*Transposition,* 167–70
*Treasure Island,* 112
Trollope, Anthony, 139
truth, 7–9, 10
    is narrow, 11
    is objective, 11, 15, 24
    self-evident truths, 35
Tumnus, Mr., 244
Twain, Mark, 38n

ultimate reality, 61
Uncle Andrew, 228–33, 236, 238
undeception, 146
University of Chicago, xiv, xviii, 26
utilitarian, 31, 111, 191, 214

Vanauken, Sheldon, 72n
verbicide, 142–43
vicarious atonement, 211
Virgil, xiin 125n 220
virtue, 41–42, 113, 231, 237

Walsh, Chad, 98, 202, 216, 221
war, 59, 103
Ward, Keith, 79n 81
the way of affirmation, 88, 91
the way of negation, 87–88, 91
Weaver, Richard, xvii, ff, xxii, 1, 7,
    26, 27, 28, 30, 42, 46–48, 60,
    64, 69, 84–85, 92–98, 100,
    109, 115–16, 130, 143, 147,
    189–91, 192, 211, 218–19,
    230, 234, 237, 239
argument, types of
    *Authority and Testimony,* xix,
        28, 32
    *Cause and Effect,* or
        *Circumstance,* xix, 27–28
    *Definition,* xix
    *Genus,* 27
    *Similitude,* xix, 27
books
    *The Ethics of Rhetoric,* 1, 26,
        28n 31, 109n 143n
    *Ideas Have Consequences,*
        xviiin, 7, 10n 17, 26, 93n 94n
        190n 208n 234, 237n
    *In Defense of Tradition,* xviiin
        26n 64n 84n 97n 100n 116n
    *Visions of Order,* 48n 95n 116n
        147n 189n 218n

dialectic, xix, xx, 26–27
essays
    "Language is Sermonic," 8, 27n
        28n 46n 47n 48n 49n 60, 69n
        85n 219n
    "The Last Metaphysical Right,"
        189–91, 192, 202, 203, 204,
        208, 211, 223, 230, 234, 238
    Metaphysical Dream, xix, 100
ultimate terms
    *devil terms,* xix, 143
    *god terms,* xix, 143
Western Tradition, xviii
Weston, 213–14, 215–16, 219, 232,
    241
    as the Unman, 218, 232
The White Witch (see, Jadis Queen
    of Charn), 124, 228, 232,
    237–38
Williams, Charles, 4, 84, 85–89, 91,
    134, 154
books
    *The Coming of Galahad,* 154n
    *The Figure of Beatrice,* 87
    *The Place of the Lion,* 4
    doctrine of romantic love, 87
Willis, John Randolph, 61
Wilson, A. N., xxi, 62, 149, 215
    *C. S. Lewis: A Biography,* 149, 152
"wish-fulfillment," 140
Woerner, Jody R., 2
Word of God:
    incarnate, 34
    written, 34
Wordsworth, William, 86, 154
World War I, 56–60
    Battle of the Somme, 56
World War II, 58, 86, 88

SCRIPTURE REFERENCES

| | |
|---|---|
| Jeremiah 18 | 70 |
| Psalm 34:8 | 159 |
| I Corinthians 10:31 | 103 n. |
| Ephesians 4:28 | 104 |
| I Thessalonians 4:11 | 104 |
| I Peter 2:5 | 70 |